D1563884

PAUL, THEN AND NOW

# PAUL, THEN AND NOW

MATTHEW V. NOVENSON

WILLIAM B. EERDMANS PUBLISHING COMPANY

GRAND RAPIDS, MICHIGAN

Wm. B. Eerdmans Publishing Co.
4035 Park East Court SE, Grand Rapids, Michigan 49546
www.eerdmans.com

28  27  26  25  24  23  22      1  2  3  4  5  6  7

ISBN 978-0-8028-8171-7

**Library of Congress Cataloging-in-Publication Data**

Names: Novenson, Matthew V., author.
Title: Paul, then and now / Matthew V. Novenson.
Description: Grand Rapids, Michigan : William B. Eerdmans Publishing
    Company, 2022. | Includes bibliographical references and index. | Summary:
    "A collection of a decade's worth of essays in which Matthew Novenson
    puts contextual understandings of Paul's letters into conversation with their
    Christian reception history"—Provided by publisher.
Identifiers: LCCN 2021051575 | ISBN 9780802881717 (hardcover)
Subjects: LCSH: Bible. Epistles of Paul—Criticism, interpretation, etc. | Paul,
    the Apostle, Saint. | BISAC: RELIGION / Biblical Studies / New Testament /
    Paul's Letters | RELIGION / Biblical Studies / New Testament / General
Classification: LCC BS2650.52 .N68 2022 | DDC 225.9/2—dc23/eng/20211117
LC record available at https://lccn.loc.gov/2021051575

*For my parents*

*The past is never dead. It's not even past.*

—WILLIAM FAULKNER,
*Requiem for a Nun*, act 1, scene 3

# CONTENTS

# ACKNOWLEDGMENTS

This is the first book of this particular kind that I have yet undertaken. It comprises some eleven essays of mine published over the past ten years or so, plus one new, programmatic essay. I explain my rationale for collecting these essays in this volume in chapter 1 below. But first things first: my most sincere thanks to the good people who helped make this book. Most importantly, I am grateful to Eerdmans editor Trevor Thompson, who saw promise in the idea, and editor-in-chief James Ernest, who made it happen. Thanks, likewise, to the whole team at Eerdmans, in particular Alexis Cutler, Laurel Draper, Laura Bardolph Hubers, and Amy Kent, and to copyeditor Cody Hinkle. The ideas included here have been worked out over a decade's worth of conversations with a wonderful group of scholar-friends scattered across the globe, in particular Frantisek Abel, John Barclay, Douglas Campbell, Cavan Concannon, Laura Dingeldein, Kathy Ehrensperger, Mark Elliott, Paula Fredriksen, Jörg Frey, John Gager, Joshua Garroway, Simon Gathercole, Beverly Gaventa, David Lincicum, Bruce Longenecker, Esau McCaulley, Margaret Mitchell, Hindy Najman, Mark Nanos, Rafael Rodriguez, Ryan Schellenberg, Benjamin Schliesser, Todd Still, Jennifer Strawbridge, Loren Stuckenbruck, Matthew Thiessen, Francis Watson, Emma Wasserman, Heidi Wendt, Benjamin White, Joel Willitts, N. T. Wright, Stephen Young, and Magnus Zetterholm. (The fingerprints of their influence are all over the footnotes to the chapters below.) Closer to home, I had sharp-minded interlocutors in my Edinburgh graduate students, many of whom have since moved on to bigger and better things: Sofanit Abebe, Lauren Barton, Brian Bunnell, Bernardo Cho, Charles Cisco, Ryan Collman (who also helped me with the indexes), Jay Thomas Hewitt, Daniel Jackson, Daniel Lam, Patrick McMurray, Alex Muir, Benj Petroelje, Manse Rim, Matthew Sharp, and Sydney Tooth. I owe a similar intellectual debt to my Edinburgh colleagues and friends Helen Bond, Paul Foster, Alison Jack, and Philippa Townsend—as well as Larry Hurtado, of blessed memory. My earliest and greatest debt, however—a debt of filial piety—is to Joseph and Barbara Novenson, to whom this book is dedicated.

A number of publishers have kindly granted permission for the republication here (with some revisions) of essays of mine previously published elsewhere. I am very grateful to them all, and I record here the details of original publication of all of the essays collected in this volume.

1. "Our Apostles, Ourselves." Not previously published.

2. "Romans 1–2 between Theology and Historical Criticism." In *According to My Gospel: Theological Explorations in Romans 1–4*. Edited by Nijay K. Gupta and John K. Goodrich. Eugene, OR: Cascade, forthcoming. Reprinted with permission.

3. "*Ioudaios*, Pharisee, Zealot." In *Handbook to the Historical Paul*. Edited by Ryan S. Schellenberg and Heidi Wendt. London: T&T Clark, forthcoming. Reprinted with permission.

4. "Did Paul Abandon Either Judaism or Monotheism?" Pp. 239–59 in *The New Cambridge Companion to St. Paul*. Edited by Bruce W. Longenecker. Cambridge: Cambridge University Press, 2020. Reprinted with permission.

5. "Romans and Galatians." Pp. 218–40 in *The Cambridge Companion to the New Testament*. Edited by Patrick Gray. Cambridge: Cambridge University Press, 2021. Reprinted with permission.

6. "The Self-Styled Jew of Romans 2 and the Actual Jews of Romans 9–11." Pp. 133–62 in *The So-Called Jew in Paul's Letter to the Romans*. Edited by Rafael Rodriguez and Matthew Thiessen. Minneapolis: Fortress, 2016. Reprinted with permission.

7. "The Messiah ben Abraham in Galatians: A Response to Joel Willitts." *Journal for the Study of Paul and His Letters* 2 (2012): 163–69. Reprinted with permission.

8. "'God Is Witness': A Classical Rhetorical Idiom in Its Pauline Usage." *Novum Testamentum* 52 (2010): 355–75. Reprinted with permission.

9. "What Eschatological Pilgrimage of the Gentiles?" Pp. 61–73 in *Israel and the Nations: Paul's Gospel in the Context of Jewish Expectation*. Edited by Frantisek Abel. Minneapolis: Fortress, 2021. Reprinted with permission.

10. "Whither the Paul within Judaism *Schule*?" *Journal of the Jesus Movement in Its Jewish Setting* 5 (2018): 79–88. Reprinted with permission.

11. "The Pauline Epistles in Tertullian's Bible." *Scottish Journal of Theology* 68 (2015): 471–83. Reprinted with permission.

12. "Anti-Judaism and Philo-Judaism in Pauline Studies, Then and Now." In *Protestant Bible Scholarship: Anti-Semitism, Philo-Semitism, and Anti-Judaism.* Edited by Arjen Bakker, Rene Bloch, Yael Fisch, Paula Fredriksen, and Hindy Najman. Leiden: Brill, forthcoming. Reprinted with permission.

# ABBREVIATIONS

All abbreviations for the names of works, ancient and modern, follow the conventions of the *SBL Handbook of Style*, 2nd ed. (Atlanta: SBL Press, 2014) and, for ancient sources not included there, the *Oxford Classical Dictionary*, 4th ed. (Oxford: Oxford University Press, 2012).

| | |
|---|---|
| AB | Anchor Bible |
| *Ad Nic.* | Isocrates, *Ad Nicoclem* |
| *Adv. Jud.* | Tertullian, *Against the Jews* |
| AGJU | Arbeiten zur Geschichte des antiken Judentums und des Urchristentums |
| AJEC | Ancient Judaism and Early Christianity |
| *An.* | Tertullian, *The Soul* |
| *Ant.* | Josephus, *Jewish Antiquities* |
| ANTC | Abingdon New Testament Commentaries |
| AYB | Anchor Yale Bible |
| AYBRL | Anchor Yale Bible Reference Library |
| *b. Ber.* | Babylonian Talmud Berakhot |
| *b. Pesaḥ.* | Babylonian Talmud Pesaḥim |
| *b. Sanh.* | Babylonian Talmud Sanhedrin |
| *Bapt.* | Tertullian, *Baptism* |
| BDAG | Danker, Frederick W., Walter Bauer, William F. Arndt, and F. Wilbur Gingrich. *Greek-English Lexicon of the New Testament and* |

|  |  |
|---|---|
|  | *Other Early Christian Literature.* 3rd ed. Chicago: University of Chicago Press, 2000 (Danker-Bauer-Arndt-Gingrich) |
| BHT | Beiträge zur historischen Theologie |
| *BibInt* | *Biblical Interpretation* |
| *Big.* | Isocrates, *On the Team of Horses* |
| BIS | Biblical Interpretation Series |
| BJRL | Bulletin of the John Rylands University Library of Manchester |
| BJS | Brown Judaic Studies |
| BNTC | Black's New Testament Commentaries |
| BRLJ | Brill Reference Library of Judaism |
| BZNW | Beihefte zur Zeitschrift für die neutestamentliche Wissenschaft |
| *C. Ap.* | Josephus, *Against Apion* |
| *Carn. Chr.* | Tertullian, *The Flesh of Christ* |
| *CBQ* | *Catholic Biblical Quarterly* |
| CBQMS | Catholic Biblical Quarterly Monograph Series |
| *CJ* | *Classical Journal* |
| *Comm. Phlm.* | Jerome, *Commentariorum in Epistulam ad Philemonem liber* |
| ConBNT | Coniectanea Neotestamentica or Coniectanea Biblica: New Testament Series |
| *Conf.* | Philo, *On the Confusion of Tongues* |
| *CQ* | *Church Quarterly* |
| CRINT | Compendia Rerum Iudaicarum ad Novum Testamentum |
| *Ctes.* | Aeschines, *Against Ctesiphon* |
| *Cult. fem.* | Tertullian, *The Apparel of Women* |
| *CurTM* | *Currents in Theology and Mission* |
| *Cyr.* | Xenophon, *Cyropaedia* |
| *De Cor.* | Demosthenes, *On the Crown* |
| *Descr.* | Pausanius, *Description of Greece* |
| *Ebr.* | Philo, *On Drunkenness* |
| *EC* | *Early Christianity* |
| ESCJ | Studies in Christianity and Judaism/Études sur le christianisme et le judaïsme |
| ET | English Translation |
| *Exh. cast.* | Tertullian, *Exhortation to Chastity* |
| *ExpTim* | *Expository Times* |
| *Fals. Leg.* | Aeschines, *On the False Embassy* |
| FAT | Forschungen zum Alten Testament |
| FRLANT | Forschungen zur Religion und Literatur des Alten und Neuen Testaments |

| | |
|---|---|
| *Fug.* | Tertullian, *Flight in Persecution* |
| HBT | *Horizons in Biblical Theology* |
| *Herm.* | Tertullian, *Against Hermogenes* |
| HNTC | Harper's New Testament Commentaries |
| HTR | *Harvard Theological Review* |
| HUCA | *Hebrew Union College Annual* |
| ICC | International Critical Commentary |
| IDB | *The Interpreter's Dictionary of the Bible.* Edited by George A. Buttrick. 4 vols. Nashville: Abingdon, 1981 |
| *Inst.* | Quintilian, *Institutio oratoria* |
| JAAR | *Journal of the American Academy of Religion* |
| JAJ | *Journal of Ancient Judaism* |
| JBL | *Journal of Biblical Literature* |
| JBT | Jahrbuch für Biblische Theologie |
| JCTCRS | Jewish and Christian Texts in Contexts and Related Studies |
| *Jejun.* | Tertullian, *On Fasting, against the Psychics* |
| JJMJS | *Journal of the Jesus Movement in Its Jewish Setting* |
| JPT | *Jahrbücher für Protestantische Theologie* |
| JQR | *Jewish Quarterly Review* |
| JRS | *Journal of Roman Studies* |
| JSHJ | *Journal for the Study of the Historical Jesus* |
| JSJ | *Journal for the Study of Judaism in the Persian, Hellenistic, and Roman Periods* |
| JSJSup | Journal for the Study of Judaism Supplement Series |
| JSNT | *Journal for the Study of the New Testament* |
| JSNTSup | Journal for the Study of the New Testament Supplement Series |
| JSPL | *Journal for the Study of Paul and His Letters* |
| JTI | *Journal for Theological Interpretation* |
| JTS | *Journal of Theological Studies* |
| *J.W.* | Josephus, *Jewish War* |
| LAB | *Liber antiquitatum biblicarum* (Pseudo-Philo) |
| LCP | Latinitas Christianorum primaeva |
| *Legat.* | Philo, *Legatio ad Gaium* |
| LNTS | Library of New Testament Studies |
| LSJ | Liddell, Henry George, Robert Scott, Henry Stuart Jones. *A Greek-English Lexicon.* 9th ed. with revised supplement. Oxford: Clarendon, 1996 |
| LXX | Septuagint |
| *m. Mak.* | Mishnah Makkot |

| | |
|---|---|
| *Marc.* | Tertullian, *Against Marcion* |
| MBT | Münsterische Beiträge zur Theologie |
| *Mem.* | Xenophon, *Memorabilia* |
| *Migr. Abr.* | Philo, *On the Migration of Abraham* |
| *Mon.* | Tertullian, *Monogamy* |
| MT | Masoretic Text |
| NA28 | *Novum Testamentum Graece.* Nestle-Aland. 28th ed. |
| NASB | New American Standard Bible |
| *Nic.* | Isocrates, *Nicocles* |
| NICNT | New International Commentary on the New Testament |
| NIGTC | New International Greek Testament Commentary |
| *NovT* | *Novum Testamentum* |
| NovTSup | Supplements to Novum Testamentum |
| NRSV | New Revised Standard Version |
| *NTS* | *New Testament Studies* |
| OECT | Oxford Early Christian Texts |
| *Off.* | Cicero, *De officiis* |
| OG | Old Greek |
| *Or.* | Tertullian, *Prayer* |
| *Pan.* | Epiphanius, *Panarion* |
| *Phal.* | Lucian, *Phalaris* |
| *Praescr.* | Tertullian, *Prescription against Heretics* |
| *Prax.* | Tertullian, *Against Praxeas* |
| Ps.-Clem. | Pseudo-Clementines |
| *Pud.* | Tertullian, *Modesty* |
| PVTG | Pseudepigrapha Veteris Testamenti Graece |
| *Quaest. Amphil.* | Photius, *Amphilochian Questions* |
| *RBL* | *Review of Biblical Literature* |
| *Res.* | Tertullian, *The Resurrection of the Flesh* |
| *Rhet.* | Aristotle, *Rhetoric* |
| *RSPT* | *Revue des sciences philosophiques et théologiques* |
| RSV | Revised Standard Version |
| SBL | Society of Biblical Literature |
| SBLDS | Society of Biblical Literature Dissertation Series |
| SBR | Studies of the Bible and Its Reception |
| SBT | Studies in Biblical Theology |
| SC | Sources chrétiennes |
| SD | Studies and Documents |
| SJHC | Studies in Jewish History and Culture |

| | |
|---|---|
| *SJT* | *Scottish Journal of Theology* |
| Smyth | Smyth, Herbert Weir. *Greek Grammar.* Cambridge, MA: Harvard University Press, 1920 |
| SNTSMS | Society for New Testament Studies Monograph Series |
| SP | Sacra Pagina |
| *SR* | *Studies in Religion/Sciences Religieuses* |
| *TDNT* | *Theological Dictionary of the New Testament.* Edited by Gerhard Kittel and Gerhard Friedrich. Translated by Geoffrey W. Bromiley. 10 vols. Grand Rapids: Eerdmans, 1964–1976 |
| *Timocr.* | Demosthenes, *Against Timocrates* |
| TSMEMJ | Texts and Studies in Medieval and Early Modern Judaism |
| *Ux.* | Tertullian, *To His Wife* |
| *Vir. ill.* | Jerome, *De viris illustribus* |
| *Virg.* | Tertullian, *The Veiling of Virgins* |
| viz. | *videlicet*, namely |
| WBC | Word Biblical Commentary |
| WUNT | Wissenschaftliche Untersuchungen zum Neuen Testament |

1

# OUR APOSTLES, OURSELVES

Rembrandt van Rijn, the seventeenth-century Dutch master, painted scores of self-portraits. But one of these self-portraits is not like the others. The face in the painting is clearly the artist's own, but he is shown holding a book and a sword, the familiar distinguishing marks of medieval icons of Saint Paul. This is Rembrandt's *Zelfportret als de apostel Paulus*, "Self-Portrait as the Apostle Paul," of 1661. The figure we see is, at the same time, both the ancient apostle and the modern artist. As in visual art, so also in literature; that is the premise of this book. A great deal of modern interpretation of the Pauline letters consists of the interpreter making Paul speak for him (or her, but usually him). Our apostles, ourselves.

The roots of this fascinating reading strategy go back to antiquity. A letter ostensibly from Seneca to Paul preserved in the ancient *Correspondence of Paul and Seneca* reads:

> When we had read your book, that is to say, one of the many letters of ad-
> mirable exhortation to an upright life which you have sent to some city or
> to the capital of a province, we were completely refreshed. These thoughts,
> I believe, were expressed not by you, but through you; though sometimes
> they were expressed both by you and through you; for they are so lofty
> and so brilliant with noble sentiments that in my opinion generations of

men could hardly be enough to become established and perfected in them. (*Correspondence of Paul and Seneca* §1)[1]

By the time the fourth-century pseudepigrapher wrote these lines in the voice of Seneca the Younger, some ten or twelve generations of readers of Paul, at least, had already come and gone. Three centuries separated the "then" of the apostle from the "now" of the pseudepigrapher. And yet, our author reckons that many more generations will still be needed to plumb the depths of the letters—and here we are, in the 2020s CE, I writing a book on the letters of Paul, and you reading it. Equally interesting is our author's notion that the words of Paul are, in a sense, not really words of Paul. They are, he believes, words of the divine muse that speaks through Paul. But if hermeneutical ventriloquism can turn Paul's words into God's words, it can also turn Paul's words into the words of Paul's later interpreters.[2] In many but not all cases, these two phenomena are directly related: the interpreter, taking Paul's words to be God's words, uses Paul's words to express what he or she, often on other grounds, believes to be divine truth.

Indeed, an enormous amount of the history of interpretation of Paul—like the history of interpretation of other parts of the Bible, but more so—consists of this very thing: the use of Paul's words to make one's own theological point.[3] Ancient pseudepigraphers (like the author of the *Correspondence of Paul and Seneca*) made Paul speak for them by putting new words in his mouth. But

1. Trans. J. K. Elliott, *The Apocryphal New Testament* (Oxford: Clarendon, 1993). For essential critical introduction, see the excellent annotated bibliography by Chance Bonar, "Epistles of Paul and Seneca," *e-Clavis: Christian Apocrypha*. http://www.nasscal.com/e-clavis-christian-apocrypha/epistles-of-paul-and-seneca/.

2. I borrow and repurpose the notion of hermeneutical ventriloquism from Robert B. Brandom, "Hermeneutic Practice and Theories of Meaning," *SATS Northern European Journal of Philosophy* 5 (2004): 1–22; Brandom, *Tales of the Mighty Dead: Historical Essays in the Metaphysics of Intentionality* (Cambridge, MA: Harvard University Press, 2002), 90–120. Differently from Brandom, however, I am not here using the term to signify any kind of malpractice. Cf. Brandom, "Hermeneutic Practice," 3: "The hermeneutic ventriloquism practiced when the author's lips move, but only the reader's voice can be heard. This is *catachresis*: doing violence to the text, forcing one's uninvited interpretive attentions on the unresisting textual corpses of the mighty dead."

3. Cavan W. Concannon, *Profaning Paul* (Chicago: University of Chicago Press, 2021), speaks movingly of how he once felt there were a lot of important theological and ethical things *he needed Paul to say for him*. Cf. the related but different phenomenon of modern interpreters casting ancient figures in their own images, as Albert Schweitzer (*The Quest of the Historical Jesus*, trans. W. Montgomery [London: Black, 1910]) famously indicted the nineteenth-century authors of lives of Jesus for doing.

the more usual way of making Paul speak for oneself, from antiquity down to the present, is simply to make the canonical words of Paul mean new things. The enormous grab bag of reading strategies traditionally called "historical criticism" remains useful today just to the extent that it helps us to keep that fact before our eyes and helps us to remember that an ancient author's words did not always mean what they eventually came to mean.[4]

With some biblical texts, modern critics have a relatively easy time remembering this; with other texts, much less so. When one reads Song of Songs as an allegory of Christ and the church, one knows without having to think too hard about it that to do so is to make a secondary (or tertiary, or quaternary) interpretive move. The many florid mentions of necks and breasts and gardens remind even the most pious reader that this poem was originally about, well, something else.[5] But when one reads Paul's Letter to the Galatians, one can easily trick oneself into thinking that the text is not about something strange and ancient, but about one's own present-day theological concerns, whatever they may be. As Robert Morgan writes about Protestant interpreters in particular, "The field of Pauline interpretation . . . is where Protestant theologians since Luther have generally heard the gospel 'clearest of all.' This is, therefore, the point at which their interpretation of the tradition and their own theology are most likely to coincide. In saying what Christianity *was* for Paul, they are often saying what it *is* for themselves."[6] This is what I mean by hermeneutical ventriloquism. Morgan's perceptive observation is especially true of Protestants (of which tribe—full disclosure—the present writer is a member), but not only of Protestants.[7] Other denominations of Christians, not to mention non-Christian readers of various stripes, have likewise found Paul's words useful for making their own points. My aim in saying this is not to throw stones at anyone for doing so. They are within their rights to use Paul's words

4. Which is to say that historical criticism *does* in fact remain useful today, some recent dismissals notwithstanding. E.g., Laura Salah Nasrallah, *Archaeology and the Letters of Paul* (Oxford: Oxford University Press, 2019), 17: "I reject the historical critical method and its faith in exegetical tools to fix, like a butterfly pinned on a wall, the people of a given time and place, to be able to say: *This is what they thought, this is what they did, this is the explanation*" (italics original). I follow Nasrallah in rejecting the kind of hubris she describes here, but I do not recognize in her description that which I would want to call historical criticism.

5. See further Ilana Pardes, *The Song of Songs: A Biography* (Princeton: Princeton University Press, 2019).

6. Robert Morgan, "Introduction: The Nature of New Testament Theology," in Morgan, ed., *The Nature of New Testament Theology*, SBT (London: SCM, 1973), 53 (emphasis original).

7. On the specifically Protestant variety of hermeneutical ventriloquism, see chapter 12 below.

in this way. And even if they were not, it would doubtless carry on happening anyway. But in such a situation as this, it is not unreasonable to pursue greater clarity about what kind of reading, exactly, any particular reader is offering.

As I point out in the following chapters (especially chapters 2 and 11), recent interpretation of Paul has witnessed quite a lot of noisy insistence that people who do not read the letters in way *x* or *y* are doomed to get Paul wrong. In contrast to all that, I would like to rise in defense of (what Jeffrey Stout calls) the relativity of interpretation:[8] the recognition that what counts as a good interpretation of the letters depends entirely on the questions and interests one brings, and that there are a great many worthwhile questions and interests one might bring (though there are also some bad questions and some blameworthy interests). Depending on the particular questions and interests at hand, very different reading strategies might be called for. Thus rightly Stout: "We might need many different *complete* interpretations of a given text to do all the explaining we want to do. This should encourage openness to the possibility that interpretations phrased in terms of Hirschian authorial intentions, Gadamerian talk of effective history, reception-theory à la Jauss, reader-response theory à la Iser, and the rest can sometimes usefully be seen as belonging to compatible explanatory projects geared to resolving different puzzles."[9] Indeed, Stout himself adduces the letters of Paul as an example in this connection. He writes:

> An apostle of a religious movement writes a letter that is later canonized. You may be interested in constructing a picture that explains what the apostle was up to. If so, you will map the letter onto your language accordingly. But you may be interested instead in the letter as a scriptural book, in the relations its words and sentences take on in its canonical setting, and in its

---

8. Jeffrey Stout, "The Relativity of Interpretation," *Monist* 69 (1986): 103–18; and relatedly Stout, "What Is the Meaning of a Text?" *New Literary History* 14 (1982): 1–12. My adoption of Stout's analysis in this connection is in the spirit of Stephen D. Moore and Yvonne Sherwood, *The Invention of the Biblical Scholar: A Critical Manifesto* (Minneapolis: Fortress, 2011), 130: "[We should] engage with and extend what philosophers, in particular, have been doing with the Bible, while resisting the temptation simply to repeat the protective mantra that they are not reading Paul, say, as they should (read: as we would)." In fact, there is no one way that one should read Paul. It depends entirely upon who the one is and for what purposes she is reading.

9. Stout, "Relativity of Interpretation," 111 (emphasis original). On fruitful uses of these and other theory-rich reading strategies for New Testament texts, see now Michal Beth Dinkler, *Literary Theory and the New Testament*, AYBRL (New Haven: Yale University Press, 2019), in particular her chapter 6 on the letters of Paul.

use as a normative document some centuries after it was authored. In that case, you will probably want an interpretation you can ascribe to the community for which the letter functions as scripture, thereby helping explain the community's behaviour under circumstances unlike the author's own.[10]

In the present volume, I am for the most part "interested in constructing a picture that explains what the apostle was up to," to use Stout's idiom. That is to say, I come with a primary interest in the original historical situation of the letters and, consequently, questions framed in such a way as to illuminate that situation. These essays are, in other words, mostly historical-critical studies of the Pauline letters (focused on the first-century "then," not the twenty-first-century "now"), although at many points throughout I also take up other, different readings of the same texts. I do so because I think that, in many cases, we can best clarify our own questions and interests by contrasting them with adjacent ones, by being as precise as possible about what we are and are not asking or claiming. This is all the more urgent with the letters of Paul because of their outsize influence in subsequent tradition. Once more Stout: "Philosophical and literary texts often enter the humanistic canon because they provide uniquely valuable occasions for normative reflection. We lavish great interpretive care upon them, but not always in order to 'get them right.' Getting them right sometimes ceases to matter. We sometimes want our interpretations to teach us something new, not so much about the text itself, its author, or its effective history as about ourselves, our forms of life, our problems."[11] As with the humanistic canon, so with the Christian canon. We might, and people very often do, read the letters of Paul in order to learn not about the letters themselves but about our own form of life.[12] But that is a very different undertaking from reading the letters in order to learn about the past, which is the burden of the present volume. And we do both jobs better if we do not confuse the one with the other.

A few years ago, I wrote that, with her book *Paul: The Pagans' Apostle*, Paula Fredriksen manages to "make Paul weird again."[13] (That essay of mine is now chapter 10 of the present volume.) The reason why that is such an important achievement is that Paul has come to seem so very not-weird, so normal,

10. Stout, "Relativity of Interpretation," 110.

11. Stout, "Relativity of Interpretation," 111.

12. See John M. G. Barclay, "What Makes Paul Challenging Today?," in *The New Cambridge Companion to St. Paul*, ed. Bruce W. Longenecker (Cambridge: Cambridge University Press, 2020), 299–318.

13. See Paula Fredriksen, *Paul: The Pagans' Apostle* (New Haven: Yale University Press, 2017).

through long centuries of Christian use. We have made Paul's words our own so many times over, in so many contexts, that we have come to view him simply as one of us.[14] But he is not one of us. He is as strange and ancient as Boudica, or Honi the Circle-Drawer, or Peregrinus Proteus.[15] The essays in the present volume try to read Paul as strange and ancient, to do what C. M. Chin calls "weird history" as opposed to "normalizing history." Chin explains:

> The historical project of making people from past worlds like us is an empathetic project, and it does useful work in many contexts, such as when we argue for the continued relevance of ancient history to the contemporary world. I would like to suggest, though, that the empathetic project of history, especially premodern history, is better served by a kind of imaginative stubbornness, a determination to remember that people living in past worlds were not always very much like us, but that we should pay attention to them anyway. And this much harder project of empathy is what I think focusing on weirdness allows us to undertake.[16]

Just so. Paul was not always very much like us, but we should pay attention to him anyway. That is my watchword in the present volume. Of course, differently from most of the premodern past about which Chin writes here, the letters of Paul come down to us as part of Christian scripture, which adds another layer of complexity to the matter (to indulge in understatement).

---

14. In this connection, Stanley Stowers rightly criticizes what he calls "academic Christian theological modernism" for assuming that "with regard to religion, morals, sociality, and subjectivity, the early Christians are the same as us. They are the same people in different clothes, with a different 'science'" (Stanley K. Stowers, "Kinds of Myths, Meals, and Power: Paul and the Corinthians," in *Redescribing Paul and the Corinthians*, ed. Ron Cameron and Merrill P. Miller [Atlanta: SBL Press, 2011], 107).

15. This point is expertly made by Troels Engberg-Pedersen, *Paul and the Stoics* (Edinburgh: T&T Clark, 2000), 19: "In spite of the fact that scholars have generally accepted the historical-critical paradigm, they often do not realize that as long as what they are elucidating is the genuinely historical meaning of Paul's [theology] . . . they cannot also behave as if they were reading Paul from within and so present their reading to its readers as a real option for them. For if scholars are truly historical in their readings, then the picture that will come out of their efforts does *not* constitute a real option for us" (emphasis original). This is *not* to say that any weird historical reading of Paul is, *eo ipso*, accurate, or that, when it comes to historical readings, the weirder the better. The point is just that to think historically is always to mind the gap.

16. C. M. Chin, "Marvelous Things Heard: On Finding Historical Radiance," *Massachusetts Review* 58 (2017): 480.

For of course, one very common approach to biblical texts is deliberately to read them as speaking to the present, not the past.[17] But even with biblical texts—and even among religious readers, I would argue—a version of Chin's rule really should stand. Recognizing that Paul belongs to the past forces us modern readers to take moral responsibility for our interpretations, which is all the more urgent for religious readers of the Bible. Contrary to a popular figure of speech, it is not the case that Paul (or Moses, or Jesus, etc.) speaks, and we just listen.[18] No, we read Paul (or Moses, or Jesus, etc.) and generate our interpretations, for which we then stand responsible.[19] Chin, again, puts the point eloquently:

> The reason that hindering our ability to draw such historical analogies is morally important is that historical analogy is not a useful substitute for direct moral reasoning. Without recourse to such analogies, we are forced into the often uncomfortable position of asking ourselves directly, is what I am doing right now, in this moment, the right thing? The weirdness of the past gives us fewer places to hide in the present. . . . Domesticating the past is a disservice to that past in a factual sense, but it is also a disservice to ourselves in an aesthetic and moral sense. The project of learning to see and write weird history is a harder empathetic task than writing normalizing history.[20]

"The weirdness of the past gives us fewer places to hide in the present." As regards the letters of Paul, the lesson here is that later readers ought to own the uses to which they put Paul's words. The buck stops with them, with us. Neither Augustine's "Sin came into the world through one person," nor Martin Luther's "righteousness from faith," nor Robert Louis Dabney's "The one called as a slave is the Lord's freedperson" is identical to what Paul meant by those words. Both Paul's and Augustine's views are "weird" (in Chin's sense), but the

---

17. This phenomenon is explained with wonderful clarity by James L. Kugel, *The Bible As It Was* (Cambridge, MA: Harvard University Press, 1997), 1–50.

18. What Dale Martin perceptively calls "the myth of textual agency" in his *Sex and the Single Savior: Gender and Sexuality in Biblical Interpretation* (Louisville: Westminster John Knox, 2006), 1–16.

19. Elisabeth Schüssler Fiorenza ("The Ethics of Biblical Interpretation: Decentering Biblical Scholarship," *JBL* 107 [1988]: 3–17) argues that interpreters of the Bible have (at least) a twofold ethical obligation, what she calls the "ethics of historical reading" and the "ethics of accountability."

20. Chin, "Marvelous Things Heard," 489–90.

one is not the other. If we mind the gap between Paul and Augustine, and the gap between Augustine and us, and the gap between Paul and us, and so on, then we stand to understand all parties better. This example reminds us that there are not just—as the hermeneutical slogan has it—two horizons: ancient text and modern reader, then and now.[21] There are myriad horizons ("thens") in between, all pressing, powerfully but often silently, upon the modern reader of Paul. Marcion, Valentinus, Tertullian, Augustine, Gregory, Lombard, Francis, Thomas, Luther, Baur, Douglass, Dabney, Harnack, Barth, Day, Weil, and King are with us whenever we read Paul. The question is whether we have eyes to see them standing there.[22]

Of course, the only kind of consciousness that any interpreter can possibly have is a historically-effected consciousness (*wirkungsgeschichtliches Bewusstsein*). We stand in the river downstream from the letters of Paul, as it were, not—to stretch the metaphor—on a ledge above looking down on them. As Gadamer puts it, "Effective-history still determines modern historical and scientific consciousness; and it does so beyond any possible knowledge of this domination. Historically effected consciousness is so radically finite that our whole being, effected in the totality of our destiny, inevitably transcends its knowledge of itself."[23] Our historically-effected consciousness is an inevitability, a necessity. But much recent research on Paul has made a virtue of this necessity, ignoring or renouncing the project of reading Paul as "weird history" and going all in on normalizing interpretation. One version of this move is very familiar from the long history of Christian theology: an argument (or, more often, simply a claim) that whatever the modern author is talking about

21. E.g., Anthony C. Thiselton, *The Two Horizons: New Testament Hermeneutics and Philosophical Description* (Grand Rapids: Eerdmans, 1980). A similar objection arises to Krister Stendahl's perceptive but insufficient distinction between what a biblical text "meant" and what it "means." See Stendahl, "Biblical Theology, Contemporary," in *IDB*, 1:418–32; and the apt criticism by Ben C. Ollenburger, "What Krister Stendahl 'Meant': A Normative Critique of 'Descriptive Biblical Theology,'" *HBT* 8 (1986): 61–98.

22. On the way biblical texts carry their afterlives around with them, see Brennan W. Breed, *Nomadic Text: A Theory of Biblical Reception History* (Bloomington: Indiana University Press, 2014). On the ancient readers of Paul who are still very much with us, see Jennifer R. Strawbridge, *The Pauline Effect: The Use of the Pauline Epistles by Early Christian Writers* (Berlin: de Gruyter, 2015); and on (some of the) modern ones, Lisa M. Bowens, *African American Readings of Paul: Reception, Resistance, and Transformation* (Grand Rapids: Eerdmans, 2020).

23. Hans-Georg Gadamer, "Foreword to the Second Edition," in Gadamer, *Truth and Method*, 2nd rev. ed., trans. Joel Weinsheimer and Donald G. Marshall (London: Bloomsbury, 2013), xxxi.

is the selfsame subject matter (*Sache*) that the apostle was talking about.[24] Thus, for instance, Stephen Westerholm's recent defense of Martin Luther from the slanders of some New Perspective critics:

> Admittedly, Luther is prone to seeing his own circumstances reflected in biblical texts (if this is a fault); and (herein lies a very great fault), when he writes polemically, his terms and tone are often monumentally lamentable. Still, one has only to read a few pages of his writings (most any will do) to realize that, in crucial respects, he inhabits the same world, and breathes the same air, as the apostle . . . Such kindredness of spirit gives Luther an inestimable advantage over many readers of Paul in 'capturing' the essence of the apostle's writings.[25]

Westerholm's initial suggestion—that it is churlish of us to fault Luther for seeing his own circumstances reflected in biblical texts—is well made. What else could we reasonably expect of a sixteenth-century clergyman reading his Bible?[26] But the further claim that Luther—in contrast to twentieth-century historical critics—"inhabits the same world as" and "breathes the same air as" the apostle Paul, making Luther uniquely able to "capture the essence" of Paul's letters, does not follow and is not true. Luther breathed sixteenth-century, Northern European air, no matter how much love he had for the letters of Paul. Now, of course, the twenty-first-century historical critic does not breathe the same air as Paul any more than Luther did. Only ancient Mediterranean people breathed that air. But a good historical reading has in its favor that it starts by recognizing this fact.

Even if we were to set aside (!) the 1,500-year and 2,000-mile gap between Paul and Luther, Westerholm's claim still begs a crucial question. It assumes what is not proven, namely, that "justification by faith," or "the divine kerygma," or "the message of God's grace in Christ," or "a massive, unremitting sense of answerability to one's Maker" (all Westerholm's terms) is in fact the *Sache* of Paul's letters, the thing itself. Claims like this may seem intuitively true to those of us who use these Pauline or Pauline-sounding phrases in our own theologi-

24. On this phenomenon, see further chapters 2 and 12 below.

25. Stephen Westerholm, "The 'New Perspective' at Twenty-Five," in *Justification and Variegated Nomism*, ed. D. A. Carson et al., WUNT 2.181 (Tübingen: Mohr Siebeck, 2001), 2:38.

26. See further David Lincicum, "Martin Luther in Modern New Testament Scholarship," in *Oxford Encyclopedia of Martin Luther*, ed. Derek R. Nelson and Paul R. Hinlicky, 3 vols. (Oxford: Oxford University Press, 2017); Stephen J. Chester, *Reading Paul with the Reformers: Reconciling Old and New Perspectives* (Grand Rapids: Eerdmans, 2017), 13–60.

cal thinking, but that intuition is subjective in the extreme. (And anyway, not all of us do use Pauline phrases in our theological thinking, or do theological thinking at all, for that matter!) This point has been well made by some practitioners of *Sachkritik* ("subject matter criticism"). Thus Robert Morgan, citing a disagreement between Käsemann and Bultmann, rightly complains, "As in all *Sachkritik*, the problem is how to avoid subjective theological judgments closing the interpreter's ear to the witness of some texts. It loads the dice in favour of the interpreter and against the text, because the criterion of criticism is the interpreter's understanding of the gospel."[27] Paul's words are part of our historically-effected consciousness, but it does not follow—nor is it the case—that any of us, even a Luther (let alone a Westerholm or a Novenson!), has privileged access to the mind of the apostle.

I said that this kind of pious claim to breathe the same air as the apostle was one version of a move to dismiss history and simply read Paul for constructive ends, but there is a second, impious version as well. Here I think, for example, of Cavan Concannon's bracing manifesto for the project of "profaning Paul."[28] He explains, "We have to kill Paul. . . . I am calling for an overthrowing of Paul as the representative of the Platonic One in favor of the creation of a vibrant, polyvalent Pauline archive, to use Peter Sloterdijk's term, that opens onto new possibilities for assembling heretofore unthought future Paulinisms. In other words, and to paraphrase Marx, let's stop interpreting Paul and start creating Paulinisms that can change the world."[29] When Concannon speaks with disapproval of "Paul as the representative of the Platonic One," he means Paul as the object of traditional historical-critical study: "Though we have had almost two hundred years of a historicized Paul, historicism has not broken free of its original conceit . . . Rather than finding Paul 'as he really was,' we keep finding Pauls who are really like us."[30]

This diagnosis of the field is spot on, but Concannon's prescribed treatment, in my view, is not. That prescription: "It is only by killing Paul and in so doing emptying his archive of the force that it wields in Christianity and the

---

27. Robert Morgan, "*Sachkritik* in Reception History," *JSNT* 33 (2010): 189.

28. Concannon, *Profaning Paul*; Concannon, "Paul Is Dead. Long Live Paulinism! Imagining a Future for Pauline Studies," *Ancient Jew Review* (1 November 2016), www.ancient jewreview.com/read/2016/11/1/paul-is-dead-long-live-paulinism-imagining-a-future-for -pauline-studies. Concannon's project is anticipated in some ways by Moore and Sherwood, *Invention of the Biblical Scholar*; and Ward Blanton, *A Materialism for the Masses: Saint Paul and the Philosophy of Undying Life* (New York: Columbia University Press, 2014).

29. Concannon, "Paul Is Dead."

30. Concannon, "Paul Is Dead."

West, that he might paradoxically be fused into an apparatus of struggle and resistance. In a repetition of Paul's own gesture of rendering the law, in Agamben's terms, 'inoperative,' a Paul who has become inoperative may become 'freely available for use' in Paulinisms that have yet to be imagined."[31] Where Concannon calls for amputation, so to speak, I think there are therapeutic options short of amputation. I sympathize with Concannon in his call to "create Paulinisms that can change the world," but I see no reason why we should have to kill Paul in order to do so. For one thing, of course, Paul is already very much dead, and has been for nearly two millennia. To say this is not just to be cheeky; it is to recall Chin's crucial point, cited above, about the weirdness of the premodern past. For another, related thing, we do not need Paulinisms to change the world. We can, and should, do that entirely apart from any appeals to Paul[32] (though some people, Christians especially, might have their own good reasons for appealing to Paul).[33] By all means, let's profane Paul, but to insist that we must *also* renounce a historical interest in him is to cut off one's nose to spite one's face.[34]

And the nose is every bit as useful as the ears or the eyes or the mouth, as a certain apostle might have said, depending whether one needs to smell or hear or see or speak. It is, once again, a matter of the relativity of interpretation. There are some legitimate questions and interests for which only a historical reading strategy will do the trick; other questions and interests will call for a theological, or feminist, or Marxist hermeneutic. The fact that modern New Testament studies have been so sloppy with their ostensibly historical readings of Paul is an indictment on us, but it is not reason to divest ourselves of what is, for its part, one quite useful reading strategy. Who knows when it might come in handy for some task or other? We ought, urgently, to denaturalize

31. Concannon, "Paul Is Dead."

32. In his *Profaning Paul*, Concannon comes down closer to this position, expressing more of a willingness simply to leave Paul out of his constructive ethical thinking.

33. On the possibility, and indeed desirability, of different constituencies having their own traditioned reasons for taking public moral action, see Jeffrey Stout, *Ethics after Babel: The Languages of Morals and Their Discontents*, 2nd ed. (Princeton: Princeton University Press, 2001); Stout, *Democracy and Tradition* (Princeton: Princeton University Press, 2004).

34. Indeed, some of the best recent profanations of Paul are conspicuous for their command of the relevant ancient history, above all Jacob Taubes, *The Political Theology of Paul*, trans. Dana Hollander (Stanford: Stanford University Press, 2004); and relatedly Giorgio Agamben, *The Time That Remains: A Commentary on the Letter to the Romans*, trans. Patricia Dailey (Stanford: Stanford University Press, 2005); but admittedly not Alain Badiou, *Saint Paul: The Foundation of Universalism*, trans. Ray Brassier (Stanford: Stanford University Press, 2003).

and relativize historical criticism, but not single it out for proscription. In the essays that follow, I take a primarily historical approach to Paul not because it is the only or the best reading strategy—it is neither—nor because we have to read historically before we can read otherwise—we do not.[35] I take the approach I do because it is one good reading strategy ("good" relative to particular questions and interests), one that promises to yield some interesting results if only we have the curiosity and the will to try it.[36]

35. This latter point is eloquently made by A. K. M. Adam, *Making Sense of New Testament Theology: "Modern" Problems and Prospects* (Macon, GA: Mercer University Press, 1995).

36. The proof of the pudding is, of course, in the eating. Readers will have to judge whether my essays below do in fact yield interesting results. But other recent historical studies of Paul have certainly done so, which gives me cause for optimism about the continuing usefulness of the approach. E.g., Caroline Johnson Hodge, *If Sons Then Heirs: A Study of Kinship and Ethnicity in the Letters of Paul* (New York: Oxford University Press, 2007); Troels Engberg-Pedersen, *Cosmology and Self in the Apostle Paul: The Material Spirit* (Oxford: Oxford University Press, 2010); John M. G. Barclay, *Pauline Churches and Diaspora Jews* (Grand Rapids: Eerdmans, 2016); Matthew Thiessen, *Paul and the Gentile Problem* (New York: Oxford University Press, 2016); Fredriksen, *Pagans' Apostle*; Emma Wasserman, *Apocalypse as Holy War: Divine Politics and Polemics in the Letters of Paul*, AYBRL (New Haven: Yale University Press, 2018); Jennifer Eyl, *Signs, Wonders, and Gifts: Divination in the Letters of Paul* (New York: Oxford University Press, 2019).

2

# ROMANS 1–2 BETWEEN THEOLOGY
# AND HISTORICAL CRITICISM

Beverly Gaventa and Benjamin Schliesser, among others, have recently offered powerful readings of certain verses and themes in Rom 1–2.[1] In this essay, by contrast, I would like to consider at a meta-level *the ways in which* and *the purposes for which* we read these two tremendously influential chapters, and how these various ways and purposes sometimes bump into each other. Hence my title: "Romans 1–2 between Theology and Historical Criticism." In one respect, this topic—the relation between theology and historical criticism—is evergreen. It takes us back to the foundations of the modern discipline of biblical studies, and it is in theory relevant to any and every biblical text.[2] In practice, however, the issue arises with some texts more than others. And I would submit that, just as Romans has occasioned more conflict between theology and historical criticism than, say, Esther or 2 Peter, so also Rom

---

1. Beverly Roberts Gaventa, "The Son of God in Power: Power and Its Places in Paul's Letter to the Romans," and Benjamin Schliesser, "The Theology of Paul in a Nutshell: A Fresh Look at the Phrase 'From Faith to Faith' (Rom 1:17)," both in Nijay K. Gupta and John K. Goodrich, eds., *According to My Gospel: Theological Explorations in Romans 1–4* (Eugene, OR: Cascade, forthcoming)

2. On this classic problem, see the disciplinary history by Michael C. Legaspi, *The Death of Scripture and the Rise of Biblical Studies* (New York: Oxford University Press, 2010); and the critical intervention of Stephen D. Moore and Yvonne Sherwood, *The Invention of the Biblical Scholar: A Critical Manifesto* (Minneapolis: Fortress, 2011).

1–2 have occasioned more than, say, Rom 5 or 6 or 12 or 15.[3] Romans 1–2 have been, and still are (in ways I shall explain below), disproportionately important sites of friction between theology and historical criticism.

Why is this the case? I can think of several possible reasons, but one stands out as especially relevant. Most Christian theologies have needed hamartiologies, accounts of sin—accounts, that is, of the plight for which Christ is the solution. And more so than most of Christian scripture, Rom 1–2 has seemed to offer a hamartiology, or at least raw material for one[4] (even if, as Beverly Gaventa pointed out to me years ago in a course on Romans, "sin" per se is almost entirely absent from these chapters, with the verb ἁμαρτάνω appearing only at 2:12 [twice] and the noun ἁμαρτία not at all, which is an observation worth reflecting on).[5] "The wrath of God is revealed from heaven upon all impiety and unrighteousness of people who suppress the truth" (1:18).[6] "They are without excuse" (1:20). "They exchanged the truth of God for falsehood" (1:25). "You who pass judgment on another person do the same things" (2:1). "You who boast in the law, do you dishonor God through transgression of the law?" (2:23) Although these lines do not add up to a doctrine of sin, they have seemed to get theologians a bit further down the road in that direction than other, more ad hoc notices of human wrongdoing scattered elsewhere across the canon. Of course, Cain, Korah, Jezebel, Manasseh, Judas, Simon Magus, Hymenaeus, and Philetus are bad apples, but theology requires a more generalizing account of the human problem, and many have found such an account in Rom 1–2.

3. For reasons having to do with the longstanding (but arguably misguided) quest for the center of Romans, whether, e.g., chapters 1–4, 5–8, 9–11, 12–15, or other permutations beside.

4. E.g., in recent research, Frank Thielman, *From Plight to Solution: A Jewish Framework for Understanding Paul's View of the Law in Galatians and Romans*, NovTSup 61 (Leiden: Brill, 1989), 87–116; Stephen Westerholm, *Understanding Paul: The Early Christian Worldview of the Letter to the Romans* (Grand Rapids: Baker, 2004), 37–64. On sin in the letters of Paul more widely, see now Bruce W. Longenecker, "What Did Paul Think Is Wrong in God's World?," in *The New Cambridge Companion to St. Paul*, ed. Bruce W. Longenecker (Cambridge: Cambridge University Press, 2020); and the essays in Nijay K. Gupta and John K. Goodrich, eds., *Sin and Its Remedy in Paul* (Eugene, OR: Cascade, 2020).

5. Stephen L. Young, "Paul the Mythmaker" (PhD diss., Brown University, 2016), has argued—persuasively to my mind—that ἁμαρτία, which becomes a main focus in Rom 5–7, is related to but different from the bad behaviour discussed in Rom 1–2, most of which Paul does not expressly call ἁμαρτία.

6. Translations of ancient sources are my own unless otherwise noted.

## WITHIN OR WITHOUT THEOLOGY

Consequently, Rom 1–2 have been made to do load-bearing work for Christian theologies, and wherever this happens, historical-critical interpretation of the relevant texts becomes proportionately more complicated. That's OK. We are professionals. We are trained to handle hermeneutical complications of this sort.[7] But in this case, there is more to it. When I speak of friction between theology and historical criticism over Rom 1–2, I mean not only conceptual friction within the mind of a single interpreter when she reads these chapters—although this is *a*, and I will argue should be *the*, paramount issue—but also polemical friction between interpreters or schools of interpreters. That is to say, recent research has witnessed forceful arguments to the effect that one cannot begin to understand Paul's indictment of people who suppress truth and worship idols (1:18–32), or his rhetorical turn to the judgmental person (2:1–16), or his rebuke of the person who goes by the name of Jew (2:17–29) *as long as one labours under the inherited baggage of theology*; and, on the other hand, equally forceful arguments to the effect that one cannot begin to understand these very same passages *otherwise than by embracing theology*. For the former school of thought, theology is the root of all misunderstanding, while for the latter, theology is the *sine qua non* for any viable interpretation. This is a head-spinning state of affairs, and in my view, an unfortunate symptom of a kind of culture-war mentality in some quarters of biblical studies.

For the Paul-*without*-theology school, I have in mind something like Stanley Stowers's tremendously and rightly influential *Rereading of Romans* (twenty-five years old as I write this essay). Stowers writes, "Romans has come to be read in ways that differ fundamentally from ways that readers in Paul's own time could have read it. More than any other writing of earliest Christianity, Romans, especially in the West, came to bear the major economies of salvation. These systems of sin and salvation reshaped the frame of reference that determined the reading of the letter."[8] And again, "[In its Christian recep-

---

7. Trained, e.g., by Elisabeth Schüssler Fiorenza, "The Ethics of Biblical Interpretation: Decentering Biblical Scholarship," *JBL* 107 (1988); 3–17; A. K. M. Adam, *Making Sense of New Testament Theology: "Modern" Problems and Prospects* (Macon, GA: Mercer University Press, 1995); Brian K. Blount, *Cultural Interpretation: Reorienting New Testament Criticism* (Minneapolis: Fortress, 1995); James L. Kugel, *How to Read the Bible: A Guide to Scripture, Then and Now* (New York: Free Press, 2007); and the essays in Markus Bockmuehl and Alan J. Torrance, eds., *Scripture's Doctrine and Theology's Bible* (Grand Rapids: Baker Academic, 2008).

8. Stanley K. Stowers, *A Rereading of Romans: Justice, Jews, and Gentiles* (New Haven: Yale University Press, 1994), 1.

tion,] Romans became a theological treatise about humanity and Christianity. Paul's situation as a Jewish 'sectarian' who preached the redemption of the gentiles became incomprehensible."[9] And again, "In the later church's moral and doctrinal instruction, the biblical texts were treated more and more as information. A text is read as information when the reader has accepted the truth of the text before reading it. . . . Rhetorical form was not important: moral and theological ideas were."[10] For the school of thought of which I am taking Stowers as a representative, theology has done terrible hermeneutical mischief with Romans, but historical criticism (leavened, perhaps, with some critical theory of religion) can put things right.[11]

For the Paul-*within*-theology school, I have in mind something like John Barclay's recent article in the journal *Early Christianity*, "An Identity Received from God," which—not coincidentally—Barclay frames as a response to one of Stowers's former students, Caroline Johnson Hodge (along with her collaborator Denise Kimber Buell).[12] In this article, Barclay argues that Paul's thought in Romans and elsewhere is "irreducibly theological" (Barclay's term), that it cannot be properly understood in terms other than the theological. He writes, "In discourse limited by anthropological or political tools of analysis, ethnicities may be represented as 'primordial' . . . or as 'processural' . . . or as a subtle mixture of the two. . . . What this analysis cannot handle (except as a mythological construct) is the specifically *theological* forms of identity evoked in the Pauline letters, which represent the believers' identity as something received from outside human agency."[13] And again, "So long as one figures Pauline identities in

9. Stowers, *Rereading*, 10.

10. Stowers, *Rereading*, 15.

11. Through the 1980s and 1990s, Stowers was above all a historical critic, while in the 2000s he became and remains increasingly a theorist of religion, albeit one focused primarily on antiquity.

12. John M. G. Barclay, "An Identity Received from God: The Theological Configuration of Paul's Kinship Discourse," *EC* 8 (2017): 354–72, which responds especially to Denise Kimber Buell and Caroline Johnson Hodge, "The Politics of Interpretation: The Rhetoric of Race and Ethnicity in Paul," *JBL* 123 (2004): 235–51; Denise Kimber Buell, *Why This New Race: Ethnic Reasoning in Early Christianity* (New York: Columbia University Press, 2005); Caroline Johnson Hodge, *If Sons Then Heirs: A Study of Kinship and Ethnicity in the Letters of Paul* (New York: Oxford University Press, 2007).

13. Barclay, "Identity Received from God," 370, emphasis original. A great deal hangs on Barclay's distinction here between "mythological" and "theological," a distinction he assumes but does not explicate in the article. On at least one common-sense reading of the two terms, they might mean almost exactly the same thing, differing only in relation to the (religious) subjectivity of the speaker or writer. See further my discussion of the ambiguity of the phrase "Pauline theology" below.

purely human terms, it seems impossible to escape the horns of the dilemma. . . .
One may, of course, take up a stance outside of Paul's own theology, and categorize his language of a God-determined identity as a form of ideological
mythology. . . . But if one reads Paul's theology on his own irreducibly *theological*
terms, one may also find in Paul the tools for a non-supersessionist construal
of ethnicity."[14] For the school of thought of which I am taking Barclay as a representative, historical criticism is certainly welcome and even necessary, but
inasmuch as it brackets out or forecloses theology, it will inevitably fail not only
(obviously) at the task of theology but also at its own task.

### PAUL'S THEOLOGY AND OURS

So which is it? Stowers and Barclay cannot both be right. I want to suggest that
in fact neither is right, at least not in the strong forms laid out in the excerpts
just quoted. With Stowers, I think that many interpreters of Romans have
mistakenly assumed, and still do, that what Paul means by "sin," "salvation,"
and the like is simply identical with what their respective Christian theologies
(be they Catholic, Lutheran, Reformed, Wesleyan, or what have you) mean by
these terms.[15] As Robert Morgan has written about Protestant exegetes, "The
field of Pauline interpretation . . . is the point at which their interpretation of
the tradition and their own theology are most likely to coincide. In saying what
Christianity *was* for Paul, they are often saying what it *is* for themselves."[16]
Moreover, also with Stowers, I think that making assumptions of this sort does
hinder one from thinking clearly about what Paul himself might have meant

---

14. Barclay, "Identity Received from God," 372, emphasis original.

15. On this point, see further Stanley K. Stowers, "Kinds of Myths, Meals, and Power:
Paul and the Corinthians," in *Redescribing Paul and the Corinthians*, ed. Ron Cameron and
Merrill P. Miller (Atlanta: SBL Press, 2011), 106–7: "The dominant approach to Paul and the
Corinthian letters I characterize as academic Christian theological modernism. . . . This
tradition is thoroughly grounded in the situation developing from the aftermath of the
Protestant Reformation, but took form as a part of the crystallization of European moder-
nity in the nineteenth century. . . . [It assumes that] with regard to science and cosmology,
the ancients and the early Christians are other in a rather absolute sense, *but with regard
to religion, morals, sociality, and subjectivity, the early Christians are the same as us.* They
are the same people in different clothes, with a different 'science.' The early Christians are
not only generally the same as modern Europeans, but also the same as the professors and
Christian scholars who study them in their focus on specialized intellectual interests, that
is, doctrines, theology, and ideas" (emphasis mine).

16. Robert Morgan, "Introduction: The Nature of New Testament Theology," in Morgan,
ed., *The Nature of New Testament Theology*, SBT (London: SCM, 1973), 53 (emphasis original).

by these and other relevant terms. To the extent that this is the case, theology has indeed done and still does hermeneutical mischief with Romans.[17] With Barclay, however, I think that those historical-critical readings that bracket out theology *in any sense of that term* effectively shut their eyes and plug their ears to a great deal of Paul's own discourse precisely in its historical context. For instance, in the relatively short space of Rom 1–2, Paul refers to God, θεός, some thirty-two times, a feature that even the least pious, most hard-nosed historical-critical or comparative-religious reading has to account for.[18]

The main problem in this whole discussion, I suspect, is a crucial ambiguity in the term "theology" and a corresponding vagueness in the ways we use it in these debates.[19] Although it is not new, this observation is important, and it is directly relevant here. The phrase "Pauline theology" can mean the theology held by the apostle himself, as best we can reconstruct and describe it: the set of ideas about gods and other non-obvious beings that this first-century person subscribed to. But "Pauline theology" can also mean any constructive Christian theology that is inspired by, takes its cues from, or speaks in the idiom of the letters of Paul. In this sense of the phrase, Augustine's theology, or Luther's, or Barth's, or, for that matter, Kwame Bediako's, or Philip Ziegler's, or Linn Tonstad's, can accurately be called a "Pauline theology." But this is a very different use of the term. To speak of theology in this latter sense is to imply something about the religious commitments of the interpreter, whereas to speak of it in the former sense is to imply no such thing.[20]

And it is at just this point that I confess that I do not understand what Barclay means—and not just Barclay, but other like-minded readers—by saying that Paul's discourse is "irreducibly theological." Is it just that any reading of Paul's letters, to be deserving of the name, owes an account of the agency

17. A point well made by Paula Fredriksen, "The Philosopher's Paul and the Problem of Anachronism," in *St. Paul among the Philosophers*, ed. John D. Caputo and Linda Martin Alcoff (Bloomington: Indiana University Press, 2009), 61–73. I discuss this dynamic further in chapter 12 below.

18. Thus rightly Nils A. Dahl, "The Neglected Factor in New Testament Theology," in Nils A. Dahl, *Jesus the Christ: The Historical Origins of Christological Doctrine*, ed. Donald H. Juel (Minneapolis: Fortress, 1991), 153–63.

19. This conceptual problem is helpfully explored by R. W. L. Moberly, "What Is Theological Interpretation of Scripture?," *JTI* 3 (2009): 161–78.

20. The distinction I am making here has certain correspondences to Krister Stendahl's famous distinction between "meant" and "means" in his "Biblical Theology, Contemporary," in *IDB*, 1:418–32. But that classic rubric, despite or perhaps because of its rhetorical power, has some crucial conceptual weaknesses. See Ben C. Ollenburger, "What Krister Stendahl 'Meant': A Normative Critique of 'Descriptive Biblical Theology,'" *HBT* 8 (1986): 61–98.

of God (and, perhaps, of Christ, Satan, angels, demons, etc.) therein? Or is it something more than this that is being insisted upon? In his article cited above, Barclay sets out the options in this way: "One may, of course, take up a stance outside of Paul's own theology, and categorize his language of a God-determined identity as a form of *ideological mythology*. . . . [Or one can] read Paul's theology on his own *irreducibly theological* terms."[21] Here, reading Paul's letters as irreducibly theological means, on Barclay's account, *for the interpreter herself to take up a stance within Paul's theology*. Now, if you happen to have postliberal sensibilities (of which I myself am not entirely innocent),[22] then this is an admittedly attractive idea, but it is also impossible, and hence cannot be a *sine qua non* for good interpretation. Much as some of us might like to take up a stance inside Paul's theology, we are constrained by our own subjectivity. We are moderns, not ancients, and nothing, not even religious commitments, can make us otherwise.[23] Many moderns, including many modern interpreters of Paul, do not stand within *any* theology, but those of us who do—including, I suspect, many of the likely readers of this book—stand within our own theologies, not Paul's, even if our theologies owe a great deal to his.

## HUMANS AND GENTILES

Let us return to Rom 1–2. Those who have read Rom 1–2 as "irreducibly theological" have typically been invested in claiming that all humanity is

21. Barclay, "Identity Received from God," 372.

22. I wrote my undergraduate thesis on George A. Lindbeck, *The Nature of Doctrine: Religion and Theology in a Postliberal Age* (Louisville: Westminster John Knox, 1984). But the idea of taking up a stance within a biblical book is closer to that strand of postliberalism represented by Hans W. Frei, *The Eclipse of Biblical Narrative: A Study in Eighteenth and Nineteenth Century Hermeneutics* (New Haven: Yale University Press, 1974). The whole movement comes under compelling criticism from Kathryn Tanner, *Theories of Culture: A New Agenda for Theology* (Minneapolis: Fortress, 1997).

23. One of the enduring points made by Rudolf Bultmann, in particular in his *New Testament and Mythology, and Other Basic Writings*, trans. Schubert M. Ogden (Philadelphia: Fortress, 1984). In fact, Barclay himself makes something very close to this point in his "What Makes Paul Challenging Today?," in Longenecker, *New Cambridge Companion to St. Paul*, 299–318, here 300: "The straight transfer of Paul's views to our own day is neither possible nor, perhaps, desirable. If Paul is to remain in any sense a constructive challenge, we will need to deploy, self-consciously, a creative theological hermeneutic." I think this claim of Barclay's is just right, but it is a very different idea from the "taking up a stance within Paul's own theology" for which he pleads elsewhere.

in view more or less from Rom 1:18 onward: "The wrath of God is revealed from heaven upon all impiety and unrighteousness of *humanity*" (1:18), they might translate. "Exchanging the glory of God for an image" (1:23) is true not only of gentiles but also of Israel (Ps 106:20), they might argue. The person who judges others in 2:1 is probably a Jew, and the so-called Ἰουδαῖος in 2:17 is certainly a Jew, so the burden of Rom 1–2 must be to stop every mouth and bring the whole human race under the judgment of God, they might reason. For this reading strategy, see not only major commentaries like Barth, Cranfield, Dunn, Moo, and Longenecker,[24] but also important monographs like John Barclay's *Paul and the Gift* or Jonathan Linebaugh's *God, Grace, and Righteousness in Wisdom of Solomon and Paul's Letter to the Romans*.[25] Meanwhile, those who have pleaded for a strictly historical-critical approach have tended to argue for a conspicuous ethnic logic to these chapters: the letter expressly addresses itself to gentiles (1:5, 13); 1:18–32 is a Hellenistic Jewish screed about gentile idolatry; 2:1–16 scolds the stock Greco-Roman character of the pretentious person; even 2:17–29 (for those who are able to receive it) indicts not a Jew, let alone *the Jews*, but a newly circumcised gentile proselyte who takes the name of "Jew" (Ἰουδαῖος ἐπονομάζῃ, Rom 2:17). For this kind of reading strategy, see the likes of Stanley Stowers, Dale Martin, Caroline Johnson Hodge, Denise Kimber Buell, Runar Thorsteinsson, or Paula Fredriksen.[26]

All this I believe to be a broadly accurate characterization of the ways Rom 1–2 have been and are being read in the recent history of research. (Exhibit A: the 2018 Society of Biblical Literature panel on the implied audience of Paul's Letter to the Romans, featuring Margaret Mitchell, John Barclay, Laura Dingeldein, and Runar Thorsteinsson.) We should note,

---

24. Karl Barth, *The Epistle to the Romans*, trans. Edwyn D. Hoskyns (London: Oxford University Press, 1933); C. E. B. Cranfield, *The Epistle to the Romans*, 2 vols., ICC (London: T&T Clark, 2010 [1975]); James D. G. Dunn, *Romans*, 2 vols., WBC (Nashville: Nelson, 1988); Douglas J. Moo, *The Epistle to the Romans*, NICNT (Grand Rapids: Eerdmans, 1996); Richard N. Longenecker, *The Epistle to the Romans*, NIGTC (Grand Rapids: Eerdmans, 2016).

25. John M. G. Barclay, *Paul and the Gift* (Grand Rapids: Eerdmans, 2015); Jonathan A. Linebaugh, *God, Grace, and Righteousness in Wisdom of Solomon and Paul's Letter to the Romans*, NovTSup 152 (Leiden: Brill, 2013).

26. Stowers, *Rereading*; Johnson Hodge, *If Sons Then Heirs*; Buell, *Why This New Race*; Dale B. Martin, "Heterosexism and the Interpretation of Romans 1:18–32," *BibInt* 3 (1995): 332–55; Runar M. Thorsteinsson, *Paul's Interlocutor in Romans 2: Function and Identity in the Context of Ancient Epistolography*, ConBNT 40 (Stockholm: Almqvist & Wiksell, 2003); Paula Fredriksen, *Paul: The Pagans' Apostle* (New Haven: Yale University Press, 2017).

however, that there is no *necessary* connection between the hermeneutical stances (theology, historical criticism, and their various possible combinations) on the one hand and these particular exegetical proposals on the other. Taking a theological approach to Rom 1–2 does not *entail* that one find there a systematic indictment of the whole human race, nor does taking a historical-critical approach *entail* that one read Rom 1–2 as a sad story of gentile dissipation. Recent interpretation has tended to run in these grooves—because of the weight of (what Stowers calls) academic Christian theological modernism—but it need not have run this way, and sometimes it has run otherwise.

One important example of it running otherwise is Krister Stendahl (of blessed memory), already his early *Paul among Jews and Gentiles*, but especially his later *Final Account* (a kind of Romans commentary in miniature).[27] Stendahl's interest in Romans was vigorously theological, and indeed ecclesiastical, and yet he pioneered an approach to the letter that put Jew/gentile questions at the forefront. A more recent and quite different example is Douglas Campbell, as proudly theological an interpreter of Paul as any I know. He has just written a *Pauline Dogmatics!*[28] How many of us have written one of those? And yet, on Rom 1–2, Campbell finds himself in the unlikely company of Stowers and others who stress the importance of rhetorical prosopopoeia, speech-in-character, in Romans. But whereas Stowers highlights prosopopoeia in Rom 7, arguing that the wretched first-person speaker is not Paul himself but an akratic gentile, Campbell detects it in Rom 1–2, placing the chauvinistic indictment of idolaters in 1:18–32 and the message of strict retributive justice in 2:6–13 not on Paul's lips but on the lips of his rival teacher.[29] I disagree with this reconstruction, but I admire Campbell's resolve to read Romans as the work of Greco-Roman rhetoric that it is, even if doing so unsettles certain familiar theological sureties. Stendahl and Campbell illustrate how many different kinds of theological readings there are, and what different results can be generated with the tools of historical criticism.

27. Krister Stendahl, *Paul among Jews and Gentiles, and Other Essays* (Philadelphia: Fortress, 1976); Stendahl, *Final Account: Paul's Letter to the Romans* (Minneapolis: Fortress, 1995).

28. Douglas A. Campbell, *Pauline Dogmatics: The Triumph of God's Love* (Grand Rapids: Eerdmans, 2020).

29. Douglas A. Campbell, *The Deliverance of God: An Apocalyptic Rereading of Justification in Paul* (Grand Rapids: Eerdmans, 2009).

## CONCLUSION

I conclude by referring you to a hundred-year-old but still brilliant discussion of the same question that I have tried, with rather less brilliance, to discuss here. In the preface to the second edition of his bombshell commentary on Romans, Karl Barth made this now-classic hermeneutical proposal:

> I have nothing whatever to say against historical criticism. I recognize it, and once more state quite definitely that it is both necessary and justified. My complaint is that recent commentators confine themselves to an interpretation of the text which seems to me to be no commentary at all, but merely the first step towards a commentary. . . . Place the work of Jülicher side by side with that of Calvin: how energetically Calvin, having first established what stands in the text, sets himself to re-think the whole material and to wrestle with it, till the walls which separate the sixteenth century from the first become transparent! Paul speaks, and the man of the sixteenth century hears. The conversation between the original record and the reader moves round the subject-matter, until a distinction between yesterday and to-day becomes impossible.[30]

Just a few short years after Barth wrote these words, and probably—if James Carleton Paget is right—responding to Barth, though not by name,[31] Albert Schweitzer prefaced his own *Mysticism of Paul the Apostle* with this quite different hermeneutical proposal:

> My methods have remained old-fashioned, in that I aim at setting forth the ideas of Paul in their historically conditioned form. I believe that the mingling of our ways of regarding religion with those of former historical periods, which is now so much practised, often with dazzling cleverness, is of no use as an aid to historical comprehension, and of not much use in the end for our religious life.[32]

Now, Barth's Romans is a virtuoso theological interpretation, easily one of the best on offer. (Origen gives him some competition, and Augustine, and

30. Barth, *Romans*, 6–7.
31. James Carleton Paget, "Schweitzer and Paul," *JSNT* 33 (2011): 223–56.
32. Albert Schweitzer, *The Mysticism of Paul the Apostle*, trans. W. Montgomery (London: Black, 1931), x.

Jacob Taubes,[33] and I am holding a spot for Beverly Gaventa's forthcoming commentary on Romans.)[34] But in one crucial respect, Schweitzer has the better end of this argument. Regarding what is most "useful for our religious life," I am not certain, and I would defer to the professional theologians. But regarding "use as an aid to historical comprehension," I think Schweitzer is right to maintain a distinction between Paul's way of regarding religion and ours. And I find this distinction helpful in Rom 1–2, because in my own exegesis of these chapters, I have come to conclude that Paul does not in fact supply all, or even most, of what Christian hamartiologies need.[35] Romans 1–2—like the rest of scripture, but more so—lies before us *between* theology and historical criticism, accessible to us by both avenues, but not at the same time. And that's OK. We are professionals. We are trained to handle complications of this sort.

33. Jacob Taubes, *The Political Theology of Paul*, trans. Dana Hollander (Stanford: Stanford University Press, 2004).

34. Beverly Roberts Gaventa, *Romans*, NTL (Louisville: Westminster John Knox, forthcoming).

35. See chapter 6 below, and a fuller account in my book *The End of the Law and the Last Man: Paul between Judaism and Christianity* (New York: Cambridge University Press, forthcoming).

3

# *IOUDAIOS*, PHARISEE, ZEALOT

According to Epiphanius, the ancient Ebionites claimed that the apostle Paul was not a born Jew at all but was actually a Greek convert (*Pan.* 30.16.8–9). Most modern critics have rightly judged this claim to be false, but the question behind it is a fair and an important one.[1] It matters for purposes of historical understanding just what ethnic categories a person is born into, migrates into, claims for herself, or has claimed for her by others. It matters, for instance, that Alexander was a Macedonian (and latterly an arch-Hellene), Philo an Egyptian Jew, Josephus a Judean Jew (and latterly a Roman), Lucian a Syrian, and so on.[2] The purpose of this essay is to consider several ethnic and related labels that get attached to the apostle Paul in the primary sources. We focus on three, in particular: Ἰουδαῖος (*Ioudaios*), Pharisee, and zealot. These three are not symmetrical with one another. Ἰουδαῖος is an ethnonym, Pharisee the name of a particular Jewish school, and zealot possibly the name of a strand of Jewish piety. Paul uses all three terms of himself in the seven undisputed letters (although what exactly he means by them requires some parsing), and all three are also used of him in early Christian sources. For the

---

1. A noteworthy exception is Hyam Maccoby, *The Mythmaker: Paul and the Invention of Christianity* (San Francisco: Harper & Row, 1986), who follows Epiphanius's Ebionites for his reconstruction of Paul.

2. On this complicated issue in ancient sources, see Jonathan M. Hall, *Ethnic Identity in Greek Antiquity* (Cambridge: Cambridge University Press, 1997).

purposes of this essay, I am primarily interested here not in the extent to which Paul's *thought* can be characterized as Jewish, Pharisaic, and so on, but rather in how *he* as a historical actor fits within these and other adjacent categories. We will consider each of the three labels in turn.

## IOUDAIOS

The Ebionite story notwithstanding, it is virtually certain that Paul was from birth what his contemporaries would have called a Ἰουδαῖος—that is, a member of the nation whose fatherland was Judea (Ἰουδαία) and whose mother-city was Jerusalem.[3] And this despite the fact that Paul's own writings place him mostly in Syria, Asia Minor, Macedonia, and Achaia. (Luke says that he was born at Tarsus in Cilicia [Acts 9:11; 21:39; 22:3], but nothing in Paul's letters either confirms or disconfirms this.) Like his distinguished coethnic Philo Judaeus (Philo the Ἰουδαῖος), who lived cradle-to-grave in Egypt, Paul was an expatriate Ἰουδαῖος, a diaspora Ἰουδαῖος,[4] the kind of person about whom the geographer Strabo wrote: "This people [the Ἰουδαῖοι] has already made its way into every city, and it is not easy to find any place in the habitable world which has not received this nation [τοῦτο τὸ φῦλον] and in which it has not made its power felt" (Strabo *apud* Josephus, *Ant.* 14.115).

Both Philo and Paul illustrate a notorious problem for translators—namely, whether Greek Ἰουδαῖος is more closely equivalent to English "Judean" or "Jew."[5] The problem only arises at all because English has two terms that are possible equivalencies, as we also do, for instance, for Ἕλλην, "Greek" or

3. Josephus reports on the currency of the ethnonym Ἰουδαῖος: "This name [Ἰουδαῖοι], by which they have been called from the time when they went up from Babylon, is derived from the tribe of Judah [ἀπὸ τῆς Ἰούδα φυλῆς]; as this tribe was the first to come to those parts, both the people themselves and the country have taken their name from it" (*Ant.* 11.173 [Josephus, *Jewish Antiquities, Volume IV: Books 9-11*, trans. Ralph Marcus, LCL (Cambridge, MA: Harvard University Press, 1937)]). I will say more below about the options for translating Ἰουδαῖος, but I will also sometimes just use the Greek in the interest of bracketing some of those debates.

4. See John M. G. Barclay, "Paul among Diaspora Jews: Anomaly or Apostate?" *JSNT* 60 (1995): 89–120; Ronald Charles, *Paul and the Politics of Diaspora* (Minneapolis: Fortress, 2014); Jill Hicks-Keeton, "Putting Paul in His Place: Diverse Diasporas and Sideways Spaces in Hellenistic Judaism," *JJMJS* 6 (2019): 1–21.

5. See the roundtable discussion by Adele Reinhartz, Steve Mason, Daniel Schwartz, Annette Yoshiko Reed, Joan Taylor, Malcolm Lowe, Jonathan Klawans, Ruth Sheridan, and James Crossley, "Jew and Judean: A Forum on Politics and Historiography in the Trans-

"Hellene," but not for most other ancient ethnonyms: Ῥωμαῖος ("Roman"), Αἰγύπτιος ("Egyptian"), Μῆδος ("Mede"), and so on. Because Paul, like Philo, operates almost entirely in the diaspora, it has been conventional in some quarters to gloss Ἰουδαῖος in his case with "Jew," and to reserve "Judean" for persons resident in the fatherland (e.g., Judah Maccabee, Jesus of Nazareth, the young Josephus). Some recent interpreters, however, have judged this convention anachronistic and argued that ancient Greek Ἰουδαῖος always means English "Judean."[6] Their key point—that Ἰουδαῖος has irreducibly ethnic and geographical overtones (as do "Roman," "Egyptian," "Mede," etc.)—is well taken. But their further suggestion that the English gloss "Jew" *lacks* these overtones is open to debate, and is in my view mistaken.[7] Hence, while I have no particular quarrel with the consistent use of "Judean" for Ἰουδαῖος, and I think that there are many texts in which "Judean" is the best gloss, I also think that recent objections to the use of the gloss "Jew" are overwrought, and thus I permit myself the use of both English terms in this essay.[8]

However we choose to gloss it, Ἰουδαῖος is in any case the most frequent and most important ethnonym used of Paul in the primary sources. The Acts of the Apostles has him expressly introduce himself as a Ἰουδαῖος: "I am a Jewish person [ἄνθρωπος . . . Ἰουδαῖος] from Tarsus in Cilicia" (Acts 21:39); and again, "I am a Jewish man [ἀνὴρ Ἰουδαῖος], born at Tarsus in Cilicia" (Acts 22:3). And other characters recognize Paul as a Ἰουδαῖος, such as when some disgruntled oracle-mongers in Philippi complain about Paul and Silas, "These people are Jews [Ἰουδαῖοι ὑπάρχοντες] and are troubling our city" (Acts 16:20). By interesting contrast, *Acts of Paul* only identifies Paul as a Christian, never as a Jew. Paul's enemies Demas and Hermogenes (cf. 2 Tim 1:15; 4:10) conspire against him, urging Thamyris, "Say that he [Paul] is a Christian, and in this way you will destroy him" (*Acts of Paul* 3.16). When Paul is in fact brought before the proconsul, he only says of himself, "I teach the things that have been revealed

lation of Ancient Texts," *Marginalia*, August 26, 2014, https://marginalia.lareviewofbooks.org/jew-judean-forum/.

6. Most importantly Steve Mason, "Jews, Judaeans, Judaizing, Judaism: Problems of Categorization in Ancient History," *JSJ* 38 (2007): 457–512.

7. With Daniel R. Schwartz, "'Judaean' or 'Jew'? How Should We Translate *Ioudaios* in Josephus?," in *Jewish Identity in the Greco-Roman World*, ed. Jörg Frey, Daniel R. Schwartz, and Stephanie Gripentrog, AJEC 71 (Leiden: Brill, 2007), 3–28.

8. With Michael L. Satlow, "Jew or Judean?," in *The One Who Sows Bountifully: Essays in Honor of Stanley K. Stowers*, ed. Caroline Johnson Hodge et al., BJS 356 (Atlanta: SBL Press, 2013), 165–75; and John M. G. Barclay, "*Ioudaios*: Ethnicity and Translation," in *Ethnicity, Race, Religion*, ed. Katherine M. Hockey and David G. Horrell (London: T&T Clark, 2018), 46–58.

to me by God" (*Acts of Paul* 3.17). The Acts of the Apostles, it turns out, has a keen theological interest in the ethnicity of Paul,[9] while *Acts of Paul* has its own, quite different set of concerns.[10]

Strikingly, whereas Luke very much likes to have Paul claim the ethnonym Ἰουδαῖος, in his own letters Paul more often self-identifies with other, related ethnonyms. One of these is Ἰσραηλίτης, "Israelite," as in Rom 11:1: "I myself am an Israelite, from the seed of Abraham, of the tribe of Benjamin." The term recurs in 2 Cor 11:22–23, where Paul measures himself against certain rivals: "Are they Hebrews? So am I. Are they Israelites? So am I. Are they seed of Abraham? So am I. Are they ministers of Christ?—I am speaking as if deranged—I more so." "Israelite" is a heritage ethnonym, an old, biblical name for descendants of the twelve sons of Jacob, also known as Israel.[11] Paul uses it not only of himself but also of all his συγγενεῖς κατὰ σάρκα, "kinfolk according to the flesh": "They are the Israelites" (Rom 9:4), whom he can also call Israel, Ἰουδαῖοι, and—via metonymy—the circumcision.

The 2 Cor 11 passage just cited evidences another of Paul's preferred ethnonyms as well: Ἑβραῖος, "Hebrew."[12] "Are they Hebrews? So am I." He uses the same term in another autobiographical passage in Phil 3:5: "[I am] circumcised on the eighth day, from the people Israel, of the tribe of Benjamin, a Hebrew from Hebrews." The expression here, Ἑβραῖος ἐξ Ἑβραίων, "a Hebrew from Hebrews," is often translated "Hebrew of Hebrews," as if it were simply superlative: "a really great Hebrew." But this is wrong. The preposition ἐξ with genitive indicates source: a Hebrew *from* Hebrews, which in this context must be a claim about parentage.[13] Paul is the Hebrew son of a Hebrew mother and father; hence his proper circumcision on the eighth day after birth, as per the law of Gen 17:12 and Lev 12:3. (Contrast the adult circumcision of the half-Jewish Timothy in Acts 16:1–3, or of any male proselyte.)[14] I strongly

---

9. See Christopher Stroup, *The Christians Who Became Jews: Acts of the Apostles and Ethnicity in the Roman City* (New Haven: Yale University Press, 2020).

10. On which see Richard I. Pervo, *The Acts of Paul: A New Translation with Introduction and Commentary* (Eugene, OR: Cascade, 2014).

11. See Graham Harvey, *The True Israel: Uses of the Names Jew, Hebrew, and Israel in Ancient Jewish and Early Christian Texts*, AGJU 35 (Leiden: Brill, 1996), 189–266.

12. On which see Harvey, *True Israel*, 104–47.

13. Thus rightly Caroline Johnson Hodge, *If Sons Then Heirs: A Study of Kinship and Ethnicity in the Letters of Paul* (New York: Oxford University Press, 2007), 79–92, esp. 81.

14. On which issue see Matthew Thiessen, *Contesting Conversion: Genealogy, Circumcision, and Identity in Ancient Judaism and Christianity* (New York: Oxford University Press, 2011); and on its particular relevance to Paul, Thiessen, *Paul and the Gentile Problem* (New York: Oxford University Press, 2016).

suspect that Paul makes this claim here because he thinks that his rivals in this passage—"the dogs, the bad workers, the mutilation" (Phil 3:2)—cannot say the same of themselves, but space prevents us from pursuing that argument further here.[15] This same phrase, "a Hebrew from Hebrews," is also invoked by modern interpreters as a claim about proficiency in Hebrew and/or Aramaic languages,[16] but this, too, is unwarranted. I can certainly imagine that Paul knew Hebrew or Aramaic or both (as Acts 21:40–22:2 portrays him), although nothing in his letters requires this conclusion. But in any case, that is certainly not his claim in Phil 3:5. In ancient Greek generally, Ἑβραΐς means Hebrew the *language* (often with διάλεκτος or φωνή, as in Acts 21:40; 22:2; 26:14; 4 Macc 12:7; 16:15), while Ἑβραῖος means Hebrew the *nationality* (often with λαός, e.g., in LXX Exodus),[17] and Paul only uses the latter term in his letters.

As Paul uses the terms, Ἰουδαῖος, Israelite, and Hebrew are for the most part coextensive. Not so φυλὴ Βενιαμίν, "tribe of Benjamin" (Rom 11:1; Phil 3:5), one of twelve tribes comprising the ancient nation of Israel. By the Roman period, Israelite tribal identity was effectively a relic of the mythical past. Jews of this period were just Jews, not Danites, Asherites, and so on. The major exception were Levites, whose ancestral right to the priesthood in Jerusalem gave them reason to maintain (at least the myth of) a distinct tribal identity.[18] Aside from Levi, only Judah and (less so) Benjamin retain some currency in Roman-period Jewish sources due to their comprising the old, biblical Southern Kingdom, centered in Jerusalem, whose territory roughly corresponded to Roman Judea. Paul is one of these few Roman-period sources attesting a specifically Benjaminite identity.[19] What exactly he intends by asserting it is not altogether

15. See Ryan D. Collman, "Beware the Dogs! The Phallic Epithet in Philippians 3:2," *NTS* 67 (2021): 105–20.

16. E.g., Martin Hengel, *The Pre-Christian Paul*, trans. John Bowden (London: SCM, 1991), 25–27; Jerome Murphy-O'Connor, *Paul: A Critical Life* (Oxford: Oxford University Press, 1996), 47–48.

17. Acts 6:1—ἐγένετο γογγυσμὸς τῶν Ἑλληνιστῶν πρὸς τοὺς Ἑβραίους, "there arose a dispute of the Hellenists with the Hebrews"—is a possible exception, but Hengel (*Pre-Christian Paul*) makes it the bedrock of his reconstruction.

18. See Menahem Stern, "Aspects of Jewish Society: The Priesthood and Other Classes," in *The Jewish People in the First Century*, vol. 2, ed. S. Safrai and M. Stern, CRINT (Assen: Van Gorcum, 1976), 561–630.

19. Another Roman-period witness to the tribe of Benjamin is the rabbinic dynasty running from Hillel through Gamaliel I to Rabbi Judah the Patriarch, which Richard Bauckham has ambitiously tried to link up to Paul's own genealogy. See Richard Bauckham, "Gamaliel and Paul," in *Earliest Christianity within the Boundaries of Judaism*, ed. Alan J. Avery-Peck, Craig Evans, and Jacob Neusner, BRLJ 49 (Leiden: Brill, 2016), 87–106.

clear. Jason Staples has proposed that Paul intends for his gentile mission to effect the ingathering of the ancient lost tribes of Israel (who are scattered among the gentiles); Paul identifies as a Benjaminite because he is one of the remnant who are not thus scattered.[20] This is not impossible, but there is arguably a simpler, more rhetorical explanation (on which see below).

In an interesting article from 2015, Glenn Snyder argues that Paul actually does not identify as a Ἰουδαῖος at all.[21] He takes Paul's two claims to membership in the tribe of Benjamin (Rom 11:1; Phil 3:5) to be an *alternative to*, not a *specification of*, identification as a Ἰουδαῖος. Snyder reasons that (what he calls) "the Jew/gentile dichotomy" is an imposition on the part of modern interpreters. He points to 1 Cor 9:20—"To the Ἰουδαῖοι, I became as a Ἰουδαῖος"—as evidence that Paul positively *denies* identification as a Ἰουδαῖος, not (as I would interpret this verse) that Paul imagines he can pneumatically rise above that identity. A fly in the ointment for Snyder's hypothesis is Gal 2:15–16, where (on most standard translations) Paul says to Cephas, "We Ἰουδαῖοι by nature, not sinners from the gentiles, knowing that a person is not rightwised from works of the law except through trust of Jesus Christ, we indeed trusted in Christ Jesus." "We Ἰουδαῖοι by nature" looks like an emphatic first-person identification, and one that expressly underlines the dichotomy with gentiles. For Snyder, however, following an argument in an unpublished paper by Jeremy Hultin, the speaker of these words is not Paul but the mysterious "people from James" (Gal 2:12).[22] Those people may believe in a Jew/gentile dichotomy, but Paul, for his part, does not. Paul is a Benjaminite, not a Ἰουδαῖος.

This is clever but, I think, finally mistaken. Admittedly, Hultin's argument is ingenious—he points out that the forms εἶδον and εἶπον in Gal 2:14 could be third-person plurals ("they saw . . . they said") rather than first-person singulars ("I saw . . . I said")—but in the end it creates more problems than it solves. All of Gal 2:11–21 makes better sense if it is Paul, not the people from James, who rebukes Cephas, as suggested by the certainly first-person singular ἀντέστην, "I opposed," in 2:11. But even if we were to concede Gal 2:15, the

20. Jason A. Staples, "What Do the Gentiles Have to Do with 'All Israel'? A Fresh Look at Romans 11:25–27," *JBL* 130 (2011): 371–90; and now also Staples, *The Idea of Israel in Second Temple Judaism: A New Theory of People, Exile, and Israelite Identity* (Cambridge: Cambridge University Press, 2021).

21. Glenn E. Snyder, "Paul beyond the Jew/Gentile Dichotomy: A Perspective from Benjamin," *Expositions* 9 (2015): 125–37.

22. Jeremy Hultin, "Who Rebuked Cephas? A New Interpretation of Gal 2:14–17" (paper presented at the Annual Meeting of the Society of Biblical Literature, Baltimore, MD, November 2013).

Jew/gentile dichotomy is still all over Paul's letters:[23] God is the god of both Jews and gentiles (Rom 3:29). God calls people from both the Jews and the gentiles (Rom 9:24). The crucified Christ is an offense to Jews and folly to gentiles (1 Cor 1:23). The good announcement is for everyone who trusts, Jew and Greek (Rom 1:16).[24] Jews and Greeks are all under sin (Rom 3:9). There is no distinction between Jew and Greek, for the same lord is over all (Rom 10:12). And so on and on. And if Paul bisects humanity asymmetrically into Jews and gentiles, as he certainly does, then there is no question on which side of the divide he himself falls. As a pneumatic, he likes to think that he can transcend this divide, condescending to be *like* the Ἰουδαῖοι or *like* the lawless gentiles (1 Cor 9:19–22).[25] But by nature, φύσει, Paul is a Ἰουδαῖος, a Hebrew, an Israelite. His Benjaminite identity is a further specification, not a rival identity. Just as Christ is an Israelite by *nation* (Rom 9:5) and a Davidide by *clan* (Rom 1:3), in the same way Paul is an Israelite by *nation* (γένος) and a Benjaminite by *tribe* (φυλή).

Why, then, does Paul prefer to name himself with the heritage terms Hebrew, Israelite, and Benjaminite rather than the more pedestrian Ἰουδαῖος? As Jennifer Eyl has recently shown, it is precisely because the latter is more pedestrian.[26] Paul happily uses Ἰουδαῖος, as his contemporaries do, as the workaday term for anyone from that nation (some 25 times in his letters).[27] But in the only three passages where he details his own ethnicity (Phil 3:4–6; 2 Cor 11:22–23; Rom 11:1), Paul writes in a highly rhetorical, competitive mode; hence the baroque heritage terms. As Eyl puts it, "In moments of self-defense,

23. See further Krister Stendahl, *Paul among Jews and Gentiles* (Philadelphia: Fortress, 1976); Stanley K. Stowers, *A Rereading of Romans: Justice, Jews, and Gentiles* (New Haven: Yale University Press, 1994); Thiessen, *Paul and the Gentile Problem*; Matthew V. Novenson, "Gentile Sinners: A Brief History of an Ancient Stereotype," in *Negotiating Identities*, ed. Anders Runesson et al. (Minneapolis: Fortress, forthcoming).

24. "Greek" is Paul's normal way of signifying a single gentile person, because the grammatical singular ἔθνος signifies a single gentile nation, not a single gentile person.

25. Which creates social problems for him, as explained by Cavan W. Concannon, *When You Were Gentiles: Specters of Ethnicity in Roman Corinth and Paul's Corinthian Correspondence*, Synkrisis (New Haven: Yale University Press, 2014).

26. Jennifer Eyl, "'I Myself Am an Israelite': Paul, Authenticity, and Authority," *JSNT* 40 (2017): 148–68.

27. Ἰουδαῖος occurs almost not at all in the disputed Pauline letters, only a single instance in Col 3:11: "There is no Greek and Jew [Ἕλλην καὶ Ἰουδαῖος], circumcision and foreskin, barbarian, Scythian, slave, free, but Christ is all, and in all" (cf. the parallels at Gal 3:28; 1 Cor 12:13). Titus 1:14 warns *against* "Jewish myths [Ἰουδαϊκοῖς μύθοις] and commandments of people who turn away from the truth."

Paul's claim to be an Israelite is a strategic discursive claim, the purpose of which is to ground his authority simultaneously in ethnic nativeness and the allure of the primordial past."[28] The rhetorical effect is all the greater because Paul writes to gentile—that is, *non*-Jewish—audiences. He performs for them a kind of exotic ethnic authenticity. In Eyl's apt comparison: "Like Brazilian capoeira instructors in Europe, Indian yogis in the modern West, and Umbrian haruspices passing themselves off as Etruscan, Paul's rhetoric of ethnic authenticity factors into the construction of his authority."[29] This is where another longstanding, influential explanation for Paul's usage—namely, that Ἰουδαῖος is an outsider term, the others insider terms—falls down.[30] In fact, contrary to what the insider/outsider rubric would suggest, it is to ethnic *outsiders* that Paul presents himself as a Hebrew and an Israelite. It is rhetoric, not linguistic code-switching, that explains his usage. Paul is a Ἰουδαῖος, and more specifically a Benjaminite. But he sometimes stands to gain by presenting himself as Hebrew or Israelite (2 Cor 11:22; Phil 3:5) or, for that matter, as Ἰουδαῖος, law-bound, lawless, or weak (1 Cor 9:20–22).


## PHARISEE


Our second term, Pharisee, presents several thorny problems. Unlike Ἰουδαῖος, an ethnonym known to people all around the ancient Mediterranean, Pharisee is an entirely inner-Jewish term (until it is appropriated by some early Christian writers, too), a name for a particular school among the Jews. Hence Josephus's explanation to his Roman audience that Pharisees are roughly equivalent to Stoics (*Life* 12). This helpful cross-cultural analogy notwithstanding, however, the actual profile of the historical Pharisees is notoriously elusive.[31]

28. Eyl, "I Myself Am an Israelite," 148–49.

29. Eyl, "I Myself Am an Israelite," 157. On this phenomenon, see further Heidi Wendt, *At the Temple Gates: The Religion of Freelance Experts in the Roman Empire* (New York: Oxford University Press, 2016), 74–113, 146–89.

30. Instances of this explanation include K. G. Kuhn, "Ἰουδαῖος," *TDNT* 3:356–69; Peter J. Tomson, "The Names Israel and Jew in Ancient Judaism and in the New Testament," *Bijdragen* 47 (1986): 120–40, 266–89; John H. Elliott, "Jesus the Israelite Was Neither a 'Jew' nor a 'Christian': On Correcting Misleading Nomenclature," *JSHJ* 5 (2007): 119–54. For apt criticism, see Nathan Thiel, "'Israel' and 'Jew' as Markers of Jewish Identity in Antiquity: The Problems of Insider/Outsider Classification," *JSJ* 45 (2014): 80–99.

31. Hengel's definition is handy but overconfident: "The Pharisees were a Palestinian lay holiness movement going back to the Hasidim of the Maccabean period, whose aim was above all the ritual sanctification of everyday life in Eretz Israel, as it was required of

Paul's declaration in Phil 3:5—"With respect to the law [I am] a Pharisee"—is the *only* extant first-person report from any ancient Pharisee, and most modern critics have not thought him representative. The next closest testimony is Josephus, who claims to have studied with the Pharisees for a time in his youth, though not to be a proper member (*Life* 10–12).[32] Most of our evidence for the Pharisees is at least second- or third-hand reporting (much of it heavily biased, on which see below). The name itself is first attested in Greek, Φαρισαῖος, but that is transliteration Greek, not an existing Greek word. As Martin Goodman puts it, "*Pharisaios* in Greek means nothing, and it must be a transliteration of an Aramaic word derived from the root *prsh*, which means 'separate': Pharisees were those who separated something from something else (quite what is separated left unstated)."[33] Unfortunately for historians, the Dead Sea Scrolls do not mention anyone called פרושים, *perushim*, but they do complain about certain people they call "seekers after smooth things" (4QpNah 3–4), who may in fact be Pharisees.[34] Rabbinic sources, all of them much later than the pre-70 CE Pharisees, do sometimes mention פרושים (*perushim*, "separatists"), but it is much disputed whether these are Pharisees. What is more, some interpreters have argued that while these talmudic פרושים are not Pharisees, the talmudic חברים (*ḥaberim*, "associates") or חכמים (*ḥakhamim*, "scholars") actually are Pharisees. In sum, rabbinic sources may yield information about some points of Pharisaic legal opinion, but they contribute vanishingly little to a social profile of first-century Pharisees.[35]

priests in the sanctuary" (Hengel, *Pre-Christian Paul*, 30). For thorough recent discussion, see Jacob Neusner and Bruce D. Chilton, eds., *In Quest of the Historical Pharisees* (Waco, TX: Baylor University Press, 2007).

32. See Steve Mason, *Flavius Josephus on the Pharisees: A Composition-Critical Study* (Leiden: Brill, 2001), 342–56. As Mason rightly points out, Josephus says that he favored the philosophy of Bannus over those of the Pharisees, Sadducees, and Essenes. About his entry into public life, he only says that he *deferred to the policies of* the Pharisees, not that he *was* a Pharisee.

33. Martin Goodman, *A History of Judaism* (Princeton: Princeton University Press, 2018), 115.

34. See James C. VanderKam, "The Pharisees and the Dead Sea Scrolls," in Neusner and Chilton, *In Quest of the Historical Pharisees*, 225–36.

35. See further Ellis Rivkin, "Defining the Pharisees: The Tannaitic Sources," *HUCA* 40 (1969): 205–49; Jacob Neusner, *The Rabbinic Traditions about the Pharisees before 70*, 3 vols. (Leiden: Brill, 1971); Solomon Zeitlin, "Spurious Interpretations of Rabbinic Sources in the Studies of the Pharisees and Pharisaism," *JQR* 65 (1974): 122–35; Shaye J. D. Cohen, "The Significance of Yavneh: Pharisees, Rabbis, and the End of Jewish Sectarianism," *HUCA* 55 (1984): 27–53; Richard Kalmin, "Pharisees in Rabbinic Literature of Late Antiquity," *Sidra* 24–25 (2010): 7–28; Annette Yoshiko Reed, "When Did Rabbis Become Pharisees? Reflec-

The Pharisees are best known from their many appearances as characters in the canonical Gospels. But the Gospels, being literary lives of Jesus,[36] have little or no interest in giving a rounded or even a strictly accurate profile of the Pharisees, who are made to play the role of opponents of Jesus.[37] (But the fact that they are Jesus's closest interlocutors may hint that, on a broad map of ancient Jewish philosophies, either Jesus himself may have been something reasonably close to a Pharisee or the Gospel authors see value in positioning him as such.)[38] Writing around the same time as the Evangelists, Josephus gives a more rounded sketch.[39] From his perspective, the Pharisees are one of several leading philosophies among the Jews, alongside Sadducees, Essenes, and a fourth group who believe in pure theocracy (*J. W.* 2.119–166; *Ant.* 13.171–173; 18.11–25). About the Pharisees, Josephus writes in *Jewish War* book 2:

> Of the two first-named schools, the Pharisees, who are considered the most accurate interpreters of the laws [οἱ μετ᾽ ἀκριβείας δοκοῦντες ἐξηγεῖσθαι τὰ νόμιμα], and hold the position of the leading sect [τὴν πρώτην ἀπάγοντες αἵρεσιν], attribute everything to Fate [εἱμαρμένη] and to God; they hold that to act rightly or otherwise rests, indeed, for the most part with men, but that in each action Fate co-operates. Every soul, they maintain, is imperishable, but the soul of the good alone passes into another body, while the souls of the wicked suffer eternal punishment. . . . The Pharisees are affectionate to each other and cultivate harmonious relations with the community. (*J. W.* 2.162–164, 166)

Here he stresses the Pharisees' role as interpreters of the laws (but gives no hint of any of their particular legal interpretations); their belief in fate and divine providence, human moral culpability, and the immortality of the soul; their social ethics; and their prominence in the Jewish community (τὴν πρώτην αἵρεσιν, "the foremost school"). A briefer reference in *Jewish Antiquities* book 13 overlaps partly with this one:

tions on Christian Evidence for Post-70 Judaism," in *Envisioning Judaism: Essays in Honor of Peter Schäfer*, ed. Ra'anan S. Boustan et al. (Tübingen: Mohr Siebeck, 2013), 2:859–96.

36. On Gospel genre, see Helen K. Bond, *The First Biography of Jesus: Genre and Meaning in Mark's Gospel* (Grand Rapids: Eerdmans, 2020).

37. See Mary Marshall, *The Portrayals of the Pharisees in the Gospels and Acts*, FRLANT 254 (Göttingen: Vandenhoeck & Ruprecht, 2015).

38. For a strong form of this argument, see Klaus Berger, "Jesus als Pharisäer und frühe Christen als Pharisäer," *NovT* 30 (1988): 231–62.

39. On which see Mason, *Flavius Josephus on the Pharisees*.

Now at this time there were three schools of thought [αἱρέσεις] among the Jews, which held different opinions concerning human affairs; the first being that of the Pharisees, the second that of the Sadducees, and the third that of the Essenes. As for the Pharisees, they say that certain events are the work of Fate, but not all; as to other events, it depends upon ourselves whether they shall take place or not. (*Ant.* 13.171–172)

Here Josephus only touches on a single point, which he thinks is of first importance for a philosophy—namely, the Pharisees' view of fate and human agency—confirming his comment on that theme in *Jewish War* book 2. A third and much fuller account comes later in *Jewish Antiquities* book 18:

The Pharisees simplify their standard of living, making no concession to luxury. They follow the guidance of that which their doctrine has selected and transmitted as good, attaching the chief importance to the observance of those commandments which it has seen fit to dictate to them. They show respect and deference to their elders, nor do they rashly presume to contradict their proposals. Though they postulate that everything is brought about by fate, still they do not deprive the human will of the pursuit of what is in man's power, since it was God's good pleasure that there should be a fusion and that the will of man with his virtue and vice should be admitted to the council-chamber of fate. They believe that souls have power to survive death and that there are rewards and punishments under the earth for those who have led lives of virtue or vice: eternal imprisonment is the lot of evil souls, while the good souls receive an easy passage to a new life. Because of these views they are, as a matter of fact, extremely influential among the towns-folk [καὶ δι᾿ αὐτὰ τοῖς τε δήμοις πιθανώτατοι τυγχάνουσιν]; and all prayers and sacred rites of divine worship are performed according to their exposition [ὁπόσα θεῖα εὐχῶν τε ἔχεται καὶ ἱερῶν ποιήσεως ἐξηγήσει τῇ ἐκείνων τυγχάνουσιν πρασσόμενα]. This is the great tribute that the inhabitants of the cities, by practising the highest ideals both in their way of living and in their discourse, have paid to the excellence of the Pharisees. (*Ant.* 18.12–15)

Here, again, we find the philosophical doctrines of fate, human agency, and the immortality of the soul. The point about Pharisaic devotion to observing the commandments handed down to them by their school is important, and may perhaps be coordinated with their being "interpreters of the laws" in *Jewish War* book 2. Likewise important is Josephus's claim that the views of the Pharisees are influential with the δῆμοι, the common-folk, so much so that—he says—public prayers and rituals are conducted according to Pharisaic protocols.[40] All of this is at least broadly consistent with Paul's potted autobiography in Gal 1:13–14: "I was advancing in Ἰουδαϊσμός beyond many contemporaries among my people, being exceedingly zealous for my ancestral traditions."[41]

Thus far in this section, we have been asking: What is a Pharisee? But the case of Paul raises a second question: What kind of animal, if it exists at all, is a *diaspora* Pharisee? Most of the (admittedly sparse) evidence points to the Pharisees being a specifically *Palestinian* Jewish school, and yet the diaspora Jew Paul says that he is one. How are we to explain this? Faced with these discordant premises, interpreters have argued in several different directions. Some jettison either one or the other of the two premises. Hyam Maccoby— noted above in connection with Epiphanius's Ebionites—argues that Paul was the furthest possible thing from a Pharisee; he only falsely presents himself as one. All diaspora, no Pharisee.[42] Recently, Michael Satlow has taken the opposite view: Paul is all Pharisee, no diaspora.[43] Or rather, Satlow argues, Paul only migrated into the diaspora in adulthood, like his contemporary Josephus did. Whereas many critics accept from Luke-Acts Paul's birth at Tarsus but reject his youth in Jerusalem, Satlow does the reverse: he accepts from Luke-Acts Paul's youth in Jerusalem but rejects the Tarsus story.[44] Satlow's Paul is a Judean Jew, full stop; hence there is no problem with him being a Pharisee.

---

40. What exactly this means—and, depending on that, whether it is true—is a notorious puzzle. See the debate among E. P. Sanders, *Jewish Law from Jesus to the Mishnah* (London: SCM, 1990); Sanders, *Judaism: Practice and Belief, 63 BCE–66 CE* (London: SCM, 1992); Jacob Neusner, "Mr. Sanders' Pharisees and Mine," *SJT* 44 (1991): 73–95; Martin Hengel and Roland Deines, "Common Judaism, Jesus, and the Pharisees," *JTS* 46 (1995): 1–70.

41. On "zealous," see further below. Ἰουδαϊσμός (derived, of course, from the ethnonym Ἰουδαῖος) is another can of worms, on which see Matthew V. Novenson, "Paul's Former Occupation in *Ioudaismos*," in *Galatians and Christian Theology*, ed. Mark W. Elliott et al. (Grand Rapids: Baker Academic, 2014), 24–39. "Ancestral traditions" here could conceivably mean specifically Pharisaic halakah, which would dovetail with Josephus's point about Pharisees' devotion to their school's teachings, but alternatively it could very well just mean the law of Moses common to all Jews.

42. Maccoby, *Mythmaker*, 50–61.

43. Michael L. Satlow, *How the Bible Became Holy* (New Haven: Yale University Press, 2014), 210–23; Satlow, "Paul, a Jew from Jerusalem," *Bible and Interpretation* (September 2014), https://bibleinterp.arizona.edu/articles/2014/09/sat388024; Satlow, "Paul's Scriptures," in *Strength to Strength: Essays in Honor of Shaye J. D. Cohen*, ed. Michael L. Satlow, BJS 363 (Providence: Brown University Press, 2018), 257–74.

44. Satlow points out that Paul never claims to have been born outside Judea; only Luke claims this for him. This is true, but neither does Paul ever claim to have been born *inside*

Most critics, however, acknowledge both premises—Paul's diaspora identity and his Pharisaism—and undertake to square the two. A very influential
solution—represented (differently) by Willem van Unnik and Martin Hengel
and anticipated by Luke-Acts—is that if the Pharisees operated in Judea, and
Paul was a Pharisee, then Paul must have had an early Judean phase.[45] That is
to say, Paul was not simply, as one might guess from the evidence of the letters
alone, a diaspora Jew. Luke makes the young Paul (giving him the Hebrew
name Saul) resident in Jerusalem (Acts 7:58–8:1) and later has Paul explain,
"I am a Jew, born at Tarsus in Cilicia, but brought up in this city [Jerusalem] at
the feet of Gamaliel, educated according to the strict manner of the law of our
fathers" (Acts 22:3). For those who, like van Unnik and Hengel, are generous
with their credence toward Luke-Acts as a source, this is an elegant solution.
But it depends on a willingness to trust Luke on a very important detail for
which there is otherwise no evidence.[46]

A different solution—associated especially with the names of Adolf Deissmann, Hans-Joachim Schoeps, and Georg Strecker—is to reason that, if Paul
was both a diaspora Jew and a Pharisee, then there must have been such a thing
as diaspora Pharisaism.[47] Paul, then, would have belonged to this context,
not to the Palestinian Pharisaism of Josephus and the Gospels. The problem
with this proposal is that Paul himself is the only secure example, so one must
extrapolate a whole set on the evidence of a single (hypothetical) member.[48]

---

Judea; Paul does not say one way or the other. Or so it seems to me. Satlow takes "tribe of
Benjamin" (Rom 11:1; Phil 3:5) to be a reference to place (viz. Jerusalem) rather than ancestry. But that is not the natural sense of φυλή, "tribe." On balance, Satlow's reconstruction
is possible but unlikely.

45. W. C. van Unnik, *Tarsus or Jerusalem? The City of Paul's Youth*, trans. George Ogg
(London: Epworth, 1962); Hengel, *Pre-Christian Paul*, 18–39.

46. But if, as Steve Mason (*Josephus and the New Testament*, 2nd ed. [Peabody, MA:
Hendrickson, 2003], 251–96) argues, Luke knows at least some of Josephus's *oeuvre*, then it
is not impossible that Luke's portrait of Paul actually echoes Josephus's self-portrait.

47. Adolf Deissmann, *St. Paul: A Study in Social and Religious History*, trans. Lionel
R. M. Strachan (London: Hodder & Stoughton, 1912); Hans-Joachim Schoeps, *Paul: The
Theology of the Apostle in the Light of Jewish Religious History*, trans. H. Knight (Philadel-
phia: Westminster, 1961); Georg Strecker, "Befreiung und Rechtfertigung," in *Rechtfertigung:
FS Ernst Käsemann zum 70. Geburtstag*, ed. J. Friedrich, Wolfgang Pöhlmann, and Peter
Stuhlmacher (Tübingen: Mohr Siebeck, 1976), 479–508.

48. Proponents sometimes appeal to Matt 23:15: "Woe to you, scribes and Pharisees,
hypocrites, for you travel over sea and dry land to make one proselyte." But tantalizing
though it may be, this verse does not clearly attest the existence of Pharisaic schools in
diaspora cities. It may, however, suggest a certain renown for the name "Pharisee" abroad,
which might provide some context for Paul's claiming that name for himself in a letter to
gentiles in Macedonia.

Schoeps, for instance, develops a fulsome profile of diaspora Pharisaic life and thought, evidently uninhibited by the problem of sample size. But a softer, more defensible form of this hypothesis is floated by E. P. Sanders (following Samuel Sandmel), who says that we simply do not know what diaspora Pharisaism looked like, but that the case of Paul suggests that there was some such thing.[49] The chief advantage of this solution is that one need not imagine an early, Palestinian phase for the apostle; one can make coherent sense of the letters as the product of a diaspora Jewish mind. This is an attractive solution; one only wishes that the sample size was rather larger.

The third and final question about Paul as Pharisee is whether he claims the affiliation for his past or his present. Most critics have tended to think the former; they contrast Saul the Pharisee (before his revelation of Christ) with Paul the apostle (after).[50] But this conclusion is by no means obvious. Paul's only express mention of his Pharisaism reads as follows: "If anyone else thinks that he has confidence in the flesh, I more so: an eighth-day circumcision, from the race of Israel, the tribe of Benjamin, a Hebrew born from Hebrews, in respect of the law a Pharisee, in respect of zeal indicting the assembly, in respect of righteousness in the law blameless" (Phil 3:4–6). Only one of these boasts—"in respect of zeal *indicting the assembly*"—has he clearly repented of: Paul no longer indicts the assembly; he edifies it (1 Cor 3:9). Most of the other boasts, however, are not things *repented of*, just *valued differently* in relation to Christ ("whatever things were gain I now consider loss" [Phil 3:7]). Paul does not *undo* his eighth-day circumcision or his Israeliteness or (I would argue) his righteousness in the law. He simply counts them as nothing relative to knowing Christ.[51] He *could* conceivably renounce or repent of his Pharisaic affiliation, but he does not do so here, the only place he mentions it. Perhaps, then, Paul the apostle is still "in respect of the law a Pharisee."

The Acts of the Apostles presents him as such.[52] Luke has Paul defend himself before the Jewish Sanhedrin: "Men, brothers, I am a Pharisee, a son

---

49. E. P. Sanders, *Paul: The Apostle's Life, Letters, and Thought* (Minneapolis: Fortress, 2015), 22–53.

50. This rubric is everywhere in the secondary literature, but the smartest, most sophisticated version of it is Alan F. Segal, *Paul the Convert: The Apostolate and Apostasy of Saul the Pharisee* (New Haven: Yale University Press, 1990).

51. A point well made by William S. Campbell, "I Rate All Things as Loss: Paul's Puzzling Accounting System," in *Celebrating Paul*, ed. Peter Spitaler, CBQMS 48 (Washington, DC: Catholic Biblical Association, 2011), 39–61; and see further Paula Fredriksen, "Paul the 'Convert'?," in *Oxford Handbook of Pauline Studies*, ed. Matthew V. Novenson and R. Barry Matlock (Oxford: Oxford University Press, forthcoming).

52. See John C. Lentz, *Luke's Portrait of Paul*, SNTSMS 77 (Cambridge: Cambridge University Press, 1993), 51–56.

of Pharisees; I am being judged on account of hope and resurrection of the dead" (Acts 23:6). This claim is strategic because, as Luke knows along with Josephus, "Sadducees say there is no resurrection or angel or *pneuma*, but Pharisees confess them all" (Acts 23:8). The Paul of Acts, like Paul himself in the letters, emphatically affirms all three, especially resurrection, as in Luke's later scene of Paul's defense before Agrippa: "I have lived as a Pharisee [ἔζησα Φαρισαῖος] according to the strictest school of our religion, and now I stand being judged for the hope of the promise given by God to our ancestors . . . [namely,] that God raises the dead [ὁ θεὸς νεκροὺς ἐγείρει]" (Acts 26:5–8). If, with Josephus and Luke, we take a hallmark of the Pharisees to be belief in immortality in general or resurrection in particular,[53] then Paul—not only in Acts but in the letters as well—certainly fits the bill, and there is no reason not to read his identification as a Pharisee in Phil 3:5 in the present tense.[54]

There is a further question about the relation of Pharisaic halakah to the circumcision controversy in the early Christ groups. Luke (though not Paul in his letters) presents the idea that gentiles-in-Christ should undergo circumcision as coming from "certain [Christ-]believers from the school of the Pharisees" (Acts 15:5). (For Luke, it is clearly possible to be both a Pharisee and a Christ-believer.) But as we have seen, Luke also portrays *Paul* as both a Pharisee and a Christ-believer. And in Luke's account, as in Paul's own letters, Paul is emphatically *against* circumcision for gentiles-in-Christ. So perhaps, Acts 15:5 notwithstanding, there is nothing specifically Pharisaic about proselyte circumcision,[55] in which case that text is no counterevidence to Paul being a Pharisee in Phil 3:5.[56] The only really formidable objection to Paul's

53. A fruitful heuristic exercise, as illustrated by G. F. Moore, "Fate and Free Will in the Jewish Philosophies according to Josephus," *HTR* 22 (1929): 371–89; and recently Jonathan Klawans, *Josephus and the Theologies of Ancient Judaism* (New York: Oxford University Press, 2012).

54. Michael B. Cover, "Paulus als Yischmaelit? The Personification of Scripture as Interpretive Authority in Paul and the School of Rabbi Ishmael," *JBL* 135 (2016): 617–37 argues plausibly that Paul's Pharisaism is further confirmed by the evidence of his interpretation of scripture.

55. Joshua D. Garroway, "The Pharisee Heresy: Circumcision for Gentiles in the Acts of the Apostles," *NTS* 60 (2014): 20–36 argues plausibly that Luke delays mentioning proselyte circumcision at all until Acts 15, and then, when he does, attributes it to Pharisees, in order to paint the notion as late, mistaken, and non-apostolic.

56. J. Andrew Overman, "*Kata Nomon Pharisaios*: A Short History of Paul's Pharisaism," in *Pauline Conversations in Context: Essays in Honor of Calvin J. Roetzel*, ed. Janice Capel Anderson, Philip Sellew, and Claudia Setzer, JSNTSup 221 (Sheffield: Sheffield Academic, 2002), 180–93 rightly criticizes modern scholarship for making Pharisaism out to be a

being a Pharisee is that his sole mention of it is part of a rhetorical boast to an audience who are not in any position to falsify the claim. At the very least, κατὰ νόμον Φαρισαῖος in Phil 3:5 means "When it comes to interpreting the law of Moses, I have the best credentials"; and it is possible (though not certain) that it means nothing more than that.

## ZEALOT

A third and final ethnic-adjacent label that Paul uses for himself is Greek ζηλω-τής, "zealot" or "champion." He writes, "I was advancing in Ἰουδαϊσμός beyond many contemporaries among my people, being exceedingly zealous for [or: a champion of] my ancestral traditions [ζηλωτὴς ὑπάρχων τῶν πατρικῶν μου παραδόσεων]" (Gal 1:14). Relatedly, Paul uses the cognate term "zeal" of his past self in Phil 3:6: κατὰ ζῆλος διώκων τὴν ἐκκλησίαν, "with respect to zeal, persecuting the assembly." I say "ethnic-*adjacent* label" because ζηλωτής is an old, widespread Greek word (attested in Plato, Aeschines, Lucian, a number of inscriptions, and more), not a specifically Jewish one, but it does acquire some particular associations in ancient Jewish usage. It is formally a noun, hence the common transliteration "zealot," and the alternate translations offered by LSJ: "emulator," "zealous admirer," "follower," and "champion." But LSJ also suggests that ζηλωτής can be used as an adjective (equivalent to ζηλωτός or ζηλότυπος, "jealous") in biblical Greek, as in Exod 20:5 LXX: θεὸς ζηλωτὴς ἀποδιδοὺς ἁμαρτίας πατέρων ἐπὶ τέκνα, "a jealous god, visiting the sins of the fathers upon the children." The English transliteration "zealot" is one reasonable gloss among others, but we should not let the magic of transliteration lull us into thinking that Greek ζηλωτής means whatever English "zealot" does.

The difficulty is compounded when we consider the particular associations of the word in the context of ancient Judaism. As illustrated, for instance, by Martin Hengel's encyclopedic study *Die Zeloten*, much modern usage and at least some ancient usage associates the term with a certain type of Jewish piety, earnest to the point of violence.[57] The archetype is Phinehas (or Pinchas) the priest in Numbers 25, who inflicts vigilante justice upon an exogamous couple

---

demon from Paul's past, but then goes astray, I think, with his constructive proposal that Paul neither is nor was ever a Pharisee.

57. Martin Hengel, *Die Zeloten* (Leiden: Brill, 1961; 3rd rev. ed., Tübingen: Mohr Siebeck, 2011); ET *The Zealots*, trans. John Bowden (Edinburgh: T&T Clark, 1989). Another recent, popular example is Reza Aslan, *Zealot: The Life and Times of Jesus of Nazareth* (New York: Random House, 2013).

caught *in flagrante delicto* and is rewarded by God with a covenant of perpetual priesthood. Because, God explains, "he was zealous for his God [ἐζήλωσεν τῷ θεῷ αὐτοῦ] and made propitiation for the sons of Israel" (Num 25:13 LXX). The zeal of Phinehas enjoys a prominent afterlife in ancient Jewish sources. When these sources discuss zeal (Hebrew קנאה, Greek ζῆλος) as a virtue, they sometimes, though not always, hark back to the legendary example of the pious, death-dealing priest (e.g., Ps 106:28–31; Sir 45:23–24; 1 Macc 2:24–26, 54; *LAB* 47).[58] Paul never mentions Phinehas, even though he quotes liberally from the Pentateuch, but some interpreters have thought that by calling himself a "zealot" Paul is painting himself after the model of Phinehas.[59] What is more, some have linked up "zealot" in Gal 1:14 with "Pharisee" in Phil 3:5 (discussed above) to yield a picture of Paul as a militant disciple of Shammai, the early first-century CE sage.[60] But this requires stretching the evidence exceedingly thin.[61]

The difficulty is compounded further still thanks to Josephus's use of ζηλωταί, "Zealots," as a name for a certain group of Jewish fighters in Jerusalem during the Great War with Rome. He first names them at *Jewish War* 4.161: "The chief priests . . . vehemently upbraided the people [of Jerusalem] for their apathy and incited them against the Zealots [ζηλωταί]; for so these miscreants called themselves, as though they were zealous in the cause of virtue and not for vice in its basest and most extravagant form." In Josephus's usage, "Zealots" is the name of one faction among several holed up in Jerusalem from 67

58. See John J. Collins, "The Zeal of Phinehas: The Bible and the Legitimation of Violence," *JBL* 122 (2003): 3–21.

59. On the whole question, see Benjamin L. Lappenga, *Paul's Language of Zelos: Monosemy and the Rhetoric of Identity and Practice*, BIS 137 (Leiden: Brill, 2016).

60. See N. T. Wright, *Paul and the Faithfulness of God*, 2 vols. (London: SPCK, 2013), 1:80–90.

61. Paul himself says nothing about his teachers, but Luke makes him a student of Gamaliel (Acts 22:3), who according to tannaitic tradition was a descendent of Hillel. Hence, e.g., the theory of Joachim Jeremias, "Paulus als Hillelit," in *Neotestamentica et Semitica: Studies in Honour of Matthew Black*, ed. E. Earle Ellis and Max Wilcox (Edinburgh: T&T Clark, 1969), 88–94. But even the relation of Hillel and Shammai to the Pharisees is a problem, as Jonathan Klawans perceptively notes: "Hillel and Shammai become Pharisees only when we employ a 'transitive property' of Pharisaism, whereby the Pharisees-to-rabbis hypothesis becomes the basis of identifying all pre-70 CE rabbinic sages as Pharisees. We do better to keep the Pharisee-rabbi connection as a hypothesis, and to refrain from inferentially identifying individual early rabbinic sages as Pharisees" (*Josephus and the Theologies of Ancient Judaism*, 34). See also Steve Mason, "N. T. Wright on Paul the Pharisee and Ancient Jews in Exile," *SJT* 69 (2016): 432–52, here 439: "The whole Pharisee/zeal-against-foreigners/Shammaite-school/Paul nexus therefore seems doubtful in every part."

until the final destruction of the city in 70. Many interpreters, however, have conflated this faction with other groups named by Josephus: the early first-century "fourth philosophy" of Judas of Galilee and his school (*Ant.* 18.23–25), the mid-century urban *sicarii* (*J.W.* 2.254–256), and even some or all of the Pharisees.[62] But as Kirsopp Lake, Morton Smith, Richard Horsley, and Steve Mason (among others) have demonstrated, "Zealot" is *not* a term of art for Jewish theocrats generally even in Josephus, let alone more widely.[63] Before, after, and apart from Josephus's highly specialized usage, ζηλωτής is a simple common noun ("follower," "champion") whose meaning is usually limited by the addition of a genitive: one can be a champion *of* a god, a philosophy, laws, traditions, virtues, or what have you.[64] It is overzealous modern interpreters who have connected the dots, so to speak, between the Pentateuch's Phinehas and Josephus's Zealots and plotted other Jewish references to "zeal" (e.g., Paul's autobiography in Gal 1) along this line, so as to make "zeal" mean nothing more or less than "killing for God."[65]

Paul never says that he killed anyone, whether for God or otherwise. We get our picture of the early Paul as homicidal almost entirely from the Acts of the Apostles, which depicts that period in lurid detail.[66] But in fact, not even

---

62. The lattermost because Josephus writes at *Ant.* 18.23: "This [Judas of Galilee's] school agrees in all other respects with the opinions of the Pharisees, except that they have a passion for liberty that is almost unconquerable, since they are convinced that God alone is their leader and master." Classic examples of this tendency to conflation include Joseph Klausner, *History of the Second Temple*, 5 vols. (Jerusalem: Ahiasaf, 1949) [Hebrew]; Hengel, *Zealots*; Wright, *Paul and the Faithfulness of God*.

63. See Kirsopp Lake, "Appendix A: The Zealots," in *The Beginnings of Christianity, Part 1: The Acts of the Apostles*, ed. F. J. Foakes Jackson and Kirsopp Lake, 5 vols. (New York: Macmillan, 1920–1933), 1:421–25; Morton Smith, "Zealots and Sicarii, Their Origins and Relation," *HTR* 64 (1971): 1–19; Richard A. Horsley, "The Zealots: The Origin, Relationships, and Importance in the Jewish Revolt," *NovT* 28 (1986): 159–92; Steve Mason, *A History of the Jewish War, AD 66–74* (New York: Cambridge University Press, 2016).

64. Paul himself writes to the Christ-believers in Corinth, "You yourselves are eager for spirits [ζηλωταί ἐστε πνευμάτων]" (1 Cor 14:12); 1 Pet 3:13 commends those who are "champions of the good [τοῦ ἀγαθοῦ ζηλωταί]"; and so on.

65. Most accounts of Paul along these lines suggest that he held such a view before his revelation, but repented of it after. E.g., Robert G. Hamerton-Kelly, *Sacred Violence: Paul's Hermeneutic of the Cross* (Minneapolis: Fortress, 1992); Seyoon Kim, "Paul and Violence," *Ex Auditu* 34 (2018): 67–89. But John G. Gager and E. Leigh Gibson, "Violent Acts and Violent Language in the Apostle Paul," in *Violence in the New Testament*, ed. Shelly Matthews and E. Leigh Gibson (London: T&T Clark, 2005), 11–21 argue that Paul remained a violent personality in his apostolic period no less than before.

66. See Murphy-O'Connor, *Paul*, 65–70.

Luke says that Paul killed anyone. Luke says that he "approved of his [Stephen's] destruction [by stoning] [συνευδοκῶν τῇ ἀναιρέσει αὐτοῦ]" (Acts 8:1); "maltreated the assembly, entering by households, dragging both men and women, and delivered them into jail [ἐλυμαίνετο τὴν ἐκκλησίαν κατὰ τοὺς οἴκους εἰσπορευόμενος, σύρων τε ἄνδρας καὶ γυναῖκας παρεδίδου εἰς φυλακήν]" (Acts 8:3); and "breathed threat and murder at the disciples of the lord [ἐμπνέων ἀπειλῆς καὶ φόνου εἰς τοὺς μαθητὰς τοῦ κυρίου]" (Acts 9:1). But for all this, Luke never depicts Paul taking a life,[67] which I suspect is significant in its precision. For his part, Paul says that he "was persecuting the assembly of God to the extreme and besieging it [καθ᾽ ὑπερβολὴν ἐδίωκον τὴν ἐκκλησίαν τοῦ θεοῦ καὶ ἐπόρθουν αὐτήν]" (Gal 1:13).[68] Many interpreters, conflating with (an over-reading of) Acts, have taken καθ᾽ ὑπερβολήν, "to the extreme," to mean "to the point of death." But if the context is synagogue discipline, a *bet din* or equivalent, then it is much more likely that καθ᾽ ὑπερβολὴν here means "to the fullest extent of the law," perhaps the thirty-nine lashes that Paul himself latterly received from the synagogue (2 Cor 11:24).[69] The early Paul certainly had no love lost for the Christ assemblies, but I can see no evidence that he acted against it extra-judicially or to the point of taking human life. It is a mistake, therefore, to classify the early Paul as a "zealot" in that much-touted sense.

But the hypothetical zealot connection has also been implicated in another theory of Paul's geographical origins. As we have seen, the letters say nothing about Paul's place of origin, while Luke places Paul's birth in Tarsus and his education in Jerusalem (Acts 22:3). There is not much else in the sources either to supplement or to contradict Luke's account. At the end of the fourth century, however, Jerome twice reports a tradition known to him that Paul's family actually came from Gischala (modern Gush Halav) in Galilee. First in his *Commentary on Philemon*: "We have heard this story. They say that the parents of the apostle Paul were from Gischala, a region of Judaea, and that, when the whole province was devastated by the hand of Rome and the Jews scattered throughout the world, they were moved to Tarsus, a town of Cilicia; the adolescent Paul inherited the personal status of his parents" (*Comm. Phlm.* on vv. 23–24). And secondly in his *On Illustrious Men*: "Paul the apostle, previ-

---

67. A point well made by Shelly Matthews, *Perfect Martyr: The Stoning of Stephen and the Construction of Christian Identity* (New York: Oxford University Press, 2010), 90–97.

68. Here I gloss διώκω with the familiar English equivalency "persecute," but it can just as well mean "chase," "drive away," "impeach," or "bring indictment."

69. Here I follow Martin Goodman, "The Persecution of Paul by Diaspora Jews," in *Judaism in the Roman World: Collected Essays*, AJEC 67 (Leiden: Brill, 2007), 145–52; Paula Fredriksen, *Paul: The Pagans' Apostle* (New Haven: Yale University Press, 2017), 77–93.

ously called Saul, was not one of the twelve apostles; he was of the tribe of Benjamin and of the town of Gischala in Judaea; when the town was captured by the Romans he migrated with his parents to Tarsus in Cilicia" (*Vir. ill.* 5).[70]

These two accounts have some apparent contradictions of detail between them,[71] and Jerome neither cites his source nor signals agreement or disagreement with it. (Theodor Zahn speculated that Jerome found this tradition in Origen's now-lost commentary on Philemon, which is an intriguing but unverifiable possibility.)[72] Neither does Jerome make any connection to Paul's hypothetical zealotism, though some modern critics have done so. Gischala is mostly unimportant in the historical record, but according to Josephus it was the last Galilean village to fall to Titus in 67 (*J.W.* 4.84–120), contributing to the radicalization of a certain John of Gischala, who went on to be one of the rebel leaders at the last stand of Jerusalem in 70 (*J.W.* 2.585–594; 4.121–127; et passim). John of Gischala, Gischala, zealotism, Paul, persecution: interpreters have strung these bits of evidence together into an inferential chain. Mark Fairchild, for instance, reasons as follows:

> Given that Jerome is correct that Paul's parents were deported to Tarsus during a Roman conquest, the passive form of the verb ('they were moved to Tarsus') implies that they were sold as slaves . . . With this past history lurking in the background, the pre-Christian Paul possessed some resentment toward the Romans. His Galilean ancestors (particularly at Gish Halav) experienced many turbulent years caused by Roman imperialism and taxation. Over the years many friends, neighbours and relatives lost their land, lives and freedom. Undoubtedly these same factors led to the Zealot aspirations of John of Gischala during the 60s. Should we find it unusual that Paul, a product of the same social and psychological conditions, would develop similar Zealot thoughts?[73]

70. Trans. Murphy-O'Connor, *Paul*, 37.

71. The ninth-century patriarch Photius (*Quaest. Amphil.* 116) tries to square Jerome's conflicting reports by reasoning that Paul was *conceived* at Gischala but *born* at Tarsus, which is ingenious but unnecessary if we concede that Jerome might simply be mistaken on at least one detail. See further Hengel, *Pre-Christian Paul*, 14, 111–12n106, who judges Photius's solution plausible.

72. Theodor Zahn, *Einleitung in das Neuen Testament*, 2 vols. (Leipzig, 1897–1900), 1:49. Ronald E. Heine, "In Search of Origen's Commentary on Philemon," *HTR* 93 (2000): 117–33 proposes that Jerome's commentary on Philemon *is* Origen's commentary on Philemon, just in Latin translation.

73. Mark R. Fairchild, "Paul's Pre-Christian Zealot Associations: A Re-examination of Gal 1:14 and Acts 22:3," *NTS* 45 (1999): 514–32, here 520. Similar but more cautious is the

But this is too speculative by half. We cannot even be certain about Luke's Tarsus and Jerusalem traditions, let alone Jerome's much later, one-off Gischala tradition. Even if they were all true, Fairchild's slave deportation hypothesis adds an additional layer of conjecture. And even if that, too, were true, we still could not hope to compare the psychology of John of Gischala with that of the young Paul. I understand the allure of a psychological profile of the early Paul's "persecuting" activity, but it is just not possible to extract one from our few, fragmentary sources. In sum, "a champion of the ancestral traditions" (Gal 1:14) is not a "zealot" in the loaded sense with which many modern critics mean that word.

## CONCLUSION

To discuss these three terms as we have done here is to think about Paul taxonomically—that is, in regard to relevant categories to which he can be said to belong. In a great many areas, perhaps all, we understand things by classing them alongside other like things. To classify is thus to compare. And to compare is to resist the siren song of uniqueness—the urge simply to declare that $x$ is $x$ and nothing else, which is to cease trying to understand.[74] By classifying Paul as a Ἰουδαῖος, for instance, we can see more clearly ways in which he is like other Ἰουδαῖοι (e.g., the Teacher of Righteousness, Jesus, Cephas, Philo, Josephus) as well as ways in which he is unlike each of them. Likewise with the category Pharisee, although we have far fewer certain members of that set with whom we can compare Paul. In the case of the category zealot, I have argued that—based on his single use of the relevant term for himself—Paul actually is not what most modern critics mean by that word when they use it in the context of ancient Judaism. But even if I am right about that, it turns out to be heuristically useful to compare Paul with Phinehas, or Judas the Galilean, or John of Gischala. And we could do still more; we could consider Paul in regard

approach of Paul McKechnie, "Paul among the Jews," in *All Things to All Cultures: Paul among Jews, Greeks, and Romans*, ed. Mark Harding and Alanna Nobbs (Grand Rapids: Eerdmans, 2013), 103–23.

74. See further Jonathan Z. Smith, *Drudgery Divine: On the Comparison of Early Christianities and the Religions of Late Antiquity* (Chicago: University of Chicago Press, 1990); Matthew V. Novenson, "Beyond Compare, or: Some Recent Strategies for Not Comparing Early Christianity with Other Things," in *The New Testament in Comparison: Validity, Method, and Purpose in Comparing Traditions*, ed. John M. G. Barclay and Benjamin G. White, LNTS 600 (London: T&T Clark, 2020), 79–94.

to the category apostle, or migrant, or thaumaturge, or philosopher, or ascetic, or otherwise.[75] And likewise for other ancients, and indeed moderns.

In addition to the many other things that he was, Paul was a Ἰουδαῖος of the diaspora who preferred to style himself a Hebrew, Israelite, or Benjaminite. He preached his Christ message to gentiles—that is, all people not Ἰουδαῖοι—around the northern and eastern Mediterranean. While doing so, he was content to conduct himself ἐθνικῶς, "gentilishly," which is perhaps how many diaspora Ἰουδαῖοι conducted themselves much of the time. He says that he belongs to the illustrious school of the Pharisees, and while this might simply be a name-dropping boast, Paul's theological and legal reasoning elsewhere does nothing to falsify the claim, as far as I can see. Because most Pharisees probably legislated for Jewish practice in the homeland, while Paul legislated for gentiles-in-Christ abroad, it is hard to say to what extent his legal interpretation is recognizably Pharisaic. His philosophical doctrines, however—divine providence, human moral agency, immortality, angels, *pneuma*—agree with those that Josephus and Luke call Pharisaic. Paul also says, and Luke reiterates, that he had earlier been "a champion of the ancestral traditions [ζηλωτὴς τῶν πατρικῶν παραδόσεων]" (Gal 1:14; cf. Acts 22:3). But ζηλωτής here is probably not a technical term, despite the surface similarity with Josephus's name for certain Jewish freedom fighters circa 67 CE. One could perhaps argue that Paul was just as zealous for certain ancestral traditions after his revelation—*mutatis mutandis*—as he had been beforehand, but Paul himself does not put it this way. In his telling, his zeal for the traditions belongs to his past,[76] while his Israeliteness (certainly) and his Pharisaism (probably) are part of his present. All three he considers fair game for boasting over his naysayers, but none is worth comparing to his imminent metamorphosis into the image of the heavenly Christ.

---

75. See the essays in Ryan S. Schellenberg and Heidi Wendt, eds., *Handbook to the Historical Paul* (London: T&T Clark, forthcoming).

76. On his rationale, see Terence L. Donaldson, "Zealot and Convert: The Origin of Paul's Christ-Torah Antithesis," *CBQ* 51 (1989): 655–82.

4

# DID PAUL ABANDON EITHER JUDAISM

# OR MONOTHEISM?

Did Socrates abandon Athenianness by propagating his controversial philosophy? Did the prophet Muhammad abandon Arabianness when he began to preach monotheism? We do not usually think about historical figures in this way, setting them over against their respective ancestral traditions. In the case of the apostle Paul, however, we do often think about him in this unusual way. The twofold question posed in this essay (Did Paul abandon either Judaism or monotheism?) arises not so much from Paul's letters themselves as from his outsize place in subsequent religious history. Because historic, catholic Christianity is (a) trinitarian[1] and (b) not Judaism, and because Paul has been widely understood as a, perhaps even *the*, founder of Christianity,[2] it has come to seem natural to ask whether these familiar features of Christianity can be traced back to the apostle—that is, whether Paul himself abandoned either Judaism or monotheism in the course of his apostolic work. What is more, again because of his outsize place in subsequent religious history, although Paul never in so many words renounces either Judaism or monotheism, some things that he does say in the letters have been taken by modern interpreters,

---

1. On most Christian accounts, of course, trinitarianism *is* monotheistic (one god, albeit in three persons), but the viability (or not) of that claim is precisely the issue in many classical Jewish and Muslim critiques of Christian trinitarianism; see further below.

2. See, e.g., the classic statement of Adolf von Harnack, *What Is Christianity?*, trans. Thomas Bailey Saunders (New York: Harper, 1957 [1901]), 176–89.

both Jewish and Christian, to imply such a renunciation. In this chapter, we must look carefully at the passages that have been so taken and ask what they actually claim. Furthermore, we must interrogate what exactly is meant by "Judaism" and "monotheism," and what would count as a renunciation, deviation, departure, violation, compromise, or abandonment of either of these isms. As in other aspects of the study of Paul, but even more so here, it is crucial to parse out what belongs to Paul and what belongs to his afterlives.[3]

## DID PAUL ABANDON JUDAISM?

The modern commonplace according to which Paul is said to have abandoned Judaism is attested already in the first great modern critic of the Pauline letters, F. C. Baur. Writing in the mid-nineteenth century, Baur summarizes Paul's gospel in this way: "Christianity is the absolute religion, the religion of the spirit and of freedom, with regard to which Judaism belongs to an inferior standpoint, from which it must be classed with heathenism."[4] According to Baur (himself a Christian), Paul abandoned Judaism, and this was a good thing. By contrast, the late nineteenth-century Jewish critic Kaufmann Kohler agrees with Baur that Paul abandoned Judaism, but he regards this to be a bad thing. Kohler writes, "His [Paul's] conception of life was not Jewish. Nor can his unparalleled animosity and hostility to Judaism as voiced in the Epistles be accounted for except upon the assumption that, while born a Jew, he was never in sympathy or in touch with the doctrines of the rabbinical schools."[5] As these examples illustrate, modern interpreters variously praise Paul or blame him for abandoning Judaism, but many agree that he did so.[6]

This agreement, however, is based on highly questionable assumptions about the supposed essences of Judaism and of Christianity and about how each came to be. In particular, it presupposes a sufficiently clear and simple concept of Judaism, from which Paul can then be shown to have deviated.

3. On this historical problem, see J. Albert Harrill, *Paul the Apostle: His Life and Legacy in Their Roman Context* (New York: Cambridge University Press, 2012).

4. F. C. Baur, *Paul the Apostle of Jesus Christ*, trans. Eduard Zeller, rev. A. Menzies, 2 vols. (London: Williams & Norgate, 1876 [1845]), 1:255.

5. Kaufmann Kohler, "Saul of Tarsus," *Jewish Encyclopedia* (New York: Funk & Wagnalls, 1906), 11:80.

6. See further Daniel R. Langton, *The Apostle Paul in the Jewish Imagination* (Cambridge: Cambridge University Press, 2010); Patrick Gray, *Paul as a Problem in History and Culture* (Grand Rapids: Baker, 2016).

For much of the modern history of research, this presupposition mostly went unchallenged, but recently it has met with some forceful objections.[7] In some recent research, it has been argued that ancient Jewish belief and practice were so diverse that we can only speak of Judaisms (plural), not Judaism (singular).[8] In an opposite direction, others have argued that Judaism did not exist at all in antiquity,[9] or, more ambitiously still, that not even religion existed in antiquity.[10] Now, in fact, these recent arguments pertain not to the social practices that we call "Judaism" or "religion," but to the concepts. That is to say, virtually no one denies that ancient Jews, for instance, worshiped the deity resident in the Jerusalem temple, but some historians argue that those ancient Jews lacked the concept "Judaism" for what they were doing.[11] That ancient Jews may have lacked such a concept is potentially relevant to the case of Paul, because Christian theology has long looked to Paul for a reification of, and principled rejection of, Judaism.[12] Let us consider the evidence of Paul's own letters, examining what he does and does not say about his ancestral religion.

The Greek word Ἰουδαϊσμός, from which we get our English word "Judaism," occurs only twice in the twenty-seven books of the New Testament, both instances in the same passage at the beginning of Paul's Letter to the Galatians. Explaining why his audience should trust that his message came from God, not humans, Paul writes, "For you heard of my former occupation in Ἰουδαϊσμός, that I was indicting the assembly of God severely, and was besieging it. And I was advancing in Ἰουδαϊσμός beyond many of my contemporaries among my people, being exceedingly zealous for my ancestral traditions. But when God was pleased . . . to reveal his son in me . . . I went away into Arabia and then returned again to Damascus" (Gal 1:13–17). The point here is that Paul's well-known about-face confirms the divine origin of his message, showing that he was not just an understudy of the chief apostles in Jerusalem. But Paul characterizes his former occupation (ἀναστροφή) as being "in Ἰουδαϊσμός,"

---

7. See in particular Michael L. Satlow, "Defining Judaism: Accounting for 'Religions' in the Study of Religion," *JAAR* 74 (2006): 837–60; Kathy Ehrensperger, *Paul at the Crossroads of Cultures: Theologizing in the Space Between* (London: T&T Clark, 2013).

8. See Jacob Neusner, "Preface," in *Judaisms and Their Messiahs at the Turn of the Christian Era*, ed. Jacob Neusner et al. (Cambridge: Cambridge University Press, 1987), ix–xiv.

9. See Daniel Boyarin, *Judaism: The Genealogy of a Modern Notion* (New Brunswick: Rutgers University Press, 2018).

10. See Brent Nongbri, *Before Religion: A History of a Modern Concept* (New Haven: Yale University Press, 2013).

11. For a lucid analysis of these arguments, see Seth Schwartz, "How Many Judaisms Were There?" *JAJ* 2 (2011): 208–38.

12. E.g., classically, Baur, *Paul the Apostle*, and his many heirs and imitators since.

from which we get (via a harmonization with the Damascus Road story in Acts 9) our centuries-long habit of thinking of Paul as a convert from Judaism to Christianity.[13] Contrary to this habit of thought, however, Paul himself never speaks of Christianity, or even of Christians.[14] What is more, Greek Ἰουδαϊσμός does not mean, as "Judaism" does in English, the religion of Jewish people. Paul calls the religion of Jewish people "the ancestral traditions" (Gal 1:14), which is what most ancient people called their respective religions, since they lacked specific names for those religions.[15] Ἰουδαϊσμός, by contrast, is what Paul calls his own exceptional activist program for the defence and promotion of those traditions (which is also what Ἰουδαϊσμός means in its few other instances in 2 Macc 2:21; 8:1; 14:38; 4 Macc 4:26). When Paul met the risen Christ, he abandoned that activist program, Ἰουδαϊσμός, but he did not abandon his ancestral traditions, which are what we call Judaism.[16]

Those ancestral traditions include, for instance, belief in the God of Abraham as the creator of all things (Rom 1:25; 1 Cor 8:6), reverence for the law of Moses as God's revelation to Israel (Rom 9:4, 31; Gal 3:19, 24), cultic worship of God in his temple in Jerusalem (Rom 9:4; 1 Cor 10:18), and belief in the future resurrection of the dead (Rom 1:4; 1 Cor 15:12) and the kingdom of God (1 Cor 6:9–10; Gal 5:21). All of these hallmarks, and many more beside, Paul has in spades.[17] Viewed from this angle, then, it is patently absurd to speak of Paul "abandoning Judaism," since he shares virtually all of the key features attested by other ancients whom we count as representing Judaism: the Qumran sect, Philo of Alexandria, Flavius Josephus, the sages of the Mishnah, and so on. The problem, if there is one, is not that Paul lacks any essential features of Judaism, but that, on top of these essential features, Paul also attests other features that later interpreters have thought put him beyond the pale. He attributes to the law of Moses a role in working wrath and effecting death (Rom 4:15; 7:5;

13. For an interrogation of this habit, see Alan F. Segal, *Paul the Convert: The Apostolate and Apostasy of Saul the Pharisee* (New Haven: Yale University Press, 1990).

14. The word "Christian" first occurs in 1 Pet 4:16; Acts 11:26; 26:28; Pliny, *Epistles* 10.96–97; Tacitus, *Annals* 15.44; and the word "Christianity" in the early second-century letters of Ignatius of Antioch.

15. A point well made by Steve Mason, "Jews, Judaeans, Judaizing, Judaism: Problems of Categorization in Ancient History," *JSJ* 38 (2007): 457–512

16. See Matthew V. Novenson, "Paul's Former Occupation in *Ioudaismos*," in *Galatians and Christian Theology*, ed. Mark Elliott et al. (Grand Rapids: Baker Academic, 2014), 24–39.

17. See Alan F. Segal, "Paul's Jewish Presuppositions," in *The Cambridge Companion to St Paul*, ed. James D. G. Dunn (Cambridge: Cambridge University Press, 2003), 159–72; Matthew V. Novenson, *Christ among the Messiahs: Christ Language in Paul and Messiah Language in Ancient Judaism* (New York: Oxford University Press, 2012).

1 Cor 15:56). He calls all kinds of human beings, gentiles as well as Jews, sons of God (Rom 8:14; Gal 3:26). He can speak of the crucified and raised messiah Jesus as if he were divine (Phil 2:6–11; 2 Cor 4:4). That Paul makes these moves is basically undisputed; the crucial question is whether they do in fact put him beyond the pale.[18] Imagine, for the sake of argument, that we had only the letters of Paul and other texts extant during Paul's lifetime (meaning, importantly, none of the other texts that are part of the New Testament,[19] let alone later Christian writers). In that case, arguably, it would never occur to us to think that any of Paul's claims, even the more provocative ones, put him beyond, outside, or against Judaism. But of course, we do have the rest of the New Testament, and the works of Justin, Irenaeus, Tertullian, Origen, Chrysostom, Augustine, Jerome, and myriad other gentile Christian writers down to the present, almost all of whom count Paul's letters as Christian scripture and therefore cite Paul's words as representing Christianity. Under this tremendous weight of tradition, it becomes very difficult for any of us to read Paul's words as representing Paul's own religion as opposed to the religion of his later Christian interpreters.[20]

Faced with this difficulty, one promising way forward is to ask whether Paul was in fact treated by others, during his own lifetime, as being beyond, outside, or against Judaism. From a social-scientific perspective, there is some evidence that Paul was regarded as deviant by other Jews who regarded themselves, and perhaps were regarded by others, as normal by comparison.[21] In a litany of traumas suffered in the course of his apostolic work, Paul writes, "Five times I received from the Jews the forty lashes less one" (2 Cor 11:24), and a few lines later, "in danger from my people, in danger from the gentiles" (2 Cor 11:26). "Danger from my people" could mean either unofficial hostility

18. For an account of these ostensibly rogue ideas, see my *The End of the Law and the Last Man: Paul between Judaism and Christianity* (New York: Cambridge University Press, forthcoming).

19. Because Paul almost certainly died by the mid-60s CE, none of his authentic letters can be later than that, while no other text in the New Testament can securely be dated earlier than 70 CE.

20. On this hermeneutical problem, see the essays collected in *Paul within Judaism: Restoring the First-Century Context to the Apostle*, ed. Mark D. Nanos and Magnus Zetterholm (Minneapolis: Fortress, 2015); and *Paul the Jew: Rereading the Apostle as a Figure of Second Temple Judaism*, ed. Gabriele Boccaccini and Carlos A. Segovia (Minneapolis: Fortress, 2016). See, too, my discussion in chapter 11 below.

21. See John M. G. Barclay, "Deviance and Apostasy: Some Applications of Deviance Theory to First-Century Judaism and Christianity," in *Pauline Churches and Diaspora Jews* (Grand Rapids: Eerdmans, 2016), 123–39.

or official punishment, but "the forty lashes less one" certainly points to formal synagogue discipline. Because the Torah had specified a maximum of forty lashes for corporal sentences (Deut 25:1–3), Jewish halakah in the early Roman period allowed for discretionary punishments of up to thirty-nine lashes (*m. Mak.* 3). Diaspora synagogues would have made use of this provision in overseeing their internal affairs, of which the case of Paul is an example. For reasons to do with the way his apostolic work was perceived by other Jews, Paul was subjected to synagogue discipline. This fact might seem to suggest a break between Paul and Judaism, but, as E. P. Sanders memorably put it, "punishment implies inclusion."[22] To submit oneself to discipline is to be still inside the fold. Diaspora synagogues had no police power. Paul could have avoided corporal punishment by absenting himself from the life of the synagogue. We know of other ancient Jews who took this step (see the famous case of Tiberius Julius Alexander in Josephus, *Ant.* 20.100).[23] Evidently, however, Paul did not do so. He stayed, and he was allowed to stay. Even in these episodes of severe social disapproval, then, Paul operated within Judaism rather than outside its bounds.[24]

Why, though, this social disapproval? What did Paul do that would have warranted synagogue punishment? He himself does not say, so interpreters have had to fill in the gaps, which they have done with zeal. One passage often invoked in this connection is a part of 1 Corinthians 9 where Paul puts himself forward as a model of accommodation to the needs of others (1 Cor 9:19–22):

> Although I am free from all people, I have enslaved myself to them all, so that I may gain more. To the Jews I became as a Jew, that I might gain Jews. To those under the law, as one under the law (though I myself am not under the law), that I might gain those under the law. To the lawless, as a lawless person (though I am not lawless with God but am in the law of Christ), that I might gain the lawless. To the weak I became a weak person, that I might gain the weak. To all people I have become all things, so that by all means I might save some.

---

22. E. P. Sanders, *Paul, the Law, and the Jewish People* (Philadelphia: Fortress, 1983), 192.

23. See E. G. Turner, "Tiberius Julius Alexander," *JRS* 44 (1954): 54–64; John M. G. Barclay, "Who Was Considered an Apostate in the Jewish Diaspora?," in *Pauline Churches and Diaspora Jews*, 141–56.

24. Here I demur from the conclusions of Udo Schnelle, "Über Judentum und Hellenismus hinaus: Die paulinische Theologie als neue Wissensystem," *ZNW* 111 (2020): 124–55.

In the wider context of 1 Corinthians 8–10, Paul's point is to persuade his gentile auditors to adjust their dietary habits to accommodate the weaker consciences of other Christ-believers, lest anyone be tempted to commit idolatry. This is the context for his saying, "I have enslaved myself to all people," and "To all people I have become all things."[25] Strikingly, though, one of the groups about whom he says that he became like them is the Jews. Since Paul is himself a Jew,[26] it is hard to see why he would have to "become as a Jew." Perhaps Paul was usually in the habit, as he says Cephas was in Gal 2, of "living gentilishly" (Gal 2:14)—that is, of observing his Jewish diet and holy days in a manner that was easily workable in great gentile cities like Antioch or Tarsus (e.g., by eating in gentile homes even in the presence of household gods). Such practice was demonstrably common among Jews in the diaspora,[27] even if some Judean Jews might have found it scandalous (e.g., Gal 2:12). If so, then "to become as a Jew" might mean to set aside one's diaspora halakah and adopt a Judean halakah when in the company of Judeans (which is precisely what Paul shames Cephas for doing in Gal 2, though in that case because gentiles-in-Christ were watching).[28]

"Living gentilishly," then, is not a likely reason for Paul's punishment at the hands of synagogue authorities. A more plausible explanation, developed in particular by Martin Goodman, is that Paul was putting the already vulnerable diaspora Jewish communities at risk from their gentile neighbours by recruiting gentiles into his Jewish movement and then teaching them to renounce their obligations to their civic and family gods.[29] This would have looked like Jewish promotion of impiety among gentiles, an understandable cause of out-

25. See Margaret M. Mitchell, "Pauline Accommodation and 'Condescension' (ΣΥ-ΓΚΑΤΑΒΑΣΙΣ): 1 Cor 9:19–23 and the History of Influence," in *Paul beyond the Judaism/ Hellenism Divide*, ed. Troels Engberg-Pedersen (Louisville: Westminster John Knox, 2001), 197–214.

26. See my argument in chapter 3 above.

27. As attested by the mountain of epigraphic and documentary evidence discussed, e.g., by Paula Fredriksen, "What 'Parting of the Ways'? Jews, Gentiles, and the Ancient Mediterranean City," in *The Ways That Never Parted: Jews and Christians in Late Antiquity and the Early Middle Ages*, ed. Adam H. Becker and Annette Yoshiko Reed (Minneapolis: Fortress, 2007), 35–63.

28. See further David J. Rudolph, *A Jew to the Jews: Jewish Contours of Pauline Flexibility in 1 Corinthians 9:19–23*, 2nd ed. (Eugene, OR: Pickwick, 2016).

29. See Martin Goodman, "The Persecution of Paul by Diaspora Jews," in *Judaism in the Roman World: Collected Essays*, AJEC 67 (Leiden: Brill, 2007), 145–52; Goodman, *A History of Judaism* (Princeton: Princeton University Press, 2018), 186–98; similarly Paula Fredriksen, *Paul: The Pagans' Apostle* (New Haven: Yale University Press, 2017), 77–93.

rage among the locals and a public relations nightmare for synagogue leaders, who would have used the means at their disposal to keep a self-authorized charismatic like Paul in line for the health and safety of the community.

In social terms, then, Paul did not abandon Judaism, but what about in theological terms? In particular, does (what Paul calls) the offense of the crucified Christ (1 Cor 1:23) entail his abandonment of Judaism? To be sure, Paul mourns that most of his co-ethnics do not recognize "the glory of God in the face of Christ" (2 Cor 4:6) as he does. From his perspective, the majority of Jews "have zeal for God, but not with recognition" (Rom 10:2), about which, Paul writes earnestly, he feels "great pain and constant anguish" (Rom 9:2). Unlike the later Christian treatises *adversus Iudaeos*, "against the Jews," however, Paul does not diagnose this as a symptom of some flaw inherent in Judaism itself. As noted above, unlike many later Christian thinkers, Paul does not reify and isolate Judaism as a thing at all; like most of his contemporaries, he only thinks in terms of "ancestral traditions," whether Jewish, Greek, Roman, or what have you.

When Paul comments on majority Jewish "distrust" or "unbelief" (ἀπιστία), he either simply notes it without any attempt at explanation or explains it with reference to a mysterious divine purpose.[30] When he himself reads the law and the prophets, of course, Paul sees the messiah Jesus plainly attested there (Rom 3:21). But he is enough of a realist to admit that when most other Jews read the same scriptures, they do not see what he sees, and this because, he says, "their thoughts were hardened" and "a veil lies over their heart" (2 Cor 3:14–15). In the Letter to the Romans, Paul attributes this noetic hardening to the agency of God himself. Quoting Isaiah, Paul writes, "God gave them a spirit of stupor, eyes not to see and ears not to hear" (Rom 11:8 citing Isa 29:10). Why would God do such a thing? Well, Paul reasons, it is an eschatological necessity that God should have mercy on all people. Gentiles had always been disobedient ("by nature," Gal 2:15), so now, quite straightforwardly, God can have mercy on them. Jews, however, had always been mostly obedient; hence God has *made* them temporarily disobedient now so that he can very soon have mercy on them, too (Rom 11:30–32).[31] This explanation may seem strange, but then, so was the phenomenon Paul was trying to explain: the Jewish messiah had appeared, but only gentiles, not Jews (for the most part), were bowing the knee to him. Desperate times call for des-

---

30. See my argument in chapter 6 below.

31. See further Stanley K. Stowers, *A Rereading of Romans: Justice, Jews, and Gentiles* (New Haven: Yale University Press, 1994), 285–316.

perate explanatory measures. None of this, however, amounts to abandoning Judaism. In fact, Rom 11 is nothing if not a manifesto against abandonment. "The gifts and the call of God are irrevocable" (Rom 11:29). Paul can no more abandon Israel than God can.[32]

The grain of truth in the old saw that Paul abandoned Judaism is the fact that Paul does sometimes speak of abandoning, or being estranged from, the entire world as we know it. Through the cross of Christ, he says, "the cosmos was crucified to me, and I to the cosmos" (Gal 6:14). Because of Christ, Paul abandons the cosmos, the universe, life itself, which technically does include (conventional, everyday) Judaism, although that is not Paul's point.[33] A similar logic is at work in another well-known passage in Philippians (3:4–9):

> If anyone else thinks that he has confidence in the flesh, I more so: an eighth-day circumcision, from the race of Israel, the tribe of Benjamin, a Hebrew born from Hebrews, in respect of the law a Pharisee, in respect of zeal indicting the assembly, in respect of righteousness in the law blameless. But whatever things were gains to me, these things I consider loss on account of Christ. What is more, I consider all things to be loss on account of the superiority of the knowledge of Christ Jesus my lord, on whose account I suffered the loss of all things, and I consider them excrement, that I may gain Christ and be found in him, not having my own righteousness from the law but that which is through Christ-faith, righteousness from God, upon faith.

Historians are grateful for these few, brief autobiographical details (e.g., Paul's Pharisaic affiliation),[34] but Paul only includes them here because apparently some rival preachers have been touting their own credentials (Phil 3:2–4). Paul one-ups these rivals by citing his own superior credentials but then undermines the whole contest by declaring all such things worthless in comparison to Christ. To be sure, this is an emphatic devaluation of certain aspects of Paul's Jewishness, but, crucially, it is a devaluation relative to other aspects of Paul's Jewishness. The comparison is not between Judaism and Christianity (the latter concept being not yet available to Paul), but between Jewish piety

---

32. On this point, see the essays collected in Todd D. Still, ed., *God and Israel: Providence and Purpose in Romans 9–11* (Waco, TX: Baylor University Press, 2017).

33. See Beverly Roberts Gaventa, "The Singularity of the Gospel," in *Our Mother Saint Paul* (Louisville: Westminster John Knox, 2007), 101–12.

34. See chapter 3 above.

in the present evil age and Jewish mythology about the perfect age to come, or in other words, between everyday Judaism and eschatological Judaism.[35] If, in the new creation, Jews and gentiles alike are all sons and heirs of God, then Benjaminite ancestry is effectively superfluous. If, in the new creation, everyone is perfectly righteous all the time, then conventional law observance, repentance, atonement, etc. are likewise effectively superfluous. And so on.

This brings us to one final passage that has been widely taken to be a direct renunciation of Judaism: "Through the law, I died to the law, that I might live to God. I have been crucified together with Christ; I am no longer alive, but Christ is alive in me" (Gal 2:19–20). Many interpreters have assumed that no good Jew could write the sentence, "I died to the law"; hence many Jewish interpreters have scolded Paul for writing it, even as many Christian interpreters have praised him for writing it (e.g., Kohler and Baur, respectively, both cited above). But their shared assumption about what a Jew would or would not say is simply false. Antinomian-sounding sentiments are in fact not infrequent in the long history of Judaism.[36] In particular, apocalyptic Jews (Jews who thought they were actually living at the end of the present age and the dawn of the age to come) have expressed, and indeed acted upon, sentiments like this.[37] Such people do of course sound strange relative to conventional, majority piety, but they are an important part of the history of Judaism, not to mention the history of religions more generally. Paul's point about "dying to the law" is not that the law makes for a bad kind of religion, but that the entire age of sin and death (over which the law exercised benevolent jurisdiction) is now over. "Living to God" here refers not to Christianity (which Paul did not live to see),[38] but to the immortal, pneumatic life of the age to come. Or, to put it

35. On which see David Novak, "Jewish Eschatology," in *The Oxford Handbook of Eschatology*, ed. Jerry L. Walls (Oxford: Oxford University Press, 2007), 113–31; and on its special relevance to Paul, see Fredriksen, *Pagans' Apostle.*

36. See Joshua D. Garroway, "Paul: Within Judaism, Without Law," in *Law and Lawlessness in Early Judaism and Early Christianity*, ed. David Lincicum et al., WUNT 420 (Tübingen: Mohr Siebeck, 2019), 49–66.

37. See the examples documented in Gershom Scholem, *Major Trends in Jewish Mysticism* (New York: Schocken, 1995 [1946]); Scholem, *The Messianic Idea in Judaism and Other Essays on Jewish Spirituality* (New York: Schocken, 1995 [1971]); and the example *par excellence* detailed in Scholem, *Sabbatai Zevi: Mystical Messiah, 1626–1676*, trans. R. J. Zwi Werblowsky (Princeton: Princeton University Press, 1973).

38. That is, Christianity in the sense that we normally use that word, e.g., as in *OED*: "A religion based on the teachings of Jesus Christ, as recorded in the New Testament, and the belief that he was the son of God; the system of doctrines and precepts taught by Jesus and his apostles."

another way: Had Paul known of such a thing as Christianity, he would have said that he had died to that, too.

## DID PAUL ABANDON MONOTHEISM?

We can think of our second question (Did Paul abandon monotheism?) as a subset of the first (Did Paul abandon Judaism?). We can think of it in this way because, in much modern discussion of the issue, monotheism has been thought to be a defining characteristic of Judaism, upon which Paul's Christology (i.e., his understanding of Jesus) supposedly infringed in one way or another. In fact, as we shall see, there are problems with both halves of this assumption, but its basic logic is clear enough. Thus, for instance, Kohler (cited above in connection with Paul and Judaism) writes about Paul and monotheism as follows: "To a Jewish mind trained by rabbinical acumen, this [viz. Paul's argument in Rom 5–8] is not pure monotheistic, but mythological, thinking. Paul's 'Son of God' is, far more than the Logos of Philo, an infringement of the absolute unity of God."[39] While historic Judaism neither has nor needs anything quite like the ancient Christian creeds (e.g., the Nicene Creed), it has long been noted that the Shema (the confession of the oneness of God from the Torah) has at least a broadly analogous kind of status: "Hear, O Israel, the Lord our God, the Lord is one" (Deut 6:4). Making this confession is among the most fundamental acts of Jewish piety, performed morning and evening by Jews everywhere from the rabbinic period to the present day. Its symbolic power is attested, for instance, by the famous story of the martyr Rabbi Akiba, who endured Roman torture and died with the Shema on his lips (b. Ber. 61b). To balk at confessing the Shema would be to put a question mark to one's Jewishness.[40]

Does Paul balk at confessing the Shema? On the face of it, certainly not. Several times, in fact, he confesses it explicitly. In Gal 3, Paul appeals to the oneness of God to explain the priority of God's promise to Abraham over God's giving of the law to Israel at Mount Sinai. He writes, "Why then the law? It was added on account of transgressions—until such time as the seed

---

39. Kohler, "Saul of Tarsus," 83.

40. On the ancient evidence, see Reuven Kimelman, "Rabbinic Prayer in Late Antiquity," in The Cambridge History of Judaism, vol. 4, ed. Steven T. Katz (Cambridge: Cambridge University Press, 2006), 573–611; and Sarit Kattan Gribetz, "The Shema in the Second Temple Period: A Reconsideration," JAJ 6 (2015): 58–84, who shows that the ritual use of the Shema in prayer is not securely attested prior to the rabbinic period.

should come to whom the promise was made—arranged through angels, in the hand of a mediator. The mediator is not of one, but God is one" (Gal 3:19–20). There are several puzzling aspects to this passage, but the central claim is clear. The oneness of God, which Paul takes as axiomatic, corresponds to God's very ancient promise to Abraham, which God made face to face and without the aid of a mediator.[41] In Rom 3, Paul again appeals to the oneness of God in order to establish another theological point: the principle that God must justify gentiles in the same way that he justifies Jews. "If God, who will justify the circumcision from faith, is one, [he will justify] also the foreskin through faith" (Rom 3:30). "God is one" (εἷς ὁ θεός). Therefore, Paul reasons, God cannot have two different strategies for justification, one for Jews and another for gentiles.[42] Here again, Paul solves a theological problem by appealing to the axiom of the oneness of God.

As with the discussion of Judaism above, so with the Shema. The problem is not that Paul ever voices any doubts about the oneness of God; he does not. In fact, he pointedly affirms it. The problem, if there is one, is that Paul also says some things about Jesus that later interpreters have thought *should* have made Paul balk at confessing the Shema. According to these interpreters, Paul himself may not have recognized that he had abandoned monotheism, but he had in fact abandoned it. A key text here is Paul's third express citation of the Shema, where he is answering the question whether it is permissible for gentiles-in-Christ to eat meat that had previously been sacrificed to idols (1 Cor 8:4–6).[43]

> So then, concerning the eating of idol sacrifices: We know that an idol is nothing in the cosmos, and that there is no god but one. For if there are so-called gods, whether in heaven or on earth—as indeed there are many gods and many lords—nevertheless for us there is one god the father, from whom are all things, and we are for him, and one lord Jesus Christ, through whom are all things, and we are through him.

On the one hand, Paul here once again affirms Deuteronomic orthodoxy ("there is no god but one") but, on the other hand, he also concedes the exis-

---

41. On this verse, see Francis Watson, *Paul and the Hermeneutics of Faith*, 2nd ed. (London: T&T Clark, 2016 [2004]), 256–58.

42. On this verse, see Richard B. Hays, "Have We Found Abraham to Be Our Forefather according to the Flesh? A Reconsideration of Rom 4:1," *NovT* 27 (1985): 76–98 at 83–85.

43. On the occasion and the argument of this passage, see the discussion in Wayne A. Meeks, *The First Urban Christians: The Social World of the Apostle Paul*, 2nd ed. (New Haven: Yale University Press, 2003 [1983]), 140–63.

tence of many other gods and lords. On the surface of it, this is confusing, not to say contradictory. But there is a logic to it. Paul says that *idols*, that is, the cult statues of gentile deities, are nothing at all. But the deities themselves do exist, as he reaffirms at the end of his discourse on idol sacrifices: "What [gentiles] sacrifice, they sacrifice to demons and not to God" (1 Cor 10:20). Unlike idols, Paul reckons, demons, gods, and lords are real things in the cosmos.[44]

What is more, one of these other lords, namely Jesus, Paul also adds to his formulaic confession of divine oneness: "For us there is one god the father . . . *and* one lord Jesus Christ."[45] Paul calls Christ a lord, not a god, which is interesting and perhaps significant (see further below), but God does at least now have a divine lieutenant, the messiah Jesus. The phrase "for us" signifies that here Paul is talking about devotion, not ontology. The point, in other words, is not that no other divine beings exist except God and Christ, but rather that only God and Christ are worthy of devotion from Paul and his co-religionists.[46] Gentiles in their natural state may sacrifice to demons, but "for us" there is only God and Christ. This is what is often called monolatry (as opposed to monotheism) in the secondary literature. If monotheism means belief in the existence of only one divine being and no others,[47] monolatry means the reservation of worship for one divine being, even if other divine beings may exist. Monolatry is often (but need not be) coordinated with henotheism—that is, belief in the existence of a pyramid of divine beings with one higher than all the rest.[48] These additional terms give us access to very helpful distinctions, but unfortunately, many scholars (not to mention laypeople) do not avail themselves of these distinctions. Many persist in using just

---

44. On the threat posed by demons here, see Dale B. Martin, *The Corinthian Body* (New Haven: Yale University Press, 1995), 179–89.

45. See N. T. Wright, *The Climax of the Covenant* (Minneapolis: Fortress, 1992), 120–36.

46. The usefulness of this devotion-versus-ontology distinction is illustrated on a large scale by Larry W. Hurtado, *Lord Jesus Christ: Devotion to Jesus in Earliest Christianity* (Grand Rapids: Eerdmans, 2003).

47. Which is the common, dictionary sense of the word. The conceptual problem is that, depending what exactly is allowed to count as a divine being, either everyone is a monotheist (because most religious cosmologies reserve space for a high god) or no one is (because even the strictest monotheisms allow angels, spirits, etc.). A good case can be made that the term itself is so problem-ridden as to be no longer useful; see Paula Fredriksen, "Mandatory Retirement: Ideas in the Study of Christian Origins Whose Time Has Come to Go," *SR* 35 (2006): 231–46.

48. On these and other configurations, see Mark S. Smith, *The Origins of Biblical Monotheism: Israel's Polytheistic Background and the Ugaritic Texts* (Oxford: Oxford University Press, 2001).

the one word "monotheism" for a number of quite different phenomena. Or they create their own bespoke distinctions, such as William Horbury's distinction between exclusive monotheism (which denies the existence of all gods but one) and inclusive monotheism (which allows that other gods exist but ranks them below the high god),[49] or Angelos Chaniotis's distinction between monotheism (only one god exists) and megatheism (one god is experienced as superior to all others).[50] Ideally, when discussing these complicated matters, we should be maximally precise while also using terms that are intelligible to the largest possible number of people. Along these lines, we might say that, in 1 Corinthians 8, Paul starts by striking an apparently monotheistic note ("there is no god but one"), but as he goes on it emerges that his position is perhaps better described as henotheistic and monolatrous (or, perhaps better, *duolatrous*): There are many gods and lords in the cosmos, but one father god is above them all, and only he and his son the messiah are worthy of devotion in Paul's assemblies.

This passage fits with a pattern whereby Paul often speaks of Christ in ways that ancients would speak of a god (invoking him, acclaiming him, delivering oracles from him, celebrating him in a ritual meal, etc.)[51] but does not actually call Christ a god, or God. Paul overwhelmingly speaks of God as the father of Jesus (Rom 15:6; 2 Cor 1:3; 11:31), not as Jesus. And, correspondingly, he speaks of Jesus as the son of God, not as God. Admittedly, Titus 2:13 arguably does call Jesus a god: "the appearing of the glory of our great god and savior Jesus Christ." But Titus is regarded by many scholars (rightly, in my view) as a pseudepigraphon—that is, a letter attributed to Paul but actually written by someone else. In the undisputedly authentic Pauline letters, there is only one passage that might conceivably call Jesus God, and it probably does not do so. The passage is Rom 9:5, and the problem for translators is how to punctuate the sentence. It reads in one of two ways: either "From the Israelites comes the messiah, according to the flesh, *who is* God over all, blessed forever, amen" or "From the Israelites comes the messiah, according to the flesh. God who is over all be blessed forever, amen." Either punctuation is technically possible.[52] But

49. William Horbury, "Jewish and Christian Monotheism in the Herodian Age," in *Herodian Judaism and New Testament Study*, WUNT 193 (Tübingen: Mohr Siebeck, 2006), 2–33.

50. Angelos Chaniotis, "Megatheism: The Search for the Almighty God and the Competition of Cults," in *One God: Pagan Monotheism in the Roman Empire*, ed. Stephen Mitchell and Peter van Nuffelen (Cambridge: Cambridge University Press, 2010), 112–40.

51. On this issue, see M. David Litwa, *Iesus Deus: The Early Christian Depiction of Jesus as a Mediterranean God* (Minneapolis: Fortress, 2014).

52. See Bruce M. Metzger, "The Punctuation of Romans 9:5," in *Christ and the Spirit in*

the second rendering is arguably the more likely, being more consistent both with Paul's usual way of writing benedictions (Rom 1:25; 2 Cor 1:3; 11:31) and with his usage of the names "God" and "Christ" elsewhere.[53]

If Paul's Christ is not identical with God the father, then what kind of divine being is he? Where, exactly, does Christ fit in Paul's cosmology? This turns out to be a rather difficult question, and it has generated a number of different, even conflicting, answers. Bart Ehrman has argued, for instance, that Paul thinks that Christ is an angel.[54] He points to Gal 4:14: "You [Galatians] received me [Paul] as an angel of God, as Christ Jesus." Ehrman takes the two parallel phrases as synonymous, but that is neither necessary nor (arguably) likely. Like an angel, Christ is a divine being who is not God the father, but there are things other than angels that fit these criteria. Elsewhere, Paul speaks of Christ much more like one would speak of a deified human being. Christ was born of a woman (Gal 4:4), from the bloodline of King David (Rom 1:3), but having died and then been raised by God, he is now immortal (Rom 6:9). These passages would seem to suggest a kind of deified king or hero (e.g., Hercules, Alexander the Great, Julius Caesar).[55] But here, too, there is more to it than that.

Paul's Christ is not identical with God, but he stands in a closer relation to God than any other divine being does.[56] In the letters of Paul, angels and demons are called angels and demons, not "sons of God," as they often are in the Hebrew Bible (e.g., Psalm 29:1; 89:7; Job 38:7). For Paul, only Christ is the son of God, with the rule-proving exception of people who get joined to Christ and thereby become sons of God themselves (Rom 8:14, 19; 9:26; Gal 3:26; 4:6–7). Christ is, moreover, "the image of God" (2 Cor 4:4), the visible representation

---

the New Testament, ed. Barnabas Lindars and Stephen S. Smalley (Cambridge: Cambridge University Press, 1973), 95–112.

53. This is how I, with many other interpreters, understand Rom 9:5. But for an exhaustive argument that Paul *does* in fact call Jesus God in this verse, see George Carraway, *Christ Is God Over All: Romans 9:5 in the Context of Romans 9–11*, LNTS 489 (London: T&T Clark, 2013).

54. Bart D. Ehrman, *How Jesus Became God: The Exaltation of a Jewish Preacher from Galilee* (San Francisco: HarperOne, 2014), 251–54.

55. On this pattern, see in particular Michael Peppard, *The Son of God in the Roman World: Divine Sonship in Its Social and Political Context* (New York: Oxford University Press, 2011).

56. What Hurtado, *Lord Jesus Christ*, calls a binitarian relation, which he regards as a "mutation" from earlier Jewish understandings of God. But for an argument that Jewish binitarianism is very ancient, see Daniel Boyarin, *The Jewish Gospels: The Story of the Jewish Christ* (New York: Free Press, 2012).

of the invisible God (analogous to the measure of the heavenly body of God [*shiʿur qomah*] in late antique Jewish mysticism). God's glory (that is, his *kavod* or bodily presence) has always been hidden in his sanctuary in Jerusalem (Rom 9:4), but in the new creation, all human beings (not only priests but also laypeople, not only Jews but also gentiles) can attain "knowledge of the glory of God in the face of Christ" (2 Cor 4:6). The divine *pneuma* (usually translated "spirit") that people receive in the new creation is, at the same time, the *pneuma* of God and the *pneuma* of Christ (Rom 8:9). Paul's Christ is the son of God, the image of God, the face of God.[57] These descriptions are tantalizingly brief, but in one passage Paul supplies a narrative within which their sense becomes a bit clearer (Phil 2:5–11):

> Christ Jesus, who, although he was in the form of God, did not consider it as spoils to be equal with God, but he emptied himself, taking the form of a slave, being in the likeness of humans; and being found as a human in regard to figure, he humbled himself, becoming obedient to the point of death, the death of a cross. Therefore indeed God highly exalted him and gave him the name higher than every name, so that at the name of Jesus every knee should bow, of beings in heaven and on earth and in the underworld, and every tongue confess that Jesus Christ is lord to the glory of God the father.

In this fascinating passage, Christ is neither God nor human, exactly. He exists in the heavenly form of God, but his likeness and figure are human. He undergoes the quintessentially human experience of death (and thus is a mortal, strictly speaking), but he receives obeisance from human and superhuman beings like a high god would.[58] Like Metatron in the Jewish mystical text *3 Enoch*, Christ in Philippians 2 is both a deified human being and the archangelic form of God.[59] If we recall that "Christ" means messiah, then this is not as strange as it might at first seem. There were a number of types of messiahs in ancient Jewish imagination: priest, king, warrior, angel, and more.

---

57. See further Paula Fredriksen, "How High Can Early High Christology Be?," in *Monotheism and Christology in Greco-Roman Antiquity*, ed. Matthew V. Novenson, NovTSup 180 (Leiden: Brill, 2020), 293–319.

58. Here, however, when *Christ* receives obeisance from human and superhuman beings, glory redounds to *God the father*, on which see further Hurtado, *Lord Jesus Christ*, 151–53.

59. See Gedaliahu G. Stroumsa, "Form(s) of God: Some Notes on Metatron and Christ," *HTR* 76 (1983): 269–88; Markus Bockmuehl, "'The Form of God' (Phil 2:6): Variations on a Theme of Jewish Mysticism," *JTS* 48 (1997): 1–23.

Nor is it at all uncommon to find features of different types mixed up in the sources, as we find in Philippians 2.

Does any of this, though, put Paul in contravention of a Jewish doctrine of God? Paul himself certainly does not think so. Strenuously to the contrary, he thinks that his gospel calls gentiles away from idolatry to the worship of the one true God, just as other Jewish Greek texts like *Letter of Aristeas* or *Wisdom of Solomon* do.[60] "You turned to God from idols, to serve a living and true God, and to await his son from heaven, whom he raised from the dead, Jesus who delivers us from the coming wrath" (1 Thess 1:9–10). Of course, Paul speaks not only of "the living and true God" but also of "his son from heaven," which *Letter of Aristeas* and *Wisdom of Solomon* do not do. But as we have seen, the idea of a heavenly lieutenant (God's son, or messenger, or chosen one, or anointed one) who will execute judgment on God's behalf is not at all unusual in Jewish texts that speculate about such things.

The conventional way of putting the question, "Did Paul abandon Jewish monotheism?" assumes that we know where Paul's Jewish contemporaries stood vis-à-vis monotheism, that they were all good, traditional monotheists, and the only question is whether Paul parted ways with them on this issue. But do we know that? We have a concept of monotheism, and we plausibly associate it with ancient Jews and their scriptures, but we often overlook the actual evidence for what Paul's contemporaries believed about God and other divine beings. As Paula Fredriksen has perceptively put it, in antiquity, even the monotheists were polytheists.[61] With very few exceptions (mostly philosophers), in the ancient world virtually everyone (Jews, Greeks, Romans, Egyptians, Arabians, Gauls, Britons, and the rest) believed that the heavens teemed with divine beings: angels, demons, spirits, gods, demigods, heroes, ancestors, and so on. All of these beings existed and therefore merited due attention from mortals, just as powerful human beings (e.g., emperors, kings, patrons) would. So if "monotheism" means denying the very existence of any divine beings save one,[62] then there were almost no monotheists in antiquity.

---

60. On these and other related texts, see Matthew V. Novenson, "The Universal Polytheism and the Case of the Jews," in *Monotheism and Christology in Greco-Roman Antiquity*, ed. Matthew V. Novenson, NovTSup 180 (Leiden: Brill, 2020), 32–60.

61. Fredriksen, *Pagans' Apostle*, 12. And see further Smith, *Origins of Biblical Monotheism*; Peter Schäfer, *Two Gods in Heaven: Jewish Concepts of God in Antiquity*, trans. Allison Brown (Princeton: Princeton University Press, 2020).

62. Which, again, is the common, dictionary sense of the term, e.g., *OED*: "the doctrine or belief that there is only one God"; *Merriam-Webster Dictionary*: "the doctrine or belief that there is but one God."

Certainly most Jews were not monotheists in this sense. Our ancient Jewish texts are full of references to divine beings, many of them even having proper names such as Michael, Gabriel, Uriel, Raphael, Metatron, Samael, Azazel, Semihazah, Satan, Belial, Beelzebub, Asmodeus, Mastema, and many more.[63] If we approach the question from this angle, then when we find Paul speaking not only of God and Christ but also of Satan, Belial, the god of this age, angels, demons, elements, spirits, rulers, authorities, powers, and more,[64] Paul suddenly looks much more like his Jewish contemporaries (and his non-Jewish contemporaries, too, for that matter), "monotheist" or not.[65]

In other words, although, in the history of interpretation, readers have been most anxious about whether Paul's view of Christ compromised monotheism, they might have done just as well to direct their anxiety toward Paul's view of other divine beings. Older scholarship often rushed to demythologize, metaphorize, or explain away these other beings, but recent scholarship has taken them more seriously and more realistically. The so-called apocalyptic school of Pauline interpretation has emphasized both the threat posed by "anti-God powers" (especially sin and death) and God's conquest over those powers in the death of Christ as features of Paul's gospel.[66] Meanwhile, from a history-of-religions perspective, other interpreters have asked whether Paul actually thinks of sin and death as demons, rulers, or authorities (see Rom 5:12–21)—that is, as particular named beings analogous to the Greek gods Planē, Thanatos, or Hades. In short, there is nowadays a greater interest in and patience with Paul's frankly rather mythological cosmology, with all its many-colored divine beings.[67]

It should be noted that Paul specifically classifies many of these divine beings as created things: "Neither death, nor life, nor angels, nor rulers, nor things that are, nor things that shall be, nor powers, nor height, nor depth,

---

63. On the mass of evidence for ancient Jewish piety directed to these beings, see Mika Ahuvia, *On My Right Michael, On My Left Gabriel: Angels in Ancient Jewish Culture* (Berkeley: University of California Press, 2021).

64. See Rom 8:37–39; 16:20; 1 Cor 4:9; 5:5; 6:3; 7:5; 10:20–21; 11:10; 12:10; 13:1; 14:12, 32; 2 Cor 2:11; 4:4; 6:15; 11:14; 12:7; Gal 1:8; 3:19; 4:14; 1 Thess 2:18.

65. See further Loren T. Stuckenbruck, "'Angels' and 'God': Exploring the Limits of Early Jewish Monotheism," in *Early Christian and Jewish Monotheism*, ed. Loren T. Stuckenbruck and Wendy E. S. North, JSNTSup 263 (London: T&T Clark, 2004), 45–70.

66. See, e.g., Beverly Roberts Gaventa, "The Cosmic Power of Sin in Paul's Letter to the Romans," *Interpretation* 58 (2004): 229–40.

67. On this mythological aspect, see Stephen L. Young, "Paul the Mythmaker" (PhD diss., Brown University, 2016); Emma Wasserman, *Apocalypse as Holy War: Divine Politics and Polemics in the Letters of Paul*, AYBRL (New Haven: Yale University Press, 2018).

nor any other creature [κτίσις] shall be able to part us from the love of God that is in Christ Jesus our lord" (Rom 8:38–39). So death, angels, powers, and rulers, at least, are created things, even if they are also superhuman (and thus divine in this latter sense). This illustrates once again a key point of confusion in the secondary literature: what exactly is meant by "god" and "divine." Some interpreters urge that these terms should only be used of the highest god, while others allow them for other immortal, celestial beings, too. Both groups of interpreters can claim warrant from Paul, who, as we have seen, gives a complicated account. For Paul, "there is no god but one"— that is, no creator but one. At the same time, however, "there are many gods and many lords" —that is, many angels, demons, rulers, powers, etc., including Satan, Belial, the god of this age, and Christ. But Christ, as we have also seen, is a special case. He is one of the lords that exist in the cosmos, but he is the one lord "for us," as Paul emphasizes. He is not God, but he is, uniquely, the son of God and the image of God. All things are *from* God the father, but all things are *through* Christ, which might suggest that Christ is not a κτίσις, a creature. This is what Richard Bauckham means by speaking of "Paul's Christology of divine identity."[68] Christ, death, angels, and archons may all be divine beings, but in respect to creation, Christ is different from all these others. They are called κτίσεις, creatures; Christ is not. Nevertheless, Paul says, at the end of all things, even Christ will ultimately be subordinated to God the father (1 Cor 15:28).[69]

In sum, Paul was just as monotheistic as his Jewish contemporaries were, which is to say, moderately monotheistic by ancient standards, but not very monotheistic by modern standards. Like most ancient Jews, Paul differed from most ancient gentiles in regarding the deity resident in Jerusalem as the creator of all things, and in theoretically reserving cultic worship for him alone. Like almost everyone in antiquity, Jew or gentile, Paul also acknowledged the existence and agency of many other divine beings. Is this monotheistic? Perhaps it is, if we stretch the concept far enough to make it fit—for instance, by allowing an "inclusive monotheism" in addition to the more familiar "exclusive monotheism" (à la Horbury), or by stipulating that "monotheism" means not belief in one god but belief in one creator (à la Bauckham). We are of course free to make moves like this, and there may be some good reasons (especially

68. Richard Bauckham, "Paul's Christology of Divine Identity," in *Jesus and the God of Israel* (Grand Rapids: Eerdmans, 2009), 182–232.

69. These subtle Pauline distinctions are part of the inheritance of the late ancient Christians who developed the doctrine of the trinity, on which see Wesley Hill, *Paul and the Trinity: Persons, Relations, and the Pauline Letters* (Grand Rapids: Eerdmans, 2015).

theological ones) for doing so. But we should also acknowledge that stretching the concept in this way makes it something other than what many people recognize as monotheism.[70] In any event, as the argument above has shown, it is not the case that the principle of monotheism was any kind of fault line separating Paul from other ancient Jews.

## CONCLUSION

For all of Socrates's conflict with the leadership of classical Athens, even to the point of his death at the hands of the state, we do not generally think of him as having abandoned Athenianness. Our intuition in the case of Socrates is right, and we should apply it also to the case of Paul. Did Paul abandon either Judaism or monotheism? We can take the latter part of the question first. Paul certainly did not abandon Judaism *by* abandoning monotheism, first because ancient Judaism itself was not monotheistic in the sense that most moderns mean that word, and second because Paul's cosmology actually agrees in most respects with the cosmologies of other ancient Jews. Like Deuteronomy, Ben Sira, Philo, and Josephus, Paul believes that the God of Abraham is the creator of the universe, but also that God is variously worshiped, assisted, and opposed by a host of lower deities. Like some (but not all) other ancient Jews, Paul believed that the messiah was one of these divine beings. So far, so conventional. The point on which most other ancient Jews disagreed with Paul (and with Peter, James, Barnabas, et al.) was the claim that the recently executed man Jesus was this messiah. That was an extreme minority opinion in ancient Judaism, but not because it was a different kind of thing from ancient Judaism.

But if not in respect of monotheism, did Paul nevertheless abandon Judaism in some other respect? Perhaps in respect of the law of Moses, since that is where modern interpreters have been most exercised? Again, at many points, Paul expressly agrees with what most other ancient Jews for whom we have evidence say about the law. God gave it to Moses on Mount Sinai. It is the patrimony of the Jews. It is altogether righteous. God has shown us how to fulfill it. And so on. In addition to these claims, however, Paul also makes some more controversial claims about the law. It works wrath. It effects death. It has

---

70. Thus rightly Chaniotis, "Megatheism," 112: "I wonder whether it really helps us to understand the religions of the Roman Empire if we modify the term monotheism beyond recognition through the addition of attributes, such as soft, pagan, inclusive, hierarchical, affective or whatever."

jurisdiction over the present age but not over the age to come. It is powerless to bring about ultimate, eschatological righteousness. He, Paul, has died to it. It is in these claims that many modern interpreters have thought they have found Paul's supposed breach with Judaism and manifesto of Christianity. To be sure, late ancient, gentile Christianity found excellent grist for its mill in these latter sayings of Paul.[71] But when, say, Marcion and Augustine use these words of Paul's, they mean quite different things from what the apostle meant when he said them.[72] In Paul's own context, even these more controversial claims about the law are recognizably, intelligibly, even familiarly Jewish. Admittedly, the closest parallel evidence comes not from everyday, conventional Jewish piety but from apocalyptic, millenarian Jewish circles, but it is no less Jewish for that. As we have learned from modern social theory of religion, ancient Judaism was whatever ancient Jews did. In short, then, Paul did not abandon Judaism. Over the course of late antiquity, Christianity abandoned Judaism, and it did so using Paul's words.[73] But that is a very different thing.

71. See my argument in chapter 11 below.

72. On this point, see the classic essay of Krister Stendahl, "The Apostle Paul and the Introspective Conscience of the West," *HTR* 56 (1963): 199–215; and my discussion in chapter 1 above.

73. On this history, see Ora Limor and Guy G. Stroumsa, eds., *Contra Iudaeos: Ancient and Medieval Polemics between Christians and Jews*, TSMEMJ 10 (Tübingen: Mohr Siebeck, 1996).

5

# ROMANS AND GALATIANS

The only instance known to me of a human being claiming a conjugal relationship with a work of literature is the case of Martin Luther with Paul's
Letter to the Galatians, about which Luther wrote, "I have betrothed myself
to it. It is my Katie von Bora" (Katie von Bora, of course, being the name of
Luther's human wife). As this quotation illustrates, historically, the example
*par excellence* of a canon within the canon is the case of Galatians and Romans
in the Protestant churches. It is in these two epistles that Protestant interpreters
have thought that they heard the word of God clearest of all.[1] Ever since F. C.
Baur in the mid-nineteenth century, critical scholars have spoken of Paul's
four *Hauptbriefe*, "chief epistles": Romans, 1 Corinthians, 2 Corinthians, and
Galatians. They are chief first of all because they are the longest; hence their
presence first in the sequence of Paul's letters in manuscripts and printed New
Testaments. But Galatians and Romans, in particular, have also been regarded
as chief in regard to their content. These letters have been thought to "push
Christ" (Luther's criterion: *was Christum treibet*, "what pushes Christ")[2] even
more than other New Testament texts do, especially because of their peculiar

1. Thus rightly Robert Morgan, "Introduction: The Nature of New Testament Theology,"
in Morgan, *The Nature of New Testament Theology*, SBT (London: SCM, 1973), 52–59.

2. On which see the discussion by Robert W. Jenson, "On the Authorities of Scripture,"
in Jenson, *The Triune Story: Collected Essays on Scripture*, ed. Brad East (Oxford: Oxford
University Press, 2019), 146–54.

emphasis on "righteousness from Christ-faith" (on which, more below). One might reasonably ask, and some have asked, whether that theme should be the gold standard for measuring the worth of a canonical text, but in any case it certainly has been in much Protestant exegesis and theology.

Further back in Christian history, Galatians and Romans did not occupy such a prominent place. Indeed, many ancient interpreters favored the Corinthian correspondence and the Pastoral Epistles, which just illustrates how canon-within-a-canon judgments are relative to the context and interests of the interpreter.[3] Luther and his successors found Paul's language in Galatians and Romans (righteousness, faith, works of the law, flesh, spirit, etc.) useful in their disputes with the early modern Catholic Church and other Protestant splinter groups.[4] What Paul meant by "righteousness from Christ-faith" is not what Luther, using Paul's words many centuries later, meant by "righteousness from Christ-faith." But that is in the nature of scriptural interpretation. Paul himself evidently arrived at this cluster of themes in his own, different polemical context. Others of Paul's letters have little or nothing to say about righteousness, faith, or law (compare, e.g., 1 Thessalonians, 2 Corinthians, Philemon),[5] but a regional controversy in Asia Minor over the prospect of gentiles-in-Christ undergoing Jewish proselyte circumcision occasioned Paul's reflection on these themes; hence their appearance in Galatians. By the time Paul wrote Romans, perhaps several years later, reports of the kind of thing he had said in Galatians had begun to cause him further trouble (see Rom 3:8); hence Romans is partly taken up with clarifying, justifying, and modifying claims first made in the Galatian controversy. We do not know whether the Galatian Christ assemblies heeded Paul's counsel against circumcision, or whether Paul ever visited the Christ-believers in Rome as he planned to do, but regardless, the influence of these two letters on later generations of readers would be hard to overstate.

## THE LETTER OF PAUL TO THE GALATIANS

Paul's usual pattern was to write a letter to the Christ assemblies (ἐκκλησίαι, *ekklēsiai*, traditionally translated "churches") in a major Mediterranean city:

---

3. See further chapter 11 below.

4. See R. Ward Holder, ed., *A Companion to Paul in the Reformation* (Leiden: Brill, 2009).

5. Which fact raises questions about our reasons for centering certain letters and marginalizing others. See further Benjamin L. White, *Remembering Paul: Ancient and Modern Contests over the Image of the Apostle*. New York: Oxford University Press, 2014.

Thessalonica, Philippi, Corinth, Rome, and so on. Galatians, by contrast, is a circular letter addressed to the Christ assemblies of an entire region. Precisely which region has long been contested. On any theory, Galatia designates a large swath of central Asia Minor (i.e., of Anatolia, modern Turkey), but Paul does not name any particular cities to which he sends the letter. The Acts of the Apostles places Paul in the cities of Antioch, Iconium, Lystra, and Derbe (Acts 13–14), which could perhaps be interpreted generously to correspond to what the letter calls Galatia, but Acts maps these cities in Pisidia and Lycaonia, not Galatia. That Paul addresses his audience in the letter as Γαλάται, "Celts" or "Gauls" (Gal 3:1) might suggest the more northerly cities of Ankyra, Pessinus, and Tavium, which, however, are not named either in Acts or in the letters (but cf. "the Galatian region" in Acts 16:6; 18:23).

In any case, Paul considers these Galatian assemblies his own, inasmuch as he first announced the good news of Christ to them, baptized them, and saw them receive the divine πνεῦμα (*pneuma*, traditionally translated "spirit": Gal 3:1–5; 4:12–20). Frustratingly for Paul, however, in the intervening months or years, other apostles have come into the Christ assemblies in Galatia, announcing what Paul calls "another good news" and "a perversion of the good news of Christ" (Gal 1:6–7). Paul never names these other apostles, other than to call them ταράσσοντες, "agitators" or "trouble-makers" (Gal 1:7; 5:10). Not until near the end of the letter does he actually specify what they are teaching; presumably he assumes that his audience knows the elephant in the room. From the opening of the letter body—"I am shocked that you are so quickly turning away from him who called you in the gift of Christ" (Gal 1:6)—through the end, the letter consists almost entirely of polemic against these rival teachers.

Most of Gal 1–2 comprises a defense, in autobiographical form, of the legitimacy of Paul's εὐαγγέλιον ("good announcement," "gospel") over against the εὐαγγέλιον taught by his rivals. He boasts, "The good news announced by me is not human, for I neither received it from a human nor was I taught it, but it came through a revelation of Jesus Christ" (Gal 1:11–12). This claim takes a feature of Paul's biography that he probably experienced as a professional liability—namely, that he had not been a student of Jesus when Jesus was alive, as the first apostles had—and turns it into an asset. His revelation of the deified Christ thus becomes his unassailable credential.[6] It is in this context that we get some precious details about Paul's early career that we would otherwise lack:

---

6. Here see Sarah E. Rollens, "'The God Came to Me in a Dream': Epiphanies in Voluntary Associations as a Context for Paul's Vision of Christ," *HTR* 111 (2018): 41–65.

his advocacy work for the defense and promotion of Jewish customs in the diaspora,[7] his mystical encounter with the son of God, his mysterious Arabian period, and his apostolic apprenticeship in Syria (Gal 1:13–17).

Paul is especially concerned to go on record with his own account of his two visits to Jerusalem subsequent to his revelation of Jesus (Gal 1:18–20; 2:1–10; cf. the four Jerusalem visits noted in Acts 9:26–30; 11:30 and 12:25; 15:4–29; 18:22). Paul's primary point about both visits is that, although the chief apostles did and do approve his apostleship, he was neither taught nor deputized by them. He has their approval, but he does not need it. They discovered his apostolic office; they did not create it. Perhaps his rivals in the Galatian assemblies were saying about him that he was only a low-level deputy of the chief apostles (see Gal 2:9). Perhaps, too, they claimed the imprimatur of the Jerusalem Christ assembly for their own gospel. About the first Jerusalem visit, three years after his revelation, Paul says only that he met Cephas (i.e., Peter) and James (Gal 1:18–19). About the second visit, fourteen years later, he gives a fuller account: He was prompted to go up by a revelation (not by an invitation from the apostles); he presented for the apostles the message that he was preaching among the gentiles; although some "false brethren" at this meeting tried to impose proselyte circumcision on Paul's gentiles-in-Christ (in the person of the gentile Titus, whom Paul had brought along), their efforts failed; and there was agreed a division of labor according to which Peter (i.e., Cephas) was recognized as apostle to the Jews and Paul as apostle to the gentiles (Gal 2:1–10).

In Gal 2:11–21, Paul narrates a subsequent episode, set not in Jerusalem but in Syrian Antioch, which is the occasion for his first mention (and indeed, the first mention anywhere in ancient literature) of the idea of "righteousness from Christ-faith and not works of the law." Curiously in light of the argument of the letter, this "Antioch incident"[8] had nothing to do with circumcision; the controversy was all about common meals among Jews and gentiles. At some unspecified point in the past, Paul and Cephas were both resident in the Christ assembly in Antioch, and they were in the practice of celebrating ritual meals together with both Jewish and gentile Christ-believers. But then, Paul says cryptically, "some people from James" arrived, and Cephas stopped eating with his gentile co-religionists on account of fear of these people, whom Paul also

7. On which see chapter 3 in the present volume.
8. On which see Magnus Zetterholm, *The Formation of Christianity in Antioch: A Sociological Approach to the Separation between Judaism and Christianity* (London: Routledge, 2003); Paula Fredriksen, *Paul: The Pagans' Apostle* (New Haven: Yale University Press, 2017), 96–99.

calls "the people from the circumcision" (i.e., probably, "people from among the Jews"). Other prominent Jews-in-Christ followed Cephas's lead, and Paul felt compelled to intervene to stop this ethnic estrangement. Paul narrates his rebuke of Cephas, which transitions seamlessly into his present exhortation to his audience in Galatia. "We know that a person is not put right from works of the law except through trust of Jesus Christ, and we have trusted in Christ Jesus, so that we might be put right from trust of Christ, not from works of the law, for from works of the law all flesh will not be put right" (Gal 2:16). The syntax of this verse is clunky, but the basic contrast Paul is drawing comes through loud and clear.

Paul had considered Cephas's shunning of his gentile co-religionists in Antioch a betrayal of the principle that righteousness comes from Christ-faith rather than works of the law. In Gal 3 and following, he insists that what the Galatian gentiles-in-Christ are contemplating (namely, proselyte circumcision, though Paul does not name it until Gal 5) is a similar betrayal. He reckons that for gentiles-in-Christ to undergo proselyte circumcision would be for them to try to get put right from works of the law. That such an outcome is impossible, however, Paul argues from the story of father Abraham in Gen 12–15. On Paul's reading of the Abraham story (which is one of many readings of the Abraham story in ancient Jewish sources), God promised to Abraham, Abraham's seed, and (indirectly) the gentiles, too, that they would one day receive righteousness and *pneuma* from trust (Paul quotes Gen 15:6 at Gal 3:6: "Abraham *trusted* God, and it was reckoned to him for righteousness").[9] This trust, Paul glosses, is the trust of Christ, and in fact, Christ himself is the "seed of Abraham" to whom God made the promises.[10] But if that was the end game, then why did God give the law to Moses at all (Gal 3:19)? God put it in place as an interim measure, Paul reasons, to superintend the evil age between the primeval promise to Abraham and the final, messianic utopia.[11] The law did and does its job, but that job is not to give eschatological righteousness and life (Gal 3:21).

Only Christ, Paul says, gives eschatological righteousness and life, but he does so, rather mysteriously, by means of his human life and ignominious death. "Christ redeemed us from the curse stipulated in the law by becoming

9. On God's promise to Abraham, see Matthew Thiessen, *Paul and the Gentile Problem* (New York: Oxford University Press, 2016), 129–60; and, differently, Esau McCaulley, *Sharing in the Son's Inheritance*, LNTS 608 (London: T&T Clark, 2019).

10. On this point see chapter 7 below.

11. On this utopia in Gal 3, see further Karin B. Neutel, *A Cosmopolitan Ideal: Paul's Declaration "Neither Jew Nor Greek, Neither Slave Nor Free, Nor Male and Female" in the Context of First-Century Thought*, LNTS 513 (London: T&T Clark, 2015).

a curse for our sake" (Gal 3:13). "God sent his son, born from a woman, born under the law, so that he might redeem those who are under the law, so that we might receive adoption" (Gal 4:4–5). All of this Paul thinks God promised to Abraham in the beginning. (Of course this meaning does not lie on the surface of the text of Genesis, but that is in the nature of scriptural interpretation in antiquity.)[12] What is more, Paul reads the subsequent story of Abraham's two sons, Ishmael by his Egyptian slave Hagar and Isaac by his aged wife Sarah (Gen 16–18; 21), as an allegory for the present situation in the Galatian Christ assemblies (Gal 4:24). There are two kinds of "children of Abraham" now being "born," so to speak: some born by the flesh into law and slavery, and others born by the promise into *pneuma* and liberty. Paul appeals to his audience that they belong to the latter group. "We are children not of the slave woman but of the free woman" (Gal 4:31).[13] But this is really an exhortation, not a simple statement of fact, as becomes clear.

In Gal 5, finally, Paul names the presenting issue in the letter: "Look, I, Paul, say to you that if you undergo circumcision, Christ will benefit you nothing. For I testify again to everyone who undergoes circumcision that he is obligated to do the whole law. You are undone away from Christ, you who are getting put right in the law, you are fallen away from the gift" (Gal 5:2–4). Significantly, Paul characterizes proselyte circumcision not as something indifferent, as an *adiaphoron*, but as a positively self-destructive course of action:[14] for these gentiles, to undergo proselyte circumcision would be to forfeit Christ. If, however, they heed Paul's warning and persevere in Christ-faith, he says, they will find themselves miraculously perfected in the virtues. The liberty into which they are "born" (cf. the allegory of the slave woman and the free woman) is a liberty not to indulge the mortal flesh but to live a perfect pneumatic life (Gal 5:13). The *pneuma* of God which gentiles-in-Christ have received allows them, or indeed compels them, to transcend the moral weakness of their corruptible bodies.[15] The *pneuma* within them yields fruit, so to speak, consisting of love, joy, peace, longsuffering, kindness, and other virtues. To "walk by the

---

12. See James L. Kugel, *The Bible As It Was* (Cambridge, MA: Harvard University Press, 1997).

13. See J. Louis Martyn, "A Tale of Two Churches," in *Theological Issues in the Letters of Paul* (Edinburgh: T&T Clark, 1997), 25–36; Thiessen, *Paul and the Gentile Problem*.

14. A crucial point well made by Beverly Roberts Gaventa, "The Singularity of the Gospel," in *Our Mother Saint Paul* (Louisville: Westminster John Knox, 2007), 101–12.

15. Here see John M. G. Barclay, *Obeying the Truth: Paul's Ethics in Galatians* (Vancouver: Regent College Publishing, 1988); Troels Engberg-Pedersen, *Paul and the Stoics* (Edinburgh: T&T Clark, 2000), 158–78; Laura B. Dingeldein, "Gaining Virtue, Gaining Christ: Moral Development in the Letters of Paul" (PhD diss., Brown University, 2014).

*pneuma*" (Gal 5:25), then, is to practice a kind of "robo-righteousness," as Christine Hayes has recently put it.[16]

Paul closes the letter by insisting that not only God and Christ but even the law itself is on his side in this dispute. "Bear one another's burdens, and in this way you will fulfill the law of Christ" (Gal 6:2), where "the law of Christ" is arguably best understood as the law, God's law, which now, in the messianic age, can be done fully and effortlessly by those who have the *pneuma*. Indeed, Paul faults his rivals for their failure in relation to the law. "Those who undergo circumcision do not themselves guard the law" (Gal 6:13), which may give some clues as to the ethnic and halakic identity of the rival teachers. Paul's combativeness toward these teachers continues right to the end of the letter. In a curious verse that later gave rise to the Christian devotional tradition of the stigmata, he writes an apotropaic warning: "Let no one cause me trouble, for I bear on my body the marks [στίγματα] of Jesus" (Gal 6:17). These στίγματα are probably wounds sustained by Paul in the course of his apostolic work, which he interprets as brands marking him as Christ's slave and signs of his solidarity with Christ's execution. "May it not be for me to boast except in the cross of our lord Jesus Christ, through whom the cosmos is crucified to me, and I to the cosmos" (Gal 6:14). The cosmos itself has been crucified and will soon be no more; all that remains is new creation (Gal 6:15).

## THE LETTER OF PAUL TO THE ROMANS

Paul's Letter to the Romans is, if anything, even more atypical than his Letter to the Galatians. Galatians is a circular letter, but at least the Christ assemblies addressed therein were Paul's own in the sense that he had first established them (Gal 4:12–16). Romans is the only letter of Paul addressed to assemblies not his own. Who first established the Christ assemblies at Rome we do not know. The names earliest associated with it are Prisca and Aquila, a Jewish wife and husband whom Paul names in 1 Cor 16:19 and again in Rom 16:3 (and cf. 2 Tim 4:19), and who appear as leaders of and refugees from the Roman Christ assembly in Acts 18 (vv. 2, 18, 26). Romans 16 includes numerous other names that contribute something to a prosopography of this group, but otherwise its origins and early years remain hidden from view.[17]

---

16. Christine Hayes, *What's Divine about Divine Law? Early Perspectives* (Princeton: Princeton University Press, 2015), 48, 140–64.

17. See Peter Lampe, *From Paul to Valentinus: Christians at Rome in the First Two Centuries* (London: T&T Clark, 2003), 1–16.

Paul writes to the people-in-Christ in Rome because, although he had not been their founder, he regards himself as their apostle, inasmuch as he is apostle to the gentiles (cf. Gal 2:7–9). He explains, "I have often intended to come to you, though I was hindered until now, so that I might have some fruit among you as also among the rest of the gentiles: Greeks and barbarians, wise and ignorant. I am obligated; hence my eagerness to announce the good news also to you who are in Rome" (Rom 1:13–15). This introduction suggests, first, that Paul perceives the Christ assemblies in Rome as being comprised mostly of gentiles and, second, that he regards them as not having had the good news fully and properly announced to them until it is announced by him. At the end of the letter, Paul explains that there are also logistical reasons for his planned trip to Rome: "I have wanted for many years to come to you as I go to Spain. For I hope to pass through and see you and to be sent onward there by you" (Rom 15:23–24). Rome would be the farthest west Paul had yet been, and an essential staging area for any onward mission to Spain.

This observation raises the classic question of the purpose of the Letter to the Romans, what has sometimes been called "the Romans debate."[18] Paul's other letters, all addressed to people familiar to him in places he himself had worked, mostly wear their purposes on their sleeves: Philemon is an intervention on behalf of Onesimus; Galatians combats the influence of rival teachers; 1 Corinthians answers questions posed in a letter from the Christ assembly in Corinth; and so on. Romans, however, is rather more opaque in this respect. While it does declare some of its reasons at its beginning and end, these reasons do not obviously fit with the sixteen chapters of material that comprise the letter, the longest of all the extant letters of Paul. Some interpreters have thought the letter a solicitation of financial support for a Spanish campaign, others a rehearsal of the *apologia pro vita sua* that Paul intends to give upon arriving in Jerusalem (Rom 15:25–32), others an intervention in local conflicts in the Roman assemblies about which Paul has heard, still others that it is what classical Christian theology has long taken it to be: Paul's own *summa theologiae*.

The letter is not a *summa theologiae*, but one can see how generations of Christian interpreters might have gotten that impression. Because Paul has not yet been to Rome, he does not meddle in local affairs as much as he does in his letters to his own Christ assemblies. And because he needs the Roman gentiles-in-Christ to receive him as their apostle, he has to introduce, explain, and justify himself to a greater extent than he does elsewhere. Consequently, although

---

18. See Karl P. Donfried, ed., *The Romans Debate*, rev. ed. (Edinburgh: T&T Clark, 1991).

Romans has an occasion as specific as any other letter has, the nature of that occasion is such that it yields something like a primer on Paulinism.[19] If, as Nils Dahl perceptively showed, the particularity of the Pauline letters posed a hermeneutical problem for the ancient church,[20] Romans at least seemed less problematic in this respect. It was more easily read as a letter addressed to the catholic church in all times and places.

If one ignores or removes Rom 16, then, with just a little squinting, it is almost possible not to notice the specifically Roman context of the letter. Probably for this very reason, a fifteen-chapter recension of the letter apparently enjoyed some circulation in late antiquity. The textual history of Romans is rather more complicated than that of any of Paul's other letters.[21] One textual unit in particular, the doxology traditionally printed at Rom 16:25–27, wanders quite conspicuously in the manuscript tradition, almost always in such a way as to mark different possible endings to the letter. It appears variously at the end of chapter 14, the end of chapter 15, the end of chapter 16, or not at all. This feature of the manuscripts dovetails with, for instance, Origen's report of a Marcionite recension of Romans having only (what we call) chapters 1–14. There was a popular twentieth-century theory, now widely though not unanimously rejected, that Rom 16 was originally the cover page of a letter of Paul to Ephesus, appended to the (ostensibly fifteen-chapter) Letter to the Romans.[22] Peter Lampe has pretty well laid this theory to rest,[23] but it just goes to show how an ancient puzzle can be evergreen.

The letter falls neatly and naturally into four main parts: chapters 1–4, 5–8, 9–11, and 12–16. Much modern scholarship has been preoccupied with deciding which of these parts is the theological center or climax of the letter. Protestant theological interpretation has long singled out chapters 1–4 for attention. In a reaction to this longstanding trend, critical scholars more interested in the relation between Jews and gentiles in Paul's thinking have pointed to chapters 9–11 as the center. Recent social history and social science approaches to Romans have focused on chapters 12–16, which offer the most

---

19. On this reason for Romans, see further John M. G. Barclay, *Paul and the Gift* (Grand Rapids: Eerdmans, 2015), 455–59.

20. Nils A. Dahl, "The Particularity of the Pauline Letters as a Problem in the Ancient Church," in *Studies in Ephesians*, WUNT 131 (Tübingen: Mohr Siebeck, 2000), 165–78.

21. See Harry Gamble, *The Textual History of the Letter to the Romans*, SD (Grand Rapids: Eerdmans, 1979).

22. E.g., T. W. Manson, "St. Paul's Letter to the Romans—and Others," in *Romans Debate*, 3–15.

23. Peter Lampe, "The Roman Christians of Romans 16," in *Romans Debate*, 216–30.

information regarding people and issues on the ground in the Roman Christ assemblies. And recent theological interpretation, weary of threadbare Protestant readings of Rom 1–4, has turned its attention to chapters 5–8 and their more cosmic, universal themes. Arguably, however, this quest for a center of the letter is neither necessary nor profitable. The letter is what it is in virtue of all its component parts. The several emphases just noted make a certain sense in the context of the history of interpretation, but we should not think that interpreting the letter means deciding which bit of it is the most important.

All of Rom 1–8 explains aspects of the good announcement that Paul preaches among the gentiles, and a few grand themes (notably righteousness, Christ, and the law) are prominent through all eight chapters. But there is also a pretty clear twofold subdivision, with Rom 1–4 focusing, in particular, on circumcision, trust (or faith), and the figure of Abraham, and Rom 5–8 on sin, *pneuma* (or spirit), and the figure of Adam.

Romans 1 begins, naturally, with an epistolary introduction: "Paul, slave of Christ Jesus, called as an apostle . . . to all the people beloved of God in Rome, called as holy ones: Grace to you and peace from God our father and the lord Jesus Christ" (Rom 1:1, 7). Paul then explains the occasion for the letter: his longstanding desire to visit the Christ assemblies in Rome, which now finally might come to pass. Because he is charged with taking the good announcement of Christ to all gentiles, and because the holy people at Rome are (apparently) mostly gentiles, Paul reckons that he needs to present them with his announcement. "I am not ashamed at the good announcement, for it is the power of God for deliverance to everyone who trusts, the Jew first and also the Greek; for in it the righteousness of God is revealed from trust to trust, as it is written, 'The righteous one shall live from trust'" (Rom 1:16–17, citing Hab 2:4).

At Rom 3:21 and following ("Now the righteousness of God is manifested . . ."), the themes headlined in Rom 1:16–17 come once again to the fore, but the logic of the intervening two chapters, everything from Rom 1:18 to 3:20, is difficult and much disputed. One reason is that this section makes heavy use of the diatribe, an ancient rhetorical convention in which an author speaks in several different voices: making a claim, then raising an objection, then defeating the objection, and so on.[24] In our passage, this process leads to the conclusion that "every mouth must be stopped and the whole cosmos become liable to God" (Rom 3:19). By "every mouth" here, Paul means both Jewish and

---

24. See Stanley K. Stowers, *The Diatribe and Paul's Letter to the Romans*, SBLDS 57 (Chico, CA: Scholars Press, 1981).

gentile mouths (cf. Rom 3:9). But probably because the letter addresses a gentile audience, most of Rom 1–3 has to do with how gentiles are under sin. (Paul will consider the Jews, speaking about them in the third person, in Rom 9–11.) In Rom 1:18–32, Paul narrates the gentiles' descent into debauchery consequent upon their decision, sometime in the primeval past, to worship statues of animals and humans.[25] In Rom 2:1–16, he scolds an imaginary gentile interlocutor who might protest that he or she is better than others. In Rom 2:17–29, raising the stakes once again, Paul addresses yet another imaginary interlocutor, a person who "calls himself a Jew." Many interpreters have thought that Paul is here criticizing Jews and Judaism, but more likely he is criticizing gentiles who "call themselves Jews," that is, who mimic Jewishness by, for instance, undergoing proselyte circumcision (see Rom 2:25–29), as in Galatians.[26] In Rom 3:1–20, finally and briefly, Paul sketches in what sense he thinks that Jews, too, are under sin: not that they are wantonly immoral like (Paul thinks) gentiles are, but oracles of scripture testify that Jews, too, are subject to sin—"so that every mouth be stopped and the whole cosmos become liable to God"—and thus in need of the eschatological deliverance that Paul announces.[27]

Paul sketches an outline of this eschatological deliverance in a short but dense paragraph at Rom 3:21–30, one of the best known parts of the letter: "But now the righteousness of God has been manifested apart from the law (though it is attested by the law and the prophets), the righteousness of God through trust of Jesus Christ to everyone who trusts. There is no distinction, for all people sinned and are bereft of the glory of God, but are put right gratuitously by his gift through the ransom which is in Christ Jesus, whom God presented as a conciliation, through trust, in his [Jesus's] blood, for a demonstration of his [God's] righteousness" (Rom 3:21–25). There is debate about the meaning of most of the key terms here, but the main lines of Paul's message are clear enough for our present purposes: God's ultimate, eschatological righteousness has just now been revealed in the death of the messiah Jesus and is accessible to humans through trust, not through the law, although the law itself bears witness to this new state of affairs. In the eschaton, God now claims his rightful place as God over all people, gentiles as well as Jews, for which reason God's

---

25. See Stanley K. Stowers, *A Rereading of Romans: Justice, Jews, and Gentiles* (New Haven: Yale University Press, 1994), 83–100.

26. See Runar M. Thorsteinsson, *Paul's Interlocutor in Romans 2: Function and Identity in the Context of Ancient Epistolography,* ConBNT 40 (Stockholm: Almqvist & Wiksell, 2003); Matthew Thiessen, "Paul's Argument against Gentile Circumcision in Rom 2:17–29," *NovT* 56 (2014): 373–91.

27. On this breakdown of Rom 1–3, see further chapter 6 below.

righteousness must ultimately be from trust. In Rom 4, a passage reminiscent in some ways of the argument of Galatians, Paul explains how Christ-faith makes all people, gentiles as well as Jews, sons and heirs of father Abraham (see further below).

As noted above, while Rom 5–8 is clearly continuous with Rom 1–4, the emphasis shifts as the ethnic signifiers "Jew" and "gentile," so prominent in Rom 1–4, drop out. Where Abraham the patriarch figured in the first part of the letter, Adam the primeval human figures in the second. Whereas Rom 1–4 was full of talk about Christ-faith and its relation to the law, Rom 5–8 is preoccupied with the *pneuma*, the divine substance now available to people-in-Christ.[28] Paul's key move in Rom 5:12–21, made disproportionately famous by the fifth-century African theologian Augustine of Hippo, is to draw an extended parallel between Adam the primeval human and Christ the originator of the eschaton: Whereas Adam's one bad deed brought sin and death to all people everywhere (in an effort to explain precisely how it did so, Augustine devised his doctrine of original sin), Christ's one good deed brings righteousness and undying life to all people everywhere. But if that is the case, then one might think that people may as well do all evil all the time, since Christ's one good deed fixes everything anyway. Paul defends himself from this inference in Rom 6, where he specifies the way in which Christ's one good deed effects righteousness and life for everyone: namely, by a mysterious (to us moderns, at least) but real and even material union between human beings and the deified Christ. "Do you not know that as many of us as were immersed into Christ Jesus, we were immersed into his death? We were, therefore, buried with him through immersion into his death, so that just as Christ was raised from the dead through the glory of the father, so too we might walk in newness of life" (Rom 6:3–4).[29]

In Rom 7, Paul struggles mightily to explain how the law of God, which is altogether righteous in its own right (Rom 7:12), nevertheless is powerless to effect final, eschatological righteousness. In Galatians, Paul had explained this phenomenon by positing a chronological scheme in the mind of God: the law was an interim measure until the seed should come, etc. (Gal 3:19–25). Here in Romans, by contrast, he explains it by appealing to (what he thinks is) the

---

28. See Beverly Roberts Gaventa, ed., *Apocalyptic Paul: Cosmos and Anthropos in Romans 5–8* (Waco, TX: Baylor University Press, 2013).

29. On the transformation effected through ritual immersion, see Jennifer Eyl, *Signs, Wonders, and Gifts: Divination in the Letters of Paul* (New York: Oxford University Press, 2019), 129–42.

psychology of gentiles who try to better themselves by adopting the law of Moses as a guide.[30] In a famous but little understood passage, Paul writes, "I do not do the good that I want, but rather the bad that I do not want, this I do" (Rom 7:19, and see all of Rom 7:7–25). This passage has provided many latter-day readers with language to represent, for instance, the experience of addiction, or of religious guilt, or of human life in general. Indeed, the sentiment expressed here is much older than Paul, going back to the classical tragedians. In Rom 7, however, Paul's specific point is that a hypothetical gentile auditor who tries to attain righteousness by following the law will find herself endlessly frustrated, because in the present evil age, even the law itself is at the mercy of sin and the passions.[31] Far from providing an escape, it only makes matters worse (Rom 7:7–12). The only release from sin and the passions is a release from mortality itself (this is the point of Rom 8): infusion with the *pneuma* of the deified Christ now and, soon, full transformation into a divine, pneumatic body. And not just that, but the transformation of the universe itself into a perfect, incorruptible state (Rom 8:18–25).

For Paul, the most pressing objection to the glorious scene that he paints here is not philosophical but empirical, and specifically demographic: If God is about to do all this, then why do the Jews mostly not believe it? Romans 9–11 is a reckoning with cognitive dissonance on Paul's own part.[32] In Gal 2, he had explained how the apostles had agreed that Peter would oversee the announcement of Christ to the Jews and Paul the announcement of Christ to the gentiles. Because the Jews have the holy books, the ancestors, the promises, the covenants, the temple service, and so on (Rom 9:4–5), Paul probably expected his own work to be hard going while Peter would likely find easy success. But as Paul is writing Romans, the demographics suggest the opposite: Paul's Christ campaign to gentiles is going from strength to strength (Rom 15:17–21), the Christ campaign to Jews much less so. "The gentiles, who do not pursue righteousness, have taken hold of righteousness, the righteousness from trust, but Israel, who pursues a law of righteousness, has not arrived at the law"

---

30. See Emma Wasserman, *The Death of the Soul in Romans 7: Sin, Death, and the Law in Light of Hellenistic Moral Psychology*, WUNT 256 (Tübingen: Mohr Siebeck, 2008).

31. See Paul W. Meyer, "The Worm at the Core of the Apple: Exegetical Reflections on Romans 7," in Meyer, *The Word in This World: Essays in New Testament Exegesis and Theology*, ed. John T. Carroll, NTL (Louisville: Westminster John Knox, 2004), 57–77.

32. See the essays in Florian Wilk and J. Ross Wagner, eds., *Between Gospel and Election: Explorations in the Interpretation of Romans 9–11*, WUNT 257 (Tübingen: Mohr Siebeck, 2010); and Todd D. Still, ed., *God and Israel: Providence and Purpose in Romans 9–11* (Waco, TX: Baylor University Press, 2017).

(Rom 9:30–31). Paul's explanation is rather tortuous, but his conclusion is clear. He cannot countenance the idea that God's promises (as he understands them) have failed. What Paul thinks must happen will happen; there is just a late plot twist: God has consigned Israel to temporary disobedience while all the gentiles come in. "God shut up all people in disobedience so that he might have mercy on all people" (Rom 11:32)—a divine comedy, as Paula Fredriksen has aptly put it.[33] These chapters, in particular Rom 9 ("So then, [God] has mercy on whom he wants, and he hardens whom he wants" [Rom 9:18]), have become a *locus classicus* for Christian theologies of predestination, prominent especially in Calvinist traditions. One can certainly see why, but this theological use of Rom 9–11 obscures both the Jew-gentile dynamic and the happy ending of Paul's discourse.[34]

Romans 12–15 is conspicuous for the sudden profusion of imperative verbs: "Do not be conformed to this age"; "Repay no one evil for evil"; "Accept one another, just as Christ accepted you"; and many more. It is characteristic of Paul to devote the latter part of a letter to paraenesis, moral instruction, in the mode of the ancient popular philosophers. But Romans is different from Paul's other letters inasmuch as his instructions here are less informed about local circumstances. Less informed, but not uninformed. Romans 12–15 suggests that Paul knows of some goings-on in the Christ assemblies in Rome. Perhaps he considers the guidance in Rom 13:1–7—"Let every soul be subjected to the governing authorities, for there is no authority except from God"—especially relevant to Christ-believers living in the capital of the Roman Empire. (This brief passage has provided fodder for manifold Christian theologies of the state, especially conservative ones, but also radical and other varieties.)[35] Romans 14, an extended exhortation on not passing judgment on brothers and sisters in Christ who have scruples about meat or wine, has tempted interpreters to speculate about Jew-gentile tensions in the Roman Christ assemblies, often in connection with the story of Claudius's expulsion of Jews from Rome (Suetonius, *Claudius* 25.4). Such reconstructions, while not impossible, are, first, speculative and, second, wanting for any actual mention of ethnic groups in Rom 14. One can just as easily imagine that the "weak" and the "strong" in

33. Paula Fredriksen, *Sin: The Early History of an Idea* (Princeton: Princeton University Press, 2012), 49.

34. Thus rightly Barclay, *Paul and the Gift*, 520–61.

35. See Jacob Taubes, *The Political Theology of Paul*, trans. Dana Hollander (Stanford: Stanford University Press, 2003); Matthew V. Novenson, "What the Apostles Did Not See," in *Reactions to Empire: Sacred Texts in Their Socio-Political Contexts*, ed. John Anthony Dunne and Dan Batovici, WUNT 2.372 (Tübingen: Mohr Siebeck, 2014), 55–72.

Rom 14 are not Jews and gentiles, respectively, but different subsets of gentiles-in-Christ (cf. 1 Cor 8–10), which would accord with the implied audience of the letter.

Romans 16 consists mostly of a lengthy list of greetings to persons known to Paul in Rome: "Greet Prisca and Aquila my fellow-workers. . . . Greet my beloved Epaenetus. . . . Greet Andronicus and Junia my kinfolk," and so on. That Paul relays so many greetings is probably related to the fact that he is writing to an assembly not his own. He has to establish a relationship with this group by appealing to such links as he has. We meet several important characters among them. Paul begins (Rom 16:1–2) with a word of commendation on behalf of Phoebe, minister of the Christ assembly at Cenchreae (near Corinth), whence Paul is writing and sending this letter. This probably means that Phoebe herself will carry the letter to Rome and read it to the gathered Christ-believers there. Tertius, the scribe who actually handwrites the letter at Paul's dictation, introduces himself at Rom 16:22. At Rome are two Jewish apostles, Andronicus and Junia (possibly though not certainly husband and wife), whose apostleship antedates Paul's and who are evidently of high status. (In some modern Christian translations the name Junia [feminine] is changed to Junias [masculine] in order to avoid the inconvenient truth that Paul here praises a woman apostle.)[36]

We have no good reasons for thinking that Paul ever made it to Spain as he had planned. Early Christian sources generally agree that he died at Rome. The Acts of the Apostles has Paul arriving at Rome, not voluntarily as per his stated intent in Rom 15, but as a prisoner arrested in Jerusalem, detained and tried at Caesarea, and finally extradited to Rome upon appeal (Acts 21–28). Acts ends with a scene of Paul imprisoned in Rome but nevertheless preaching boldly (Acts 28:16–31). Because Acts was written a generation or two after Paul's death, the author probably knows the tradition that Paul died at Rome but ends his story the way he does so as to portray Paul as a forerunner rather than a martyr. *Acts of Paul* tells a story of Paul being beheaded at Rome under Nero, and 2 Timothy is perhaps a pseudonymous testament imagining Paul in these circumstances ("I am already being poured out as a libation, and the time of my departure has come" [2 Tim 4:6]). Romans, then, is perhaps (depending on the date of Philippians) the last text that we have from Paul himself and

---

36. See further Bernadette Brooten, "'Junia . . . Outstanding among the Apostles' (Romans 16:7)," in *Women Priests: A Catholic Commentary on the Vatican Declaration*, ed. Leonard Swidler and Arlene Swidler (New York: Paulist, 1977), 141–44; Eldon Jay Epp, *Junia: The First Woman Apostle* (Minneapolis: Fortress, 2005).

reflects his durable confidence that God would see him all the way around the Mediterranean basin before the kingdom of God arrived.

## THEMES COMMON TO BOTH LETTERS

Galatians and Romans have long been discussed together, and are being discussed together here, because, as already indicated by the surveys above, a number of key themes are common to both and not (for the most part) to Paul's other letters. One of these themes is δικαιοσύνη, "righteousness" or "justice."[37] The classic doctrinal term "justification" comes from the same root, although Paul himself uses that particular form, δικαίωσις, "justification," only twice (Rom 4:25; 5:18). Δικαιοσύνη, "righteousness," is an attribute or a state of affairs, while its cognate verb δικαιόω means either to put things right, to rectify them, or to declare someone to be in the right, to vindicate her. In Romans, but not in Galatians, Paul speaks of the δικαιοσύνη θεοῦ, "the righteousness of God," an attribute God demonstrates by sending his son Jesus (Rom 1:17; 3:5, 21, 22, 25, 26; 10:3; and cf. 2 Cor 5:21). Elsewhere in Romans, but more conspicuously in Galatians, δικαιοσύνη is an eschatological state of affairs,[38] one that only obtains in the new creation that Paul thinks is dawning (Gal 2:21; 3:21; 5:5; Rom 5:21; 6:18–20; 10:4, 6; 14:17). This latter usage is closely related to his use of the verb δικαιόω, "to put right," with a person or people as direct object, which he sometimes, following the example of LXX Genesis, glosses with λογίζομαι δικαιοσύνην, "to reckon righteousness [to someone]" (Rom 4:3–22; Gal 3:6). This is the thing that Paul famously insists happens only from Christ-faith and not from works of the law (Gal 2:16; 3:11, 24; Rom 3:28; also Phil 3:9).

Which brings us to a second key theme common to Galatians and Romans: πίστις, "faith" or, better, "trust."[39] Πίστις is a very old, sturdy Greek word for the social virtue of trust, trustworthiness, loyalty, or fidelity, and Paul uses the word broadly along these traditional lines. But, as he does with "righteousness," he also claims that πίστις in some perfect, maximal sense has only just

37. On the quite particular sense in which Paul means "righteousness," see Albert Schweitzer, *The Mysticism of Paul the Apostle*, trans. W. Montgomery (New York: Seabury, 1968), 205–26.

38. On which see Andrew K. Boakye, *Death and Life: Resurrection, Restoration, and Rectification in Paul's Letter to the Galatians* (Eugene, OR: Pickwick, 2017).

39. On which see Teresa Morgan, *Roman Faith and Christian Faith: Pistis and Fides in the Early Roman Empire and Early Churches* (Oxford: Oxford University Press, 2015).

arrived in the cosmos with God's sending of the messiah Jesus. "Before trust came, we were kept watch over by the law" (Gal 3:23). The present age, the age of the law of Moses, was not characterized by this eschatological πίστις (Gal 3:12). This perfect, maximal kind of trust Paul sometimes calls πίστις Χριστοῦ, "trust of Christ" or "Christ-faith" (Gal 2:16; 3:22; Rom 3:22; Phil 3:9). There is a notorious grammatical ambiguity here. Πίστις Χριστοῦ can mean "faithfulness *of* Christ"—that is, "the trustworthiness with which Christ himself is trustworthy"—or alternatively "faith *in* Christ"—that is, "the trust with which mortals trust Christ." Or it can be used precisely in such as way as not to distinguish between those two ideas; hence the perennial debate. Paul never unambiguously says that Christ is πιστός, "faithful," or exercises πίστις, "faithfulness," although something like Gal 1:4 ("Christ gave himself for our sins to deliver us from the present evil age") might indicate some such idea. Paul does sometimes expressly say that mortals do and should trust in Christ (Gal 2:16; cf. Rom 9:33; 10:9, 11; 1 Thess 4:14), although more often he says they should trust in God, as father Abraham did (Rom 4:3, 5, 17, 24; Gal 3:6).

Yet another key theme in Galatians and Romans comes from the second half of Paul's polemical maxim: A person is put right from Christ-faith, *not from works of the law.*[40] But the abbreviated, abstracted form "faith, not works" is better known in the Protestant tradition, and is found already in Eph 2:8–9 ("By grace you have been saved, through faith, not from works, lest anyone should boast"), which, however, was probably written by a next-generation disciple of Paul, not the apostle himself. In Galatians and Romans, the faith in question is Christ-faith, and the works in question are works of the law. But what are works of the law? Luther and his heirs, following Ephesians, took this phrase to mean moral achievements in general, and there is admittedly a foothold for this idea in Paul's discussion of Abraham in Rom 4:2–5 (and cf. Rom 3:27). But overwhelmingly in Galatians and Romans, "works *of the law*" suggests upright acts prescribed by the law of Moses. In Galatians, only one such act is really at issue—namely, ritual circumcision of male worshipers. Notably, however, while circumcision is indeed an act prescribed by the Torah, it is not a moral achievement in the way that chastity or almsgiving is. Hence it is remarkable that, in the long history of interpretation, Paul's maxim came to be applied so often and so earnestly to the latter kind of works. Interpreters still disagree whether "works of the law" in Galatians and Romans refers to

---

40. See Jörg Frey, "Contextualizing Paul's 'Works of the Law': MMT in New Testament Scholarship," in Frey, *Qumran, Early Judaism, and New Testament Interpretation: Kleine Schriften III*, ed. Jacob N. Cerone, WUNT 424 (Tübingen: Mohr Siebeck, 2019), 743–62.

any and all stipulations of the Torah or just a few symbolic *mitzvot*. More on that debate below; the key thing to note is that, in our two letters, works are *works of the law*, and the law is the *law of Moses*.

I have already mentioned, however, the partial exception to this rule in the discussion of Abraham in Rom 4. And the figure of Abraham is yet another theme common to Galatians and Romans and no other Pauline letters (excepting one mention in 2 Cor 11:22). Abraham occupies most of Gal 3–4, all of Rom 4, and appears briefly again in Rom 9–11. Most of this material is preoccupied with Abraham's role as ancestor and the corollary question who count as his offspring, sons, or heirs, and by what means they do so.[41] In Gal 3, Paul's key move is to claim that Christ alone is the singular "seed" or offspring of Abraham (Gal 3:16 citing Gen 13:15; 17:8; 24:7), with the consequence that all who are "in Christ" (Paul's formulation) count as Abraham's seed and therefore heirs. In Gal 4, Paul interprets the story of Abraham's two sons—Ishmael by his Egyptian slave Hagar and Isaac by his aged wife Sarah—as an allegory for two covenants: flesh and promise, present Jerusalem and Jerusalem above, slavery and liberty, respectively. The discussion in Rom 4 continues these themes but also complicates them. There is no longer any mention of the mothers of Abraham's sons. "Abraham is the father of us all," both those who are from the law and those who are from trust (Rom 4:16). But Rom 4 insists, as Galatians does not, that a son of Abraham "walks in the footsteps of father Abraham" (Rom 4:12) by trusting in God for righteousness just as Abraham did (Rom 4:5). This latter argument makes Abraham look more like an exemplar than an ancestor, which is in fact how he has been understood in much Protestant interpretation of Romans.

A fifth theme common to Galatians and Romans (and, in this case, 1–2 Corinthians as well) is also a relative weak spot in that conventional Protestant interpretation—namely, πνεῦμα, *pneuma*, which came over into Latin as *spiritus* and thence into English as "spirit," which is unfortunately a bit misleading. Whereas English "spirit" tends to conjure Platonic-inflected images of something immaterial or ghostly, *pneuma* for Paul, as in much ancient popular philosophy (especially but not only Stoic), signifies a divine or heavenly substance,

---

41. See Caroline Johnson Hodge, *If Sons Then Heirs: A Study of Kinship and Ethnicity in the Letters of Paul* (New York: Oxford University Press, 2007). Paul is just one of many ancient authors who spent a great deal of intellectual energy on the question of Abrahamic ancestry; see the essays in Martin Goodman et al., eds., *Abraham, the Nations, and the Hagarites: Jewish, Christian, and Islamic Perspectives on Kinship with Abraham* (Leiden: Brill, 2010).

an extremely fine, pure, and therefore imperishable kind of matter.[42] Paul, of course, speaks of the *pneuma* of God and of Christ (e.g., Rom 8:9), and this idiom would provide fodder for the late antique doctrine of the Trinity,[43] but in Paul's letters *pneuma* is not yet a discrete divine person, but rather the stuff of God and of Christ, the stuff that makes them immortal and, when conferred on humans, allows them, too, to attain immortality: "God will make alive your mortal bodies through his *pneuma* dwelling in you" (Rom 8:11). But how does this *pneuma* motif relate to the other themes noted above? In Gal 3, Paul reasons that, long ago, God promised father Abraham not only righteousness from faith (Gal 3:8) but also the divine *pneuma*, so that Abraham's offspring would one day be immortal and godlike (Gal 3:14; cf. Rom 4:17–18).[44] Paul's gentiles-in-Christ have received this promised *pneuma* in their bodies, although their full and final pneumatic transformation awaits the resurrection of the dead (1 Cor 15:12–58). Meanwhile, the *pneuma* inside them already allows them to transcend their flesh, perfect the virtues (Gal 5:22–23), and fulfill the moral ideals of the law of God (Gal 5:13–14; Rom 8:4).

Righteousness, trust, works of the law, Abraham, and *pneuma*. We could say much more about each of these themes, and we could add others as well, but this is enough. The past half-century of research, from the 1960s to the present, has seen the emergence of several schools of thought which interpret each of these themes somewhat differently.[45] Prior to the 1960s—extending back a century and a half to the birth of modern criticism of the Pauline letters, and further back to the Protestant reformers and the medieval schoolmen— most interpreters of Galatians and Romans assumed that these letters represented Christianity (Paul's version of it, and most often the interpreter's own version, too), defined over and against Judaism. "Judaism," in this tradition of interpretation, was defined as the sum total of all the views and habits that Paul opposes: trying to establish a righteousness of one's own, saying that a person is justified from works of law, spying out other people's freedom in Christ, bringing people under a yoke of slavery, and so on. Hence, for example, F. C. Baur's theory that Paul delivers Christianity from the carnal, nationalistic confines

---

42. See Troels Engberg-Pedersen, *Cosmology and Self in the Apostle Paul: The Material Spirit* (New York: Oxford University Press, 2010).

43. As traced by Wesley Hill, *Paul and the Trinity: Persons, Relations, and the Pauline Letters* (Grand Rapids: Eerdmans, 2015).

44. As argued by Thiessen, *Paul and the Gentile Problem*, 129–60.

45. See Magnus Zetterholm, *Approaches to Paul: A Student's Guide to Recent Scholarship* (Minneapolis: Fortress, 2009); N. T. Wright, *Paul and His Recent Interpreters: Some Contemporary Debates* (Minneapolis: Fortress, 2015).

of Judaism,[46] or Rudolf Bultmann's theory that Paul assails the Jewish meta-sin of trying to obey God's law.[47] This was Christian theology done by way of artificial contrast. Since the 1980s, this centuries-long interpretive tradition has often been called "the Lutheran view," and Luther's own writings do illustrate it in many respects, both for good and for ill. But in fact this tradition is older than Luther, and many of its exemplars are not Lutheran in any meaningful sense, so the label is dubious.[48] This was just the mainstream of centuries of medieval and modern Christian interpretation of Paul.

In 1982, James Dunn coined the label "the New Perspective on Paul" in an eponymous lecture, which was published the following year under the same title.[49] What was new about the New Perspective, for Dunn, was E. P. Sanders's demonstration in his 1977 *Paul and Palestinian Judaism* that the view of ancient Jewish piety assumed by most modern New Testament scholars as a background to and target of Paul's polemics was demonstrably false.[50] (Dunn gives due recognition to the likes of George Foot Moore in the 1920s, W. D. Davies in the 1950s, and Krister Stendahl in the 1960s for anticipating this claim.) If, as per Sanders, late Second Temple Judaism was not in fact an anemic, petty, legalistic system of religion, and if Paul knew this, then many, even most classic Pauline texts cannot mean what they had long been taken to mean by Christian interpreters. By "the New Perspective," Dunn meant the perspective of himself and others who were trying to make new sense of Paul after abandoning a centuries-old Christian caricature of ancient Judaism.

Since the early 1980s, most interpreters of Paul now presuppose Sanders's central claim as a point of departure, but not all of these scholars identify with the "New Perspective" label. (Indeed, Sanders himself, in his subsequent writings, does not.) That label attaches, rather, to a very particular kind of post-Sanders rereading of Paul, a kind represented by Dunn and N. T. Wright, especially.[51] The key feature of this particular kind of rereading is a quest

46. F. C. Baur, *Paul the Apostle of Jesus Christ*, trans. Eduard Zeller, rev. A. Menzies, 2 vols. (London: Williams & Norgate, 1876 [1845]), 2:182–227.

47. Rudolf Bultmann, *Theology of the New Testament*, trans. Kendrick Grobel, 2 vols. (New York: Scribner's, 1951–1955), 1:259–269, esp. 264.

48. Thus rightly Stephen Westerholm, *Perspectives Old and New on Paul: The "Lutheran" Paul and His Critics* (Grand Rapids: Eerdmans, 2004); David Lincicum, "Martin Luther in Modern New Testament Scholarship," in *Oxford Encyclopedia of Martin Luther*, ed. Derek R. Nelson and Paul R. Hinlicky, 3 vols. (Oxford: Oxford University Press, 2017).

49. James D. G. Dunn, "The New Perspective on Paul," *BJRL* 65 (1983): 95–122.

50. E. P. Sanders, *Paul and Palestinian Judaism: A Comparison of Patterns of Religion* (Philadelphia: Fortress, 1977).

51. See James D. G. Dunn, *The New Perspective on Paul*, rev. ed. (Grand Rapids: Eerd-

for some feature of ancient Jewish piety *other than* petty legalism that would explain Paul's supposed criticism thereof. Crucially, Dunn and Wright agree with earlier generations of Christian interpreters that Paul's claims about righteousness, faith, law, etc. are indeed meant as a critique of Judaism. But having followed Sanders in rejecting the classical caricature, they need some other deficiency in ancient Judaism to which Paul's polemical claims can stick.[52] Enter national righteousness, the New Perspective's answer to the old bugbear of works righteousness. National righteousness, for Dunn and Wright, is a kind of ethnic-theological chauvinism: the idea that the people Israel, by virtue of their election by God, enjoy a status in relation to God that other people (namely, gentiles) do not, cannot, and should not enjoy. On this New Perspective account, "justification from works of law" does not mean striving to win God's favour through one's own moral effort but rather presuming upon God's favor because one is part of the chosen people.

Since the early 2000s, another school has questioned whether the New Perspective was radical enough in its rejection of Christian anti-Judaism. Not coincidentally spearheaded by a number of Jewish scholars (e.g., Pamela Eisenbaum, Mark Nanos, Paula Fredriksen), as well as others, this school initially was and sometimes still is called the "radical new perspective," a name that gives the mistaken impression that it is like the New Perspective, only more so. But in fact, this school (now usually called the "Paul within Judaism school") roundly rejects the idea that Paul's polemics were aimed at his ancestral religion in any respect (whether as works righteousness, national righteousness, or otherwise). For these interpreters, Paul stands entirely *within* Judaism and not in any respect *against* Judaism.[53] By their lights, the "justification from works of law" that Paul rejects is only a possible course of action *for gentiles.* On Judaism itself, Paul has nothing to say. Whereas previous generations tended to assume that Paul wrote to mixed-ethnic assemblies of Jewish and gentile Christ-followers (in line with the portrayal of Paul in Acts), the Paul within Judaism school strongly emphasizes Paul's claim to be an apostle to

---

mans, 2005); N. T. Wright, *The Climax of the Covenant: Christ and the Law in Pauline Theology* (Edinburgh: T&T Clark, 1991); Wright, *Paul and the Faithfulness of God*, 2 vols. (London: SPCK, 2013).

52. This logic is rightly diagnosed by Matthew Thiessen, "Conjuring Paul and Judaism Forty Years after *Paul and Palestinian Judaism*," *JJMJS* 5 (2018): 6–20.

53. See Mark D. Nanos and Magnus Zetterholm, eds., *Paul within Judaism: Restoring the First-Century Context to the Apostle* (Minneapolis: Fortress, 2015); also Gabriele Boccaccini and Carlos A. Segovia, eds., *Paul the Jew: Rereading the Apostle as a Figure of Second Temple Judaism* (Minneapolis: Fortress, 2016).

the gentiles (Gal 2:7–9; Rom 1:5; 11:13), reasoning that his letters are addressed entirely to gentiles (e.g., Gal 4:8; 1 Cor 12:2; Rom 1:5–6, 13–15; 11:13; 15:15–16). When, therefore, we read Paul ostensibly pointing out some deficiency in the law of Moses, according to this school, we should always read an implied "as it pertains to gentiles": "The law effects death [for gentiles]"; "Christ redeemed [gentiles] from the curse of the law"; and so on. Beyond this emphasis on gentile audience and the watchword that Paul stands within Judaism, this school's members disagree among themselves on many, even most, particulars. But in view of the long, fraught history of research, their shared watchword is significant enough to make a movement.[54]

Meanwhile, Christian theological interpretation of Galatians and Romans proceeds apace. And while some of it still operates with pre-E. P. Sanders stereotypes about Jews and Judaism, most of it has taken on board, more or less successfully, Sanders's lessons about Christian anti-Judaism in New Testament exegesis. Among recent Christian theological interpretation, one movement in particular stands out for its vigor and generativeness—namely, the so-called apocalyptic school. The forerunners of this school were Karl Barth and Ernst Käsemann, its founders J. Christiaan Beker and J. Louis Martyn, and its leading lights include Martinus De Boer, Beverly Roberts Gaventa, John Barclay, Alexandra Brown, and Susan Eastman.[55] These interpreters, working especially from Galatians and Romans, argue that Paul's apostolic announcement is not about the forgiveness of sins, nor even about the inclusion of gentiles among the people of God, but about God's triumph over evil powers and redemption of the cosmos. There has been some debate over the label "apocalyptic" as used by this school, especially regarding how it relates to the more usual use of that term in Jewish studies. Critics have argued that this school's claims about apocalyptic are mostly untethered from actual ancient Jewish (and Christian) apocalypses.[56] While some proponents have contested this criticism, others have effectively conceded it and simply noted their desire to use the term in a quite specific sense internal to Christian theology. Theological interpretation of Ga-

54. See my discussion in chapter 10 below.
55. E.g., Martinus C. De Boer, *The Defeat of Death: Apocalyptic Eschatology in 1 Corinthians 15 and Romans 5*, JSNTSup 22 (Sheffield: JSOT Press, 1988); J. Louis Martyn, *Galatians: A New Translation with Introduction and Commentary*, AYB (New Haven: Yale University Press, 2004); Alexandra R. Brown, *The Cross and Human Transformation: Paul's Apocalyptic Word in 1 Corinthians* (Minneapolis: Fortress, 1995); Gaventa, *Our Mother Saint Paul*.
56. E.g., J. P. Davies, *Paul among the Apocalypses? An Evaluation of the "Apocalyptic Paul" in the Context of Jewish and Christian Apocalyptic Literature*, LNTS 562 (London: T&T Clark, 2016).

latians and Romans will doubtless enjoy a long and variegated future, but for now, at least, the apocalyptic school is its most interesting representative.

## CONCLUSION

The reception history of a biblical text is part of that text's story, and thus eminently worthy of the attention of any student of the text. To read Galatians and Romans in the twenty-first century is necessarily to reckon with the Augustinian doctrine of original sin, the Lutheran doctrine of justification by faith, and other key moments in the afterlives of those letters.[57] Even so, the first and most important rule of historical criticism is that biblical texts did not always mean what they eventually came to mean, that to read a biblical text in its original historical context is to discover a strange, new world of signification. And never was this rule truer than in the case of Galatians and Romans. Romans 5 does not just "mean" original sin, nor does Gal 2 just "mean" justification by faith. Augustine, Luther, and other interpreters before, between, and after them used Paul's words to make their own points in their own contexts. They sometimes hit on something very close to the first-century sense of the words, other times not. We cannot pretend that the long history of interpretation never happened, but neither can we naively assume that Augustine or Luther always got Paul right. In any given instance, Paul and, say, Luther may or may not be talking about the same subject matter. The only way to tell is rigorously to interrogate the historical context and ideological interests of each, as we have tried briefly to do here.

The fact that the famous themes noted above (righteousness, faith, works, etc.) appear only or mostly in Galatians and Romans has been the rationale for the vaunted canon-within-a-canon status of those letters. But we can just as well run that reasoning in the opposite direction. If these themes appear only or mostly in Galatians and Romans, then perhaps these themes were not as all-important to Paul as they were to Luther or are to us. Albert Schweitzer famously made this point in the early twentieth century when he suggested that, for Paul, righteousness from faith is only a "subsidiary crater within the rim of the main crater" (a curious metaphor, but it makes the point), which is mystical participation in Christ.[58] E. P. Sanders seconded this view in the

---

57. This is expertly done, e.g., by John Riches, *Galatians through the Centuries* (Oxford: Wiley Blackwell, 2007).

58. Schweitzer, *Mysticism of Paul the Apostle*, 225.

1970s, characterizing Paul's pattern of religion as a kind of "participationist eschatology."[59] We might put the point this way: righteousness, faith, and works may only appear here and there in the letters of Paul, but Christ appears in almost every paragraph. Thus, if we insist on speaking of Paul's thought in terms of center, margins, etc., we might do better to start with Christ and work our way around to these other themes. The present writer has argued elsewhere that Paul's "Christ" (Greek for "messiah" or "anointed") makes good sense in the context of ancient Jewish messianism.[60] Paula Fredriksen has recently offered a fully rounded account of Paul's life and letters in the context of ancient Jewish apocalypticism.[61] If we take this route, then not only Galatians and Romans but all the other letters as well begin to come into clearer focus as the ancient artifacts that they first were.

59. Sanders, *Paul and Palestinian Judaism*, 552 and passim.
60. Matthew V. Novenson, *Christ among the Messiahs: Christ Language in Paul and Messiah Language in Ancient Judaism* (New York: Oxford University Press, 2012).
61. Fredriksen, *Pagans' Apostle*.

6

# THE SELF-STYLED JEW OF ROMANS 2 AND
# THE ACTUAL JEWS OF ROMANS 9–11

If one wants to test the controversial hypothesis that Paul's rhetorical interlocutor in Rom 2 is a gentile, not a Jew, against the wider context of the letter, then Rom 9–11 presents a golden opportunity.[1] For, while the ethnicity of the person who "calls himself a Jew" in Rom 2:17 is open to question, the ethnicity of the people in view from Rom 9:1 to 11:36 is not. "They are my kinfolk according to the flesh" (Rom 9:3). "They are the Israelites" (Rom 9:4). They are "Israel," defined precisely in contrast to "the gentiles" (Rom 9:30–31; 11:25).[2] Admittedly, what it is, exactly, that Paul claims about them in these chapters is subject to debate, but the identity of the "them" is clear. We stand to gain, therefore, from a close comparison of the self-styled Jew of Rom 2 with the actual Jews of Rom 9–11. My project in this chapter is to undertake such a comparison, beginning with a brief discussion of several relevant contributions to recent research which figure in my argument.

1. I presented a version of this essay at the Cambridge New Testament Seminar, where I received sage feedback from James Carleton Paget, Simon Gathercole, Morna Hooker, William Horbury, and James Prothro. I also benefited from incisive reader comments from Jay Thomas Hewitt, Daniel Jackson, Benjamin Petroelje, Rafael Rodriguez, and Matthew Thiessen, and I worked through parts of the argument in conversation with my colleague Philippa Townsend. Wherever my argument succeeds, it is thanks in large part to these colleagues; wherever it fails, it is my fault alone.

2. One possible exception is Rom 11:26 ("and in this way all Israel will be saved"), which in my view is not an actual exception.

## SOME RECENT CONTRIBUTIONS

One point of departure for this chapter is an observation that one finds here and there in the secondary literature to the effect that Paul's comments about "the Jew" in Rom 2 and "the Jews" in Rom 9–11 seem not to match up. Thus E. P. Sanders, for instance, comments, "The manner in which Paul can roundly condemn the Jews for flagrant disobedience (2:17–24) also causes some surprise, since in Rom. 10:2 he characterizes his kin as zealous for the law, and in Gal. 2:15 he contrasts Jews with 'Gentile sinners.' The exaggerated description of Gentile sexual immorality in 1:18–32 is not too surprising in light of such passages as 1 Cor. 6:9–11, but the description of Jewish behavior in 2:17–24 is unparalleled."[3] Similarly Lloyd Gaston: "In Rom 9:4–5 Paul gives a list of what characterizes Israelites, a list with which Jews could agree. His list here [Rom 2:17–29], however, is quite different."[4] And Francis Watson: "Romans 2 is not typical, for elsewhere Paul does acknowledge the Jewish pursuit of 'works of law' and does not suggest a fundamental imbalance between knowing and doing."[5] I take it that these interpreters are right to perceive a mismatch in content between Rom 2 and Rom 9–11.[6] Paul characterizes the "one who calls himself a Jew" in one way and "the Jews" in quite a different way. While he could be making different points about the same group, of course, we should not too hastily dismiss the alternative hypothesis, that the respective passages have in view altogether different groups.

In recent research, no one has done more to pursue this hypothesis than Runar M. Thorsteinsson. In his 2003 monograph *Paul's Interlocutor in Romans 2*, Thorsteinsson makes the case that Paul's rhetorical interlocutor throughout Rom 2 is best understood as a gentile judaizer—that is, not an actual Jew but a self-styled Jew.[7] He writes, "It is quite possible that Paul's address in Romans 2:17 is aimed, not at a Jew (or any Jew) who is so in name only, but at a gentile who calls himself, or wants to call himself, a Jew, i.e. a person who 'acts the part of a Jew' and is thought of either as a proselyte or a potential one."[8] Thorsteinsson

---

3. E. P. Sanders, *Paul, the Law, and the Jewish People* (Philadelphia: Fortress, 1983), 124.

4. Lloyd Gaston, "Israel's Misstep in the Eyes of Paul," in *Paul and the Torah* (Vancouver: University of British Columbia Press, 1987), 138.

5. Francis Watson, *Paul, Judaism, and the Gentiles*, rev. ed. (Grand Rapids: Eerdmans, 2007), 202.

6. Other interpreters propose various thematic connections between the two passages, but most such proposals seem to me rather strained (see further below).

7. Runar M. Thorsteinsson, *Paul's Interlocutor in Romans 2: Function and Identity in the Context of Ancient Epistolography*, ConBNT 40 (Stockholm: Almqvist & Wiksell, 2003).

8. Thorsteinsson, *Paul's Interlocutor in Romans 2*, 204.

argues his case especially on the grounds of epistolary structure, encoded audience, and diatribe style, in addition to certain features of the discourse of Rom 2 itself (on which see further below). The argument is learned and sophisticated throughout, and it has received deservedly respectful comment from reviewers,[9] but it has not so far brought about widespread change of opinion on the issue in question.[10] For my part, I do not follow Thorsteinsson at all points, but I do find that his reading of Rom 2:17–29—above all his explication of the puzzling phrase Εἰ δὲ σὺ Ἰουδαῖος ἐπονομάζῃ (Rom 2:17)—opens up promising interpretive possibilities, possibilities that might be confirmed or disconfirmed with further evidence from the broader social and historical contexts of the epistle.

Some such evidence has been marshaled by Matthew Thiessen in his 2011 monograph *Contesting Conversion*.[11] Thiessen challenges the *communis opinio* that, from the Hasmonean period onward, Jewishness was an ethno-religious property theoretically available to gentile proselytes who, in the case of males, were willing to undergo circumcision. According to this *communis opinio*, for Jewish communities in the late-Hellenistic and Roman periods, the rite of circumcision allowed for the possibility of what we moderns would call—but ancients did not call—conversion.[12] Thiessen grants that many ancient texts do indeed attest such an understanding, but he also shows that certain other texts reject it, some of them vehemently.[13] He concludes that there was fundamental disagreement among late Second-Temple Jewish thinkers about the very pos-

9. See Andrie du Toit, review of Thorsteinssen, *Paul's Interlocutor in Romans 2*, *Neot* 38 (2004): 152–54; James Sweeney, review of Thorsteinssen, *Paul's Interlocutor in Romans 2*, *RBL* (2004); Bryan D. Lee, review of Thorsteinsson, *Paul's Interlocutor in Romans 2*, *RBL* (2005); Stanley K. Stowers, review of Thorsteinsson, *Paul's Interlocutor in Romans 2*, *JTS* 56 (2005): 561–65; and Friedrich Wilhelm Horn, review of Thorsteinssen, *Paul's Interlocutor in Romans 2*, *TLZ* 130 (2005): 786–89.

10. In addition to the reviews cited above, see the criticism by Watson, *Paul, Judaism, and the Gentiles*, 188, 200–201. The minority who have followed Thorsteinsson include William S. Campbell, *Paul and the Creation of Christian Identity*, LNTS 322 (London: T&T Clark, 2006), esp. 105–8; Matthew Thiessen, "Paul's Argument against Gentile Circumcision in Rom 2:17–29," *NovT* 56 (2014): 373–91; and Rafael Rodriguez, *If You Call Yourself a Jew: Reappraising Paul's Letter to the Romans* (Eugene, OR: Cascade, 2014).

11. Matthew Thiessen, *Contesting Conversion: Genealogy, Circumcision, and Identity in Ancient Judaism and Christianity* (New York: Oxford University Press, 2011).

12. The definitive treatment is Shaye J. D. Cohen, *The Beginnings of Jewishness: Boundaries, Varieties, Uncertainties*, Hellenistic Culture and Society 31 (Berkeley: University of California Press, 1999), esp. 109–238.

13. Shaye Cohen (review of Thiessen, *Contesting Conversion*, *CBQ* 75 [2013]: 379–381) objects that Thiessen's key primary texts have only native Israelites in view, but it seems to me that, if we understand the modern redescriptions "native" and "conversion" in a suitably

sibility of gentile conversion.[14] Among the many texts that figure in Thiessen's argument, perhaps the most instructive example is Jubilees 15, an alternate account of the establishment of the covenant of circumcision in Gen 17.[15] At one point, Jubilees 15 explicates the circumcision commandment as follows:

> This law is for all the generations for ever, and there is no circumcision of the days, and no omission of one day out of the eight days; for it is an eternal ordinance, ordained and written on the heavenly tables. And every one that is born, the flesh of whose foreskin is not circumcised on the eighth day, belongs not to the children of the covenant which the Lord made with Abraham, but to the children of destruction; nor is there, moreover, any sign on him that he is the Lord's, but (he is destined) to be destroyed and slain from the earth, and to be rooted out of the earth, for he has broken the covenant of the Lord our God. (Jubilees 15.25–26; trans. Charles, modified)[16]

For Jubilees as for Genesis, transgression of the circumcision commandment amounts to a grievous breach of covenant (Gen 17:14; Jubilees 15:14). But what exactly constitutes transgression of this commandment? For both texts, certainly, failure to circumcise Israelite sons does so. But for Jubilees, significantly, any circumcision other than eighth-day circumcision amounts to the same: "There is no circumcision of the days, and no omission of one day out of the eight days" (Jubilees 15:25). We may compare Gen 17:14 MT: "Any uncircumcised male who is not circumcised in the flesh of his foreskin shall be cut off from his people"; and Jubilees 15:14: "The uncircumcised male who is not circumcised in the flesh of his foreskin *on the eighth day*, that soul will be cut off from his people, for he has broken my covenant." What is more, just here LXX Genesis agrees with Jubilees against MT Genesis: "The uncircumcised male, who has not circumcised the flesh of his foreskin *on the eighth*

---

nuanced way, then Thiessen has the better end of this argument (in this connection, see John Marshall, review of Thiessen, *Contesting Conversion*, *JTS* 64 [2013]: 617–20).

14. See Thiessen, *Contesting Conversion*, 85: "While the Hellenizers of 1 and 2 Maccabees desired to join with the other nations by rejecting the separatist legislation of Moses, other Jews in the second century BCE desired to achieve similar ends through quite different means. Instead of rejecting the Mosaic Law, some desired to encourage (or even impose) law observance upon non-Jews. . . . For the author of *Jubilees*, however, conversion was impossible. *Jubilees* links law observance inextricably with birth and therefore with genealogy."

15. On the relation between these two parallel accounts, see further Jacques T. A. G. M. van Ruiten, *Abraham in the Book of Jubilees: The Rewriting of Genesis 11:26–25:10 in the Book of Jubilees 11:14–23:8*, JSJSup 161 (Leiden: Brill, 2012), 137–67.

16. R. H. Charles, *The Book of Jubilees* (London: SPCK, 1917).

*day*, that life shall be eliminated from among his tribe, for he has broken my covenant" (Gen 17:14 LXX).[17] Thus the rejection of post-eighth-day circumcisions as non-covenantal is not just an idiosyncrasy on the part of Jubilees. It is enshrined in the main textual tradition of the Greek Bible, which is of course significant for Hellenophone Jews like Paul who read the holy books in that language.[18] As I see it, one felicitous result of Thiessen's argument is that it provides an intelligible inner-Jewish rationale for the position taken by Thorsteinsson's Paul in Rom 2:17–29.[19]

One more relevant development in recent research is Hans Arneson's proposal for the translation of Rom 2:28–29, that difficult passage at the end of Rom 2 in which Paul introduces the distinction between "the Jew on display" and "the Jew in secret" (ὁ ἐν τῷ φανερῷ Ἰουδαῖος and ὁ ἐν τῷ κρυπτῷ Ἰουδαῖος, respectively).[20] The text, according to NA28, reads: οὐ γὰρ ὁ ἐν τῷ φανερῷ Ἰουδαῖός ἐστιν οὐδὲ ἡ ἐν τῷ φανερῷ ἐν σαρκὶ περιτομή, ἀλλ' ὁ ἐν τῷ κρυπτῷ Ἰουδαῖος, καὶ περιτομὴ καρδίας ἐν πνεύματι οὐ γράμματι, οὗ ὁ ἔπαινος οὐκ ἐξ ἀνθρώπων ἀλλ' ἐκ τοῦ θεοῦ. Modern versions and commentators typically supplement this terse Greek sentence with numerous explanatory additions. Thus, for instance, the RSV: "For *he is not a real* Jew who is one outwardly, nor is *true* circumcision something external and physical. *He is a Jew who* is one inwardly, and *real* circumcision is a matter of the heart, spiritual and not literal. His praise is not from men but from God" (emphasis added). Arneson, by contrast, deftly manages a translation which, first, does not supply any more verbs than the sense demands and, second and more importantly, does not smuggle in the artificial notion of "the true Jew" or "the real Jew." In light of Arneson's compelling account of the syntax of this sentence, I propose translating Rom 2:28–29 as follows: "For it is not the Jew on display, nor the circumcision on display in the flesh, but the Jew in secret, and the circumcision of the heart in *pneuma*, not in letter, whose praise [is] not from people but

---

17. The Samaritan Pentateuch is also on the side of Jubilees and LXX Genesis here, while the Syriac and the Vulgate follow MT. On the text-critical problem, see further Matthew Thiessen, "The Text of Genesis 17:14," *JBL* 128 (2009): 625–42.

18. It is interesting to note, however, that neither Paul nor any other New Testament writer actually quotes Gen 17:14.

19. Thiessen himself does not make this connection in *Contesting Conversion*, but he does further develop his position vis-à-vis Thorsteinsson's in his "Paul's Argument against Gentile Circumcision."

20. See Hans K. Arneson, "Revisiting the Sense and Syntax of Romans 2:28–29," forthcoming.

from God."[21] This, it seems to me, gets the syntax exactly right. A translation of Rom 2:28–29 along the lines that Arneson suggests really should become standard, regardless of one's interpretation of Rom 2 as a whole. It fits especially well, however, with the reading of Rom 2 that I offer in what follows. Onward, then, to that reading.

## THE SELF-STYLED JEW OF ROMANS 2

The key text for our purposes is Rom 2:17–29, which I translate as follows:

> But if you call yourself a Jew and rest upon the law and boast in God and know the [divine] will and approve the good, having been catechized from the law, and you are confident that you are a guide to the blind, a light to those in darkness, a trainer of the foolish, a teacher of children, having the form of knowledge and of truth in the law—You, therefore, who teach another, do you not teach yourself? You who preach not to steal, do you steal? You who say not to commit adultery, do you commit adultery? You who detest idols, do you commit sacrilege? You who boast in the law, do you, through transgression of the law, dishonor God? For as it is written, "On account of you the name of God is slandered among the gentiles" [Isa 52:5]. For circumcision confers benefit if you practice the law, but if you are a transgressor of the law, your circumcision becomes a foreskin. If then a foreskin[ned person] keeps the regulations of the law, will not his foreskin be reckoned as a circumcision? And the natural-born foreskin[ned person] who completes the law will judge you who through the letter and circumcision are a transgressor of the law. For it is not the Jew on display, nor the circumcision on display in the flesh, but the Jew in secret, and the circumcision of the heart in *pneuma*, not in letter, whose praise [is] not from people but from God.

---

21. My translation also takes a cue from John M. G. Barclay, "Paul and Philo on Circumcision: Romans 2.25–9 in Social and Cultural Context," *NTS* 44 (1998): 554: "It is important to note the precise terms Paul uses: he does not say that the Jew is one 'inwardly' (despite many translations to this effect) nor does he precisely use the 'inner'–'outer' contrast. . . . In Platonic thought the word-pair 'invisible' and 'visible' were integral to an axiomatic contrast between noetic, incorporeal truths and sensible, corruptible matter. Paul does not adopt that conceptual or linguistic framework. What is 'hidden' for Paul is not what is, by constitution, invisible and incorruptible, but simply what is not (presently) accessible to human eyes."

This passage is part of a larger diatribe form, a rhetorical back-and-forth with one or more imagined interlocutors by means of which Paul develops his argument.[22] In the near context, Paul's central claim is that his gospel is the deity's means of deliverance for all people, Jews as well as Greeks (Rom 1:16), who are alike under sin (Rom 3:9) and thus liable to divine judgment (Rom 3:19). Most interpreters take it that in 2:17 and following, Paul's interlocutor is Jewish, since the word Ἰουδαῖος appears in 2:17, 28, 29. They only dispute whether he is also identical with the interlocutor named in 2:1 ("you, everyone who passes judgment").[23] Most older commentators take this so-called Jew to represent the Jews as such, while many recent readers, by contrast, specify that he is a Jewish teacher of or missionary to gentiles (Rom 2:19–22).[24]

In fact, however, Paul does not actually concede that the figure in 2:17 is a Jew, as some interpreters rightly note. Thus, for instance, Leander Keck: "Instead of 'But if you are a Jew . . . ,' he writes, 'But if you call yourself a Jew,' thus hinting that the man's self-image does not square with reality."[25] This apt observation goes back at least as far as Origen, who writes in his commentary on Romans at this point: "First of all it must be observed that he has not said of him, 'But if you are a Jew,' but rather 'if you call yourself a Jew.' This is because to be a Jew and to be called a Jew are not the same thing" (Origen, *Comm. Rom.* 2.11.4).[26] Both Origen and Keck go on to conclude that the interlocutor should be understood as an ethnic Jew, but one whom, on account of his moral

22. Rom 2:17–29 itself comprises only an address to, not a response from, the interlocutor. On the diatribe form, see further Stanley K. Stowers, *The Diatribe and Paul's Letter to the Romans*, SBLDS 57 (Chico, CA: Scholars Press, 1981), which improves upon Rudolf Bultmann, *Der Stil der paulinischen Predigt und die kynisch-stoische Diatribe*, FRLANT 13 (Göttingen: Vandehoeck & Ruprecht, 1910).

23. See, e.g., Barclay, "Paul and Philo on Circumcision," 544n11: "Since the identity of the [dialogue] partner is made explicit only in 2.17, it is possible that the earlier verses have wider reference (to any 'righteous' person), while subsequently proving to be of specific relevance to Jews."

24. Cf., on the one hand, C. H. Dodd, *The Epistle to the Romans*, MNTC (London: Hodder & Stoughton, 1932), 38: "Paul now turns directly to the Jew, with a fiercely satirical attack upon his complacent self-satisfaction, which elaborates the charge made in verse 3"; and, on the other hand, Douglas A. Campbell, *The Deliverance of God* (Grand Rapids: Eerdmans, 2009), 560: "The hypocrite targeted beginning in 2:1 and then beginning in 2:17 is not a generic Jew representative of Judaism in general but a representative of an elite group of literate Jewish males who are learned in the law and various Jewish traditions, into which the Teacher falls."

25. Leander E. Keck, *Romans*, ANTC (Nashville: Abingdon, 2005), 83.

26. Origen, *Commentary on the Epistle to the Romans, Books 1–5*, trans. Thomas P. Scheck, FC 103 (Washington, DC: Catholic University of America Press, 2001).

failings (Rom 2:21–27), Paul denies the right to claim the name "Jew." But this is a strange line of reasoning. For one thing, "Jew," unlike "philosopher" or "free person" or "good person," is a conventional ethnic name, not a claim of merit such as are disputed in philosophical dialogues. Granted, in some later Christian texts, "the true Israel" (but not usually "the true Jew") becomes a contested title,[27] but whether that is the case here is precisely the question. Even relative to the near context, it is a strange line of reasoning, since the point to which Paul is driving is not that all people fall short of the name "Jew" but that all people are under sin (Rom 3:9). In fact, ironically, this line of reasoning actually releases rather than entraps the interlocutor, since *ex hypothesi* he is not a gentile, and by the time we get to Rom 2:29 he is no longer a "Jew"!

Enter Thorsteinsson, who presses the question whether Paul's use of the verb ἐπονομάζω here might have a more prosaic sense: Perhaps this person calls himself but is not, in the regular, ethnic sense, a Jew.[28] The verb form in Rom 2:17 is ἐπονομάζῃ, a present middle-passive indicative. (Both middle and passive forms of ἐπονομάζω are amply attested elsewhere, so the morphology is not decisive.)[29] The lexical form ἐπονομάζω occurs only here in the New Testament (except as a *varia lectio* for ὀνομάζω in Codex Bezae at Luke 6:14), but the simple cognate ὀνομάζω, *sans* prefix, is relatively common.[30] Paul uses the latter at Rom 15:20 ("to preach the gospel not where Christ has already been named [ὠνομάσθη]") and, a closer parallel to our text, at 1 Cor 5:11: "I wrote to you not to associate yourselves or eat with someone if he calls himself a brother [ἐάν τις ἀδελφὸς ὀνομαζόμενος] yet is an adulterer or a greedy person or an idolater or a slanderer or a drunk or a thief." The point here is that such a person calls himself a brother (that is, a member of the Christ group) but is not one, on account of which Paul exhorts, "Exclude the evil person from among

27. On this development, see Graham Harvey, *The True Israel: Uses of the Names Jew, Hebrew, and Israel in Ancient Jewish and Early Christian Literature*, AGJU 35 (Leiden: Brill, 1996).

28. Cf. David Frankfurter, "Jews or Not? Reconstructing the 'Other' in Rev 2:9 and 3:9," *HTR* 94 (2001): 419: "We might ask, who 'calls oneself' a Jew anyway? Certainly not someone who is *recognized* as Jewish by birth or by community. Rather, this suggestion of self-chosen Jewishness would denote a Gentile who has taken to practicing certain elements of Jewish observance and thereby has come to claim that self-definition" (emphasis original).

29. Lionel J. Windsor, "The Named Jew and the Name of God," *NovT* 63 (2021): 229–48 concedes this point, but reports that he cannot find the middle used reflexively ("to call *oneself*") elsewhere. Cf. Ryan D. Collman, "Apostle to the Foreskin: Circumcision in the Letters of Paul" (PhD diss., University of Edinburgh, 2021) for an argument that it can be so used.

30. See Mark 3:14; Luke 6:13, 14; Acts 19:13; Rom 15:20; 1 Cor 5:11; Eph 1:21; 3:15; 5:3; 2 Tim 2:19.

you" (1 Cor 5:13, citing Deut 17:7). This self-styled brother is an impostor. He calls himself (ὀνομαζόμενος) something that he is not.[31] This parallel is not decisive, but it is instructive. It provides warrant for a thought experiment: Granted that the words Εἰ δὲ σὺ Ἰουδαῖος ἐπονομάζῃ could, on their own, signify a non-Jew who assumes for himself the name "Jew," let us inquire, first, whether such a scenario is socially plausible and, second, whether it yields a compelling reading of Rom 2.

In fact, this social phenomenon, the assumption of the name "Jew" by non-Jews, is relatively well attested in sources from the early Roman period.[32] The most proximate parallel, which is itself an interpretive puzzle, is the double mention in Revelation of certain persons τῶν λεγόντων ἑαυτοὺς Ἰουδαίους εἶναι καὶ οὐκ εἰσίν, "who say they are Jews and are not" (Rev 2:9; 3:9). John of Patmos roundly condemns such persons in his addresses to the assemblies in Smyrna (Rev 2:8–11) and Philadelphia (Rev 3:7–13). A formidable case can be made that these mysterious people are local synagogue Jews whom John denies the name "Jews" so as to claim it exclusively for the Jesus group.[33] But the other main possibility, which I think has much to commend it, is that they are people who are not in fact Jews but say, for reasons of religious identity, that they are. They are, in other words, a subset of "Christians" (to use a convenient misnomer) whom John finds objectionable, perhaps for reasons having to do with their ritual impurity, which he sees as a threat to the eschatological readiness of the Jesus group.[34]

It may be, then, that Revelation attests the phenomenon of non-Jews calling themselves Jews, but in any case, other sources close in time and place certainly attest it. Thus Epictetus, the great Stoic sage from Phrygia in Asia Minor, active

31. See Wayne A. Meeks, *The First Urban Christians: The Social World of the Apostle Paul*, 2nd ed. (New Haven: Yale University Press, 2003), 130: "To shun the offender, especially at common meals—the Lord's Supper and others—would be an effective way of letting him know that he no longer had access to that special fellowship indicated by the use of the term *brother.*"

32. For a thorough treatment of the many ancient references, see Cohen, *Beginnings of Jewishness*, 25–68.

33. Among recent interpreters, see, e.g., Adela Yarbro Collins, "Insiders and Outsiders in the Book of Revelation," in *To See Ourselves as Others See Us: Christians, Jews, "Others" in Late Antiquity*, ed. Jacob Neusner and Ernest S. Frerichs (Chico, CA: Scholars Press, 1985), 187–218; Collins, "Vilification and Self-Definition in the Book of Revelation," *HTR* 79 (1986): 308–20.

34. For an argument along these lines, see Frankfurter, "Jews or Not?" and, rather differently, John W. Marshall, *Parables of War: Reading John's Jewish Apocalypse*, ESCJ 10 (Waterloo, Ontario: Wilfred Laurier University Press, 2001), 12–16.

in the late first and early second centuries CE, discusses the person who "acts the part of a Jew" (ὑποκρίνεται Ἰουδαῖον) on analogy to the way a person might sample the way of life of a philosophy before finally committing to it.[35] Epictetus's comment, according to Arrian, reads as follows:

> Why, then, do you call yourself a Stoic, why do you deceive the multitude, why do you act the part of a Jew, when you are a Greek [τί ὑποκρίνῃ Ἰουδαῖον ὢν Ἕλλην]? Do you not see in what sense men are severally called Jew, Syrian, or Egyptian? For example, whenever we see a man halting between two faiths, we are in the habit of saying, 'He is not a Jew, he is only acting the part [οὐκ ἔστιν Ἰουδαῖος, ἀλλ᾽ ὑποκρίνεται].' But when he adopts the attitude of mind of the man who has been baptized and has made his choice, then he is both a Jew in fact and is also called one [τότε καὶ ἔστι τῷ ὄντι καὶ καλεῖται Ἰουδαῖος]. So we also are counterfeit 'baptists,' ostensibly Jews, but in reality something else [λόγῳ μὲν Ἰουδαῖοι, ἔργῳ δ᾽ ἄλλο τι], not in sympathy with our own reason, far from applying the principles which we profess, yet priding ourselves upon them as being men who know them. (Epictetus, *Discourses* 2.9.19–22)[36]

Epictetus knows of people who "act the part of Jews," "call themselves Jews," or are "Jews ostensibly but not really." By his lights, such behavior is less than ideal inasmuch as it indicates a hesitancy to commit to one's principles, but it is at any rate not pernicious. One can imagine, however, how native Jews of a certain halakic perspective might find this social category ethically problematic.

Writing in a different context, Dio Cassius, the second- to third-century CE Roman historian, gives an account of the relation of the ethnic name Ἰουδαῖος to the place name Ἰουδαία, noting that, while the name "Jews" obviously attaches to people of Judean extraction, it is also regularly used of foreigners, non-Jews, who choose to follow the laws and customs of the Jews:[37]

> They have also another name that they have acquired [in addition to Palestina]: The country has been named Judaea, and the people themselves Jews

---

35. On this text, see Menahem Stern, *Greek and Latin Authors on Jews and Judaism*, 3 vols. (Jerusalem: Israel Academy of Sciences and Humanities, 1974–1984), 1:542–44.

36. Epictetus, *Discourses*, trans. W. A. Oldfather, LCL (Cambridge, MA: Harvard University Press, 1925).

37. On this text, see Stern, *Greek and Latin Authors*, 2:349–353.

[ἥ τε γὰρ χώρα Ἰουδαία καὶ αὐτοὶ Ἰουδαῖοι ὠνομάδαται]. I do not know how this title [ἐπίκλησις] came to be given them, but it applies also to all the rest of mankind, although of alien race, who affect their customs [τοὺς ἄλλους ἀνθρώπους ὅσοι τὰ νόμιμα αὐτῶν, καίπερ ἀλλοεθνεῖς ὄντες, ζηλοῦσι]. This class exists even among the Romans, and though often repressed has increased to a very great extent and has won its way to the right of freedom in its observances. (Dio Cassius, *Roman History* 37.17.1)[38]

The conduct of these non-Jewish "Jews," Dio notes, incurs the disapproval of some but gained a degree of recognition all the same on account of its popularity. There are even some Romans, Dio says, who call themselves "Jews" in this sense, which brings us around again to the apostle Paul and his letter to the Christ assemblies in Rome.

Dio's description of foreigners who go by the name "Jews"—"people who, although they are of alien race, affect the customs of the Jews"—is strikingly reminiscent of the situation in Paul's assemblies in Galatia and Philippi, where gentiles-in-Christ were contemplating taking upon themselves certain νόμιμα, "customs" or "laws," of the Jews: circumcision above all (Gal 5:2–4; 6:12–13; Phil 3:2–3), but perhaps also Sabbath and festival observances (Gal 4:8–10; and cf. food regulations in Gal 2:11–14). In contrast to Dio, Paul does not say that gentiles who affect such customs adopt the name "Jew" (unless, of course, that is what he is saying in Rom 2), but he does say that they ἰουδαΐζειν, "judaize" or "act Jewishly" (Gal 2:14).[39] In Galatians and Philippians, Paul's objection is not to what his gentiles call themselves but to what they do; it is the affecting of the customs that poses the problem. (Indeed, on one very influential interpretation with which I happen to disagree, it is Paul himself who presumes to give to non-Jews the name "Jews" [Rom 2:28–29], or at least the names "Israel" [Gal 6:16; Rom 11:26] and "the circumcision" [Phil 3:3].[40] I think that

38. Dio Cassius, *Roman History*, vol. 3, trans. Earnest Carey, LCL (Cambridge, MA: Harvard University Press, 1914).

39. On judaizing, see Cohen, *Beginnings of Jewishness*, 175–97. On this issue in Galatians, see Matthew V. Novenson, "Paul's Former Occupations in *Ioudaismos*," in *Galatians and Christian Theology*, ed. Mark W. Elliott et al. (Grand Rapids: Baker Academic, 2014), 24–39.

40. E.g., N. T. Wright, *The Climax of the Covenant: Christ and the Law in Pauline Theology* (Minneapolis: Fortress, 1992), 250: "Paul actually began the whole section ([Rom] 9.6) with just such a programmatic distinction between two 'Israels,' and throughout the letter (e.g. [Rom] 2.25–9) as well as elsewhere (e.g. Philippians 3.2–11) he has systematically transferred the privileges and attributes of 'Israel' to the Messiah and his people. It is therefore greatly preferable to take 'all Israel' in [Rom 11] v. 26 as a typically Pauline polemical redefinition, as in Galatians 6.16 (though that is of course also controversial), and in line

this interpretation is mistaken, but that is a topic for another time.)[41] Romans 2 adds to the mix the issue of the name "Jew" (Ἰουδαῖος ἐπονομάζῃ), but it is otherwise quite consistent with Galatians and Philippians in focusing on the adoption of Jewish customs (νόμος in Rom 2:17–24), above all circumcision (περιτομή in Rom 2:25–29).

How, then, would our passage work on the premises of this thought experiment? My own reading would go something like this: Paul identifies his interlocutor in Rom 2:17 as "one who calls himself a Jew." In continuity with the figure in 2:1–16 who presumed to judge others, the figure in this passage presumes to teach others, but the claim to the name Ἰουδαῖος introduces a new layer. This person rests on the law [of Moses], boasts in [the Jewish] God, knows the [divine] will, and approves the good, on account of his having been catechized in the law (2:17–18). There is not yet any charge of hypocrisy. In 2:19–21, the emphasis falls on the interlocutor's self-appointed role as instructor of others: a guide to the blind, a light to those in darkness, and so on. Here, as noted above, many recent interpreters have reasoned that this figure is not just any Jew but a Jewish teacher of gentiles. Fair enough. But this hypothetical social category, the Jew who proactively exhorts gentiles to adopt Jewish ancestral law, is not nearly as well attested as the one discussed above, the gentile judaizer.[42] Thus it is at least as easy to imagine that this self-appointed law teacher is a gentile as it is to imagine that he is a Jew.

We find further reason to imagine a gentile judaizer in the following section, vv. 21–23, which make the the notoriously difficult accusation that the interlocutor teaches others to obey the law while transgressing it himself. In particular, Paul lodges three illustrative charges: theft, adultery, and sacrilege. "You who preach not to steal, do you steal? You who say not to commit adultery, do you commit adultery? You who detest idols, do you commit sacrilege?" (Rom 2:21–22). As many interpreters have noted, it is hard to see how these charges would stick to a representative Jewish interlocutor.[43] Of course, Paul

---

also with Philippians 3.2ff., where the church is described as 'the circumcision'"; and similarly Daniel Boyarin, *A Radical Jew: Paul and the Politics of Identity* (Berkeley: University of California Press, 1997), 1–12 et passim.

41. I discuss this issue at length in my *The End of the Law and the Last Man: Paul between Judaism and Christianity* (New York: Cambridge University Press, forthcoming).

42. On the notion of an ancient Jewish mission to gentiles and, in particular, the scarcity of evidence for any such thing, see Martin Goodman, *Mission and Conversion: Proselytizing in the Religious History of the Roman Empire* (Oxford: Clarendon, 1994).

43. See C. K. Barrett, *The Epistle to the Romans*, 2nd ed., BNTC (London: Black, 1991), 53: "Paul's argument is lost if he is compelled to rely on comparatively unusual events, and

might have made an accusation that was simply nonsense, but a more elegant interpretation would be preferable. The notion of a Jewish interlocutor can perhaps be made to work by appeal to Philo's list of sins in *Conf.* 163[44] (but Jews are not specifically in view here) or to Josephus's account of the swindling of the Roman proselyte Fulvia in *Ant.* 18.81–84[45] (but here there is no mention of ἱεροσυλία), but these are subtler maneuvers than I would like to have to make. The hypothesis of a gentile interlocutor is arguably more economical.

The former two charges, theft and adultery, both plucked straight from the Decalogue (Exod 20:14–15; Deut 5:18–19), are stereotypically gentile vices such as Paul catalogues summarily in 1 Cor 6:9–10 (μοιχοί, κλέπται) and elaborately in Rom 1:18–32. Paul could conceivably say that "gentile sinners" (Gal 2:15) do such things without having to defend the claim. The third charge, ἱεροσυλία, "pillaging temples," or better, "sacrilege," is puzzling on any reading,[46] but if our interlocutor is a gentile judaizer, then he might conceivably be associated with

---

it is simply not true that the average Jewish missionary acted in this way"; Heikki Räisänen, *Paul and the Law* (Philadelphia: Fortress, 1986), 99: "Logically Paul's argument proves no more than that circumcision is of no avail to a Jew who is guilty of serious transgressions of the law. . . . That this should demonstrate that all are 'under sin' is another *petitio principii*."

44. Philo, *Conf.* 163: "This is a sign of a soul lacking good sense, which finds no obstacle in all that lies between it and its sin. For he who is not far gone in mortal error would pray that all the promptings of his mind's purposes should fail him, so that when he attempts to commit theft or adultery, or murder or sacrilege [κλέπτειν ἢ μοιχεύειν ἢ ἀνδροφονεῖν ἢ ἱεροσυλεῖν], or any similar deed, he should not find an easy path but rather a host of obstacles to hinder its execution" (*Philo*, vol. 4, trans. F. H. Colson and G. H. Whitaker, LCL [Cambridge, MA: Harvard University Press, 1932]).

45. Josephus, *Ant.* 18.82: "He [a Jewish scoundrel living in Rome] enlisted three confederates not a whit better in character than himself; and when Fulvia, a woman of high rank who had become a Jewish proselyte, began to meet with them regularly, they urged her to send purple and gold to the temple in Jerusalem. They, however, took the gifts and used them for their own personal expenses, for it was this that had been their intention in asking for gifts from the start" (Josephus, *Antiquities*, trans. Louis Feldman, LCL [Cambridge, MA: Harvard University Press, 1965]). The appeal to this story as an *explanans* for Rom 2:21–24 has recently been championed by Jan Dochhorn, "Der Vorwurf des Tempelraubs in Röm 2,22b und seine politischen Hintergründe," *ZNW* 109 (2018): 101–17, but I remain sceptical.

46. See Etienne Trocmé, "The Jews as Seen by Paul and Luke," in *To See Ourselves as Others See Us*, 145–61, here 153: "They abhor idols and at the same time commit an act which our old translators rendered as 'sacrilege' (ἱεροσυλεῖς) and which nowadays we do not really know how to translate. (No great loss, perhaps, as we do not have the slightest idea to what action it might refer.)" This is a wonderful comment on the history of interpretation of this verse, but the final clause is an overstatement. It is simple enough, by consulting the standard lexicons, to get an idea of the sense of ἱεροσυλία; the only difficulty is teasing out how the charge is meant in Rom 2:22.

sacrilege in regard to the cult of the Jerusalem temple. Most modern English versions render ἱεροσυλεῖς in Rom 2:22 "Do you rob temples?" (thus, e.g., RSV, NSRV, NASB), reasoning etymologically from the roots ἱερόν, "sacred precinct" or "sanctuary," and συλάω, "despoil" or "pillage." But in this instance the old King James Bible is better: "Dost thou commit sacrilege?" When heads of state (e.g., kings, generals) do it, ἱεροσυλία signifies the actual despoiling of temples by force of arms (e.g., Menelaus and Lysimachus in 2 Macc 4:39, 42; Antiochus IV in 2 Macc 9:2). But when common people do it, ἱεροσυλία can signify just the infringement upon or violation of sacred precincts by foreigners. So it is in Acts 19, where Paul himself is accused of ἱεροσυλία at the temple of Artemis in Ephesus: τοὺς ἄνδρας τούτους οὔτε ἱεροσύλους οὔτε βλασφημοῦντας τὴν θεὸν ἡμῶν, "These men have neither committed sacrilege nor blasphemed our goddess" (Acts 19:37). A Jewish analogy might be the charge against Paul and Trophimus the Ephesian when they are spotted in the vicinity of the Jerusalem temple in Acts 21:27–29:Ἕλληνας εἰσήγαγεν εἰς τὸ ἱερὸν καὶ κεκοίνωκεν τὸν ἅγιον τόπον τοῦτον, "This man [Paul] brought Greeks [Trophimus] into the sanctuary and has profaned this sacred place" (Acts 21:28), although admittedly Luke does not call this ἱεροσυλία. Another example might be the fanciful rabbinic story of the gentile who sneaked into the Second Temple and ate the Passover sacrifices but was subsequently discovered and put to death (b. Pesaḥ. 3b).[47] If Paul's "you who call yourself a Jew" in Rom 2:17 is a gentile judaizer, he might conceivably incur the charge of sacrilege for presuming upon a natural-born Jew's right of access to the cult of Yahweh headquartered in Jerusalem.[48] By presuming to take upon himself the law of the Jews (Rom 2:17, 18, 23), he actually transgresses that very law.[49]

This is an apt transition to the second half of our passage, Rom 2:25–29, where the issue of circumcision suddenly comes to the fore: "Circumcision confers benefit if you practice the law, but if you are a transgressor of the law, your circumcision becomes a foreskin" (Rom 2:25), and so on. This turn in the

---

47. On this story, see the discussion of Cohen, *Beginnings of Jewishness*, 62–66.

48. See Josephus, *Ant.* 15.417: "Such, then, was the first court [of Herod's temple]. Within it and not far distant was a second one, accessible by a few steps and surrounded by a stone balustrade with an inscription prohibiting the entrance of a foreigner [ἀλλοεθνῆ] under threat of the penalty of death"; and cf. Josephus, *J. W.* 5.193; 6.124; Philo, *Leg.* 31. See further the discussion by Elias J. Bickermann, "The Warning Inscriptions of Herod's Temple," *JQR* 37 (1946–1947): 387–405.

49. For a related but rather different interpretation of these verses, see Matthew Thiessen, "Paul's So-Called Jew and Lawless Lawkeeping," in *The So-Called Jew in Paul's Letter to the Romans*, ed. Rafael Rodriguez and Matthew Thiessen (Minneapolis: Fortress, 2016), 59–84.

discourse is striking, and it suggests the possibility that the sense in which our mysterious interlocutor "calls himself a Jew" has to do with this initiation rite in particular. Just here Thiessen's argument about the different ancient Jewish views on the possibility and permissibility of gentile conversion sheds valuable light. Texts like 1 Maccabees view gentile circumcision as the first, best step toward incorporation into the covenant people, while texts like Jubilees view gentile circumcision as a damnable breach of the covenant. Both kinds of texts think that they are interpreting the covenant of circumcision in Gen 17 faithfully, but they come to exactly opposite conclusions.[50]

In this connection, it is significant that Paul characterizes his interlocutor in Rom 2 as σὲ τὸν διὰ γράμματος καὶ περιτομῆς παραβάτην νόμου, "you who through the letter and circumcision are a transgressor of the law" (Rom 2:27). Modern versions and commentators often render the prepositional phrase as a disjunctive, as in the RSV: "you who have the written code and circumcision *but* break the law," as if this person were a transgressor in spite of his fulfillment of the circumcision commandment. What Paul writes, however, is a straightforward διά-plus-genitive construction, which under normal circumstances would be rendered "through such-and-such" and taken to express means by which (see BDAG, s.v. διά, A3; BDF §223).[51] On this more grammatically natural reading, the interlocutor becomes a transgressor of the law precisely through, not in spite of, his circumcision. By undergoing circumcision, he violates the circumcision commandment. Relative to our conventional ways of reading Rom 2, this might sound strange, but in view of the rejection of proselyte circumcision on halakic grounds in Jubilees, it actually makes good sense. We know that there were Jews who would say that a gentile who undergoes adult circumcision becomes a transgressor precisely by his mistaken effort to obey the circumcision commandment. Perhaps Paul was one of them.

If so, this might also suggest a solution to the notorious puzzle of the righteous pagan in Rom 2:26–27, "the natural-born foreskinned person who fulfills the law." Romans 2:27 reads: καὶ κρινεῖ ἡ ἐκ φύσεως ἀκροβυστία τὸν νόμον τελοῦσα σὲ τὸν διὰ γράμματος καὶ περιτομῆς παραβάτην νόμου, "The natural-born foreskin[ned person] who completes the law will judge you who through the letter and circumcision are a transgressor of the law." Interpreters have agonized over whether this remarkable person, a foreskinned person who fulfills the law, could really be a pagan in his natural habitat or whether,

---

50. See Thiessen, *Contesting Conversion*, 67–86.
51. Thus rightly Thiessen, "Paul's Argument against Gentile Circumcision," 385–86.

instead, he must be a so-called "gentile Christian."[52] But this classic debate bumps up against the familiar, obstinate fact that Paul characteristically distinguishes between Jews and gentiles, circumcised people and foreskinned people, not between "Christians" and "non-Christians." Thus the question as typically put misses the point. In Rom 2, it seems to me, "the natural-born foreskin[ned person] who completes the law" is the gentile who rightly remains in his foreskinned state (cf. 1 Cor 7:18). He avoids transgressing the eighth-day circumcision commandment and thus "fulfills the law." "He will judge you" in the sense that he is blameless with respect to that commandment, while "you," the gentile judaizer, are guilty of transgressing it.

The end of our passage, Rom 2:28–29, has been taken by many to be the key moment at which Paul polemically redefines Jewishness in spiritual as opposed to genealogical terms, as in the RSV: "He is not a *real* Jew who is one outwardly. . . . He is a Jew who is one inwardly," and so on.[53] A lot of theological mileage has been gotten out of this translation, but it is suspect on old-fashioned grammatical grounds. In the syntax of these verses, the question (or, in formal terms, the predicate) is not, Who is a real Jew? but rather, Who receives praise from God?[54] As noted above, following Arneson's proposal, I translate this sentence as follows: "For it is not the Jew on display, nor the circumcision on display in the flesh, but the Jew in secret, and the circumcision of the heart in *pneuma*, not in letter, whose praise [is] not from people but from God." Paul's interlocutor would be a "Jew" on display, inasmuch as he has adopted on his body ("flesh") a distinguishing mark on the grounds of which he claims the name "Jew." But this kind of Jewishness on display, Paul suggests, wins praise only from people (cf. Gal 1:10; 5:11; 6:12). By contrast, praise from God (not "true Jewishness") comes to Jews who are what they are in secret, not on display, and who are circumcised of heart, in good biblical fashion (Deut 10:16; 30:6; Jer 4:4; cf. Matt 6:1–18).

---

52. See the incisive discussion of Räisänen, *Paul and the Law*, 101–9.

53. See especially Boyarin, *A Radical Jew*, 94–95: "[In Rom 2:28–29] Paul introduces his major concern throughout his ministry: producing a new, single human essence, one of 'true Jews' whose 'circumcision' does not mark off their bodies as ethnically distinct from any other human bodies. . . . 'True Jewishness' ends up having nothing to do with family connection (descent from Abraham according to the flesh), history (having the Law), or maintaining the cultural/religious practices of the historical Jewish community (circumcision), but paradoxically consists of participating in a universalism, an allegory that dissolves those essences and meanings entirely."

54. The importance of this theme, but not this aspect of the syntax of the verse, is rightly noted by Barclay, "Paul and Philo on Circumcision," 546–51.

Now, we might be inclined to doubt that Paul could take Jubilees' side on the circumcision commandment because of our well-worn image of the apostle as a libertine with respect to Torah. But halakic perspectives do not map onto a simple continuum from rigorist on one end to libertine on the other. In 1 Maccabees, Mattathias and his sons aggressively enforce circumcision among the peoples under their jurisdiction (1 Macc 2:46), but they relax the Sabbath commandment to allow for warfare on the seventh day (1 Macc 2:29–41). Philo of Alexandria allegorizes commandments of Moses by the score, but he nevertheless insists on the proper, traditional observance of the Sabbath, feast days, and circumcision (*Migr. Abr.* 89–93). By the same token, one can readily imagine Paul concluding that, in light of the present messianic ingathering of the gentiles, Jews may—indeed, must—violate certain interpretations of kashrut in order to share in the one table of the lord (see Gal 2:11–21), and yet, at the same time, insisting that the eighth-day circumcision commandment is not to be violated, and in fact, for precisely the same eschatological reason: Jews enter the kingdom as Jews, gentiles as gentiles, but all share in the one messianic banquet.[55]

Perhaps, then, it is not such a stretch to think of Paul agreeing with Jubilees that non-eighth-day circumcision contravenes the commandment and thus makes the self-styled Jew a transgressor. This reconstruction is broadly consistent with Paul's own self-presentation, at several points in his letters, as a relative rigorist:[56] "an eighth-day circumcision, from the race of Israel, the tribe of Benjamin, a Hebrew born from Hebrews, in respect of the law a Pharisee, in respect of zeal indicting the assembly, in respect of righteousness in the law blameless" (Phil 3:5–6; cf. Gal 1:14). It is also possible—but this takes us further afield—that this reconstruction helps explain some of Paul's more cryptic comments in Galatians about the "agitators" who were urging circumcision upon his gentiles-in-Christ. "I testify to every person who undergoes circumcision that he is obligated to do the whole law" (Gal 5:3); "Those who undergo circumcision do not even keep the law themselves; rather, they want you to be circumcised so that they may boast in your flesh" (Gal 6:13). Such comments might suggest not just a pique of anger, although they do suggest that, but also a claim to the halakic high ground.[57] Not only do the agitators

55. On this latter point, see Paula Fredriksen, "Judaizing the Nations: The Ritual Demands of Paul's Gospel," *NTS* 56 (2010): 232–52. On the subtleties of Paul's halakic reasoning, see Peter J. Tomson, *Paul and the Jewish Law: Halakha in the Letters of the Apostle to the Gentiles*, CRINT (Assen: Van Gorcum, 1990), esp. 55–96, 259–81.

56. Thus rightly Räisänen, *Paul and the Law*, 175–76.

57. Thus perceptively Johannes Munck, *Paul and the Salvation of Mankind*, trans. Frank

fail as models of virtue; their policy positively violates the very commandment they ostensibly want to safeguard.

So far, so good. One potentially damning objection remains, however, not from within the passage itself but rather from the near context, in particular, Rom 3:9: "What then? Are we at an advantage?[58] Not at all, for we charged previously that all people, both Jews and Greeks, are under sin." On the conventional reading, the main verb of this sentence, προῃτιασάμεθα, refers to the immediately preceding argument: Paul indicts the gentiles in 1:18–32 and the Jews in 2:1–3:8; thus he can say in 3:9 that he has previously charged that all are under sin.[59] On my reading, however, Paul has not in fact indicted the Jews in Rom 2. How, then, can he say προῃτιασάμεθα? The answer lies in what follows, to wit: a litany of scripture citations presenting a kaleidoscope of impiety: "There is no one righteous, not even one; there is no one who comprehends, no one who seeks after God," and so on (Rom 3:10–18).[60] Paul concludes this catena of oracles with a hermeneutical pronouncement: "We know that whatever the law says it speaks to those who are in the law, so that every mouth be shut and the whole cosmos be answerable to God" (Rom 3:19). I propose that "those who are in the law" are the Jews (cf. Gal 2:14–16; 1 Cor 9:20; Rom 3:28–29; 9:4). These indictments from the law speak to them, shutting their mouths and making them answerable to God. In other words, it is the sacred books of old, not Paul himself in the preceding paragraph, that "previously charged" the Jews with being under sin.[61] That the gentiles are

Clarke (London: SCM, 1959), 87–134. The polemic in Phil 3 arguably admits of a similar interpretation: "Beware the dogs, beware those who effect harm, beware the excision. For we are the circumcision" (Phil 3:2–3). For an interpretation of this passage along these lines, see Michele Murray, "Romans 2 within the Broader Context of Gentile Judaizing in Early Christianity," in *The So-Called Jew in Paul's Letter to the Romans*, 163–82; Ryan D. Collman, "Beware the Dogs! The Phallic Epithet in Philippians 3:2," *NTS* 67 (2021): 105–20.

58. For a fine discussion of the grammatical difficulties with the verb προεχόμεθα here, see Joshua D. Garroway, "Paul's Gentile Interlocutor in Romans 3:1–20," in *The So-Called Jew in Paul's Letter to the Romans*, 85–100. I agree with Garroway on the ethnicity of the rhetorical interlocutor in Rom 3, but I take a different view of the way this question fits in the discourse.

59. See Räisänen, *Paul and the Law*, 97: "When Paul states in 3.9 that all, Jew and Greek alike, are under sin, he says that he has set forth this charge before (προῃτιασάμεθα). He must, then, think that this has taken place in the section 1.18–2.29."

60. See the form-critical study of Leander E. Keck, "The Function of Rom 3:10–18: Observations and Suggestions," in *God's Christ and His People: Studies in Honour of Nils Alstrup Dahl*, ed. Jacob Jervell and Wayne A. Meeks (Oslo: Universitetsforlaget, 1977), 141–57.

61. Here I agree with Thorsteinsson, *Paul's Interlocutor in Romans 2*, 236: "It seems to me that the verb προῃτιασάμεθα [in Rom 3:9] refers not to what Paul himself had previously

under sin is empirically demonstrable, which is the point not only of Rom 1:18–32 but also of 2:1–29.[62] That the Jews are under sin is known from the testimony of the law, that is to say, from scripture rather than experience.[63] As Paul himself writes in Gal 3:22, συνέκλεισεν ἡ γραφὴ τὰ πάντα ὑπὸ ἁμαρτίαν, "Scripture shut up all things under sin." Thus far the self-styled Jew of Rom 2. What, then, about the actual Jews of Rom 9–11?

### THE ACTUAL JEWS OF ROMANS 9–11

"Romans 9–11 is as full of problems as a hedgehog is of prickles," N. T. Wright has aptly commented,[64] and it is neither possible nor necessary for us to address all of them here. For the purposes of this essay, we are specifically concerned with the question of how Paul assesses his Jewish kinfolk—that is, on what points he variously praises and blames them, which is a big enough problem on its own, and which on any interpretation of these chapters lies very close to the heart of the discourse. Gone are the days when interpreters regarded Rom 9–11 as an ill-fitting digression from an otherwise elegant argument.[65] Since the 1970s especially, it has become a scholarly commonplace to note the thematic connections between this section and the rest of the letter, a development

---

said in his letter but to what had previously been stated in the Jewish scriptures about all being under sin." For a different solution, see Garroway, "Paul's Gentile Interlocutor in Romans 3:1–20."

62. Thus rightly Stanley K. Stowers, *A Rereading of Romans: Justice, Jews, and Gentiles* (New Haven: Yale University Press, 1994), 156: "Paul assumes that gentiles normally have the status of sinners . . . and that Jews normally do not."

63. Most of the oracles comprising the catena in Rom 3:10–18 come from the Psalter and in their original contexts indict "the wicked," irrespective of ethnicity, in contrast to the righteous psalmist. There is a significant exception in the penultimate oracle, Rom 3:15–17, which cites Isa 59:7–8, part of an oracle against the people Israel. For his part, Paul takes the whole series of oracles to indict all people (Rom 3:9), but especially the Jews whose scriptures they are (Rom 3:19–20).

64. Wright, *Climax of the Covenant*, 231.

65. E.g., famously, Dodd, *Romans*, 149: "It [viz. Rom 9–11] is the kind of sermon that Paul often must have had occasion to deliver, in defining his attitude to what we may call the Jewish question. It is quite possible that he kept by him a MS. of such a sermon, for use as occasion demanded, and inserted it here. As we have seen, the epistle could be read without any sense of a gap if these chapters were omitted." More radically, Francois Refoulé ("Unité de l'Épitre aux Romains et histoire du salut," *RSPT* 71 [1987]: 219–42) entertained the possibility that the whole of Rom 9–11 is a post-Pauline interpolation into the text of the letter.

which I regard as entirely salutary.[66] The crucial question, however, is precisely what connections there are. One might think, and many have thought, that in Rom 9:1 Paul picks up again the critique of Judaism that he began in Rom 2:17 (or 2:1, as the case may be).[67] But if, first, the interlocutor in Rom 2:17–29 is actually a gentile judaizer, and second, Paul's claims about Israel in Rom 9–11 differ meaningfully from his claims about that figure, then the longstanding interpretation of Rom 2 and 9–11 under the rubric of "Paul's critique of Judaism" suffers proportionately. Let us see whether this is in fact the case.

At Rom 9:1, Paul's letter takes a turn into lament: "I might wish that I myself were accursed, [cut off] from the messiah for the sake of my brothers, my kinfolk according to the flesh, who are the Israelites, whose are the establishment as sons, and the glory, and the covenants, and the giving of the law, and the [temple] service, and the promises, whose are the ancestors, and from whom, according to the flesh, is the messiah. (God, who is over all, be blessed forever, amen.) But it is not as though the word of God had fallen, for not all of those from Israel are Israel" (Rom 9:3–6), and so on. It is an oft-noted problem that Paul does not spell out exactly what he thinks has gone wrong with the people Israel.[68] He is aggrieved for them, he would become anathema for their sake,

---

66. Thus influentially Krister Stendahl, *Paul among Jews and Gentiles* (Philadelphia: Fortress, 1976), 4: "To me the climax of Romans is actually chapters 9–11. . . . In this letter Paul's focus really is the relation between Jews and Gentiles, not the notion of justification or predestination and certainly not other proper yet abstract theological topics." In fact, this view was advocated already by F. C. Baur, *Paul the Apostle of Jesus Christ*, 2 vols. (London: Williams & Norgate, 1873–1875 [German original 1845]), 1:327: "The centre and pith of the whole, to which everything else is only an addition, would then be comprised in that part of the Epistle which is contained in the three above-named chapters [viz. Rom 9–11]: here we must take our stand, place ourselves in harmony with the original conception of the Apostle, from which is developed the whole organism of the Epistle as it is presented to us."

67. E.g., in the nineteenth century, Matthew Arnold, *St. Paul and Protestantism*, pop. ed. (London: Smith & Elder, 1887), 63–64: "The second [chapter] is to the Jews—its purport is: No more have you [righteousness], though you think you have. . . . The ninth, tenth, and eleventh chapters uphold the second chapter's thesis—so hard to a Jew, so easy to us—that righteousness is not by the Jewish law"; and scores of other interpreters in the twentieth and twenty-first centuries as well.

68. Lloyd Gaston ("Israel's Enemies," in *Paul and the Torah*, 92) makes a great deal of this silence: "How is that people can say that chapter 9 deals with the unbelief of Israel when it is never mentioned?" On Gaston's account, Paul's only complaint with Israel is that they do not endorse his apostolic mission to the gentiles (see Gaston, "Israel's Misstep in the Eyes of Paul," in *Paul and the Torah*, 135–50). But cf. the cogent criticism of Heikki Räisänen, "Paul, God, and Israel: Romans 9–11 in Recent Research," in *The Social World of Formative Christianity and Judaism: Essays in Tribute to Howard Clark Kee*, ed. Jacob Neusner et al.

he is aware that the state of affairs—whatever it is—might give the impression that the divine word had somehow failed. The Jews as such, the people Israel, are certainly in view here (Rom 9:4–5), and the grandeur of their ancestral institutions underlines the extremity of Paul's anguish: In view of all the benefits their god has conferred upon them, their present enmity toward that god's purposes (Rom 11:28) is altogether shocking. Just here, it is striking that in Rom 9:1–5 the Israelites' rightful claim upon their god and their ancestral law is presented as a plain fact ("theirs is the glory . . . theirs the giving of the law" [Rom 9:4]), not, as with the figure in Rom 2:17–29, a presumption ("You who boast in the law, do you dishonor God through transgression of the law?" [Rom 2:23]).

Beginning from 9:6 and on through 9:29, the argument is preoccupied with vindicating the divine word from the charge of failure ("It is not as though the word of God had fallen" [9:6]), especially via appeal to scriptural oracles that attest the motif of divine election, God's prerogative to choose for his purposes a few from among many. Only at Rom 9:30 does Paul finally get around to explaining what is presently happening, as he sees it, among his Jewish kinfolk on the one hand and the gentiles on the other: "What then shall we say? The gentiles, who do not pursue righteousness, have taken hold of righteousness, the righteousness from trust, but Israel, who pursues a law of righteousness, has not arrived at the law" (Rom 9:30–31). Paul generalizes here about what gentiles and Jews stereotypically do: Gentiles do not pursue righteousness. They are sinners by nature (Gal 2:15), prone to all manner of idol-worship and immorality (1 Thess 4:5; 1 Cor 6:9–11; Rom 1:18–32). Not so with Jews. Not being idol-worshippers, they are not naturally predisposed to gross immorality.[69] On the contrary, they pursue a law of righteousness, as indeed they should do, since "they were entrusted with the oracles of God" (Rom 3:2).[70]

---

(Philadelphia: Fortress, 1988), 180: "No other reason [than unbelief of the gospel] makes sense. If Israel merely lacks understanding or faithfulness 'with respect to the Gentile mission,' why should Paul have such deep sorrow in his heart? Paul goes even further. In v. 3 he expresses the unreal wish that he could be 'accursed [ἀνάθεμα] and cut off from Christ' for the sake of his kinsmen. This implies that they must be 'in a plight as serious as the one he is willing to enter for their sake.'"

69. See Stowers, *Rereading of Romans*, 116: "*Natural* refers to a feature of life that the writer regards as self-evident, unarguable, or taken for granted. From Paul's perspective, being uncircumcised belongs to the essential nature of gentiles but not that of Jews"; and 156: "Paul assumes that gentiles normally have the status of sinners . . . and that Jews normally do not."

70. Thus rightly J. Ross Wagner, *Heralds of the Good News: Isaiah and Paul in Concert in the Letter to the Romans*, NovTSup 101 (Leiden: Brill, 2003), 152.

In the present moment, however, the normal propensities of both groups have been frustrated: The gentiles who care not a whit for righteousness have suddenly found themselves rightwised, and the Jews have somehow not caught up with or grasped (what Paul sees as) the point of their own ancestral law, which point Paul will spell out in Rom 10:4 ("The messiah is the end of the law unto righteousness"). The former plot twist is to be explained as the result of sheer divine mercy. Fair enough. But why the latter? "Because not from trust but as if from works" (Rom 9:32a). This Greek sentence is elliptical, having neither stated subject nor stated verb. It must, therefore, take its subject and verb from the preceding clause: [Israel pursued their righteous law] not from trust but as if from works. This is now syntactically clear, but conceptually still rather vague. Interpreters have tried to dispel the vagueness by appealing to their own respective theories of "works" (e.g., establishing a moral claim upon God, or excluding ethnic others from fellowship, or what have you). Paul himself adds some clarity, at least, in the form of a metaphor in the following clause: "They stumbled at the stone of stumbling" (Rom 9:32b). Israel's pursuing the law as if from works rather than trust is explicated in terms of their figuratively stumbling over some cause of offense.

But what is the "rock of offense" at which they stumbled? The majority answer over the long history of interpretation of Romans is that the rock is Christ (but not in the sense that "the rock was Christ" in 1 Cor 10:4). Some, however, have suggested that the rock in this metaphor is the law itself, which makes a certain sense in the immediate context, although it also confuses the metaphor.[71] Still others have settled the dispute by ruling in favor of both sides. Thus Wright: "The Torah is therefore, in a sense, the stone over which Israel has now stumbled, just as in another sense it is the crucified Messiah over which she has now stumbled."[72] This lattermost solution seems to me too conciliatory. Yes, the themes of law and messiah are profoundly interrelated in this passage, but it does not follow that both are the stone of stumbling.

Despite the legitimate near-context arguments in favor of the law, there are more and stronger factors pointing in the direction of the messiah. First, the parallel to 1 Cor 1:23 is too exact to be an accident: ἡμεῖς δὲ κηρύσσομεν Χριστὸν ἐσταυρωμένον, Ἰουδαίοις μὲν σκάνδαλον, ἔθνεσιν δὲ μωρίαν, "We proclaim a crucified messiah, an offense to Jews, and folly to gentiles" (1 Cor 1:23). Paul comments only very rarely on the mainstream Jewish posture toward the Jesus movement (understandably, since his oeuvre consists of letters to gentile

---

71. As noted by Wagner, *Heralds of the Good News*, 155–57.
72. Wright, *Climax of the Covenant*, 244.

assemblies), but when he does so in 1 Cor 1, he expresses his assessment that the Jews find the apostolic message of a crucified messiah to be a σκάνδαλον, "offense." Thus, when Paul says in Rom 9:32–33, in a discourse which has entirely to do with the mainstream Jewish posture toward the Jesus movement, that Israel stumbled over the "rock of offense," the "offense to Jews" posed by the crucified messiah in 1 Cor 1:23 suggests itself as an obvious intertext, and one would want extraordinary reasons for hypothesizing another, altogether different "offense to Jews," in this context of all contexts.

Second and even more decisive is the scripture citation in Rom 9:33, a conflation of two oracles from Isaiah, 28:16 and 8:14: καθὼς γέγραπται· ἰδοὺ τίθημι ἐν Σιὼν λίθον προσκόμματος καὶ πέτραν σκανδάλου, καὶ ὁ πιστεύων ἐπ᾽ αὐτῷ οὐ καταισχυνθήσεται, "As it is written, 'Behold, I am placing in Zion a stone of stumbling, a rock of offense; and the person who trusts in it will not be put to shame.'" There are interesting text-critical and hermeneutical issues here,[73] but the crucial point for our purposes is that, in Paul's conflated citation, the "stone of stumbling" or "rock of offense" is identified as the object of trust (ὁ πιστεύων ἐπ᾽ αὐτῷ). Trusting the messiah is of course a leitmotif in Romans (see 3:22; 10:4, 17), not to mention elsewhere in Paul (1 Cor 15:17; Gal 2:16, 20; 3:22, 26), while the law—holy, righteous, and good though it is (Rom 7:12)—is never said to be an object of trust, and is sometimes actually contrasted with trust, as in Gal 3:23: "Before trust came, we were guarded under the law." Furthermore, in the very next paragraph Paul again cites Isa 28:16, "The person who trusts in him will not be put to shame" (Rom 10:11), this time specifying that the αὐτῷ of the citation is not it but him, the lord—that is, Jesus (Rom 10:9: κύριον Ἰησοῦν). All of this points to the conclusion that the "rock of offense" over which Israel stumbled and in which they do not presently trust (ἀπιστία in Rom 3:3; 11:20, 23) is the crucified messiah.[74]

Following the Isaiah citation, Rom 10:1–4 commences a new period but continues Paul's assessment of the piety of his co-ethnics: "Brothers, the goodwill of my heart and my petition to God on their behalf is for deliverance. For I testify for them that they have the zeal of God, but not with understanding. For not recognizing the righteousness of God, and seeking to establish their own, they did not submit to the righteousness of God. For the messiah is the

---

73. On which see Wagner, *Heralds of the Good News*, 120–57.

74. Thus rightly Nils A. Dahl, "The Future of Israel," in *Studies in Paul: Theology for the Early Christian Mission* (Minneapolis: Augsburg, 1977), 150: "Paul interprets what has actually happened. The crucified Messiah became an offense to Jews but brought salvation to the Gentiles. . . . For Paul, however, this does not mean that God's promise of salvation is taken from Israel and given to the Gentiles, but only that the order of events has been reversed."

end of the law unto righteousness for everyone who trusts" (Rom 10:1–4). Here again, the "they" in view is the people Israel. Paul resolves and pleads for their deliverance (σωτηρία), which implies both the direness of the situation as Paul sees it but also the prospect of a reversal of fortune. The saying in Rom 10:2 is the closest thing anywhere in Paul to a summary assessment of the religion of the Jewish ethnos: "They have the zeal of God, but not with understanding." (Note that, unlike in Rom 2, there is nothing at all here about boasting in the law, much less a flagrant transgression of it.) The Jews' putative lack of understanding (ἐπίγνωσις) in 10:2 Paul immediately specifies in 10:3: "not recognizing [ἀγνοοῦντες] the righteousness of God, and seeking to establish their own." Their pious zeal is deficient just to the extent that they failed to recognize the righteousness of God when it appeared. And "the righteousness of God" (Rom 10:3) as Paul uses it in Romans is a metonym for the coming of the messiah (Rom 1:16; 3:21–26; 10:4).

Krister Stendahl famously observed about our passage, "It is stunning to note that Paul writes this whole section of Romans (10:17–11:36) without using the name of Jesus Christ."[75] This observation has the merit of being *almost* true, and it has a renewed currency in the very interesting discussion surrounding the so-called radical new perspective on Paul.[76] But I fear that the manifest brilliance of Stendahl's groundbreaking essay has lulled us into certain lazy assumptions about the logic of Paul's argument in Rom 9–11, especially with regard to the ostensible unimportance of Christ thereto. Several points are germane. First, Paul *does* actually use the name of Christ in Rom 10:17: "Trust is from hearing, and hearing through the message of Christ." Second, we should not too hastily dismiss the possibility that the citation of Isa 59:20 in Rom 11:26—"The deliverer will come from Zion"—is another direct reference to the messiah, only (as is frequently the case in Paul) not by name.[77] Third, there are other long blocks of text in which Paul happens not to use the words "Jesus" or "Christ"—2 Cor 7, or all of 1 Cor 13–14, for example—where we do not therefore conclude that Paul means to exclude Christ from the mythological picture. Fourth and finally, the relevant discourse unit is not just Rom 10:17–11:36 but all of Rom 9–11 (not to mention the wider context), in which three chapters

---

75. Stendahl, *Paul among Jews and Gentiles*, 4.

76. On which see chapter 10 in the present volume.

77. Thus rightly Sanders, *Paul, the Law, and the Jewish People*, 194: "Since Paul thought Jesus was the Jewish messiah and, more, Lord of the living and the dead . . . it is likely that he thought of Christ as coming at the end, before the kingdom was handed over to God. . . . [But] it matters little whether he understands 'the Deliverer' to be God or Christ; for it is incredible that he thought of God apart from Christ."

Christ figures early, often, prominently, and in direct relation to Israel (9:5, 32–33; 10:4, 6–7, 9, 11, 14, 17; 11:26). The fashion for reading Christ out of Rom 9–11 thus simplifies the logic of the passage at the expense of falsifying it.

The big picture of Rom 9–11 is, as Paula Fredriksen has written, a divine comedy.[78] The gifts of God and the call of God are irrevocable (Rom 11:29), and all Israel will indeed be saved (Rom 11:26). But Rom 9:1–4 is not a feint. Paul is genuinely anguished for his kinfolk, and he is quite serious in laying charges of enmity, unbelief, and disobedience at their feet. But the disobedience with which Paul charges Israel is of a very particular sort.[79] It is neither gross moral turpitude, as in Rom 1–2, nor a perverse use of the law for either egotistic or jingoistic ends. Rather, it is disobedience to the εὐαγγέλιον, the apostolic announcement of the messiah: οὐ πάντες ὑπήκουσαν τῷ εὐαγγελίῳ, "Not all [of Israel] obeyed the gospel" (Rom 10:16). And again, κατὰ μὲν τὸ εὐαγγέλιον ἐχθροὶ δι᾽ ὑμᾶς, "With respect to the gospel they [Israel] are enemies for your [gentiles'] sake" (Rom 11:28). Or, another way of saying the same thing: ἀγνοοῦντες γὰρ τὴν τοῦ θεοῦ δικαιοσύνην, "They did not recognize the righteousness of God" (Rom 10:3). This is a subtle but important point. It is not that Israel failed to recognize the righteousness of God because they were already in the bad habit of boasting in the law while flouting it, or of wielding the law as a cudgel to keep gentiles away.[80] Rather, just to the extent that they did not recognize the righteousness of God—that is, did not trust the messiah—they established an alternative righteousness. The law of Moses is of course a law of righteousness (Rom 2:26; 7:12; 8:4; 9:31), so by simply carrying on with that law as if the eschatological righteousness of God had not appeared, in the nature of the case, Israel established a righteousness of their own (Rom 10:3). Their stumbling is neither expected (Rom 9:1–5) nor unanimous (Rom 9:6–29;

---

78. Paula Fredriksen, *Sin: The Early History of an Idea* (Princeton: Princeton University Press, 2012), 49: "Paul thus envisages a divine comedy, a cosmic happy ending. And he—like John the Baptizer and like Jesus before him—is convinced that these events will happen *soon*" (emphasis original).

79. On this point, see Stephen L. Young, "Paul's Eschatological Myth of Judean Sin," *NTS* (forthcoming).

80. Contra Wright, *Climax of the Covenant*, 240: "Israel's rejection of Jesus as Messiah simply *is* the logical outworking of her misuse of the Torah, her attempt to treat it as a charter of automatic national privilege" (emphasis original). For one thing, Paul does not say that Israel misused the law, only that they pursued it in the wrong way, and for another, he charges them with "establishing their own righteousness" only at, not prior to, the appearing of the righteousness of God.

11:1–10) nor malicious (Rom 9:30–10:4) nor final (Rom 11:11–12, 25–32), but, by Paul's lights, it is a stumbling nonetheless.[81]


CONCLUSION

A comparison of Paul's rhetorical address to a self-styled Jew in Rom 2:17–29 with his lament for his actual Jewish kinfolk in Rom 9–11 turns out to be quite instructive. Paul charges the self-styled Jew in Rom 2 with κλέπτειν, "theft" (Rom 2:21), μοιχεύειν, "adultery," ἱεροσυλία, "sacrilege" (Rom 2:22, ἱεροσυλεῖς), and παράβασις τοῦ νόμου, "transgression of the law" (Rom 2:23, 25, 27), all under the heading of "teaching another but not teaching oneself" (Rom 2:21). If we read Rom 2:17–29 as a continuation of the dialogue in Rom 2:1–16, then we should add to this list τὰ αὐτὰ πράσσεις ὁ κρίνων, "doing the very things for which one judges others" (Rom 2:1). By contrast, Paul says about the actual Jews of Rom 9–11 that they οὐκ ἐκ πίστεως ἀλλ᾽ ὡς ἐξ ἔργων, "[pursued the law] not from trust but as if from works" (Rom 9:32); προσέκοψαν, "stumbled" (Rom 9:32; and cf. 11:11); ζῆλον θεοῦ ἔχουσιν ἀλλ᾽ οὐ κατ᾽ ἐπίγνωσιν, "have the zeal of God but without understanding" (Rom 10:2); ἀγνοοῦντες γὰρ τὴν τοῦ θεοῦ δικαιοσύνην, "did not recognize the righteousness of God" (Rom 10:3); τὴν ἰδίαν ζητοῦντες στῆσαι, "sought to establish their own [righteousness]" (Rom 10:3); τῇ δικαιοσύνῃ τοῦ θεοῦ οὐχ ὑπετάγησαν, "did not submit to the righteousness of God" (Rom 10:3); and οὐ πάντες ὑπήκουσαν τῷ εὐαγγελίῳ, "did not obey the gospel" (Rom 10:16). More tersely, Paul charges Israel with ἀπιστίᾳ, "unfaithfulness" or "unbelief" (Rom 11:23), κατὰ μὲν τὸ εὐαγγέλιον ἐχθροί, "enmity with respect to the gospel" (Rom 11:28), and ἠπείθησαν, "disobedience" (Rom 11:31). To these we may add by way of corroboration Rom 3:3: ἠπίστησάν τινες, "some [of the Jews] were unfaithful," which corresponds exactly to Rom 11:23.

The differences are striking. The self-styled Jew is addressed in the second person, whereas Paul only ever speaks of "the Jews" and "Israel" in the third person (Rom 3:1–3; 9–11). The self-styled Jew, like, or perhaps as, the presumptuous person introduced in Rom 2:1, is guilty of gross infractions of the

81. Sanders's summary statement (*Paul, the Law, and the Jewish People*, 185) is, I think, basically right: "Paul was an apostle to Gentiles, his mission was a success, the mission to the Jews was relatively unsuccessful, he addresses that failure as a fresh problem for the first time in Romans 9–11, he rearranges the eschatological sequence so that it accords with the facts, and only indirectly does he give himself a role in the salvation of Israel."

law despite his evident busyness exhorting other people to obey it. The Jews of Rom 9–11 (and Rom 3:3) come in for criticism, but not at all in the same way. Not only is it "they" rather than "you," and thus in the mode of diagnosis rather than rebuke;[82] what is more, there is nothing at all about transgression in Rom 9–11. The reproach of Israel in Rom 9–11 has to do entirely with the apostolic announcement, the gospel: "Some did not obey the gospel" (Rom 10:16); "They are enemies with respect to the gospel for your sake" (Rom 11:28). More tersely, Paul writes, the Jews are presently "unfaithful" or "unbelieving" (Rom 11:23) and "disobedient" (Rom 11:31), but again with respect to the gospel. One key passage that might be taken to hint otherwise—"Israel did not attain to the law of righteousness" (Rom 9:31)—means not that Israel transgressed the law (contra RSV: "did not succeed in fulfilling"), but rather, as Paul says in so many words, that she failed to apprehend its *telos*—namely, the messiah (Rom 10:4). I would therefore respectfully suggest that the longstanding interpretive tradition of reading Rom 2 and 9–11 under the rubric of "Paul's critique of Judaism" should be laid to rest. In Paul's letter to the Romans, there are "Jews," and there are Jews, and the former are not the latter.

---

82. On this point, see further Garroway, "Paul's Gentile Interlocutor in Romans 3:1–20."

# THE MESSIAH BEN ABRAHAM
# IN GALATIANS

This essay is framed as a response to Joel Willitts's thoughtful assessment of my book *Christ among the Messiahs*[1] and his constructive account of how the messiahship of Jesus figures in the argument of Paul's Letter to the Galatians.[2] Both Willitts's and my contributions are part of a wider discussion in recent Pauline studies about the adequacy of the conventional view of the messiahship of Jesus in Pauline theology.[3] I find Willitts's particular account of

---

1. Matthew V. Novenson, *Christ among the Messiahs: Christ Language in Paul and Messiah Language in Ancient Judaism* (New York: Oxford University Press, 2012).

2. Joel Willitts, "Davidic Messiahship in Galatians: Clearing the Deck for a Study of the Theme in Galatians," *JSPL* 2 (2012): 143–61. Willitts is well positioned to speak to these questions, having demonstrated his mastery of the relevant sources with his *Matthew's Messianic Shepherd-King: In Search of "the Lost Sheep of the House of Israel,"* BZNW 147 (Berlin: de Gruyter, 2007).

3. Other recent reassessments include Dieter Zeller, "Zur Transformation des Χριστός bei Paulus," in *Der Messias*, ed. Ingo Baldermann et al., JBT 8 (Neukirchen-Vluyn: Neukirchener Verlag, 1993), 155–67; Stanley K. Stowers, *A Rereading of Romans: Justice, Jews, and Gentiles* (New Haven: Yale University Press, 1994), 213–16; Richard B. Hays, "Christ Prays the Psalms: Israel's Psalter as Matrix of Early Christology," in *The Conversion of the Imagination: Paul as Interpreter of Israel's Scripture* (Grand Rapids: Eerdmans, 2005), 101–18; Adela Yarbro Collins, "Jesus as Messiah and Son of God in the Letters of Paul," in John J. Collins and Adela Yarbro Collins, *King and Messiah as Son of God: Divine, Human, and Angelic Messianic Figures in Biblical and Related Literature* (Grand Rapids: Eerdmans, 2008), 101–22; James A. Waddell, *The Messiah: A Comparative Study of the Enochic Son of Man*

the Christology of Galatians promising but not entirely persuasive, so I offer this essay by way of advancing what I think is a very worthwhile discussion.

First, regarding Willitts's review, he gives my book a commendably fair, attentive reading, and I am gratified to learn that he finds my argument largely persuasive, even if he also disagrees with some of my conclusions. His distillation of several central claims from my book differs from my own summary of the argument, but this is a quibble about relative degrees of emphasis.[4] The nature of his criticisms suggests that, on a broad spectrum of Pauline scholarship on this issue, Willitts's position and mine are quite close to one another.

Because of this proximity, however, our points of disagreement are particularly illuminating. As I understand it, Willitts's principal criticism of my book has to do with the degree of discursive freedom that I attribute to Paul in his use of messiah language. He writes, "Novenson doesn't seem to adequately take into account the Davidic shape of Paul's messianic language."[5] Willitts concedes that I do acknowledge the point that he makes here, quoting my claim that "in Paul's case, his scriptural source texts are overwhelmingly associated with the house of David rather than, say, the Aaronic priesthood or Daniel's visions."[6] But of course, in discussions like this one the crucial question is how much emphasis it takes to count as adequate, and for Willitts my account does not go far enough.

Articulating an account that he thinks does go far enough, Willitts writes, "Once Paul embraced the Davidic interpretation of the Messiah texts of the Jewish Scriptures . . . his Messianic expectations would be shaped by the Davidic imprint." And again, "I propose that Paul's messianism is laden with Davidic freight."[7] Now, if by the terms "Davidic imprint" and "Davidic freight" Willitts means just a cluster of biblical traditions associated with the ancient Judahite house of David, then he is surely right. Paul thinks that Jesus is the messiah son of David and is therefore rhetorically constrained in certain ways by the available biblical resources for talking about such a figure. But when Willitts says "Davidic imprint" he means something else, something more; that is the point of his claim that my book does not take Davidic messiahship

---

*and the Pauline Kyrios*, JCTCRS 10 (London: T&T Clark, 2011); N. T. Wright, *Paul and the Faithfulness of God*, 2 vols. (London: SPCK, 2013); Joshua W. Jipp, *Christ Is King: Paul's Royal Ideology* (Minneapolis: Fortress, 2015); Paula Fredriksen, *Paul: The Pagans' Apostle* (New Haven: Yale University Press, 2017); J. Thomas Hewitt, *Messiah and Scripture: Paul's 'in Christ' Idiom in Its Ancient Jewish Context*, WUNT 2.522 (Tübingen: Mohr Siebeck, 2020).

4. For my own summary, see Novenson, *Christ among the Messiahs*, 174–78.

5. Willitts, "Davidic Messiahship," 150.

6. Novenson, *Christ among the Messiahs*, 173.

7. Willitts, "Davidic Messiahship," 151.

seriously enough. For Willitts, these various biblical David traditions comprise a discrete model of the messiah, a model that Paul, like *Psalms of Solomon* before him, adopts in full. Once Paul adopts that model, his portrait of Jesus is largely (although not entirely) scripted for him.

Willitts suggests that if I had seen the implications of my own argument, I would have arrived at his position. But in fact, in *Christ among the Messiahs* I do consider something very much like Willitts's position and find it wanting for evidence.[8] As I see it, there simply is no such thing as "the Davidic interpretation" of scripture or "the Davidic imprint." There is a cluster of texts and traditions associated with the house of David, but from this cluster Paul picks and chooses at will in ways that suit his other theological beliefs and his various rhetorical purposes. What is more, as I argue in the book, this is not a peculiarly Pauline phenomenon. It is the way that all ancient messiah texts, Jewish and Christian, normally work.[9] The manifest diversity even among Davidic messiahs demonstrates that this is the case. Paul has a Davidic messiah who dies and rises from the dead (Rom 1:3–4). *Fourth Ezra* has a Davidic messiah who dies but does not rise from the dead (*4 Ezra* 7:28–29). The Qumran *Community Rule* has a Davidic messiah who is an accessory to a priestly messiah (1QS IX, 11). The Epistle to the Hebrews has a Davidic messiah who is himself a priestly messiah (Heb 7:11–17). Bavli Sanhedrin even has a Davidic messiah who judges cases by a divinely inspired sense of smell (*b. Sanh.* 93b). All of these texts represent defensible ancient interpretations of certain biblical house of David texts, but they do not remotely constitute a single model of the Davidic messiah. Willitts and I agree that there is variety among a number of ancient models of the messiah, but I also maintain, against Willitts, that there is great variety even within the notion of a Davidic messiah.[10]

To the extent that, in his view, I give too loose a description of Davidic messianism, to that extent Willitts finds something lacking in my reading of

---

8. See Novenson, *Christ among the Messiahs*, 34–63, esp. 41–47. More recently, I have again had almost exactly this argument with N. T. Wright. See his "Messianic Grammar? A Response to Matthew V. Novenson, *The Grammar of Messianism: An Ancient Jewish Political Idiom and Its Users*," *ExpTim* 129 (2018): 295–302; and my response "On *The Grammar of Messianism*, in Dialogue with N. T. Wright," *ExpTim* 129 (2018): 303–6, here 305: "At the risk of oversimplifying, I think that people tell stories; Wright thinks that stories tell people."

9. I make this case at length in my *The Grammar of Messianism: An Ancient Jewish Political Idiom and Its Users* (New York: Oxford University Press, 2017).

10. On the literary character of David as a kind of muse for ancient Jewish textual production, see Eva Mroczek, *The Literary Imagination in Jewish Antiquity* (New York: Oxford University Press, 2016), esp. 51–85.

Paul. It is not altogether clear, however, just what Willitts wants to claim about Davidic messianism in Paul. He criticizes me (and N. T. Wright, too, for that matter) for not taking the motif in question seriously enough. But what, precisely, does he think is missing in Wright's and my accounts? What would one have to do, on Willitts's view, to treat the theme adequately? Responding to me Willitts writes, "It is not enough to query why Paul would have used the term χριστός. It must be asked more particularly, why would he have made use of language of a Davidic χριστός?"[11] Similarly, responding to Wright he writes, "The question . . . remains: What significance does the adjective 'Davidic' have for Paul with respect to his understanding of Jesus' messiahship? Why a Davidic messiah?"[12] If these statements are representative, I take it that what Willitts wants is an answer to the question: Why does Paul identify Jesus as a Davidic messiah rather than another type of messiah?

If so, then an answer is close at hand. Paul uses Davidic messiah language for talking about Jesus because, to put it plainly, he is stuck with such language.[13] He inherited it from those who were in Christ before him (Rom 16:7). Indeed, from the first time that Paul encountered the notion that Jesus might be identified as the messiah (that is, in the period before his revelation, when he was still an opponent of the ἐκκλησία [Gal 1:13–14]), that notion already included an association with the house of David (Rom 1:3–4). Consequently, Paul never had the opportunity to decide for himself which category of messiah Jesus best fit. It simply never occurred to him to think of Jesus as any other kind of messiah than a Davidic messiah. That is not to say that Paul does not give his own interpretations of the Davidic messiahship of Jesus. He certainly does so, and the study of Paul's messianism consists precisely in the explication of these interpretations. But to the question of why Paul thinks of Jesus as a specifically Davidic messiah, the answer is straightforward and proportionately uninteresting.

Second, then, regarding Willitts's reading of Galatians, as Willitts notes, in the book I say less about Galatians than other Pauline epistles, so I find his soundings in the Christology of Galatians welcome and his observations illuminating. He and I concur that the few often cited messiah Christology texts in Paul (e.g., Rom 1:3; 9:5) are not random aberrations from Paul's ostensibly real Christology. Rather, they are occasional, context-generated clarifications of

---

11. Willitts, "Davidic Messiahship," 150.
12. Willitts, "Davidic Messiahship," 151n25.
13. As ancient messiah texts often are. On this point see Novenson, *Grammar of Messianism*, 65–113.

how Paul means the word "Christ" whenever and wherever he uses it. Willitts is methodologically right, therefore, to inquire how the messiahship of Jesus factors in the argument of Galatians. (The answer to that question, however, is not predetermined by the content of the concept "messiah" or even Willitts's more nuanced concept "Davidic messiah.") Willitts begins by adducing for his thesis several pieces of "circumstantial evidence"—namely, Luke's account of Paul's synagogue sermon at Pisidian Antioch (Acts 13:13–47) and 2 Timothy's reference to "Jesus Christ, raised from the dead, from the seed of David, according to my gospel" (2 Tim 2:8). I would dispute Willitts's claim that the citation of Isa 49:6 in Acts 13:47 ("I have set you to be a light for the gentiles")[14] is a "Davidic messianic text"; I think that Luke's citation identifies Paul himself, not Christ, as the Isaianic servant whom God appoints as a light to gentiles. As for the Acts 13 sermon, as well as the "seed of David" reference in 2 Tim 2:8, I agree that these constitute evidence for a widespread early Christian messiah Christology,[15] but I disagree that they tell us anything about Paul's own Christology in Galatians.

Willitts's test case for reading Christology in the epistolary greeting of Galatians (1:1–4) is promising, but his argument for intertextual echoes in the phrase "to deliver us from the present evil age" is not finally persuasive. Willitts argues that Paul intends (and, an even more ambitious claim, that the Galatian assemblies would recognize) a reference to the messiah ben David in the use of the verb ἐξαιρέομαι in Gal 1:4: τοῦ δόντος ἑαυτὸν ὑπὲρ τῶν ἁμαρτιῶν ἡμῶν, ὅπως ἐξέληται ἡμᾶς ἐκ τοῦ αἰῶνος τοῦ ἐνεστῶτος πονηροῦ, "He [Christ] gave himself for our sins so as to deliver us out of the present evil age." On Willitts's account, the verbal idea of "delivering" is a component part of the Davidic messiah model that Paul adopts: "The delivering action of Jesus Messiah from forces both spiritual and physical, irrespective of the manner of the rescue, was certainly in line with what we know of the general messianic expectations of Paul's day."[16] And again, "In Galatians we have a description of the work of the Davidic Messiah, that of delivering from the grasp of an enemy."[17] And further, "Paul presents Jesus as the Davidic Messiah by means of his action of deliverance. The Galatian readers would know that this was the Davidic Messiah by what Jesus Messiah did for them."[18]

14. My translation, here as elsewhere.
15. On which see now Joshua W. Jipp, *The Messianic Theology of the New Testament* (Grand Rapids: Eerdmans, 2020).
16. Willitts, "Davidic Messiahship," 155.
17. Willitts, "Davidic Messiahship," 156.
18. Willitts, "Davidic Messiahship," 156.

To be sure, the verbal idea of delivering from hostile forces is consonant with the notion of a messiah (Davidic or otherwise), but there is nothing in the biblical usage of the verb ἐξαιρέομαι that makes the connection necessary or even especially suggestive. Most significantly, in the LXX/OG ἐξαιρέομαι never occurs in conjunction with χριστός.[19] This in itself would not be decisive if it were the case that ἐξαιρέομαι occurs especially in royal ideology texts, but it does not. As Willitts notes, by far the most frequent subject of the verb is God, but many human subjects also "deliver" in a variety of contexts. Reuben delivers Joseph from their homicidal brothers (Gen 37:21–22). The Israelite congregation may deliver a person guilty of manslaughter from a blood avenger (Num 35:25). The Hebrew spies agree to deliver Rahab and her family from the siege of Jericho (Josh 2:13). Joshua delivers the Gibeonites from destruction at Israelite hands on account of their sartorial ruse (Josh 9:26). Jerubbaal delivers the Israelites from the Midianite hoards (Judg 9:17), and so on. Of these many human "deliverers," David and his descendants feature no more often or more prominently than any others.

Willitts rightly identifies the three passages in which either David or a descendant of David is the subject of the pertinent verb. In 1 Kgdms 30:8, 18, the brigand David "delivers" his own wives and possessions from Amalekite raiders. In 2 Kgdms 19:10–11, the mutinied tribes of Israel say among themselves, "David the king rescued us from all our enemies, and he delivered us from the hand of foreigners [αὐτὸς ἐξείλατο ἡμᾶς ἐκ χειρὸς ἀλλοφύλων], and now he has fled from the land and from his kingdom, away from Absalom. And Absalom, whom we anointed over us [ὃν ἐχρίσαμεν ἐφ᾽ ἡμῶν], has died in the conflict." Here David "delivers," but ironically the usurper Absalom is the "messiah." Finally, in OG Jer 21:11–22:5, an oracle against "the king of Judah, who sits on the throne of David," the prophet twice exhorts the king: ἐξαιρεῖσθε διηρπασμένον ἐκ χειρὸς ἀδικοῦντος αὐτόν, "Deliver the victim from the hand of the one who wrongs him" (OG Jer 21:12; 22:3). The point of this passage is that the Davidic king is not doing any delivering, whereas in the prophet's view he ought to be.

Read in isolation, the second passage (2 Kgdms 19:10–11) might be taken to suggest an archetype of David the deliverer, but in context it does not do so. On the contrary, in 2 Kgdms 19:5, just after the death of Absalom, Joab scolds David because the king's servants have had to "deliver" him, not the other way around. In short, there are only three biblical passages in which

---

19. But cf. ἐξαιρέομαι in conjunction with χρίω in Num 35:25 and 2 Kgdms 19:10–11, neither of which, however, makes "delivering" a prerogative of an "anointed one."

David or a son of David "delivers" anyone, and none of those passages figures in the substantial and influential royal ideology tradition (cf. 2 Sam 7; Isa 11; Ps 72; and so on). Willitts acknowledges that these three passages comprise a meager evidence base, but he pleads for the significance of the fact that many other Septuagintal uses of ἐξαιρέομαι occur in "Davidic contexts," in particular psalms of David (namely, OG Pss 30:2–3; 36:40; 58:2; 63:2; 70:2; 90:15; 139:2, 5; 142:9; 143:7, 11).[20] As Willitts himself notes, however, in every one of those psalm instances the subject of the verb is God, and the "David" of the psalm is not delivering but being delivered, which actually weighs against a generalizing portrayal of David as an archetypal deliverer. Consequently, Willitts's claim that "a quarter of all the uses of the verb ἐξαιρέω in the Jewish Greek Scriptures are Davidic" is not sustainable.[21] This is not to say that Jesus's "delivering" activity in Gal 1 is not messianic, only that there are no biblical reasons for thinking of "delivering" as a uniquely messianic activity. There is no archetypal Davidic deliverer whom Paul could have invoked by saying that "Christ delivers us from the present evil age."

Even so, Willitts's observation that the messiahship of Jesus comprises part of the argument of Galatians is right. Precisely how it functions in the argument is a matter for further research;[22] but Willitts has given us some valuable programmatic suggestions. Summarizing these suggestions, he writes, "When we read Galatians with Davidic eyes, Galatians 1:1–4 brims with Davidic elements."[23] This statement is true, but it is true by definition. The eyes with which one chooses to read a text can of course determine what one finds there. But Willitts sells himself short here; he could have claimed more. In fact, the Davidic messiahship of Jesus emerges as a theme in the Pauline letters (Galatians included) regardless of the eyes with which one chooses to read the texts (with the exception of determinedly anti-messianic eyes, of which there have admittedly been many in the history of interpretation). It is a feature of the letters, not of the eyes.

20. Willitts also cites several psalm instances of ἐξαιρέομαι that are not in fact psalms of David, viz. OG Pss 49:15 (Asaph); 81:4 (Asaph); 114:8 (anonymous); 118:153 (anonymous).

21. Willitts, "Davidic Messiahship," 158.

22. The few existing treatments include Paula Fredriksen, "Judaism, the Circumcision of Gentiles, and Apocalyptic Hope: Another Look at Galatians 1 and 2," *JTS* 42 (1991): 532–64; N. T. Wright, "Messiahship in Galatians?," in *Galatians and Christian Theology*, ed. Mark W. Elliott et al. (Grand Rapids: Baker Academic, 2014), 3–23; J. Thomas Hewitt, "Ancient Messiah Discourse and Paul's Expression *achris hou elthe to sperma* in Galatians 3:19," *NTS* 65 (2019): 398–411; and Esau McCaulley, *Sharing in the Son's Inheritance*, LNTS 608 (London: T&T Clark, 2019).

23. Willitts, "Davidic Messiahship," 160.

The messiahship of Jesus features differently in each letter, however, depending on the particular issue at stake. (For this reason, I take exception to Willitts's claim that Paul "has not said anything in Galatians that he did not say elsewhere."[24]) In Galatians, where there is a heated dispute concerning the grounds on which gentiles may be reckoned as children of Abraham (Gal 3:7; 4:22), Paul explicates his messiah Christology with the curious claim that σπέρμα Ἀβραάμ ἐστιν Χριστός, "The seed of Abraham is the messiah" (Gal 3:16). This claim is curious because at one level it is entirely uncontroversial, even tautologous, while at another level (the one that comprises the rhetorical context of the letter) it is quite radical. The messiah ben David is self-evidently a descendant of Abraham (inasmuch as all descendants of David are descendants of Abraham), but Paul takes this truism to imply that gentiles-in-Christ are, as such, children of Abraham in good standing and therefore need not—indeed, must not—join the people Israel in the conventional way.[25] As ever, Paul's Christ is the messiah son of David, but in Galatians the crucial move is the claim that this messiah ben David is also the messiah ben Abraham.

---

24. Willitts, "Davidic Messiahship," 152.

25. On Paul's reasoning here, see Matthew Thiessen, *Paul and the Gentile Problem* (New York: Oxford University Press, 2016), 129–60.

8

# THE CLASSICAL RHETORICAL IDIOM
# "GOD IS WITNESS" IN ITS PAULINE USAGE

Five times in the undisputed letters Paul invokes God as guarantor of the truth of a claim with a form of the phrase θεὸς μάρτυς, "God is witness" (Rom 1:9; 2 Cor 1:23; Phil 1:8; 1 Thess 2:5, 10).[1] These sayings present a problem for interpretation in that their exact rhetorical force is not immediately clear; there is more than one way in which God might be understood to function as a witness in these contexts. A few interpreters of Paul have noticed this point of ambiguity, but no one has yet given close attention to the Greek rhetorical tradition of divine testimony as a plausible context for these Pauline sayings.[2] This bibliographical anomaly provides the occasion for this essay.

Methodologically, I follow that school of thought that Margaret Mitchell has called historical rhetorical criticism, which is to be distinguished from the New Rhetoric and other synchronic forms of analysis.[3] In a variation on Mitchell's

1. Twice Paul writes μάρτυς μού [ἐστιν] ὁ θεός, "God is my witness" (Rom 1:9; Phil 1:8); twice simply θεὸς μάρτυς, "God is witness" (1 Thess 2:5, 10); and once the more elaborate ἐγὼ δὲ μάρτυρα τὸν θεὸν ἐπικαλοῦμαι ἐπὶ τὴν ἐμὴν ψυχήν, "I call upon God as witness upon my life" (2 Cor 1:23). The full text and context of each of these sayings are provided and discussed below. All translations are my own unless otherwise noted.

2. Commentators have usually pointed to Israelite oaths as parallels, while rhetorical critics have usually focused on other formal issues (esp. τάξις or arrangement) rather than on particular figures of speech like this one.

3. See Margaret M. Mitchell, *Paul and the Rhetoric of Reconciliation: An Exegetical Investigation of the Language and Composition of 1 Corinthians* (Tübingen: Mohr Siebeck, 1991), 6: "The rhetoric of [Paul] will be studied in the light of the Greco-Roman rhetorical tradition which was operative and pervasive at the time of the letter's composition. Thus the re-

approach, I follow Stanley Stowers in applying historical rhetorical criticism not only to whole literary units but also to smaller forms.[4] My thesis is that the Pauline phrase "God is witness" is not a self-imprecatory oath at all, but rather a figure of speech with roots in the rhetoric of classical Greece and a long tradition in postclassical pagan, Jewish, and Christian literature.[5] In this figure of speech, God is not testifying against Paul in case Paul should default on a promise; rather, God is testifying for Paul that Paul's character can be trusted.

### SELF-IMPRECATORY OATHS?

Commentators have long identified the Pauline "God is witness" sayings as self-imprecatory oaths after a pattern attested in the Hebrew Bible. For example, Ernst Käsemann comments on Rom 1:9 ("God is my witness . . . that unceasingly I remember you always in my prayers") that its literary form is an "oath, which occurs in 1 Sam 12:6 LXX and which is a common formula in Paul."[6] C. K. Barrett comments on the same verse that it represents "an Old Testament form of asseveration."[7] Likewise, Gordon Fee writes about Phil 1:8 ("God is my witness that I long for you all in the affection of Christ Jesus") that it is a "mild oath" whose form "probably derives from the OT practice of calling on God as witness between two parties."[8] Examples might be multiplied, but these are sufficient to illustrate a pattern of interpretation.[9] According to

---

sources drawn upon in reconstructing this rhetorical tradition are the ancient Greco-Roman handbooks, speeches and letters themselves." On the New Rhetoric, see Chaim Perelman and Lucie Olbrechts-Tyteca, *The New Rhetoric: A Treatise on Argumentation* (Notre Dame: University of Notre Dame Press, 1969).

4. For a model of the micro-rhetorical-critical approach that I take here, see Stanley K. Stowers, *The Diatribe and Paul's Letter to the Romans*, SBLDS 57 (Chico, CA: Scholars Press, 1981).

5. Per convention, and despite the ideological liabilities of the word, I use "pagan" as a shorthand term for the enormous variety of Greek and Roman cultural traditions that are neither Jewish nor Christian.

6. Ernst Käsemann, *Commentary on Romans* (Grand Rapids: Eerdmans, 1980), 18.

7. C. K. Barrett, *A Commentary on the Epistle to the Romans*, HNTC (New York: Harper & Row, 1957), 24.

8. Gordon D. Fee, *Paul's Letter to the Philippians*, NICNT (Grand Rapids: Eerdmans, 1995), 93–94.

9. More recent examples include Frank J. Matera, *II Corinthians: A Commentary*, NTL (Louisville: Westminster John Knox, 2003), 57; Robert Jewett, *Romans: A Commentary*, Hermeneia (Minneapolis: Fortress, 2007), 120; Victor Paul Furnish, *1 Thessalonians, 2 Thessalonians*, ANTC (Abingdon: Nashville, 2007), 55; John Reumann, *Philippians: A New Translation with Introduction and Commentary*, AYB (New Haven: Yale University Press, 2008), 120–121.

this pattern of interpretation, when Paul says, "God is my witness," what he means is, "May God testify against me if what I am saying is false."

There is certainly precedent for such an idiom in the Hebrew Bible.[10] Distributed across the Torah, Prophets, and Writings are a number of instances in which people appeal to God as a witness between or against parties in the striking of promissory agreements. So in Gen 31:50, Laban makes a pact with Jacob saying, "If you abuse my daughters, or if you take wives in addition to my daughters, although no one is with us, see, God is witness between me and you (אלהים עד ביני ובינך)."[11] The sense of the statement אלהים עד, "God is witness," is determined by the conditional clause אם תענה . . . ואם תקח, "If you abuse . . . and if you take"; that is, God will testify against Jacob in case Jacob should violate the agreement.

Likewise in Jer 42, in the wake of the Babylonian conquest of Judah, the remnant of the people ask Jeremiah what they should do, promising to abide by whatever word God sends:

יהי יהוה בנו לעד אמת ונאמן אם לא ככל הדבר אשר ישלחך יהוה אלהיך
אלינו כן נעשׂה

"May YHWH be a true and faithful witness against us if we do not act according to all the word with which YHWH your God sends you to us" (Jer 42:5). The Greek translator renders the expression very closely: ἔστω κύριος ἐν ἡμῖν εἰς μάρτυρα δίκαιον καὶ πιστόν, εἰ μὴ κατὰ πάντα τὸν λόγον, ὃν ἂν ἀποστείλῃ

---

The traction of this interpretation is due in part to Gustav Stählin's oft-cited 1962 article "Zum Gebrauch von Beteuerungsformeln im Neuen Testament," *NovT* 5 (1962): 115–143, here 132: "Mit dieser Art von Selbstrechtfertigung vor den Seinen . . . tritt Paulus in die Fussstapfen Samuels [1 Sam 12:5]. Die hier skizzierte Szene zeigt zugleich den juristischen Vorgang, in dem die Formel μάρτυς μου ὁ θεός ihren Ursprung hat. Verwandt mit ihr sind auch die Formeln der Vertragsszenen in [Gen 31:50; 1 Sam 20:23, 42; Judg 11:10; Josh 22:22]. . . . Paulus steht mit seinem Zeugenaufruf Gottes also einerseits ganz auf dem Boden des Alten Testaments."

10. But not only in the Hebrew Bible. For a parallel in classical Greek tragedy, cf. Euripides, *Hipp.* 1028–1031: ἦ τἄρ' ὀλοίμην ἀκλεὴς ἀνώνυμος / [ἄπολις ἄοικος, φυγὰς ἀλητεύων χθόνα,] / καὶ μήτε πόντος μήτε γῆ δέξαιτό μου / σάρκας θανόντος, εἰ κακὸς πέφυκ' ἀνήρ, "May I perish with no name or reputation, / [citiless, homeless, wandering the earth an exile] / and may neither sea nor earth receive / my body when I am dead if I am guilty!" (text and trans. David Kovacs, *Euripides*, LCL (Cambridge, MA: Harvard University Press, 1995). On ancient Greek oaths, see the essays in *Oaths and Swearing in Ancient Greece*, ed. Alan H. Sommerstein and Isabelle C. Torrance (Berlin: de Gruyter, 2014). As Sommerstein and Torrance point out, formal Greek oaths, like Israelite ones, invariably include a conditional self-imprecation, either explicit (μὰ Δία, "by Zeus!"; μὰ τοὺς θεούς, "by the gods!") or implicit (ναὶ μὰ τόν, "surely, by [Zeus]!"; ὄμνυμι, "I swear").

11. Gen 31:50 LXX has a minus here, lacking an equivalency for the clause.

σε κύριος πρὸς ἡμᾶς, οὕτως ποιήσομεν (Jer 49:5 OG). Here, as in the oath between Laban and Jacob, God is invoked as witness against a party in case that party should fail to carry out a promised future course of action (MT אל סא . . . השׁען; OG εἰ μὴ . . . ποιήσομεν; "if we do not do").[12]

In 1 Sam 20:12 the same idiom is implied, albeit without the word עד, "witness." There Jonathan promises David that he will inquire after his father Saul's attitude toward David, saying, יהוה אלהי ישׂראל כי אחקר את אבי, literally, "YHWH the God of Israel, that I will sound out my father." The Greek translator supplies the verb οἶδεν, so: κύριος ὁ θεὸς Ισραηλ οἶδεν ὅτι ἀνακρινῶ τὸν πατέρα μου, "The Lord God of Israel knows that I will sound out my father" (1 Kgdms 20:12).[13] In favor of reading this as an ellipsis for our oath formula is the following verse, where Jonathan adds a self-imprecation:

כה יעשׂה יהוה ליהונתן וכה יסיף

"May YHWH do the same to Jonathan, and even more," in case Jonathan should fail to alert David to danger from Saul's hand.[14] Here, as in the instances cited above, God is named as witness to future acts to be undertaken in fulfillment of a promise. The form of the sayings is conditional: "if you mistreat my daughters," "if we do not do as you say," "if I do not inform you." If these circumstances should obtain, if one party should default on her promise, then God will be witness against that party that she is guilty.

In an extension of this idiom, there are a few places at which God is named as witness against a party not in case of future wrongdoing but rather for past wrongdoing. For example, Jeremiah's letter to Babylon in Jer 29:1–23 includes a condemnation of two false prophets, about whose many crimes the oracle

---

12. Judg 11:10 may also be relevant here. There the Gileadites accept Jephthah's terms for going to war against the Ammonites saying,

יהוה יהיה שׁמע בינותינו אם לא כדברך כן נעשׂה

"YHWH will be a hearer between us if we do not do according to your word" (Judg 11:10). It is significant that this passage does not use עד, "witness," but rather the qal participle of שׁמע, "to hear"; so either, if substantive, "YHWH will be a hearer" (cf. OG κύριος ἔσται ὁ ἀκούων), or, if periphrastic, "YHWH will hear." The NRSV translates, "The LORD will be witness," but when שׁמע is used elsewhere in judicial contexts, the person who does the hearing is not the witness but rather the judge (as in "to hear a case" [cf. Deut 1:17; 2 Sam 14:17; 1 Kgs 3:11; Job 31:35]). If so, then God is perhaps not a witness at all in this passage.

13. The RSV assumes an implied עד, "witness," so "The LORD, the God of Israel, be witness!" The NRSV, more economically, translates "By the LORD, the God of Israel!"

14. Rendered in the optative mood in 1 Kgdms 20:13: τάδε ποιήσαι ὁ θεὸς τῷ Ιωναθαν καὶ τάδε προσθείη.

says, ואנכי הוידע ועד נאם יהוה, "I am the one who knows,[15] and I am witness, says YHWH" (Jer 29:23). Either due to a textual minus or a condensed translation, Jer 36:23 OG lacks an equivalency for הוידע, reading simply ἐγὼ μάρτυς, φησὶν κύριος, "I am witness, says the Lord." The force of the idiom, however, is unaffected by this difference. God is a witness against these wrongdoers by virtue of his having knowledge of their crimes. This is also the sense of the prophetic oracles at Mic 1:2 ("Hear, all you peoples, listen, O earth and all that is in it, let the Lord YHWH be a witness against you [ויהי אדני יהוה בכם לעד; OG ἔσται κύριος ἐν ὑμῖν εἰς μαρτύριον]") and Mal 3:5 ("I will draw near to you for judgment, I will be a swift witness [והייתי עד ממהר; OG ἔσομαι μάρτυς ταχύς] against the sorcerers, against the adulterers," etc.). With Jer 29:23, these passages attest a form of the idiom used in oracles of judgment wherein God is spoken of as both judge and witness, both the executor of the sentence and the one who confirms the guilt of the guilty.

There are two possible exceptions to this otherwise consistent pattern. At 1 Sam 12:5, in Samuel's speech ceding authority to the newly coronated Saul, Samuel insists that he has been upright in all his dealings with the nation. He says, עד יהוה בכם ועד משיחו היום הזה כי לא מצאתם בידי מאומה, "YHWH is witness against you, and his anointed is witness this day, that you have not found anything in my hand." The Greek translator renders closely: μάρτυς κύριος ἐν ὑμῖν καὶ μάρτυς χριστὸς αὐτοῦ σήμερον ἐν ταύτῃ τῇ ἡμέρᾳ ὅτι οὐχ εὑρήκατε ἐν χειρί μου οὐθέν (1 Kgdms 12:5). Here God is called upon to vindicate Samuel, not to condemn him. Formally, however, even here God is a witness against a party: "YHWH is witness against you (בכם; but cf. OG ἐν ὑμῖν)." That is, Samuel's vindication consists in God's condemning the Israelites if they should try to falsely accuse him. The only genuine exception, then, is Job 16:19, where Job protests his innocence to his friends, saying that God will vouch for his upright manner of life: גם עתה הנה בשמים עדי ושהדי במרומים, "Even now, behold, my witness is in heaven; my advocate is on high." Likewise in Greek: καὶ νῦν ἰδοὺ ἐν οὐρανοῖς ὁ μάρτυς μου, ὁ δὲ συνίστωρ μου ἐν ὑψίστοις (Job 16:19 OG). Here God is a witness for Job, not against him.[16] Everywhere else, though, God is a witness between parties by being a witness against either party in case it should violate the agreement.[17]

15. The *ketiv* here, as per my citation of BHS above, is הוידע, but the *qere* is היודע, hence "the one who knows." It may be that this textual problem accounts for the minus in the OG.

16. The exception represented by Job 16:19, like the converse case of Euripides, *Hipp.* 1028–1031 (n. 10 above), shows that this is not simply a case of a Semitic idiom versus a Greek one.

17. On self-imprecatory oath formulae in the Hebrew Bible, see further Paul Sanders, "So May God Do To Me!" *Bib* 85 (2004): 91–98.

Not surprisingly, this figure of speech endures after the biblical period, as well. So in *Testament of Levi* (ca. second century BCE), the dying patriarch charges his sons to live according to the law of the Lord. Upon their promise to do so, Levi names a series of witnesses to the vow: μάρτυς κύριος, καὶ μάρτυρες οἱ ἄγγελοι αὐτοῦ, καὶ μάρτυς ἐγώ, καὶ μάρτυρες ὑμεῖς περὶ τοῦ λόγου τοῦ στόματος ὑμῶν, "The Lord is witness, and his angels are witnesses, and I am witness, and you are witnesses concerning the word of your mouth" (*T. Levi* 19:3).[18] In keeping with the biblical pattern, the point of these witnesses is that they can testify against the oath-takers in case they fail to make good on their promise. It is clear that the Israelite self-imprecatory oath has a rich biblical and post-biblical history. The question is whether, in our five passages, Paul participates in this history.[19]

## THE PAULINE "GOD IS WITNESS" SAYINGS

In the epistolary opening of the Letter to the Romans, following the greeting, Paul begins with thanksgiving for the renowned faith of the believers in Rome.[20] It is in the context of this thanksgiving that he assures his hearers of their place in his prayers: μάρτυς γάρ μού ἐστιν ὁ θεός . . . ὡς ἀδιαλείπτως μνείαν ὑμῶν ποιοῦμαι, "God is my witness . . . that unceasingly I remember you always in my prayers" (Rom 1:9). Paul names God as his μάρτυς, in this case with the simple copulative ἐστίν; formally, this is a statement of fact, not an appeal. Also, μάρτυς is modified by the first person possessive pronoun; God is Paul's witness. The thing to which God is witness is Paul's constant remembrance of the Romans in prayer. This relation is expressed with ὡς plus an independent clause, where ὡς functions essentially like ὅτι, introducing the fact, not (as the English "how" might suggest) the degree of the sentiment

18. Greek text ed. Marinus de Jonge, *Testamenta xii patriarcharum*, 2nd ed., PVTG 1 (Leiden: Brill, 1970).

19. The assumption that he does so has raised questions about ethical positions on oath-taking in different quarters of the early Jesus movement. As is well known, both the Gospel of Matthew (5:34) and the Epistle of James (5:12) are sharply critical of oath-taking. If the Pauline "God is witness" sayings are oaths, then apparently Paul either does not know, disagrees with, or fails to comply with this tradition (see, e.g., James D. G. Dunn, *Romans 1–8*, WBC [Dallas: Word, 1988], 28). If these Pauline sayings are not oaths, though, then the observation is not really to the point.

20. On the Pauline thanksgivings generally, see Paul Schubert, *The Form and Function of the Pauline Thanksgivings* (Berlin: Töpelmann, 1939); and Peter T. O'Brien, *Introductory Thanksgivings in the Letters of Paul*, NovTSup 49 (Leiden: Brill, 1977).

expressed.[21] In short, Paul expresses his desire to visit his hearers by informing them of the content of his prayers, concerning which God, who alone hears them, is the only qualified witness.

The "God is witness" saying in Phil 1:8 is very much like that in Rom 1:9. It, too, falls in the thanksgiving section of the epistolary opening and functions to verify the apostle's goodwill toward his hearers. Paul has great confidence in God's work among the Philippian believers (1:6), who are his co-participants in grace and whom he holds in his heart (1:7). In fact, Paul writes, μάρτυς γάρ μου ὁ θεὸς ὡς ἐπιποθῶ πάντας ὑμᾶς ἐν σπλάγχνοις Χριστοῦ Ἰησοῦ, "God is my witness that I long for you all in the affection of Christ Jesus" (1:8). Here, as in Rom 1:9, God is named as Paul's witness using the copulative and the possessive pronoun. Here, too, the thing attested is introduced by ὡς expressing "that-ness." In Phil 1:8, though, the thing attested is not the content of a prayer but rather a particular emotion; God can testify that Paul feels profound affection for the believers in Philippi. Paul's emotions, like his prayers, are things that God is in a unique position to know; therefore God is the appropriate witness to the claim.

First Thessalonians 2 contains a pair of "God is witness" sayings in close proximity. Following the epistolary introduction, 1 Thess 2:1–12 comprises an extended defense of the uprightness of Paul's ministry in Thessalonica.[22] He comments in some detail on the various virtues that he practiced and vices that he shunned while he was among the Thessalonians. For example, Paul says, so far from any error, uncleanness, or guile (2:3), he behaved like a nurse tending to her children (2:7). It is in this context that Paul makes a twofold denial in 2:5: Οὔτε γάρ ποτε ἐν λόγῳ κολακείας ἐγενήθημεν, καθὼς οἴδατε, "We did not ever come in a word of flattery, as you know"; οὔτε ἐν προφάσει πλεονεξίας, θεὸς μάρτυς, "nor [did we come] in a pretext of greed, God is witness." Here καθὼς οἴδατε, "as you know," and θεὸς μάρτυς, "God is witness," are parallel

---

21. See BDAG, s.v. ὡς 5; LSJ, s.v. ὡς B.I; Smyth §§2577, 2578.c, 2579, 3000. Cf. Homer, *Od.* 5.423; Andocides 2.14; Isocrates, *Ad Nic.* 3; *Nic.* 10; *Big.* 11, 15; Aeschines, *Fals. leg.* 35; Demosthenes, *Timocr.* 139; Thucydides 3.88; 5.45; Xenophon, *Mem.* 1.1.1; *Cyr.* 5.4.20. For a discussion of the Pauline instances, see O'Brien, *Introductory Thanksgivings*, 214n75.

22. There continues to be a lively debate whether 1 Thess 2:1–12 is an *apologia* in response to actual accusations brought by actual opponents (see the discussion among Karl P. Donfried, Rudolf Hoppe, Traugott Holtz, Johan S. Vos, Otto Merk, and Jeffrey A. D. Weima in *The Thessalonians Debate*, ed. Karl P. Donfried and Johannes Beutler [Grand Rapids: Eerdmans, 2000], 31–131). As Abraham Malherbe has shown, however, it is at least not necessarily so. Formally, 1 Thess 2:1–12 is very much along the lines of the self-presentations of the popular philosophers, and so may simply reflect a standard rhetorical means of communicating the teacher's goodwill toward his disciples (see Abraham J. Malherbe, "'Gentle as a Nurse': The Cynic Background to 1 Thessalonians 2," *NovT* 12 [1970]: 203–17; Malherbe, *The Letters to the Thessalonians*, AB [New York: Doubleday, 2000], 153–63).

expressions. Because they heard Paul's words, the Thessalonians can attest that Paul did not speak flatteringly, and God, because he knows Paul's motives, can attest that he harbored no secret hope of getting rich.

Again in 1 Thess 2:10 Paul writes more generally, ὑμεῖς μάρτυρες καὶ ὁ θεός, ὡς ὁσίως καὶ δικαίως καὶ ἀμέμπτως ὑμῖν τοῖς πιστεύουσιν ἐγενήθημεν, "You and God are witnesses that we came to you believers in holiness and righteousness and blamelessness." Here God and the Thessalonians are co-witnesses to the same thing—namely, the total uprightness of Paul's pattern of life among them. In 2:5 the designation of God as witness is syntactically independent, while in 2:10 we find the familiar ὡς plus independent clause expressing the thing attested. In neither case does Paul use the first person possessive pronoun, as he does in Rom 1:9 and Phil 1:8, and in both cases God is a co-witness along with the addressees themselves.

It is fitting to discuss 2 Cor 1:23 last of all because of its formal differences from the other four sayings. Like them, it falls near the beginning of the letter, although (as in 1 Thessalonians) not technically in the epistolary introduction. On the heels of the introduction proper (1:1–11), Paul turns to explain his decision not to visit Corinth as he had originally planned. "I wanted to come to you first" (1:15), he assures the Corinthians, but the course of events has belied this intention, and the apostle's delinquency has apparently raised questions about his character. Is he guilty of ἐλαφρία, "vacillation," in his dealings with the Corinthians (1:17)? No, Paul insists, there was an honorable reason for his delay: φειδόμενος ὑμῶν οὐκέτι ἦλθον εἰς Κόρινθον, "In order to spare you I did not yet come to Corinth" (1:23). But it is not just the apostle's word against the Corinthians' suspicions in this matter. Paul prefaces his explanation with an invocation of a divine witness: Ἐγὼ δὲ μάρτυρα τὸν θεὸν ἐπικαλοῦμαι ἐπὶ τὴν ἐμὴν ψυχήν, "I call upon God as witness upon my life" that concern for the Corinthians was the reason for the delay.

Despite the familiar "God is witness" motif, 2 Cor 1:23 differs from our other passages in several important respects. Only here does Paul formally invoke (ἐπικαλοῦμαι) God as μάρτυς, rather than simply identifying him as such.[23] Only here is the thing witnessed to introduced by ὅτι rather than ὡς.[24] As in 1 Thess 2:5, the thing attested is an intention or motive, something that the addressees had no way of knowing but that God did. Last of all, only in 2 Cor 1:23 does a participial phrase qualify μάρτυς—namely, ἐπὶ τὴν ἐμὴν

---

23. Cf. Lucian, *Phal.* 1.1: καλῶ δὲ ὧν ἐρῶ τὸν θεὸν αὐτὸν μάρτυρα, "I call upon the god himself as witness"; Josephus, *Ant.* 1.243: ἐπικαλοῦνται τὸν θεὸν μάρτυρα, "They call upon God as witness" (on both of which, see further below).

24. But on the negligible difference, see O'Brien, *Introductory Thanksgivings*, 214n75.

ψυχήν, literally "upon my life." The translation of the preposition is a problem that bears heavily on the question of the meaning of the saying as a whole. Both the RSV and the NRSV, reading the verse as a self-imprecatory oath, translate ἐπί as "against." The commentaries tend to agree. Frank Matera translates, "I call upon God as my witness—staking my life on this," and explains, "The sense is that if Paul is speaking falsely, then let God take his life."[25] Likewise Jan Lambrecht comments, "The clause means that he is willing to give his life in case he is not telling the truth."[26]

The formal differences from our other four passages are significant. The explicit invocation and, even more so, the self-referential participial phrase have been reason for many interpreters to read this verse as a variation on the Israelite self-imprecatory oath. But even these features are not decisive. The invocation ἐπικαλοῦμαι is not determinative, since it is attested in "God is witness" sayings that are not self-imprecatory oaths.[27] As for the participial phrase ἐπὶ τὴν ἐμὴν ψυχήν, it might mean "against my life" in the sense of "with my life at stake"; but it might equally well mean "concerning my life" in the sense of "concerning my way of life."[28] If the latter, it would be entirely in keeping with the pattern we have observed elsewhere, in which the apostle calls God to testify, as only God can, that his moral character in relation to the assemblies is above reproach.[29]

In light of these features of the Pauline "God is witness" sayings, while the oath interpretation has remained the dominant one, some interpreters have noticed that the category is not a perfect fit. Joseph Fitzmyer, in a note on Rom 1:9, writes, "His formulation echoes OT usage . . . [but] in this case Paul is not using a conventional formula."[30] Likewise Earl Richard, commenting on 1 Thess 2:5, can find no biblical precedent for the Pauline formula. "Paul, in a Hellenistic manner, calls on God as the only witness to the missionaries' interior motives."[31] But those who have noticed that the Pauline sayings do not fit the biblical pattern have not pursued the question further to identify a

---

25. Matera, *II Corinthians*, 57.

26. Jan Lambrecht, *Second Corinthians*, SP (Collegeville, MN: Liturgical Press, 1999), 30.

27. E.g., Lucian, *Phal.* 1.1, on which see further below.

28. For both senses of ἐπί with the accusative, see Smyth §1689 3.d.

29. The pattern established by the other four passages makes this reading of 2 Cor 1:23 compelling, in my view, but the possibility remains that it is an exception.

30. Joseph A. Fitzmyer, *Romans*, AB (New York: Doubleday, 1993), 245.

31. Earl J. Richard, *First and Second Thessalonians*, SP (Collegeville, MN: Liturgical Press, 1995), 81, but without further specifying the "Hellenistic manner" of Paul's turn of phrase.

more fitting linguistic context for them. When such an inquiry is undertaken, however, it turns out that a fitting linguistic context presents itself.

## DIVINE TESTIMONY IN THE GRECO-ROMAN RHETORICAL TRADITION

As is well known, the testimony of witnesses (μάρτυρες) was a prominent feature of the Athenian legal system in which the forms of argument that would become hallmarks of Greco-Roman rhetoric were first developed.[32] The function of the μάρτυς was to stand and speak in verification of a claim made by the speaker who summoned him. So in the speeches the calling of the witness is often prefixed by ὅτι ταῦτ᾽ ἀληθῆ λέγω, "To prove that I am telling the truth," or the like. One example from a forensic context is Lysias 1.29, where the defendant Euphiletus claims that the man he killed, Eratosthenes, had admitted his guilt in the presence of Euphiletus and his neighbors. In support of this claim, Euphiletus summons some of those who heard the confession: καί μοι ἀνάβητε τούτων μάρτυρες, "Will my witnesses to these things come forward?" (29).[33] The words of the witnesses are not preserved in the text of Lysias; it is the fact of their testimony, the content of which is understood to be identical with the speaker's claim, that matters.

The summoning of witnesses is a standard feature not only of forensic but also of deliberative rhetoric. So, for example, in Demosthenes's *On the Crown*, Demosthenes levels a charge of treason at his opponent Aeschines, claiming that he was caught meeting with the Macedonian spy Anaxinus. Not content to let such a charge stand on its own, Demosthenes says, καὶ ὅτι ταῦτ᾽ ἀληθῆ λέγω, κάλει μοι τούτων τοὺς μάρτυρας, "To prove that I am telling the truth, please call my witnesses of these things" (*De Cor.* 137).[34] Here, as in Lysias, the words of the witnesses are not preserved; the point is that they said what Demosthenes had said, thereby verifying it.

---

32. See the treatments of S. H. Humphreys, "Social Relations on Stage: Witnesses in Classical Athens," *History and Anthropology* 1 (1985): 313–69; David C. Mirhady, "Athens' Democratic Witnesses," *Phoenix* 56 (2002): 255–74. As happened with other features of classical Athenian rhetoric, this rhetorical *practice* was codified for purposes of rhetorical *training* and subsequently received as a feature of the rhetorical *culture* that flourished in Greco-Roman antiquity.

33. Greek text ed. Umberto Albini, *Lisia. I discorsi* (Florence: Sansoni, 1955).

34. Greek text ed. S. H. Butcher, *Demosthenis orationes*, 3 vols. (Oxford: Clarendon, 1903; repr. 1966).

As this last example shows, witnesses are often employed where the quality of a person's character is under consideration. Such cases are especially relevant for our purposes, since this is precisely the issue in all five Pauline "God is witness" sayings. Another good example is Demosthenes, *De Cor.* 267–268, where Demosthenes demonstrates the uprightness of his public life by recounting his many liturgies on behalf of the city. These he substantiates not by summoning live witnesses (μάρτυρες) but by having the clerk read written testimonies (μαρτυρίαι). After the μαρτυρίαι, the text of which has not come down to us, are read aloud, Demosthenes concludes plainly, Ἐν μὲν τοίνυν τοῖς πρὸς τὴν πόλιν τοιοῦτος, "Such is my character in matters pertaining to the city" (*De Cor.* 268). That is, the testimonies to his particular public services bear out his claim to be a beneficent person.

Greek μάρτυρες included not only live human beings and their written statements; the gods were thought to be as qualified, or more so, to give official testimony.[35] The testimony of the gods often came in the form of oracles (μαντεῖαι or χρησμοί). So, for example, in Aeschines's *Against Ctesiphon*, the speech to which Demosthenes's *On the Crown* is a response, Aeschines relates a version of Demosthenes's career that amounts to a litany of offenses against the people of Athens and the gods. In one place, Aeschines charges that Demosthenes sinned against Apollo by accepting a bribe from the people of Amphissa, who were illegally farming the plain of Cirra, a place that the Pythia at Delphi had said should lie fallow as consecrated ground. In support of this charge, Aeschines asks that the actual text of the oracle in question be read aloud in the assembly:[36] Ὅτι δ᾽ ἀληθῆ λέγω, ἀνάγνωθι τὴν τοῦ θεοῦ μαντείαν, "To prove that I am telling the truth, please read the oracle of the god" (*Ctes.* 112).[37] That is, Aeschines invokes a divine testimony in oracular form, the authority of which is recognized by the assembly.

The earliest major rhetorical handbook, Aristotle's *Rhetoric*, does not address the testimonies of the gods, but it does give pride of place to the "testimonies of the ancients."[38] Under the heading of ἄτεχνοι πίστεις, "inartistic

---

35. See Donald B. King, "The Appeal to Religion in Greek Rhetoric," *CJ* 50 (1955): 363–76.

36. In this case, the MSS actually preserve the text of an oracle at this point, but it is almost certainly a later addition borrowed from Pausanias's account of the Cirra incident (Pausanias, *Descr.* 10.37.6).

37. Greek text ed. V. Martin and G. de Budé, *Eschine. Discours*, vol. 2 (Paris: Belles Lettres, 1928; repr. 1962).

38. The relation of Aristotle's handbook to the actual practice of the classical lawcourts is a difficult question, but see J. C. Trevett, "Aristotle's Knowledge of Athenian Oratory," *CQ* 46 (1996): 371–79.

proofs," Aristotle includes a section on μάρτυρες. These he groups into two classes, ancient and recent, the former being generally more reliable than the latter and alone qualified to speak to the moral quality of an act:[39]

περὶ δὲ μαρτύρων, μάρτυρές εἰσιν διττοί, οἱ μὲν παλαιοὶ οἱ δὲ πρόσφατοι, καὶ τούτων οἱ μὲν μετέχοντες τοῦ κινδύνου οἱ δ' ἐκτός. λέγω δὲ παλαιοὺς μὲν τούς τε ποιητὰς καὶ ὅσων ἄλλων γνωρίμων εἰσὶν κρίσεις φανεραί.

Concerning witnesses: Witnesses are of two kinds: ancient and recent; and of the latter, some share the risk [of being brought to trial] while others do not. I call "ancient witnesses" the poets and any other well-known persons whose judgments are clear. (Aristotle, *Rhet.* 1.15.13)

καὶ οἱ μετέχοντες τοῦ κινδύνου, ἂν δόξωσι ψεύδεσθαι. οἱ μὲν οὖν τοιοῦτοι τούτων μόνον μάρτυρές εἰσιν, εἰ γέγονεν ἢ μή, εἰ ἔστιν ἢ μή, περὶ δὲ τοῦ ποῖον οὐ μάρτυρες, οἷον εἰ δίκαιον ἢ ἄδικον, εἰ συμφέρον ἢ ἀσύμφορον· οἱ δ' ἄπωθεν περὶ τούτων πιστότεροι, πιστότατοι δ' οἱ παλαιοί· ἀδιάφθοροι γάρ.

There are some [recent witnesses] who share the risk [of being brought to trial], if they should appear to perjure themselves. Such persons are only witnesses of whether or not something has happened—that is, whether or not something is the case; they are not witnesses to the quality of the act—of whether it was just or unjust, or whether it conferred advantage or not. On such matters, outsiders are more credible witnesses, and ancient ones the most credible; for they are incorruptible. (Aristotle, *Rhet.* 1.15.16–17)

Ideal ancient witnesses, Aristotle explains, are figures like Homer and Solon, "well-known persons whose judgments are clear." Such figures are wise enough in their own right and distant enough from the events of a case to give trustworthy judgments on the quality of acts. They are especially qualified to act as witnesses because they are ἀδιάφθοροι, "incorruptible."

What Aristotle calls παλαιοὶ μάρτυρες, "ancient witnesses," the first-century CE Roman rhetorician Quintilian calls *auctoritates*, "authorities," and among them he expressly includes *divina testimonia*, "the testimonies of the gods." Quintilian writes:[40]

---

39. Greek text ed. W. D. Ross, *Aristotelis ars rhetorica* (Oxford: Clarendon, 1959; repr. 1964).

40. Latin text ed. Michael Winterbottom, *M. Fabi Quintiliani Institutionis oratoriae libri duodecim*, 2 vols. (Oxford: Clarendon, 1970).

Ponitur a quibusdam, et quidem in parte prima, deorum auctoritas, quae
est ex responsis, ut "Socraten esse sapientissimum." Id rarum est, non sine
usu tamen. . . . Quae cum propria causae sunt, divina testimonia vocantur,
cum aliunde arcessuntur, argumenta.

Under this head, and even as the first item, some put the authority of the
gods, which is derived from oracles, like the one that said that Socrates
was the wisest of people [Plato, *Apol.* 21A]. This is rare, but nevertheless
useful. . . . When these belong to the cause, they are called "divine testimonies"; when adduced from elsewhere, they are "arguments." (Quintilian,
*Inst.* 5.11.42)

Lest the clarity of the *divina testimonia* be obscured by haphazard appeals
not only to oracles but also to augury, astrology, and other types of less con-
trolled divination, Quintilian codifies the practice, which had been in effect at
least since the time of Demosthenes, whereby divine testimony is officially ad-
missible and rhetorically persuasive in the lawcourt and in the assembly.[41]

In light of the evidence of both the speeches and the handbooks, we may
draw a few conclusions about the divine testimony motif in the Greek rhetorical tradition. While it is by no means monolithic, certain recognizable
features do emerge. The speeches and the handbooks jointly suggest, first, the
prominence of witnesses generally in the Greek rhetorical tradition; second,
their special use in establishing the good or bad character of a speaker; and
third, the particular status accorded to ancient and divine testimonies in such

41. Elsewhere Quintilian addresses the problem of evaluating *divina testimonia*, distinguishing different types and corresponding manners of treatment: "His adicere si qui
volet ea quae divina testimonia vocant, ex responsis oraculis ominibus, duplicem sciat esse
eorum tractatum: generalem alterum, in quo inter Stoicos et Epicuri sectam secutos pugna
perpetua est regaturne providentia mundus, specialem alterum circa partis divinationum,
ut quaeque in quaestionem cadet. Aliter enim oraculorum, aliter haruspicum augurum
coniectorum mathematicorum fides confirmari aut refelli potest, cum sit rerum ipsarum
ratio diversa." "If anyone wishes to add what are called 'divine testimonies'—from responses,
oracles, and omens—he should know that there are two ways of handling these: a general
treatment, including the perpetual dispute between the Stoics and the Epicureans as to
whether the world is governed by providence, and a special treatment relevant to the type
of divination that pertains to the question. Trustworthiness is either confirmed or disproved
in one way for oracles, in another way for soothsayers, another for augurs, another for
diviners, and another for astrologers, because the principles of the things themselves are
different." (*Inst.* 5.7.35–36)

cases. Only in the context of this history can we explain the continued use of divine witness language in the Hellenistic and Roman periods.

## DIVINE TESTIMONY IN HELLENISTIC- AND ROMAN-PERIOD LITERATURE

Almost four hundred years separate Demosthenes from Paul, the orator from the apostle, but many rhetorical patterns of language survived, even thrived, from the classical into the Hellenistic and Roman periods.[42] So it is in the case of the divine testimony motif. Pagan authors certainly continued to make use of it.[43] For example, at the beginning of Lucian's *Phalaris*, the emissaries of the notorious tyrant Phalaris deliver a message to the men of Delphi, wherein Phalaris defends what sort of person he is (ὁποῖός εἰμι) against what he insists are slanderous rumors.[44] In this context, Lucian has Phalaris call Apollo as witness: καλῶ δὲ ὧν ἐρῶ τὸν θεὸν αὐτὸν μάρτυρα, "I call the god himself as witness to the things I am about to say" (*Phal.* 1.1)—namely, that Phalaris is not as wicked a person as he is reputed to be.

By the beginning of the Common Era, however, the "God is witness" motif appears rather less frequently in pagan authors like Lysias and increasingly frequently in their Jewish and Christian counterparts.[45] By the time of Paul, it is

42. The long afterlife of the classical rhetorical tradition has been well documented by George A. Kennedy, *Classical Rhetoric and Its Christian and Secular Tradition from Ancient to Modern Times*, 2nd ed. (Chapel Hill: University of North Carolina Press, 1999).

43. The idiom at Polybius 11.6.4 (ὑμεῖς δὲ τότε τοὺς θεοὺς ἐπικαλέσεσθε μάρτυρας, ὅταν μήτε τῶν θεῶν βούληται μήτε τῶν ἀνθρώπων ἔτι δύνηται βοηθεῖν ὑμῖν μηδείς, "Then you will call upon the gods as witnesses, when no god is willing, and no person able any longer to help you" [Greek text ed. Ludwig August Dindorf and Theodorus Büttner-Wobst, *Polybii Historiae* (Stuttgart: Teubner, 1967–1985)]), while related, is not directly relevant here, since there "witness" has the sense of "helper," "witness of the wrongs one is suffering."

44. Greek text ed. A. M. Harmon, *Lucian*, vol. 1 (Cambridge, MA: Harvard University Press, 1913; repr. 1961).

45. This is not to say that forensic rhetoric, or rhetoric as a whole, fell out of use in the Roman period. The relative lack of extant forensic speeches from that period has to do with the differences between the legal systems of classical Athens and imperial Rome (on this see, e.g., Malcom Heath, *Menander: A Rhetor in Context* [Oxford: Oxford University Press, 2004]). For the persistence of the "God is witness" motif in forensic rhetoric of the Roman period, see Cicero's warning that a magistrate must not violate justice by ruling in favor of a friend if the friend is guilty: *Cum vero iurato sententia dicenda erit, meminerit deum se adhibere testem*, "When he delivers the verdict under oath, he should remember to summon

already a Jewish literary commonplace to speak of God as a witness in matters relating to character, because in such matters only God is a qualified witness. We find the idea in the para-scriptural Jewish literature of the first century BCE. The early chapters of the Wisdom of Solomon praise personified Wisdom for all her virtues. So, for example, Wis 1:6: "Wisdom is a kindly spirit, and will not free the blasphemer from his words." This is so, the sage explains, because τῶν νεφρῶν αὐτοῦ μάρτυς ὁ θεὸς καὶ τῆς καρδίας αὐτοῦ ἐπίσκοπος ἀληθὴς καὶ τῆς γλώσσης ἀκουστής, "God is the witness of his inmost thoughts, and the true overseer of his heart, and the hearer of his tongue."[46] That is, Wisdom is a just judge because God is a trustworthy witness. Whether originally composed in Hebrew or in Greek, formally this is classic Hebraic *parallelismus membrorum*, where the three phrases are mutually interpretive.[47] For God to be the μάρτυς τῶν νεφρῶν means that he is uniquely qualified to be a character witness, to vouch for or against the thoughts and intentions of the human heart.[48]

The great Jewish writers of the first century CE attest the motif as well. In his treatise *On Drunkenness*, Philo explains that Moses speaks of wine figuratively to represent five different conditions (folly, insensibility, greed, cheerfulness, and nakedness), which Philo expounds in turn. In the section on folly, Philo considers God's command to Aaron and his sons not to drink wine when they enter the tabernacle, lest they die (Lev 10:9). The tabernacle, Philo explains, represents the idea of virtue generally, and the altar particular virtues. But why, Philo wonders, is the tabernacle sometimes called σκηνὴ μαρτυρίου, the tent of witness? Perhaps, he suggests, because ὁ ἀψευδὴς θεὸς ἀρετῆς ἐστι μάρτυς, "God who does not lie is the witness of virtue" (*Ebr.* 139).[49] The ascription μάρτυς ἀρετῆς, "witness of virtue," which appears nowhere in the LXX/OG with reference to God (or anyone else, for that matter), is nevertheless very much at home in the thought of Philo.

Philo is not alone in thinking of God as the μάρτυς ἀρετῆς. In a very different context, at the conclusion of *Against Apion*, Josephus summarizes all that he

---

the god himself as witness" (*Off.* 3.10.44 [Latin text ed. C. F. W. Müller, *M. Tullii Ciceronis Scripta quae manserunt omnia recgonovit* (Leipzig: Teubner, 1879)]).

46. Greek text ed. A. Rahlfs, *Septuaginta*, 9th ed., 2 vols. (Stuttgart: Deutsche Bibelstiftung, 1935; repr. 1971).

47. For a thorough discussion concluding in favor of an entirely Greek original, see David Winston, *The Wisdom of Solomon*, AB (New York: Doubleday, 1979), 14–18.

48. Cf. Acts 15:8 (but without the formulaic θεὸς μάρτυς), where Peter says of the newly added gentile believers, ὁ καρδιογνώστης θεὸς ἐμαρτύρησεν αὐτοῖς δοὺς τὸ πνεῦμα τὸ ἅγιον καθὼς καὶ ἡμῖν, "God who knows the heart bore witness for them, giving them the holy spirit just as he did us."

49. Greek text ed. P. Wendland, *Philonis Alexandrini opera quae supersunt* (Berlin: Reimer, 1897; repr. de Gruyter, 1962).

has said to vindicate the Jews from the slanderous charges of their detractors. They say, among other things, that Moses was a vulgar person. But, Josephus counters, Moses has for his own μάρτυς ἀρετῆς first of all God and also time itself: τῷ δὲ τῆς ἀρετῆς πάλαι μὲν ὁ θεός, μετ' ἐκεῖνον δὲ μάρτυς ὁ χρόνος εὕρηται γεγενημένος, "Of [Moses's] virtue, from of old, God, and after him, time, is found to be witness" (*C. Ap.* 2.290).[50] That is, God is not only the μάρτυς ἀρετῆς in general, but particularly of Moses's ἀρετή when it is called into question.

In addition, Josephus frequently speaks of God as witness in matters of good or bad character, even in the absence of the word ἀρετή. At *Ant.* 5.113, in Josephus's retelling of the Israelite occupation of Canaan, the Reubenites, Gadites, and Manassites protest that the altar they have built is not an alternative altar from the one in the tabernacle but simply a non-functioning copy, a memorial identifying them with their kinfolk across the Jordan (cf. Josh 22:21–29). That such was their reason for building the altar, they say, μάρτυς . . . γένοιτο ὁ θεὸς ἀξιόχρεως, "may God be a sufficient witness" (*Ant.* 5.113). Josephus is unique in using the optative "may God be" here, but the content is very much in keeping with what we have seen so far. There is a moral question concerning the αἰτία, "motive," of the three tribes in building the altar. Only God can, and God in fact does, attest their righteous intention in the matter.

Again, book 1 of *Jewish War* includes an account of a conspiracy by Pheroras and Antipater to poison Herod the Great. After Pheroras has died and Herod learns of the failed plan, the king interrogates Pheroras's widow. Terrified, the woman pleads for an honest hearing from the king and from θεὸς ὁ μάρτυς ἐμοὶ τῆς ἀληθείας πλανηθῆναι μὴ δυνάμενος, "God the witness to the truth of my words who cannot be deceived" (*J.W.* 1.595). God is an ideal witness because he cannot be deceived; one thinks here of Aristotle, for whom ancient witnesses are ideal because they are ἀδιάφθοροι, "incorruptible" (*Rhet.* 1.15.17). Similarly, a bit later on in the same story, Antipater's last words before his execution are: θεός ἐστίν μοι τοῦ μηδὲν ἀδικεῖν μάρτυς, "God is my witness that I have done no wrong" (*J.W.* 1.639).

In one place Josephus even calls God to be his own μάρτυς ἀρετῆς, when his ἀρετή appears to be suspect. The famous scene in *Jewish War* in which Josephus evades his part in the suicide pact at Jotapata begins with Josephus's prayer wherein he agrees to surrender to the Romans. Since God has abandoned the Jews, and since he has chosen Josephus as his prophet to the Romans, Josephus agrees to surrender to Nicanor. But, he adds in haste, μαρτύρομαι δὲ ὡς οὐ προδότης, ἀλλὰ σὸς εἰμι διάκονος (*J.W.* 3.354). Thackeray translates aptly, "I

---

50. For Josephus, I follow the Greek text of B. Niese, *Flavii Iosephi opera* (Berlin: Weidmann, 1895; repr. 1955).

take thee to witness that I go, not as a traitor, but as thy minister."[51] While it is possible, in theory, for μαρτύρομαι to have a simple middle sense, "I testify concerning myself," in practice it almost always has the technical meaning, "I call to witness."[52] That is, the subject of the verb does not himself testify; rather, he summons someone else to do so. In Josephus's case, the verb is addressed to God. Josephus calls God to witness to his righteous motives in this (admittedly morally questionable) act. God is his μάρτυς ἀρετῆς.

There is, however, one exception in Josephus to the pattern we have identified. When Josephus tells the story of Abraham's sending a servant to secure a wife for Isaac (Gen 24:1–9), he briefly explains the Israelite custom of swearing an oath by placing one's hand under the thigh of the other party. With their hands so placed, Josephus says, ἐπικαλοῦνται τὸν θεὸν μάρτυρα τῶν ἐσομένων, "they invoke God as witness to the things they are about to do" (*Ant.* 1.243). Significant for our purposes is that Josephus speaks of God as witness in the setting of an Israelite oath. But in keeping with biblical usage, and unlike the Pauline sayings, here God is called as witness to future acts (τῶν ἐσομένων) that are promised by the parties involved. This exception, then, tends to confirm rather than undermine the rule.

We know, too, that this motif is still in use well after the first century CE. It is attested twice in the third-century CE Pseudo-Clementine Homilies. In the second homily, Nicetas assures Clement that he, Nicetas, and Aquila, although they accompanied the wicked Simon, they were not party to any of his evil deeds. Nicetas insists, μάρτυς ὁ θεὸς ὡς οὐδὲν αὐτῷ ἡμεῖς συνειργασάμεθα ἀσεβές, "God is witness that we committed no impiety together with him" (Ps.-Clem. Hom. 2.27).[53] The thirteenth homily consists largely of a long speech by Peter on chastity. In the conclusion to this speech, Peter compares adultery to murder, arguing that the former is a worse sin than the latter. In support of this claim he says, μάρτυς θεός, πολλοὶ φόνοι μοιχεία μία, "God is witness, many murders are like one act of adultery" (Ps.-Clem. Hom. 13.19). Here it is not Peter's own morals, but rather a question of moral principle, to which God is called to testify.

In the mid-fourth century CE, in a very different religious milieu, the emperor Julian wrote a *Hymn to the Mother of the Gods*, an ode to the Phrygian Cybele who was worshiped by the Romans as Magna Mater.[54] At the end of the

---

51. Josephus, *The Jewish War, Volume II: Books 3–4*, trans. H. St. J. Thackeray, LCL (Cambridge, MA: Harvard University Press, 1927).

52. See LSJ, s.v. μαρτύρομαι.

53. Greek text ed. J. Irmscher, F. Paschke, and B. Rehm, *Die Pseudoklementinen I. Homilien*, 2nd ed., GCS 42 (Berlin: Akademie Verlag, 1969).

54. On Julian's association with the cult of Cybele, see Rowland Smith, *Julian's Gods:*

hymn, the emperor excuses himself for breaking off the discourse where he does: "What then remains for us to say? Especially since it was permitted me to compose this in a breath, in a short part of a night, having neither done prior reading nor researched the subject, nor even intended to speak on these matters before asking for these writing tablets. The goddess is witness of what I say [μάρ-τυς δὲ ἡ θεός μοι τοῦ λόγου]" (*Orations* 5.19).[55] Lest the reader think that Julian left off where he did for some irresponsible reason, he protests that he wrote the whole thing in the space of a night with no prior preparation. But how can the reader know this? The goddess, the Magna Mater, is witness to what he says.

It is perhaps no surprise to find Julian, that great enthusiast of classical culture, employing this idiom of classical rhetoric. It might be less obvious to some why the apostle Paul should do so. But when we find the motif in the Jewish tradition before Paul, other Jewish writers contemporary with Paul, and Christian authors after Paul, a rhetorical context emerges in which the Pauline sayings fit quite naturally. In this rhetorical context, that of the Greco-Roman divine testimonies, the speaker names the god as a witness on his behalf. It is therefore the god, not the speaker, who swears.

## CONCLUSION

In closing, we have shown that the self-imprecatory oath is a poor fit for the rhetorical context of the Pauline "God is witness" sayings (the history of interpretation notwithstanding). In all five instances, the apostle's time reference is past rather than future. In no case does he promise to fulfill some course of action; rather, he insists upon the uprightness of his past behavior. In no case is God a witness between parties or against a party; God is always a witness for the apostle. We have seen, instead, that the Greek rhetorical tradition of divine testimonies, as it was received and adapted in Judaism of the Hellenistic and Roman periods, provides a very plausible rhetorical context for these sayings. For Paul, as for Demosthenes, Aristotle, Philo, and Josephus, when the moral quality of an act or intention is in question, a speaker may rightly appeal to the testimony of God, the only truly incorruptible witness. In such appeals, Paul is not swearing anything; rather he is inviting God to swear concerning him.

---

*Religion and Philosophy in the Thought and Action of Julian the Apostate* (London: Routledge, 1995), esp. chs. 5–6.

55. Greek text ed. G. Rochefort, *L'empereur Julien. Oeuvres complètes*, vol. 2.1 (Paris: Belles Lettres, 1963).

To put it differently, "God is witness" is close in meaning to another Pauline expression that appears in similar contexts: "God knows." An example is 2 Cor 11:11, where Paul expresses his affection for the troublesome saints in Corinth, saying, διὰ τί; ὅτι οὐκ ἀγαπῶ ὑμᾶς; ὁ θεὸς οἶδεν, "Why? Because I do not love you? God knows [that I do]." That is, though some might doubt whether Paul really loves his Corinthian auditors, God knows that he does, and God's knowing it verifies that it is so. Again, a bit further on in the same chapter, Paul relates a litany of personal weaknesses in which he ironically boasts. Lest this litany sound somehow contrived, though, Paul prefaces it thus: ὁ θεὸς καὶ πατὴρ τοῦ κυρίου Ἰησοῦ οἶδεν, ὁ ὢν εὐλογητὸς εἰς τοὺς αἰῶνας, ὅτι οὐ ψεύδομαι, "The God and father of the lord Jesus, who is blessed forever, knows that I am not lying" (2 Cor 11:31).[56]

This is not to say that Paul never takes an oath, nor that he does not invoke the name of God in self-imprecation.[57] Rather, what I have shown in this essay is that, in the five places at which Paul names God as his witness, this is not what he is doing. In these instances, Paul is participating in a rhetorical tradition as old as the Athenian assembly, one that took on a particularly monotheistic cast in the Jewish literature of the Hellenistic and Roman periods, and survived for centuries thereafter. For Paul, the God of Israel is the μάρτυς ἀρετῆς, the one uniquely qualified to vouch for one's character when it is in question.

---

56. Cf. 2 Cor 5:11: θεῷ δὲ πεφανερώμεθα· ἐλπίζω δὲ καὶ ἐν ταῖς συνειδήσεσιν ὑμῶν πεφανερῶσθαι, "We are known to God, and I hope we are also known to your consciences." Conscience, like God, is a qualified witness to such claims in Paul, as in Rom 9:1 (Ἀλήθειαν λέγω ἐν Χριστῷ, οὐ ψεύδομαι, συμμαρτυρούσης μοι τῆς συνειδήσεώς μου ἐν πνεύματι ἁγίῳ, "I am telling the truth in Christ, I am not lying, as my conscience also bears witness in the holy spirit") and 2 Cor 1:12 (τὸ μαρτύριον τῆς συνειδήσεως ἡμῶν, ὅτι ἐν ἁπλότητι καὶ εἰλικρινείᾳ τοῦ θεοῦ . . . ἀνεστράφημεν ἐν τῷ κόσμῳ, περισσοτέρως δὲ πρὸς ὑμᾶς, "the witness of our conscience that we conducted ourselves in the world, and even more so toward you, with generosity and godly sincerity").

57. Gal 1:20 may be such an expression. There Paul protests that he did not receive his apostolic commission from the pillars in Jerusalem, having visited Cephas and James only briefly. He then adds, ἃ δὲ γράφω ὑμῖν, ἰδοὺ ἐνώπιον τοῦ θεοῦ ὅτι οὐ ψεύδομαι, "In what I am writing you, look, before God, I am not lying." Because ἐνώπιον plus the genitive is sometimes used in oath formulae (e.g., with ὁρκίζω at 4 Kgdms 11:4), this may be an oath in the strict sense, albeit elliptically expressed.

# WHAT ESCHATOLOGICAL PILGRIMAGE
# OF THE GENTILES?

It shall come to pass in the latter days that the mountain of the house of the LORD shall be established as the highest of the mountains, and shall be raised above the hills; and all the nations shall flow to it, and many peoples shall come, and say: "Come, let us go up to the mountain of the LORD, to the house of the God of Jacob; that he may teach us his ways and that we may walk in his paths." (Isa 2:2–3 = Mic 4:1–2 RSV)

On this mountain the LORD of hosts will make for all peoples a feast of fat things, a feast of wine on the lees, of fat things full of marrow, of wine on the lees well refined. And he will destroy on this mountain the covering that is cast over all peoples, the veil that is spread over all nations. (Isa 25:6–7 RSV)

And the foreigners who join themselves to the LORD, to minister to him, to love the name of the LORD, and to be his servants, every one who keeps the sabbath, and does not profane it, and holds fast my covenant—these I will bring to my holy mountain, and make them joyful in my house of prayer; their burnt offerings and their sacrifices will be accepted on my altar; for my house shall be called a house of prayer for all peoples. (Isa 56:6–7 RSV)

I am coming to gather all nations and tongues; and they shall come and shall see my glory, and I will set a sign among them. And from them I will send survivors to the nations, to Tarshish, Put, and Lud, who draw the bow, to Tubal and Javan, to the coastlands afar off, that have not heard my fame or seen my glory; and they shall declare my glory among the nations. And they shall bring all your brethren from all the nations as an offering to the LORD, upon horses, and in chariots, and in litters, and upon mules, and upon dromedaries, to my holy mountain Jerusalem, says the LORD, just as the Israelites bring their cereal offering in a clean vessel to the house of the LORD. (Isa 66:18–20 RSV)

Many peoples and strong nations shall come to seek the LORD of hosts in Jerusalem, and to entreat the favor of the LORD. Thus says the LORD of hosts: In those days ten men from the nations of every tongue shall take hold of the robe of a Jew, saying, "Let us go with you, for we have heard that God is with you." (Zech 8:22–23 RSV)

Then everyone that survives of all the nations that have come against Jerusalem shall go up year after year to worship the King, the LORD of hosts, and to keep the feast of booths. (Zech 14:16 RSV)

These are all justly famous, rhetorically powerful oracles from the classical Hebrew prophets envisioning an eschatological future when gentiles will forsake their idols and their weapons of war and make pilgrimage to Jerusalem to worship the living God and learn his ways.[1] But Paul, apostle to the gentiles and a virtuosic interpreter of the prophets, cites precisely none of these texts. None at all. Not so much as an allusion or an echo.[2]

---

1. Inasmuch as no other classical prophetic texts clearly attest all of these features, this list can be said to be comprehensive. (But on the afterlives of these oracles, see further below). A very fine discussion of this whole tradition is given by Heikki Räisänen, "Zion Torah and Biblical Theology: Thoughts on a Tübingen Theory," in *Jesus, Paul, and Torah: Collected Essays*, trans. David E. Orton, JSNTSup 43 (Sheffield: Sheffield Academic, 1992), 225–51.

2. By my count. The non-occurrence of citations is demonstrable. The one near-miss is 1 Cor 15:54, where Paul quotes (what we recognize as) the Theodotian text of Isa 25:8, "Death is swallowed up in victory," but nothing from the preceding verses that mention gentile pilgrimage (Isa 25:6–7). The non-occurrence of allusions is harder to establish, but I think it is quite clear. The editors of NA28, more generous than I in this respect, identify three in their "Loci Citati vel Allegati": Isa 56:7 in Phil 4:18 ("Their burnt offerings and their sacrifices will be accepted on my altar"//"I received from Epaphroditus the gifts you sent, a fragrant offering, a sacrifice acceptable and pleasing to God"); Isa 66:20 in Rom 15:16 ("They shall bring all your brethren from all the nations as an offering to the LORD"//"[Paul's] priestly service of the gospel of God, so that the offering of the gentiles may be acceptable"); and

What are we to make of this fact? It would seem that the apostle has missed a trick. Given Paul's urgent need to justify his gentile mission,[3] these classic eschatological pilgrimage texts are low-hanging fruit, surely. And yet, Paul never avails himself of any of them. That is to say, Paul never actually makes the interpretive move that many modern critics have thought must have lay at the back of his mind. As E. P. Sanders—to cite one preeminent example—has written, "Paul's entire work, both evangelizing and collecting money, had its setting in the expected pilgrimage of the Gentiles to Mount Zion in the last days."[4]

Others before me have pointed out this curious feature of Pauline intertextuality, most importantly Terence Donaldson in his excellent 1997 book *Paul and the Gentiles*.[5] Donaldson goes on to conclude that, because Paul does not cite these texts or invoke this tradition, he must have thought of his gentile mission not as a performance of an eschatological script at all but rather as a form of Jewish proselytizing, only proselytizing for *Christ*-adherents rather

---

Zech 8:23 in 1 Cor 14:25 ("Ten men from the nations of every tongue shall take hold of the robe of a Jew, saying, 'Let us go with you, for we have heard that God is with you'"//"Falling on his face, [the unbeliever] will worship God and declare that God is really among you"). But in none of these cases would Paul have needed the supposed prophetic source text in order to say what he says. They only look like allusions if one presupposes that Paul has an eschatological gentile pilgrimage motif in mind, which is precisely the question before us.

3. On which see J. Ross Wagner, *Heralds of the Good News: Isaiah and Paul in Concert in the Letter to the Romans*, NovTSup 101 (Leiden: Brill, 2002); and John M. G. Barclay, *Paul and the Gift* (Grand Rapids: Eerdmans, 2015), 449–561.

4. E. P. Sanders, *Paul, the Law, and the Jewish People* (Philadelphia: Fortress, 1983), 171. This view is very widespread in the secondary literature, including—to cite just a few leading lights—Hans-Joachim Schoeps, *Paul: The Theology of the Apostle in the Light of Jewish Religious History*, trans. H. Knight (Philadelphia: Westminster, 1961); Ferdinand Hahn, *Mission in the New Testament*, SBT 47 (London: SCM, 1965); Halvor Moxnes, *Theology in Conflict: Studies in Paul's Understanding of God in Romans*, NovTSup 53 (Leiden: Brill, 1980); Markus Barth, *The People of God*, JSNTSup 5 (Sheffield: Sheffield Academic, 1983); Peter Stuhlmacher, *Paul's Letter to the Romans*, trans. Scott J. Hafemann (Louisville: Westminster John Knox, 1994 [German original 1989]); Karl-Wilhelm Niebuhr, *Heidenapostel aus Israel: Die jüdische Identität des Paulus nach ihrer Darstellung in seinen Briefen*, WUNT 62 (Tübingen: Mohr Siebeck, 1992); Paula Fredriksen, *Paul: The Pagans' Apostle* (New Haven: Yale University Press, 2017).

5. Terence L. Donaldson, *Paul and the Gentiles: Remapping the Apostle's Convictional World* (Minneapolis: Fortress, 1997), here 194: "Paul's statements about the Gentile mission stubbornly resist any attempt to force them into the Procrustean bed of eschatological pilgrimage patterns of thought. . . . [Note] the virtual absence of eschatological pilgrimage texts. Such texts were plenteous and close at hand. Given Paul's desire to ground the Gentile mission in scripture, there would have been plenty of opportunity to cite such texts if he had so desired."

than *Torah*-adherents.[6] I disagree with Donaldson's conclusion (because I think there are other eschatological scripts Paul might have been performing; more on this below), but we have Donaldson to thank for troubling the eschatological-pilgrimage-of-the-gentiles hypothesis, which was in need of troubling. The solution, I argue in this essay, is not to take the eschatological pilgrimage tradition as a given and to reject it (as Donaldson does), but rather to refuse to take it as a given, to interrogate and deconstruct it, and then to see what options lie open to us.

Hence the title of this essay: "*What* eschatological pilgrimage of the gentiles?" This is one of those secondary-literature stock phrases that we use thinking we know what we mean by it, but, I want to suggest, in fact we do not. The phrase papers over a great deal of actual diversity in the relevant texts from the classical prophets, few or none of which (depending how we count them) Paul himself actually cites anyway. What we have here is a conspicuous mismatch between *explanans* and *explanandum*, between the putative prophetic tradition on the one hand and the relevant Pauline texts on the other. It is this mismatch that I want to explore and, hopefully, to resolve.

To be sure, there is such a thing as an eschatological-pilgrimage-of-the-gentiles tradition, attested in a number of texts from the Second Temple period.[7] But—I would want to insist—to be deserving of the name, a text should clearly attest all three aspects: eschatology, pilgrimage, and gentiles (as the marquee oracles from Isaiah, Micah, and Zechariah cited above all do). And we find all three aspects, for instance, in Tobit's address to the city of Jerusalem in the prayer of Tob 13:

> O Jerusalem, the holy city, he will afflict you for the deeds of your sons, but again he will show mercy to the sons of the righteous. Give thanks worthily to the Lord, and praise the King of the ages, that his tent may be raised for you again with joy. May he cheer those within you who are captives, and love those within you who are distressed, to all generations for ever. Many nations will come from afar to the name of the Lord God, bearing gifts in their hands, gifts for the King of heaven. (Tob 13:9–11 RSV)

6. Donaldson, *Paul and the Gentiles*, 304: "Both before and after his conversion, he was convinced that [gentiles'] one hope of salvation was to become part of the people of Israel. His conversion can be understood as a shift from a paradigm in which membership in Israel was determined by Torah, to one in which it was determined by Christ."

7. On which see Terence L. Donaldson, *Judaism and the Gentiles: Jewish Patterns of Universalism (to 135 CE)* (Waco, TX: Baylor University Press, 2007), 670–78.

And in the Hellenistic Jewish prophecy of Sibylline Oracles 3:

> And then all the islands and cities will say . . . "Come, let us fall on the
> ground and entreat the immortal king, the great eternal God. Let us send to
> the temple, since he alone is sovereign, and let us all ponder the law of the
> Most High God." . . . From every land they will bring incense and gifts to
> the house of the great God. There will be no other house among men, even
> for future generations to know, except the one which God gave to faithful
> men to honour. (Sib. Or. 3.715–719, 772–775; trans. Collins)[8]

And probably also in a climactic scene near the end of the Animal Apocalypse:

> The Lord of the sheep brought a new house, larger and higher than the
> first one, and he erected it on the site of the first one. . . . And all the sheep
> were within it. And I saw all the sheep that remained. And all the animals
> on the earth and all the birds of heaven were falling down and worshiping
> those sheep and making petition to them and obeying them in everything.
> (1 Enoch 90:29–31; trans. Nickelsburg and VanderKam)[9]

These and other related texts have all been much discussed.[10] I take what
I think is an uncontroversial majority view that these texts carry the baton,
so to speak, of the eschatological pilgrimage of the gentiles ideal from Isaiah,
Micah, and Zechariah before them. So far, so good.

The problems arise when we come to Paul. As I have said, although he cites
the prophets (especially Isaiah) copiously,[11] Paul never cites any of the classic

---

8. John J. Collins, trans., "Sibylline Oracles," in *The Old Testament Pseudepigrapha*, ed.
James H. Charlesworth, 2 vols. (New York: Doubleday, 1983), 1:317–472.

9. George W. E. Nickelsburg and James C. VanderKam, *1 Enoch: A New Translation*
(Minneapolis: Fortress, 2004).

10. See Jill Hicks-Keeton, "Already/Not Yet: Eschatological Tension in the Book of Tobit,"
*JBL* 132 (2013): 97–117; Andrew Chester, "The Sibyl and the Temple," in *Templum Amicitiae:
Essays on the Second Temple Presented to Ernst Bammel*, ed. William Horbury, JSNTSup 48
(Sheffield: Sheffield Academic, 1991), 37–69; Devorah Dimant, "Jerusalem and the Temple in
the *Animal Apocalypse* (1 Enoch 85–90) in Light of the Qumran Community Worldview," in
*From Enoch to Tobit*, FAT 114 (Tübingen: Mohr Siebeck, 2017 [Hebrew original 1983]), 119–37.

11. See Dietrich-Alex Koch, *Die Schrift als Zeuge des Evangeliums*, BHT 69 (Tübingen:
Mohr Siebeck, 1986); Richard B. Hays, *Echoes of Scripture in the Letters of Paul* (New Haven:
Yale University Press, 1989); Christopher D. Stanley, *Paul and the Language of Scripture*,
SNTSMS 74 (Cambridge: Cambridge University Press, 1992); Timothy H. Lim, *Holy Scrip-*

eschatological pilgrimage texts noted above. Nor does he bring all three of our key elements—eschatology, pilgrimage, and gentiles—together anywhere in his own prose. Paul's letters are full of eschatology, and of gentiles, but none of those gentiles ever takes hold of the hem of the robe of a Jew for directions, none of them ever makes *aliyah* to Mount Zion. (Admittedly, there is the case of Titus in Gal 2:1–3: "I went up to Jerusalem with Barnabas, bringing Titus along." But Titus does not go up. Paul goes up, and brings Titus along with him. And he goes up not to worship at the temple but, apparently, to show Titus off to the chief apostles.)

One might possibly see—and quite a few interpreters have seen—a hint of the eschatological gentile pilgrimage motif in Paul's collection of money from the gentile Christ assemblies abroad to give aid to the poor among the saints in Jerusalem (mentioned in 1 Cor 16:1–4; 2 Cor 8:1–9:15; Rom 15:25–31). Indeed, ever since the mid-twentieth-century works of Johannes Munck and Dieter Georgi, this account of Paul's collection has become quite influential, even standard.[12] As David Downs has argued, however, Paul nowhere portrays the gathering or the delivery of the collection as a pilgrimage of the gentiles.[13] Most importantly, it is Paul himself, not the gentile donors, who will bring the offering to Jerusalem.[14] And he will deliver it not to the temple on Mount Zion but to the Jerusalem Christ assembly, for distribution to its poorest members.[15]

---

ture in the Qumran Commentaries and Pauline Letters (Oxford: Clarendon, 1997); Florian Wilk, *Die Bedeutung des Jesajabuches für Paulus*, FRLANT 179 (Göttingen: Vandenhoeck & Ruprecht, 1998); Wagner, *Heralds of the Good News*.

12. See Johannes Munck, *Paul and the Salvation of Mankind*, trans. Frank Clarke (Atlanta: John Knox, 1959 [German original 1954]); Dieter Georgi, *Remembering the Poor: The History of Paul's Collection for Jerusalem* (Nashville: Abingdon, 1992 [German original 1965]); Keith F. Nickle, *The Collection: A Study in Paul's Strategy*, SBT 48 (Naperville, IL: Allenson, 1966); Burkhard Beckheuer, *Paulus und Jerusalem* (Frankfurt: Peter Lang, 1997).

13. David J. Downs, *The Offering of the Gentiles: Paul's Collection for Jerusalem in Its Chronological, Cultural, and Cultic Contexts* (Grand Rapids: Eerdmans, 2016), 3–9. See also the earlier criticism levelled by Leander Keck, "The Poor among the Saints in the New Testament," *ZNW* 56 (1965): 100–129.

14. One might invoke as counterevidence 1 Cor 16:3: "When I [Paul] arrive, I will send those whom you [Corinthians] accredit by letter to carry your gift to Jerusalem." But the stated purposes of these Achaean couriers is safekeeping, not symbolic pilgrimage. And in any case, by the time he writes Rom 15, Paul has apparently resolved to deliver the collection himself.

15. Rom 15:25–28: "At present, I am going to Jerusalem with aid for the saints. For Macedonia and Achaia have been pleased to make some contribution for the poor among the saints at Jerusalem; they were pleased to do it, and indeed they are in debt to them, for if

Some recent interpreters—even ones who are otherwise deeply skeptical of Luke-Acts as a historical source—have thought that the rumor in Acts 21:28–29 that Paul sneaked his gentile companion Trophimus past the court of gentiles into the inner courts of the temple[16] is a smoking gun: Paul actually tried to trigger the eschaton by dragging a newly holy-in-Christ gentile across the sacred boundary.[17] But one lone Ephesian does not a pilgrimage make. And anyway, this is Luke's story, not Paul's. (And even Luke says it was a rumor, that Paul did not actually do it.) And nothing Paul himself says hints at such a scheme. According to his travel itinerary in Rom 15, Paul will go up to see the brothers-in-Christ in Jerusalem, as he has done several times before (Gal 1–2). Only this time, he will come bearing gentile money.

But if the collection for the poverty-stricken saints in Jerusalem is not an eschatological pilgrimage of gentiles, what then? Well, there is one other key text that we have yet to consider. I have claimed that Paul never cites any of the eschatological pilgrimage texts from scripture, but some of my colleagues would say that this claim of mine is an error of fact. I have missed, they would say, Paul's crucial citation of Isa 11:10 at Rom 15:12:[18] "And again Isaiah says: 'There shall be the root of Jesse, even he who rises to rule over the gentiles, in him the gentiles will hope.'" This is a crucial citation, indeed, but it is not an exception to the rule that Paul never cites any of the eschatological pilgrimage texts from scripture. Here is one of those instances where, I think, we do not really know what we mean by the phrase "eschatological pilgrimage of the gentiles." Or, if we do know what we mean, then we are using it sloppily. We are either confused or willfully imprecise. Let us consider this imprecision.

---

the gentiles have come to share in their spiritual blessings, they ought also to be of service to them in material blessings. When therefore I have completed this, and have delivered to them what has been raised, I shall go on by way of you [in Rome] to Spain."

16. Acts 21:28–29: "[Jews from Asia] cried out, 'Men of Israel, help! This is the man who is teaching men everywhere against the people and the law and this place; moreover he also brought Greeks into the temple, and he has defiled this holy place.' For they had previously seen Trophimus the Ephesian with him in the city, and they supposed that Paul had brought him into the temple."

17. E.g., J. Albert Harrill, *Paul the Apostle: His Life and Legacy in Their Roman Context* (New York: Cambridge University Press, 2012), 72–74; Fredriksen, *Pagans' Apostle*, 244.

18. Indeed, this very point was made to me by Christopher Zoccali at an SBL session on the topic. Zoccali has argued that Rom 15:12/Isa 11:10 is indeed evidence of an eschatological gentile pilgrimage motif in Paul (Christopher Zoccali, *Reading Philippians after Supersessionism* [Eugene, OR: Cascade, 2017], 35–44). He is quite right about the importance of the citation, but not about its connection to a pilgrimage motif, for the reasons I adduce here.

One of my muses for the argument of this essay is the Hebrew Bible scholar J. J. M. Roberts, in particular his excellent 2004 article "The End of War in the Zion Tradition."[19] Roberts argues that even the bona fide eschatological pilgrimage oracles noted at the beginning of this paper presuppose a starkly imperialistic vision of divine governance. About Isa 2 (=Mic 4)—"Many peoples shall come, and say: 'Come, let us go up to the mountain of the LORD.' . . . He shall judge between the nations, and shall decide for many peoples; and they shall beat their swords into plowshares, and their spears into pruning hooks" (Isa 2:3–4)—Roberts writes: "The reason the nations can discard their weapons of war is that they are all vassals of Yahweh, and as his vassals, they are not permitted to go to war against one another to settle their disputes; instead their disputes will be settled by Yahweh's binding arbitration issued from the imperial capital in Jerusalem."[20] For his part, Roberts is particularly concerned to argue against those interpreters who see the "swords into plowshares" image as a straightforwardly pacifist ideal.[21]

What is more, Roberts also differentiates between this ideal politeia in Isa 2 and the related but different one in Isa 11. About Isa 11:10—"In that day, the root of Jesse shall stand as a sign to the peoples; him shall the nations seek, and his dwellings shall be glorious"—Roberts writes: "Rather than the divine mountain being exalted to catch the attention of the nations, it is the king from the root of Jesse who stands out like a flag, and it is to him that the nations go to inquire."[22] Isaiah 2 (like the other passages cited at the beginning of this chapter) has a gentile pilgrimage to Zion but no messiah. Isaiah 11 has a messiah but no gentile pilgrimage. It is surely no accident that Paul cites the one oracle and not the others.

And in fact, Paul cites not the proto-MT Hebrew (as represented, e.g., in 1QIsaiah[a]) but the Old Greek version of Isa 11:10, which has even more messiah and even less gentile pilgrimage than its Hebrew *Vorlage*. Whereas in the Hebrew the Davidic king rises עַמִּים לְנֵס, "as a sign to the peoples," in the Greek he rises ἄρχειν ἐθνῶν, "to rule over the gentiles" (perhaps mistaking נֵס, "sign, flag," for נָשִׂיא, "prince, ruler"). And whereas in the Hebrew the nations "inquire after him" (יִדְרֹשׁוּ), in the Greek they "hope in him" (ἐλπιοῦσιν). It

19. J. J. M. Roberts, "The End of War in the Zion Tradition," *HBT* 26 (2004): 2–22. And see Roberts's other essays on related themes in his *The Bible and the Ancient Near East: Collected Essays* (Winona Lake, IN: Eisenbrauns, 2002).

20. Roberts, "End of War," 6.

21. See in particular H. W. Wolff, "Swords into Plowshares: Misuse of a Word of Prophecy?" *CurTM* 12 (1985): 133–47.

22. Roberts, "End of War," 11.

is this Greek version that Paul cites in Rom 15:12, painting a picture not of the eschatological pilgrimage of the gentiles to Zion but rather of the eschatological subjection of the gentiles to the messiah.[23] The full passage reads as follows:[24]

> Christ became a servant of circumcision for the sake of the truthfulness of God, so as to confirm the promises to the patriarchs, and [a servant] with respect to the gentiles for the sake of his mercy, so as to glorify God, as it is written:
>
>> For this reason I will confess you among the gentiles,
>> and I will sing to your name. [OG Ps 17:50 = 2 Kgdms 22:50]
>
> And again it says:
>
>> Rejoice, O gentiles, with his people. [LXX Deut 32:43]
>
> And again:
>
>> Praise the lord, all you gentiles,
>> and let all the peoples praise him. [OG Ps 116:1]
>
> And again Isaiah says:
>
>> There shall be the root of Jesse,
>> even he who rises to rule over the gentiles,
>> in him the gentiles will hope. [OG Isa 11:10]
>
> (Rom 15:8–12)

This catena of four scripture citations is meant to bear out Paul's claim in v. 9 that Christ became a servant of the *gentiles* for the sake of God's mercy: The one thing that all four scriptural excerpts have in common is the keyword ἔθνη, "gentiles." In addition, the first and the last excerpts have in common the theme of the Davidic messiah in his role vis-à-vis the gentiles, the latter excerpt obviously ("the root of Jesse . . . rises to rule"), and the former in its

---

23. On these aspects of OG Isa 11, see further Wagner, *Heralds of the Good News*, 317–27; Matthew V. Novenson, "The Jewish Messiahs, the Pauline Christ, and the Gentile Question," *JBL* 128 (2009): 357–73. And on the theology of Old Greek Isaiah more generally, see J. Ross Wagner, *Opening the Sealed Book: Old Greek Isaiah and the Problem of Septuagint Hermeneutics*, FAT 88 (Tübingen: Mohr Siebeck, 2013).

24. My translation. On the difficult syntax of the opening sentence, I follow J. Ross Wagner, "The Christ, Servant of Jew and Gentile: A Fresh Approach to Rom 15:8–9," *JBL* 116 (1997): 473–85. With Wagner, and *pace* Joshua Garroway ("The Circumcision of Christ: Romans 15:7–13," *JSNT* 34 [2012]: 303–22), I think it most likely that διάκονον περιτομῆς, "servant of circumcision," here means *not* "agent of circumcision," i.e., "circumciser," but rather "servant of the people Israel." But see Garroway's ingenious argument to the contrary as developed in his *Paul's Gentile-Jews: Neither Jew nor Gentile, but Both* (New York: Palgrave Macmillan, 2012).

immediate context: "For this reason I will confess you among the gentiles, and I will sing to your name, O Lord, who magnifies deliverances for his king, and does mercy for his christ [i.e., messiah, anointed], for David and his seed forever" (OG Ps 17:50–51 = 2 Kgdms 22:50–51).[25]

My point here is that the citation of Isa 11:10 in Rom 15:12 cannot accurately be called an eschatological pilgrimage reference. And because no other citation is even in the vicinity of the eschatological pilgrimage motif, I think we are better off not appealing to that motif at all for the purposes of interpreting Paul's gentile mission. There is, however, an eschatological script here,[26] just not the particular script that we usually hear mentioned in this connection. There is nothing here about the gentiles making pilgrimage to Zion, but everything about their being subjected to the messiah. The messiah rises to rule the gentiles, and the gentiles obey him. As Paul himself puts it later in the same chapter, "Christ works in me to bring about the obedience of the gentiles [ὑπακοὴν ἐθνῶν]" (Rom 15:18).[27] Paul mentions "Zion" only twice, both times in Isaiah quotations (Isa 28:16 in Rom 9:33; Isa 59:20 in Rom 11:26),[28] both expressly with reference to Israel, *not* the gentiles.[29] Gentiles-in-Christ (like Jews-in-Christ, presumably) have the Jerusalem *above* as their metropolis (Gal 4:26), not the present Jerusalem (Gal 4:25), which perhaps is why Paul does not exhort them to make pilgrimage to the latter.[30]

I do not know why the eschatological-pilgrimage-of-the-gentiles hypothesis has come to command such wide assent in the field. I would speculate, though,

25. On this text, see Novenson, "Jewish Messiahs."

26. *Pace* Donaldson, *Paul and the Gentiles.*

27. On this under-appreciated theme, see the classic discussion by Paul S. Minear, *The Obedience of Faith: The Purposes of Paul in the Epistle to the Romans* (London: SCM, 1971).

28. "[Israel] stumbled over the stumbling stone, as it is written, 'Behold, I am laying in Zion a stone that will make men stumble, a rock that will make them fall; and he who believes in him will not be put to shame' [Isa 28:16]" (Rom 9:33); "In this way all Israel will be saved, as it is written, 'The deliverer will come from Zion, he will banish impiety from Jacob' [Isa 59:20]" (Rom 11:26).

29. On Zion in Rom 9–11, see further Wagner, *Heralds of the Good News.*

30. On the Jerusalem above in Gal 4, see Michael B. Cover, "Now and Above, Then and Now (Gal 4:21–31): Platonizing and Apocalyptic Polarities in Paul's Eschatology," in *Galatians and Christian Theology*, ed. Mark Elliott et al. (Grand Rapids: Baker Academic, 2014), 220–29. With thanks to Paula Fredriksen for helping me clarify this, I understand Paul to expect that, at the imminent parousia of Jesus and resurrection of the righteous dead, all people-in-Christ will be translated directly to the Jerusalem above. The cosmology and anthropology underlying such a scenario are brilliantly explained by Matthew Thiessen, *Paul and the Gentile Problem* (New York: Oxford University Press, 2016), 129–60.

that it has to do with a popular and intuitively sensible—but, I think, finally mistaken—threefold rubric of ancient Jewish views of the fate of gentiles. This rubric goes roughly as follows: Some ancient Jews thought that gentiles would be destroyed in the final judgment (e.g., Jubilees; 4 Ezra); others that gentiles would, or could, become proselytes and thus be saved (e.g., Judith; Joseph and Aseneth); still others that gentiles would remain gentiles but renounce idolatry and make pilgrimage to Zion (Isa 2; Zech 8; etc.). Given those three options, many of us have, of course, opted for the lattermost as the closest fit with Paul: He clearly does not believe that all gentiles will be destroyed; but he equally clearly opposes gentiles becoming proselytes via circumcision; hence he must hold to the eschatological pilgrimage paradigm.

The mistake is thinking that there are only three options. In fact, there are more, even *many* more, depending how finely one wants to parse it. Some "gentile destruction" texts imagine the gentiles being dispatched judicially (in a last judgment), others extra-judicially (in a last battle). Some "gentile conversion" texts reason that gentiles must convert in the quotidian present, others that they will have an eschatological opportunity to do so. Some "gentiles remain gentiles" texts imagine that individual gentiles *who keep the Noahide laws* will be spared, others that individual gentiles *who have Christ-faith* will be spared, still others that gentiles *from nations that did not oppress Israel* will be spared. And however they are spared, some of our texts imagine them being subdued by the messiah, others imagine them licking the dust of the feet of the Jews (with no messiah to be seen), and still others imagine them making pious pilgrimage to Mount Zion. And so on. My point is that our texts make a very wide range of creative moves,[31] and we only hamstring ourselves as interpreters if we reduce them all to just a few simple templates.

In Paul's discourse, we find eschatology and gentiles, to be sure, but not pilgrimage. And this is a problem for the eponymous hypothesis, because pilgrimage in particular is the hallmark of this putative tradition. Paul's gentile mission, I think, aimed to bring about not the eschatological *pilgrimage* of the gentiles but rather their eschatological *obedience*.[32] Of course, a combination of these two ideas is easily conceivable, and was in fact conceived of by, for instance, Psalms of Solomon and the Animal Apocalypse. In those texts— arguably, but one has to argue the case—the gentiles *both* make pilgrimage to Mount Zion *and* obey the messiah. I would say, however, that Psalms of

---

31. Many of which are detailed in the essays in *Israel and the Nations: Paul's Gospel in the Context of Jewish Expectation*, ed. Frantisek Abel (Minneapolis: Fortress, 2021).

32. See further Novenson, "Jewish Messiahs."

Solomon and the Animal Apocalypse are simply more creative than Paul is in this respect. Although Paul surely knew Isa 2 and 11 equally well, he only chose to appeal to the latter in interpreting his gentile mission. I strongly suspect, though I cannot prove, that he did so because only the latter text has the root of Jesse, the messiah from the seed of David, which is the one thing Paul's gospel cannot do without.[33]

---

33. I have made this case in full in my *Christ among the Messiahs: Christ Language in Paul and Messiah Language in Ancient Judaism* (New York: Oxford University Press, 2012). Other important interpretations of the messiah motif in Paul include Stanley K. Stowers, *A Rereading of Romans: Justice, Jews, and Gentiles* (New Haven: Yale University Press, 1994); Joshua W. Jipp, *Christ Is King: Paul's Royal Ideology* (Minneapolis: Fortress, 2015); Fredriksen, *Pagans' Apostle*.

10

# WHITHER THE PAUL WITHIN
# JUDAISM *SCHULE*?

It was in Atlanta in November 2010 that the Paul and Judaism Consultation (latterly the Paul within Judaism Section) of the Society of Biblical Literature, newly sprung—like Athena from the head of Zeus—from the heads of Mark Nanos and Magnus Zetterholm, first assembled. Several years later, the section saw published an eponymous volume of essays representing the fruit of its work during that initial period: *Paul within Judaism: Restoring the First-Century Context to the Apostle.*[1] The research undertaken by this group had some notable twentieth-century antecedents, especially in the work of Krister Stendahl, Lloyd Gaston, John Gager, and Stanley Stowers. But something emerged in the 2010s that might be, and has been, called a *Schule*: a team of scholars jointly advancing the large-scale hypothesis that Paul should be understood as operating entirely within Judaism. Rather differently from the New Perspective on Paul, so christened by James Dunn in 1982,[2] this twenty-first-century *Schule* has been slower to develop a consistent brand. In its infancy it was sometimes called just "the radical school" or, in a kind of portmanteau, "the radical new perspective on Paul."[3] But with an established SBL section

1. Mark D. Nanos and Magnus Zetterholm, eds., *Paul within Judaism: Restoring the First-Century Context to the Apostle* (Minneapolis: Fortress, 2015).
2. James D. G. Dunn, "The New Perspective on Paul," *BJRL* 65 (1983): 95–122.
3. See, e.g., in Pamela Eisenbaum, "Paul, Polemics, and the Problem of Essentialism," *BibInt* 13 (2005): 224–38; Magnus Zetterholm, *Approaches to Paul: A Student's Guide to Recent Scholarship* (Minneapolis: Fortress, 2009), 127–63.

157

came the need for a proper name, and Paul within Judaism it was. We know, then, whence came this very interesting development in recent Pauline studies. But whither is it going? The present chapter attempts a partial answer to this question by means of an engagement with two recent books from representatives of the *Schule*.

In the course of researching and writing this chapter, I reread the preface to Paula Fredriksen's Princeton PhD thesis "Augustine's Early Interpretation of Paul,"[4] in which she thanks her supervisor—John Gager—for pushing her "to get my languages in order, and to take full responsibility for my own intellectual development." So the two important new books on Paul here under discussion are also a remarkable snapshot of an academic genealogy. Nowadays, Fredriksen and Gager are often mentioned together in print as representatives of the obstinately name-resistant radical new perspective on Paul, or Paul within Judaism *Schule*. This shared reputation of theirs is well earned, and I expect that both are happy to own it. But the appearance of these two important books around the same time also demonstrates the very interesting diversity of views within this *Schule* and, furthermore, provides an occasion for us to imagine possible futures for the scholarly discussion of Paul. More on this later, but first, I offer some comments on each book, in turn.

## ON PAULA FREDRIKSEN'S PAUL

I think it is fair to say that, until 2017, Paula Fredriksen was the most important contemporary interpreter of Paul who had never written a book about Paul. She had written important books about Jesus, early Christology, Augustine, and sin (to mention some highlights),[5] and in some of these books the apostle played a supporting role. Meanwhile, though, and especially through the 2010s, Fredriksen authored a number of articles that quickly became touchstones in contemporary Pauline studies, for instance: "Judaism, the Cir-

---

4. Paula Fredriksen, "Augustine's Early Interpretation of Paul" (PhD diss., Princeton University, 1979).

5. Paula Fredriksen, *From Jesus to Christ: The Origins of the New Testament Images of Jesus* (New Haven: Yale University Press, 1988); Fredriksen, *Jesus of Nazareth, King of the Jews: A Jewish Life and the Emergence of Christianity* (New York: Knopf, 1999); Fredriksen, *Augustine and the Jews: A Christian Defense of Jews and Judaism* (New Haven: Yale University Press, 2010); Fredriksen, *Sin: The Early History of an Idea* (Princeton: Princeton University Press, 2012).

cumcision of Gentiles, and Apocalyptic Hope";[6] "Judaizing the Nations: The Ritual Demands of Paul's Gospel";[7] and "Paul's Letter to the Romans, the Ten Commandments, and Pagan Justification by Faith."[8] Reading, citing, and interacting with those articles, I (like many other interpreters, I am sure) have often wished that I had a fuller account from Fredriksen: one that included her reading of this or that passage, or her engagement with this or that scholar. And now, at last, we have it. With *Paul: The Pagans' Apostle*,[9] Fredriksen does for Paul what she had done for Jesus and for Augustine. She gives him a full and sympathetic reading, but one that situates him squarely in his ancient (read: strange, foreign) ideological context. She makes Paul weird again.

Her chosen subtitle, "the pagans' apostle," is jarring, and intentionally so. Even as many of us have been put off using the term "pagan" by warnings (from the likes of Christopher Jones and others)[10] that it concedes to ancient Christian apologists and heresiologists their rhetorical claims to superiority, Fredriksen undertakes to resuscitate the term as a translation for Greek ἔθνος (plural ἔθνη). She points out that our usual rendering of ἔθνη as "gentiles" leaves out the sense of religious obligation to ancestral deities that was everywhere assumed in antiquity—the idea that "gods run in the blood," as she memorably puts it. The term "pagans," precisely because it has these religious overtones, captures the dilemma faced by the apostle Paul's ἔθνη-in-Christ. They were (in theory, at least) no longer proper gentiles, but not yet (indeed, not ever) Jews. They were "ex-pagan pagans," to use another Fredriksenism. And Paul was their apostle.

Fredriksen makes her case as follows. A brief introduction takes us from Jesus announcing the kingdom of God to Paul (a few years later) announcing the risen Jesus, sketching how the proclaimer became the proclaimed. Chapter 1, "Israel and the Nations," is Fredriksen's account of the imagined scriptural world within which Paul sees himself operating: the stories of the nations and their gods, Israel and its god, kingdom, exile, and hope for redemption. Chapter 2, "Fatherland and Mother City," is her account of the actual social world

6. Paula Fredriksen, "Judaism, the Circumcision of Gentiles, and Apocalyptic Hope," *JTS* 42 (1991): 532–64.

7. Paula Fredriksen, "Judaizing the Nations: The Ritual Demands of Paul's Gospel," *NTS* 56 (2010): 232–52.

8. Paula Fredriksen, "Paul's Letter to the Romans, the Ten Commandments, and Pagan Justification by Faith," *JBL* 133 (2014): 801–8.

9. Paula Fredriksen, *Paul: The Pagans' Apostle* (New Haven: Yale University Press, 2017).

10. E.g., Christopher P. Jones, *Between Pagan and Christian* (Cambridge, MA: Harvard University Press, 2014).

within which Paul operated, a world where Jews frequented pagan places (the agora, hippodrome, gymnasium, etc.) and pagans Jewish places (the court of the gentiles in Jerusalem, and urban synagogues everywhere). Chapter 3, "Paul: Mission and Persecution," considers why Paul would have harassed the Christ assemblies before his revelation and why he found himself on the receiving end of such harassment after. She especially emphasizes the agency of hostile gentile gods in this picture. Chapter 4, "Paul and the Law," is a sure-footed and economical treatment of the thorny problems surrounding righteousness, law, and faith in Paul. Fredriksen argues that δικαιοσύνη, "righteousness," refers to the second table of the Decalogue, and that Paul's gentiles, once rightwised by Christ-faith, become capable of keeping it. Chapter 5, "Christ and the Kingdom," emphasizes the frantically eschatological context of Paul's apostolic labours. Here Fredriksen argues that the controversy surrounding gentile circumcision was an accident occasioned by the unforeseen, ever-lengthening delay of the kingdom. A postscript briefly, provocatively argues that next-generation, gentile Christian thinkers such as Valentinus, Marcion, and—lest one think the proto-orthodox are being let off the hook—Justin Martyr all get Paul wrong in the same way: they identify the (middle-Platonic) transcendent high god as someone other than the god of Abraham.

In terms of its overall outlook, *Paul: The Pagans' Apostle* reminds me a great deal (indeed, far more than any other recent treatment of Paul does) of Albert Schweitzer's classic *Mysticism of Paul the Apostle*.[11] Almost ninety years ago, Schweitzer wrote, "The fact that even the second [Christian] generation does not know what to make of his [Paul's] teaching suggests the conjecture that he built his system upon a conviction which ruled only in the first generation. But what was it that disappeared out of the first Christian generation? What but the expectation of the immediate dawn of the messianic kingdom of Jesus?"[12] And now Fredriksen: "Why, how . . . can Paul still be so sure that he knows the hour on God's clock? This is the question that drives the present study. It will lead us into a Jewish world incandescent with apocalyptic hopes. . . . Only in [this context] can we begin to see Paul as he saw himself: as God's prophetic messenger, formed in the womb to carry the good news of impending salvation to the nations, racing on the edge of the End of time."[13] Fredriksen, more than any other contemporary interpreter, perhaps more than any interpreter

---

11. Albert Schweitzer, *Die Mystik des Apostels Paulus* (Tübingen: Mohr, 1930); ET *The Mysticism of Paul the Apostle*, trans. W. Montgomery (London: Black, 1931).

12. Schweitzer, *Mysticism*, 39.

13. Fredriksen, *Pagans' Apostle*, xii.

since Schweitzer, reads Paul unflinchingly in terms of thoroughgoing eschatology. This is, in my opinion, a great triumph. It also generates sharp conflict
with readings that Fredriksen calls Christian-theological, ones that identify
the *Sache* of Paul's message with something other than the imminent kingdom of God.[14] But is this sharp conflict also inevitable? This is a fascinating
question to which I genuinely do not know the answer. I can conceive of a
Christian reading of Paul that grasped the nettle of thoroughgoing eschatology, but empirically I can think of almost none that do so.[15] Fredriksen's
fundamental disagreement with some of the most important recent works by
Christian interpreters of Paul[16] highlights a significant rift within our subfield.
Rapprochement may be possible, but not, I think, otherwise than by following
Fredriksen's argument all the way through to the end.

### ON JOHN GAGER'S PAUL

John Gager's new book *Who Made Early Christianity? The Jewish Lives of the
Apostle Paul*[17] had its genesis in the author's prestigious American Lectures
in the History of Religions for 2013, and the book appears in the eponymous
series from Columbia University Press (in the distinguished company of Peter
Brown's *The Body and Society* and Wendy Doniger's *The Implied Spider*, among
others).[18] Gager has for more than 30 years been one of the architects of a

---

14. E.g., Fredriksen, *Pagans' Apostle*, 230n43: "Two of the most recent—and longest—
works arguing that Paul is a Christian theologian who repudiates Judaism, Wright ([*Paul
and the Faithfulness of God*] 2013, 1,660 pages) and Barclay ([*Paul and the Gift*] 2015, 656
pages)—do not bring Paul's vivid eschatology into view at all in their respective depic-
tions. . . . Seeing Paul's letters as examples of 'Christianity,' they fail to consider eschatology
as an important factor shaping Paul's message, and they see him as addressing his theology
to Jews as well as to gentiles." And similarly Fredriksen, *Pagans' Apostle*, 228n36: "[According
to Barclay,] Paul the Christian theologian 'radically redefines' Jewish identity and thinks
that fleshly circumcision is of no consequence for Jews as well as for gentiles. . . . Barclay's
Paul, like Wright's, is a Christian theologian."

15. A remarkable nettle-grasping exception, Fredriksen rightly reminds me, is Krister
Stendahl, *Final Account: Paul's Letter to the Romans* (Minneapolis: Fortress, 1995).

16. Esp. N. T. Wright, *Paul and the Faithfulness of God*, 2 vols. (London: SPCK, 2013);
and John M. G. Barclay, *Paul and the Gift* (Grand Rapids: Eerdmans, 2015).

17. John G. Gager, *Who Made Early Christianity? The Jewish Lives of the Apostle Paul*,
American Lectures in the History of Religions (New York: Columbia University Press, 2015).

18. My comments on Gager's book here appear in slightly different form in my published
review in *Theology Today* 73 (2017): 396–97.

putatively new or radical perspective on the apostle Paul. The fourth and final part of Gager's landmark 1983 monograph *The Origins of Anti-Semitism* was a close consideration of "the case of Paul."[19] And his *Reinventing Paul* (2000) offered a book-length exposition of what Gager calls "the new view of Paul," taking stock of developments in the 1980s and 1990s (especially Stowers's 1994 *Rereading of Romans*).[20] The newness or radicalism of Gager's interpretation of the apostle has to do with his central claim that Paul was not the father of Christian anti-Judaism, nor indeed a Christian at all, but simply a Jew, full stop. (Thus the author's answer to the question posed in the title of this new book—Who made early Christianity?—is: not Paul.)[21]

This newest book is a further contribution to Gager's revisionist project, but from a quite different angle. Of the six chapters that comprise the book, only one does any first-order interpretation of the Pauline letters. The rest are concerned with what Gager calls "the Jewish lives of the apostle Paul"—that is, the reception and assessment of Paul in a number of relatively lesser known Jewish sources from across the centuries. Perhaps the closest bibliographical peer to this book is Daniel Langton's fine 2010 study *The Apostle Paul in the Jewish Imagination*.[22] But whereas Langton examines the many post-Enlightenment Jewish readers of Paul, Gager mines the late antique, medieval, and early modern archives for Jewish perceptions of Paul attested in Pseudo-Clementines, Toledot Yeshu, Abd al-Jabbar, Profiat Duran, and Jacob Emden (as well as modern Jewish critics including Graetz, Klausner, Buber, Taubes, Lapide, Flusser, and Wyschogrod). Gager's key finding is that the familiar Jewish image of Paul as an apostate is actually a nineteenth-century innovation. Prior to that time, Gager argues, most Jewish thinkers ignored Paul altogether, and those few who took notice mostly recognized him as a co-religionist in good standing.[23]

19. John G. Gager, *The Origins of Anti-Semitism: Attitudes toward Judaism in Pagan and Christian Antiquity* (New York: Oxford University Press, 1983), 193–264.

20. John G. Gager, *Reinventing Paul* (New York: Oxford University Press, 2000); and see Stanley K. Stowers, *A Rereading of Romans: Justice, Jews, and Gentiles* (New Haven: Yale University Press, 1994).

21. Gager, *Who Made Early Christianity*, 12–13: "Not only did Paul not make early Christianity, he had no conception of what we call Christianity. . . . What we call Christianity is not just post-Pauline; it is un-Pauline."

22. Daniel R. Langton, *The Apostle Paul in the Jewish Imagination: A Study in Modern Jewish-Christian Relations* (New York: Cambridge University Press, 2010).

23. See Gager, *Who Made Early Christianity*, 40: "My claim here is that . . . [1] There is no perennial Jewish debate with or about Paul through the centuries. [2] The Jewish view of Paul before the modern period is anything but negative. [3] Numerous Jewish thinkers

The book unfolds as follows: An introduction shows that the classical narrative of the supersession of Judaism by Christianity is given the lie already by Origen, Jerome, and Augustine, and (the book will argue) by Paul himself. Chapter 1, "Was the Apostle to the Gentiles the Father of Christian Anti-Judaism?" briefly rehearses the argument of Gager's *Reinventing Paul*: that Paul's supposedly anti-Jewish sayings are actually directed only at gentile judaizing. Chapter 2, "The Apostle Paul in Jewish Eyes: Heretic or Hero?" argues that the so-called new view of Paul—that he remained ever a Jew in good standing—is in fact well attested among Jews in the middle ages, so far as we can tell from the patchy sources. Chapter 3, "Let's Meet Downtown in the Synagogue: Four Case Studies," argues from Acts and from remains at Antioch, Aphrodisias, Sardis, and Dura-Europos that, against the protestations of some bishops and rabbis, Jews and Christians co-mingled long into late antiquity. Chapter 4, "Two Stories of How Early Christianity Came to Be," posits a choice between two narratives of Christian origins: first, the classical narrative of the rise of Christianity and attendant decline of Judaism and, second, an alternate narrative of "the ways that never parted," abuzz with liminal groups of Jewish Christians, Christian judaizers, and others. Chapter 5, "Turning the World Upside Down: An Ancient Jewish Life of Jesus," is a brief but thorough account of the Toledot Yeshu, arguing that its longer recensions portray Peter and Paul as Jewish sleeper agents among the Christians. An epilogue makes the case that the thesis argued in the book is no mere historical curiosity but stands to aid the contemporary ethical project of extirpating anti-Semitism.

Gager's revisionist interpretation of Paul is, still today as in 1983, both powerful and controversial. Glenn Bowersock, reviewing *Who Made Early Christianity?* in *The New York Review of Books*, comments, "The new Paul, both Jewish and universalist, as . . . Gager and others have delineated him, is attractive, but Paul's own writings remain an immovable obstacle to accepting this view. The contradictions and inconsistencies in his preaching still provide ample support for the old Paul, the Paul of Tertullian, who was the apostle of the heretics, and the Paul of Harnack, who delivered Christianity from Judaism."[24] Now, there is an important idea worth discussing here,[25] but Bowersock's review also misses Gager's point in *Who Made Early Christianity?*

---

have sought to reclaim Paul as a Jew—and in the process have managed to recover what I take to be the core of his original preaching."

24. G. W. Bowersock, "Who Was Saint Paul?" *New York Review of Books* (November 5, 2015).

25. Margaret Mitchell gets at this idea quite perceptively in her essay "Paul and Judaism Now, *Quo vadimus?*" *JJMJS* 5 (2018): 55–78.

Gager does not merely reiterate his well-known account of Paul (although he certainly stands by that account) but rather shows that account to be not in fact new, but very old indeed. Gager's excavation of Jewish perceptions of Paul in the Middle Ages and early modern period is a genuinely novel contribution, one that must now figure in the lively discussion of the apostle's place in the intertwining histories of Judaism and Christianity.

## A BIOPSY

Reading Fredriksen's and Gager's books together raised for me a number of interesting questions. I conclude by posing two of them for the reader's consideration. First, what do these two books tell us about the present state and the possible futures of the Paul within Judaism *Schule*? Both of the authors under review here are leading lights in that *Schule*, and yet, reading them closely side by side, one becomes aware of many particular texts and issues in Paul about which they differ, sometimes quite significantly. For Fredriksen, it is crucial that Paul thinks of Jesus as the messiah son of David who will usher in the kingdom of God; for Gager, it is equally important that Paul *not* think of Jesus as the messiah of Israel, but only of the nations. For Fredriksen, Paul's gentile mission may be (in certain respects) law-free, but Paul himself is altogether law-observant; for Gager (following Lloyd Gaston), Paul strategically transgresses Torah, making himself an apostate for the sake of his gentiles-in-Christ. And I could cite other examples.

Perhaps, as with the so-called New Perspective on Paul, there never really was just *one* radical new perspective. Rather, there was and is a network of interpreters reading Paul together in new (or perhaps very old) directions, in parallel but not actually in agreement with one another. In hindsight, we can now see how, say, E. P. Sanders's and James Dunn's accounts of Paul together moved the field in a certain direction, but when it comes to actually interpreting any particular text, Sanders often differs from Dunn at least as much as either of them differs from Bultmann. And perhaps the same is true of Fredriksen and Gager, and, for that matter, Magnus Zetterholm, Mark Nanos, Pamela Eisenbaum, and the rest. All of these scholars (and many others, myself included) can rally around the claim that Paul lived his life and discharged his apostolic office within the ambit of his native Judaism. But in fact, it seems to me, radical new perspective scholars actually mean many different things by that (very broad) claim—for example, that Paul's cosmology and eschatology were Jewish not Christian (Fredriksen), or that the social context of Paul's

Christ assemblies was the synagogue rather than the household (Nanos), or that Paul himself kept kosher (Karin Hedner Zetterholm), or that Paul opposed any Christ mission to Jews (Gager). But none of these more precise subclaims entails any of the others, and in fact radical new perspective scholars disagree vigorously about all of them. So how far is it useful for us to continue to think of *a* perspective or *a Schule*?

Second question: What is the place of *Wirkungsgeschichte* in Pauline studies today? Before reading these two books, I imagined a relatively tidy division in our subfield between those who think the future of the study of Paul lies in mining his reception history and those who think it lies in bracketing out that history and pressing back *ad fontes*. Under the former heading, I would have cited Cavan Concannon's clever essay "Paul Is Dead. Long Live Paulinism!" and recent books by Benjamin White (*Remembering Paul*), Jennifer Strawbridge (*The Pauline Effect*), and T. J. Lang (*From Paul to the Second Century*).[26] Under the latter heading, I would have cited both Fredriksen ("How Later Contexts Affect Pauline Content, or: Retrospect Is the Mother of Anachronism") and Gager (his broadside against "the traditional view of Paul"), as well as Stanley Stowers, Albert Harrill, the new SBL Consultation on "The Historical Paul," and more.[27] In fact, I would have classed most or all of the Paul within Judaism *Schule* among those who put no confidence in reception history. But reading these two books disabused me of that (perhaps naive) diagnosis of the field. Indeed, Gager's book positively exploded it. *Who Made Early Christianity?* is just as much a reception history of Paul as Benjamin White's and Jennifer Strawbridge's books are. It is just that Gager focuses on a different group of recipients: not Tertullian and Augustine but the Toledot Yeshu and Profiat Duran. Fredriksen's book does not scupper my tidy twofold rubric quite so obviously, but it does do so more subtly. Make no mistake: In this book Fredriksen's watchword is still "retrospect is the mother of anach-

---

26. Cavan Concannon, "Paul Is Dead. Long Live Paulinism! Imagining a Future for Pauline Studies," *Ancient Jew Review* (November 1, 2016); Benjamin L. White, *Remembering Paul: Ancient and Modern Contests over the Image of the Apostle* (New York: Oxford University Press, 2014); Jennifer Strawbridge, *The Pauline Effect: The Use of the Pauline Epistles by Early Christian Writers*, SBR 5 (Berlin: de Gruyter, 2015); T. J. Lang, *Mystery and the Making of a Christian Historical Consciousness: From Paul to the Second Century*, BZNW 219 (Berlin: de Gruyter, 2015).

27. Paula Fredriksen, "How Later Contexts Affect Pauline Content, or: Retrospect Is the Mother of Anachronism," in *Jews and Christians in the First and Second Centuries: How to Write Their History*, ed. Peter J. Tomson and Joshua Schwartz, CRINT 13 (Leiden: Brill, 2014), 17–51; Gager, *Reinventing Paul*; Stowers, *Rereading*; J. Albert Harrill, *Paul the Apostle: His Life and Legacy in Their Roman Context* (New York: Cambridge University Press, 2012).

ronism." She dedicates the book to the blessed memory of Krister Stendahl, who of course taught us not to assume that Paul understood himself the way Augustine, using Paul's words, understood himself.[28]

And yet. Here we recall that Fredriksen wrote her PhD on Augustine's early interpretation of Paul, and that her first published book was a Latin edition and English translation of Augustine's *Propositions on the Epistle to the Romans* and *Unfinished Commentary on the Epistle to the Romans.*[29] And it turns out that, at a few key moments in this new book, Fredriksen appeals to Augustine's commentaries over against standard modern interpretations of passages in Paul. One of the cruces, on which she has persuaded me entirely, is Rom 1:4, where Fredriksen, citing Augustine, argues that Christ is appointed son of God in power not *at the moment of his resurrection from the dead* but *by virtue of his effecting the general resurrection of the dead.*[30] This is an ingenious reading, with very important consequences for Paul's understanding of Jesus, and it was there in Augustine's secondhand Latin all along. So perhaps, with apologies to Cavan Concannon, Paul is not dead after all, and perhaps we have Paulinism to thank for resuscitating him.

28. Most famously in Krister Stendahl, "The Apostle Paul and the Introspective Conscience of the West," *HTR* 56 (1963): 199–215.

29. Paula Fredriksen, ed. and trans., *Augustine on Romans* (Chico, CA: Scholars Press, 1982).

30. See Fredriksen, *Pagans' Apostle,* 141–45.

# THE PAULINE EPISTLES IN
# TERTULLIAN'S BIBLE

The question of the fate of Paulinism in late antiquity, a point of controversy in early Christian studies especially since Adolf von Harnack, has
benefited from fresh attention in recent research, even as, simultaneously,
there is ever less agreement among New Testament scholars on the question
what Paulinism actually is. This state of affairs comes sharply into focus in
Todd Still and David Wilhite's edited volume *Tertullian and Paul*, the first in
a new series from T&T Clark on the reception of Paul in the church fathers.[1]
Reading and assessing *Tertullian and Paul* is a sometimes dizzying experience
of intertextuality. The reader encounters, for example, Margaret MacDonald
reading Elizabeth Clark reading Tertullian reading Paul. What is more, Paul
himself is reading, for example, Second Isaiah, who is reading First Isaiah, who
is reading parts of the Pentateuch, and so on. One thinks of Derrida's notion
of *différance*, in which any given text refers to other texts, which refer to still
other texts, which refer to still other texts, and so on, ad infinitum.[2]

---

1. Todd D. Still and David E. Wilhite, eds., *Tertullian and Paul* (London: T&T Clark,
2013). This essay has been revised in light of valuable comments from Markus Bockmuehl,
David Eastman, Mark Elliott, Todd Still, Benjamin White, and David Wilhite. Any remaining deficiencies are my own responsibility.

2. See Jacque Derrida, "Différance," in *Margins of Philosophy*, trans. Alan Bass (Chicago:
University of Chicago Press, 1982), 1–28.

READING TERTULLIAN READING PAUL

But to call the encounter with Still and Wilhite's book dizzying is not to call it fruitless. On the contrary, their well-advised project of gathering experts from patristics and New Testament studies around a fictive seminar table allows the reader to see things in both Paul and Tertullian that she would not otherwise be in a position to see. This is the book's unique contribution to this interdisciplinary field of research. To date, we have, on the one hand, studies of Tertullian that give some attention to his interpretation of Paul (e.g., Holl, Lortz, O'Malley, Osborn, and Dunn);[3] and, on the other hand, studies of the *Rezeptionsgeschichte* of the Pauline epistles that give some attention to Tertullian's exegesis (e.g., Aleith, Wiles, Lindemann, Rensberger, Pervo, Eastman, and White).[4] Closest to Still and Wilhite's project, we have a number of short studies dedicated to Paul and Tertullian (e.g., Barth, Rambaux, Sider, Lieu, and Bain).[5] These studies have been largely—although not entirely—preoccupied with the question whether Tertullian gets Paul right or wrong, a question to

3. Karl Holl, "Tertullian als Schriftsteller," in *Gesammelte Aufsätze zur Kirchengeschichte*, vol. 3 (Tübingen: Mohr, 1928 [1897]), 1–12; Joseph Lortz, *Tertullian als Apologet*, 2 vols., MBT 9–10 (Münster: Aschendorff, 1927–1928); T. P. O'Malley, *Tertullian and the Bible: Language, Imagery, Exegesis*, LCP 21 (Nijmegen: Dekker & Van De Vegt, 1967); Eric Osborn, *Tertullian: First Theologian of the West* (Cambridge: Cambridge University Press, 1997); Geoffrey D. Dunn, *Tertullian* (London: Routledge, 2004).

4. Eva Aleith, *Paulusverständnis in der alten Kirche*, BZNW 18 (Berlin: Töpelmann, 1937); Maurice F. Wiles, *The Divine Apostle: The Interpretation of St. Paul's Epistles in the Early Church* (Cambridge: Cambridge University Press, 1967); Andreas Lindemann, *Paulus im ältesten Christentum*, BHT 58 (Tübingen: Mohr Siebeck, 1979); David K. Rensberger, "As the Apostle Teaches: The Development of the Use of Paul's Letters in Second-Century Christianity" (PhD diss., Yale University, 1981); Richard I. Pervo, *The Making of Paul: Constructions of the Apostle in Early Christianity* (Minneapolis: Fortress, 2010); David L. Eastman, *Paul the Martyr: The Cult of the Apostle in the Latin West* (Atlanta: SBL Press, 2011); Benjamin L. White, "Imago Pauli: Memory, Tradition, and Discourses on the 'Real' Paul in the Second Century" (PhD diss., University of North Carolina, 2011); White, *Remembering Paul: Ancient and Modern Contests over the Image of the Apostle* (New York: Oxford University Press, 2014).

5. Fritz Barth, "Tertullians Auffassung des Apostels Paulus und seines Verhältnisses zu den Uraposteln," *JPT* 8 (1882): 706–56; Claude Rambaux, "La composition et l'exégèse dans les deux lettres *Ad uxorem*, le *De exhortations castitatis*, et le *De monogamia*, ou la construction de la pensée dans les traités de Tertullien sur la remarriage," *REA* 22 (1976): 3–28; 201–17; and 23 (1977): 18–55; Robert D. Sider, "Literary Artifice and the Figure of Paul in the Writings of Tertullian," in *Paul and the Legacies of Paul*, ed. William S. Babcock (Dallas: Southern Methodist University Press, 1986), 99–120; Judith M. Lieu, "'As Much My Apostle as Christ Is Mine': The Dispute over Paul between Tertullian and Marcion," *EC* 1 (2010):

which we will return. Still and Wilhite's book, while it does perpetuate that classic debate, also allows space for finer-grained comparative analysis of Paul and Tertullian on topics in which both were keenly interested: the nature of God, the threat of persecution, the management of women, and other such.

Which raises the very interesting question, How should an editor go about structuring a book like this? What are the topics in which both Paul and Tertullian were interested? At one level the construction of a table of contents is a mundane editorial decision, but at another level it cuts to the core of the religious thought of both ancient figures, respectively. A book like this one, but organized according to Paul's literary rubric, would proceed city by city around the eastern Mediterranean—a chapter on the church in Thessalonica, a chapter on the church in Corinth, and so on. A book like this one, but organized according to Tertullian's literary rubric, would be a strange animal, by turns doctrinal (on the trinity, the soul, the resurrection, etc.) and practical (on dress, remarriage, fasting, etc.), but almost always polemical (against Jews, pagans, Marcionites, Valentinians, etc.). Still and Wilhite's decision to organize the book according to an artificial modern rubric is therefore very sensible. Wilhite explains in his introduction, "The following essays are topical. For the sake of convenience, the subjects treated follow a roughly systematic outline, beginning with God and concluding with eschatology."[6] This is true, although a number of the chapters in between (e.g., on Israel, on martyrs, on women, on heresy) do not correspond to familiar loci from systematic theology. The table of contents actually represents a mix of conventional theological categories (e.g., the holy spirit) and other analytical topoi (e.g., gender), all of which suit the two ancient corpora in question, as different as those two corpora are from one another in other respects.

In their explanations of the rationale for the book, Still and Wilhite naturally emphasize the similarities between Paul's and Tertullian's respective projects.[7] One might question, however, whether these similarities are really as deep as they may at first appear. Still writes, "Paul and Tertullian were both ancient, occasional, pastoral theologians";[8] but not, I think, in the same way. Paul is pastoral in the sense that he performs the function of an itinerant

---

41–59; Andrew M. Bain, "Tertullian: Paul as Teacher of the Gentiles," in *Paul and the Second Century*, ed. Michael F. Bird and Joseph R. Dodson, LNTS 412 (London: T&T Clark, 2011).

6. David E. Wilhite, "Introduction: Reading Tertullian Reading Paul," in Still and Wilhite, *Tertullian and Paul*, xxi.

7. Wilhite, "Introduction"; Todd D. Still, "Afterword: Tertullian and Pauline Studies," in Still and Wilhite, *Tertullian and Paul*, 282–84.

8. Still, "Afterword," 283.

minister to his own Christ assemblies, and he is occasional in the sense that his literary oeuvre consists entirely of ad hoc letters to those assemblies. Tertullian also writes on topics of pastoral concern, but he does not have episcopal responsibility for any ecclesial body (*Exh. cast.* 7.3; *Mon.* 12.1–4);[9] and while his treatises are occasional in the sense that they address current issues, they are proper theological treatises nonetheless. But the most important difference between Paul and Tertullian, for our purposes, is precisely the fact that Paul is himself a source for Tertullian. And not a source just in the way that Justin Martyr's *Dialogue with Trypho* is a source for Tertullian's *Against the Jews*, but a biblical source, a source with authority virtually equal to the Gospels (*Praescr.* 4.1; *Marc.* 5.1) and greater than the Torah (*Marc.* 4.1). Whereas Paul's Bible consists of the law and the prophets (Rom 3:21), Tertullian's Bible consists of the Old Testament and the New Testament (*Prax.* 15.1; *Marc.* 3.14.3; 4.6.1).

### TERTULLIAN'S CORPUS PAULINUM

With this observation in mind, and in dialogue with Still and Wilhite and their contributors, it will be helpful to make several salient points regarding the Pauline Epistles in Tertullian's Bible. First of all, with respect to the history of the New Testament canon, it is very significant that Tertullian's thirteen-letter *corpus Paulinum*, unlike other ancient recensions, corresponds exactly with ours. On the one hand, Tertullian famously denounces Marcion's ten-letter edition of Paul, writing, "This epistle alone [viz. Philemon] has so profited by its brevity as to escape Marcion's falsifying hands. As however he has accepted this letter to a single person, I do not see why he has rejected two written to Timothy and one to Titus about the church system. I suppose he had a whim to meddle even with the number of the epistles [*Affectavit, opinor, etiam numerum epistularum interpolare*]" (*Marc.* 5.21).[10] On the other hand, however, Tertullian also differs from those of his contemporaries who attribute to Paul more than the thirteen letters. Unlike his Alexandrian counterparts Clement and Origen, Tertullian does not count Hebrews among the Pauline epistles. In a fascinating passage in *Modesty*, after first adducing apostolic evidence in favor of sexual abstinence, Tertullian supplements this with sub-apostolic

---

9. Perhaps he should be counted among the North African *seniores laici*, "lay elders," but this is neither clear nor agreed upon.

10. Text and trans. Ernest Evans, *Tertullian: Adversus Marcionem*, 2 vols., OECT (Oxford: Clarendon, 1972).

evidence: "I wish redundantly to superadd the testimony likewise of a particular comrade of the apostles, which is aptly suited for confirming, by most proximate right, the discipline of his masters. For there is extant also an Epistle to the Hebrews under the name of Barnabas—a man sufficiently accredited by God, as being one whom Paul has stationed next to himself in the uninterrupted observance of abstinence: *Do not Barnabas and I alone have the power of working?* [1 Cor 9:6]" (*Pud.* 20).[11] Tertullian proceeds to quote Heb 6:4-8 ("It is impossible to restore again to repentance those who have fallen away . . .") as Barnabas's corroborating testimony against the possibility of postbaptismal repentance for fornicators. Hebrews is, for Tertullian, a sub-apostolic letter.

Relatedly, Tertullian provides one of our earliest examples of the detection and rejection of Pauline apocrypha. In *Baptism*, arguing against the idea that Paul permits women to perform baptisms, Tertullian writes, "If certain Acts of Paul, which are falsely so named [*Acta Pauli quae perperam scripta sunt*], claim the example of Thecla for allowing women to teach and to baptize, let men know that in Asia the presbyter who compiled that document, thinking to add of his own to Paul's reputation [*presbyterum qui eam scripturam construxit, quasi titulo Pauli de suo cumulans*], was found out, and though he professed he had done it for love of Paul, was deposed from his position" (*Bapt.* 17.5).[12] This text is a *locus classicus* for the discussion of early Christian attitudes toward pseudepigraphy and an obvious difficulty for the view that the practice was considered benign by ancient readers.[13] In view of his attitude toward *Acts of Paul*, Tertullian's inclusion in his *corpus Paulinum* of letters that are now widely regarded as pseudonymous (e.g., Ephesians, 1 Timothy, 2 Timothy, Titus) is somewhat ironic. But of course, Tertullian could not have predicted that sea

11. Latin text ed. Charles Munier, *La pudicité*, 2 vols., Sources chrétiennes 394–395 (Paris: Cerf, 1993). Trans. alt. from Thelwall in ANF. Our text of 1 Cor 9:6 (per NA28) reads ἢ μόνος ἐγὼ καὶ Βαρναβᾶς οὐκ ἔχομεν ἐξουσίαν μὴ ἐργάζεσθαι; "Or do only Barnabas and I not have the right to refrain from working?" But Tertullian's text of the verse reads *Aut ego solus et Barnabas non habemus operandi potestatem?* which lacks an equivalency for the μή in the last phrase and so exactly reverses the sense of the verse.

12. Text and trans. Ernest Evans, *Tertullian's Homily on Baptism* (London: SPCK, 1964).

13. For the latter view see Bruce M. Metzger, "Literary Forgeries and Canonical Pseudepigrapha," *JBL* 91 (1972): 3–24; and against it see now Bart D. Ehrman, *Forgery and Counterforgery: The Use of Literary Deceit in Early Christian Polemics* (New York: Oxford University Press, 2013). Note that Tertullian's objection to *Acts of Paul* has to do not with pseudonymity but rather with inauthenticity. Those who favored *Acts of Paul* claimed not that Paul wrote the text but that it was a true account of his acts, and it is this latter claim that Tertullian disputes.

change in scholarly opinion. And if he had encountered it, one suspects that he would have mounted a spirited defense of the authenticity of these letters.

With respect to the epistles of Paul to the churches, although Tertullian knows them as part of his Bible, he also attests the tradition that each of the original Pauline assemblies preserved a master copy of its letter from the apostle. In *Prescription against Heretics*, Tertullian writes:

> Go through the apostolic churches, where the very thrones of the apostles at this very day preside over their own districts, where their own genuine letters are read [*apud quas ipsae authenticae litterae eorum recitantur*], which speak their words and bring the presence of each before our minds. If Achaia is nearest to you, you have Corinth. If you are not far from Macedonia, you have Philippi. If you can travel into Asia, you have Ephesus. Or if you are near to Italy, you have Rome, where we too have an authority close at hand. (*Praescr.* 36.1–2)[14]

It is possible that, as Bruce Metzger suggests, *ipsae authenticae litterae* here means to refer to the actual autographs of Paul's letters.[15] Alternatively, one could perhaps interpret the phrase to mean simply "uncorrupted versions" in contrast to the recensions in circulation among the heretics.[16] In any case, for Tertullian the Pauline epistles are not only a canonical deposit enshrined in the New Testament but also the inheritances of the several apostolic churches.

Thus far the canon and the text of Tertullian's *corpus Paulinum*. But how, more specifically, does Tertullian use his Pauline and other biblical sources? The scripture index prepared by Dekkers et al. in the Corpus Christianorum edition confirms Adolf von Harnack's claim that Tertullian's scriptural citations run upward of three thousand, which is actually, by my count, a very conservative estimate.[17] Tertullian is well known, of course, for his two-testament Christian Bible (*Prax.* 15.1; *Marc.* 3.14.3; 4.6.1), but fully two-thirds

---

14. Latin text ed. R. F. Refoulé, *Traité de la prescription contre les hérétiques*, Sources chrétiennes 46 (Paris: Cerf, 1957). Trans. alt. from T. H. Bindley, *Tertullian: On the Testimony of the Soul and On the Prescription of Heretics* (London: SPCK, 1914).

15. Bruce M. Metzger, *The Canon of the New Testament: Its Origin, Development, and Significance* (Oxford: Clarendon, 1987), 4n4.

16. But *ipsae* may suggest that the former interpretation is the more defensible.

17. Adolf von Harnack, "Tertullians Bibliothek christlicher Schriften," *Sitzungsberichte der königlich preussischen Akademie der Wissenschaften* 10 (1914): 303–34, here 308n1. For his estimate Harnack follows the index prepared by Franz Oehler, *Q. S. F. Tertulliani opera omnia*, 3 vols. (Leipzig, 1851–1854) as well as the study of Hermann Roensch, *Das neue Testament Tertullians* (Leipzig, 1871).

of his scriptural citations come from the New Testament. Of those New Testament citations, roughly forty percent come from his *corpus Paulinum*, which is noticeably but not vastly disproportionate. By far the most frequently cited Pauline letter is 1 Corinthians, which is cited more than twice as often as its nearest competitor, Romans, three times as often as 2 Corinthians, Galatians, or Ephesians, and more than seven times as often as any other Pauline letter.[18] The shorter epistles are all reasonably well represented, with the exception of Philemon, which Tertullian recognizes (*Marc.* 5.21) but does not cite.[19] Tertullian's most frequently cited chapter of Paul is 1 Cor 15, the discourse on the resurrection of the dead, which he uses heavily in *The Flesh of Christ* and *The Resurrection of the Flesh* as well as in book 5 of *Against Marcion*. A strong second most frequently cited chapter is 1 Cor 7, Paul's counsel regarding sexual desire and marriage, which features prominently in *Exhortation to Chastity*, *The Veiling of Virgins*, *Monogamy*, and *To His Wife*.

Tertullian's most frequently cited Pauline verses follow a similar trend. The most cited verses, with ten citations each, are 1 Cor 7:29, "From now on, let those who have wives live as though they had none . . .";[20] 1 Cor 11:19, "There must be sects among you in order that those who are genuine may be recognized . . .";[21] and 1 Cor 15:50, "Flesh and blood cannot inherit the kingdom of God . . ."[22] Next in line with nine citations is 1 Cor 15:53, "This perishable nature must put on the imperishable . . ."[23] And finally, passages cited eight times include 1 Cor 1:27, "God chose what is foolish in the world to shame the wise . . .";[24] 1 Cor 7:9, "It is better to marry than to burn . . .";[25] 1 Cor 7:39, "A wife is bound to her husband as long as he lives . . .";[26] 1 Cor 10:4, "They drank from the spiritual rock which followed them, and the rock was Christ . . .";[27] 1 Cor 11:5, "Any woman who prays or prophesies with her head

---

18. So rightly Sider, "Literary Artifice," 119: "Tertullian's Paul, it would seem, emerges more from the Epistles to the Corinthians than from the Epistles to the Romans and the Galatians."

19. Dekkers et al. suggest an allusion to Phlm 10 in the phrase *onesimum aeonem* at *Val.* 32.4, but this is unlikely. Oehler proposes, quite plausibly in my view, that *onesimum* may be a corruption for the numerical name of an aeon ending with the superlative -issimum (F. Oehler, *Q. S. F. Tertulliani opera omnia* [Leipzig, 1854], 3:888).

20. *Exh. cast.* 4.2; 6.1; *Cult. fem.* 2.9.6; *Marc.* 1.29.4; 5.7.8; 5.8.7; *Mon.* 3.2; 7.4; 11.4; *Ux.* 1.5.4.

21. *An.* 3.1; *Herm.* 1.1; *Praescr.* 4.6; 30.4; 39.1; 39.7; *Prax.* 10.8; *Res.* 40.1; 63.8; *Val.* 5.2.

22. *Carn. Chr.* 13.3; *Marc.* 5.10.11; 5.10.15; 5.12.6; 5.14.4; *Res.* 48.1; 49.9; 50.3; 51.4; 51.7.

23. *Marc.* 5.10.14; 5.12.3; *Res.* 42.2; 50.5; 51.8; 54.2; 54.4; 57.9; 60.4.

24. *Bapt.* 2.3; *Carn. Chr.* 4.5; *Fug.* 2.1; *Marc.* 5.5.10; 5.19.8; *Praescr.* 7.1; *Prax.* 10.7; *Res.* 57.11.

25. *Exh. cast.* 3.6; 3.9; 3.10; *Marc.* 5.7.6; *Mon.* 3.4; *Pud.* 1.15; 16.15; *Ux.* 1.3.3.

26. *Exh. cast.* 4.4; *Cor.* 13.5; *Marc.* 5.7.8; *Mon.* 11.1; 11.3; 11.10; 11.11; *Ux.* 2.2.3.

27. *Bapt.* 9.3; *Adv. Jud.* 9.22; *Marc.* 3.5.4; 3.16.5; 4.35.15; 5.5.9; 5.7.12; *Pat.* 5.24.

unveiled dishonors her head . . .";[28] 2 Cor 5:17, "If any one is in Christ, there is new creation . . .";[29] and Eph 6:12, "We contend not against flesh and blood but against the principalities and powers . . ."[30]

Of course, a scripture index is not an infallible guide to a writer's theology, but in the matter before us it is an important piece of evidence. Strikingly, and not coincidentally, Tertullian's most well-worn Pauline texts have to do with women's bodies, personal eschatology, and false teaching. In view of this pattern, there is some truth in Hans von Campenhausen's comment: "Tertullian does not study the Bible in order to derive from it personal enlightenment, edification, or secret knowledge. He loves it for its hard, practical realism, he loves in particular the inexorable clarity of its demands on which salvation depends."[31] It is instructive to consider, by contrast, Pauline texts that Tertullian passes over in silence. As far as I have been able to tell, he never cites Gal 3:28, "There is neither Jew nor Greek, there is neither slave nor free . . ."; Gal 5:22, "The fruit of the spirit is love, joy, peace, patience . . ."; 1 Cor 13:13, "Faith, hope, love abide, these three; but the greatest of these is love . . ."; Rom 3:21, "But now the righteousness of God has been manifested apart from law . . ."; or Rom 5:12, "Just as sin came into the world through one man and death through sin . . . ," to name several interesting examples. On the other hand, Tertullian does cite the bewildering 1 Cor 15:29, "If the dead are not raised, why are people baptized on their behalf?" twice (*Marc.* 5.10.1; *Res.* 48.11) and the textually questionable 1 Cor 14:34–35, "It is shameful for a woman to speak in church . . ." four times (*Bapt.* 17.4; 17.5; *Marc.* 5.8.11; *Virg.* 9.1). Tertullian's preference for these Pauline texts rather than others is just the kind of thing that modern critics have in mind when they say, as many have said, that Tertullian did not really understand Paul.

## PAULINISM IN LATE ANTIQUITY

Which brings us back to the question to which I promised to return—namely, Did Tertullian get Paul right or wrong? A useful way into this question is to consider, for instance, the answer of one eminent scholar of early Christianity who receives some attention in Still and Wilhite's book. Gilles Quispel writes:

28. *Cor.* 6.1; 14.1; *Marc.* 5.8.11; *Or.* 22.1; 22.4; *Virg.* 4.1; 8.2; 11.1.

29. *Jejun.* 14.2; *Marc.* 4.1.6; 4.11.9; 4.33.8; 5.2.1; 5.4.3; 5.12.6; 5.19.11.

30. *Fug.* 1.5; 12.3; *Jejun.* 17.8; *Marc.* 3.14.3; 5.18.12; 5.18.13; *Praescr.* 39.1; *Res.* 22.11.

31. Hans von Campenhausen, *The Formation of the Christian Bible*, trans. J. A. Baker (Philadelphia: Fortress, 1972 [German original 1968]), 275.

Joseph Lortz as early as 1928 observed that the religiosity of St. Paul represented only one type of primitive Christian piety and the rational, monotheistic approach of the Apologists another equally valid and valuable type. This phenomenological approach should be supplemented by the historical observation that Paul never came to Africa and that his letters were never really understood there. Tertullian and Cyprian and their descendants, the Donatists, as well as the Catholics until St. Augustine preached the New Law and did not really understand what 'the rightwising of the ungodly' or 'suffering with Christ' or 'Christ is the end of the law' really meant.[32]

Quispel represents the majority view from the mid-nineteenth to the mid-twentieth century: that Tertullian fundamentally fails to understand Paul's central theological ideas (for Quispel, "the rightwising of the ungodly," "suffering with Christ," and "Christ is the end of the law"). Quispel, following Lortz, attributes Tertullian's misunderstanding to a prevailing misunderstanding of Paul in ancient African Christianity generally, but there are other explanations on offer. Echoing F. C. Baur, Fritz Barth argues that Tertullian strips Paul of his theological genius in order to make him conform to the rest of the apostolic tradition.[33] Eva Aleith suggests that Tertullian was unable to understand Paul because of his own fundamentally different religious sensibilities.[34] Claude Rambaux argues that Tertullian willfully misrepresents Paul's sexual ethics because of his own personal pathologies.[35] Most recently, Calvin Roetzel follows Barth in criticizing Tertullian for filing down the apostle's brilliant rough edges.[36]

The last half-century of scholarship, however, has witnessed a reaction against this dim view of Tertullian's grasp of Paul. Maurice Wiles counters that it is really only Protestantism, not Paulinism, that is lacking in the church

---

32. Gilles Quispel, "African Christianity before Minucius Felix and Tertullian," in *Actus: Studies in Honour of H. L. W. Nelson*, ed. J. den Boeft and A. H. M. Kessels (Utrecht: Institute of Classical Languages, 1982), 257–335, here 297. Quispel's initial reference is to Lortz, *Tertullian als Apologet*, 2:20–30. This comment of Quispel's is discussed by Andrew B. McGowan, "God in Christ: Tertullian, Paul, and Christology," in Still and Wilhite, *Tertullian and Paul*, 1–2.

33. Barth, "Tertullians Auffassung."

34. Aleith, *Paulusverständnis*, 49–61; similarly Quispel, "Christianity in Africa."

35. Rambaux, "La composition et l'exégèse." See further Rambaux, *Tertullien face aux morales des trois premiers siècles* (Paris: Belles Lettres, 1979).

36. Calvin J. Roetzel, "Paul in the Second Century," in *The Cambridge Companion to St Paul*, ed. James D. G. Dunn (Cambridge: Cambridge University Press, 2003), 227–41, esp. 235–37.

fathers prior to Augustine.[37] Andreas Lindemann argues that Tertullian is not simply reacting to Marcion but has his own coherent account of Pauline theology.[38] Robert Sider suggests that, if we give due consideration to Tertullian's literary project, then he is really not so far from Paul, after all.[39] The contributors to Still and Wilhite's book take different views on this vexed question, but as a group they are broadly sympathetic with the recent resuscitation of Tertullian's reputation as an interpreter of Paul. And yet, not a few of them—in particular, John Barclay, Elizabeth Clark, Bruce Longenecker, and Todd Still—justifiably indict Tertullian for some quite serious misreadings of key Pauline texts.[40] This persistent feature of the secondary literature raises the meta-level question, What exactly is Tertullian doing when he cites Paul? What kind of textual activity is it? By what criteria do we call any given instance of Tertullian citing Paul a use, misuse, abuse, or otherwise? Just here, I would like to make a modest proposal.

Scholars working in philosophy (and in cognate branches of religious studies) sometimes use the handy concept of rational reconstruction, in which we imagine what a great dead thinker might say in response to a contemporary question of ours. This is to be distinguished from historical reconstruction, which describes and explains the views of the dead thinker in his own historical context (which is what biblical scholars usually mean by "exegesis"). As Richard Rorty puts it, "Analytic philosophers who have attempted 'rational reconstructions' of the arguments of great dead philosophers have done so in the hope of treating these philosophers as contemporaries, as colleagues with whom they can exchange views. They have argued that unless one does this one might as well turn over the history of philosophy to historians."[41] And

37. Wiles, *Divine Apostle*, 132–39.

38. Andreas Lindemann, *Paulus Apostel und Lehrer der Kirche: Studien zu Paulus und zum frühen Paulusverständnis* (Tübingen: Mohr Siebeck, 1999), 294–322; and Lindemann, *Paulus im ältesten Christentum*, 378–95.

39. Sider, "Literary Artifice."

40. John M. G. Barclay, "Tertullian, Paul, and the Nation of Israel: A Response to Geoffrey D. Dunn," in Still and Wilhite, *Tertullian and Paul*, 98–103; Elizabeth A. Clark, "Status Feminae: Tertullian and the Uses of Paul," in Still and Wilhite, *Tertullian and Paul*, 127–55; Bruce W. Longenecker, "Did Tertullian Succeed? Reflections on Tertullian's Appropration of Paul in His Response to Marcion," in Still and Wilhite, *Tertullian and Paul*, 247–58; Todd D. Still, "Martyrdom as Sacrament: Tertullian's (Mis)Use of 'the Apostle' (Paul)," in Still and Wilhite, *Tertullian and Paul*, 119–26.

41. Richard Rorty, "The Historiography of Philosophy: Four Genres," in *Philosophy in History: Essays on the Historiography of Philosophy*, ed. Richard Rorty et al. (Cambridge: Cambridge University Press, 1984), 49.

again, "[We] want to imagine conversations between ourselves . . . and the mighty dead. We want this not simply because it is nice to feel one up on one's betters, but because we would like to be able to see the history of our race as a long conversational interchange."[42] Rational reconstructions, then, include things like Giorgio Agamben's Pauline political philosophy or Eric Gregory's Augustinian ethic of democratic citizenship.[43] It seems to me that one possible way around the impasse over the question whether Tertullian gets Paul right or wrong is to think of Tertullian's interpretive project as a rational reconstruction of Paul rather than a historical reconstruction, a thought experiment rather than a disciplined exegesis.[44] Of course, Tertullian himself does not make this modern distinction, although he does make an analogous distinction between a biblical text's original context and its subsequent ecclesiastical contexts (*Praescr.* 8; cf. *An.* 35.2; *Res.* 33.5).[45] In other words, Tertullian is aware of a degree of historical distance between Paul and himself, even if he also believes that his interpretation of Paul is incontrovertibly right: *tam meum apostolum quam et Christum*, "as much my apostle as Christ is mine" (*Marc.* 5.1.8).

In this connection, it is instructive to consider Mark Elliott's recent essay "The Triumph of Paulinism by the Mid-Third Century," in which he contends that there is in fact a robust strand of catholic Pauline exegesis running right through Irenaeus, Clement, Tertullian, and Origen. Elliott echoes the argument of Maurice Wiles, who wrote, "The theory that the thought of Paul was totally lost in obscurity of a dark Pelagian world until the shining of the

42. Rorty, "Historiography of Philosophy," 51.

43. Giorgio Agamben, *The Time That Remains: A Commentary on the Letter to the Romans*, trans. Patricia Dailey (Stanford: Stanford University Press, 2005); Eric Gregory, *Politics and the Order of Love: An Augustinian Ethic of Democratic Citizenship* (Chicago: University of Chicago Press, 2010).

44. Cf. Michael F. Bird, "Paul, Tertullian, and the God of the Christians: A Response to Andrew B. McGowan," in Still and Wilhite, *Tertullian and Paul*, 20: "If there is one category that best describes what Tertullian is doing with Paul it is probably 'theological exegesis.'" As I see it, theological exegesis is an accurate but insufficiently specific descriptor for Tertullian's use of Paul. Closer to my notion of rational reconstruction is Sider, "Literary Artifice," 120: "Tertullian's experiment in a Christian literary art whose ends the apostle was made to serve should in itself command our attention. But out of his rhetorical art a figure of the apostle emerges worthy also of our interest, a figure capable of change and growth, rendered present to the reader in the sound of his voice and the touch of his flesh, but at the same time a figure with the power and authority appropriate to a haloed saint."

45. On which see R. P. C. Hanson, "Notes on Tertullian's Interpretation of Scripture," *JTS* 12 (1961): 273–79; Geoffrey D. Dunn, "Tertullian's Scriptural Exegesis in *De praescriptione haereticorum*," *JECS* 14 (2006): 141–55.

great Augustinian light is one deserving to be dismissed to that very limbo of outworn ideas in which it would itself seek to place the early patristic commentaries on the writings of the divine apostle."[46] For my part, I would demur from saying that Paulinism had triumphed by the third century CE, since this seems to suggest an identity between the Paulinism of, say, Tertullian and the Paulinism of Paul himself. I agree with Elliott that a version of Paulinism was ascendant by the third century, and also that this version has at least as strong a claim to "authenticity" (defining which, of course, is precisely the problem) as Marcion's or Augustine's version of Paulinism. But to the extent that Tertullian needs Paul to speak to his own turn-of-the-third-century, proto-orthodox, African Christian problems, his Paulinism is not identical with Paul's own Paulinism, nor could it possibly have been. One thinks of Arnaldo Momigliano's characterization of Tertullian's idiosyncrasies: "He was more afraid of original sin . . . than reassured by the Eucharistic sacrifice. . . . He understood punishment more readily than atonement. . . . He saw more devils than angels."[47] Tertullian's Paulinism is, to use Rorty's term, a rational reconstruction, which is no insult to Tertullian.

In closing: At least two contributors to Still and Wilhite's book quote Harnack's famous bon mot: "Marcion was the only Gentile Christian who understood Paul, and even he misunderstood him."[48] In view of the subject matter of this book, Harnack's comment is obviously apropos. As Andrew McGowan reminds us in his contribution, however, according to Harnack's contemporary and critic Franz Overbeck, this immortal comment originally occurred in the context of polite banter at a dinner party, where Overbeck claims that he said it to Harnack with reference to the nineteenth-century disciples of Hegel.[49] In any case, the "Marcionite" version of the comment found its way into Harnack's influential *History of Dogma* and has been a commonplace in discussion of second-century Christianity ever since.[50] Yet, while it is a brilliant epigram,

46. Wiles, *Divine Apostle*, 139.

47. Arnaldo Momigliano, review of Timothy D. Barnes, *Tertullian: A Historical and Literary Study*, in *JRS* 66 (1976): 273–76.

48. Adolf von Harnack, *History of Dogma*, trans. Neil Buchanan, 7 vols. (London: Williams & Norgate, 1894–1899), 1:89. Harnack's comment is cited and discussed by McGowan, "God in Christ," 1–2; and Stephen Cooper, "Communis Magister Paulus: Altercation over the Gospel in Tertullian's *Against Marcion*," in Still and Wilhite, *Tertullian and Paul*, 227.

49. Franz Overbeck, *Christentum und Kultur: Gedanken und Anmerkungen zur modernen Theologie* (Basel: Benno Schwabe, 1919; repr. 1963), 218–19; noted by Metzger, *Canon of the New Testament*, 93n32; and thence McGowan, "God in Christ," 1.

50. The fuller context of the famous saying runs as follows: "The dependence of the Pauline Theology on the Old Testament or on Judaism is overlooked in the traditional

as an analytical tool Harnack's comment is virtually useless. To say simply that a later thinker understood or misunderstood an earlier one is as imprecise as, well, dinner party banter. Granted, Marcion grasps Paul's conviction that a radically new state of affairs was effected by the death and resurrection of Jesus, but Marcion infers from this that the God of Israel is an evil demon, which is an egregiously un-Pauline conclusion. Tertullian, for his part, denies Paul's conflict with the Jerusalem apostles, erases Paul's distinction between psychic bodies and pneumatic bodies, and turns Paul's ethical concessions into prohibitions, among other interpretive liberties. On the other hand, he grasps Paul's conviction that the law and the prophets testify to the gospel and so makes the fateful decision to retain Paul's Bible as part of the Christian Bible. In fact, both Marcion and Tertullian understand Paul, and both Marcion and Tertullian misunderstand Paul, but on different issues and in different respects. To say, as Harnack does, that Marcion's misunderstanding of Paul was better than Tertullian's (or vice versa) is a pledge of theological allegiance, not a historical judgment. What we need is a subtler, less dogmatic, more historically specific approach to comparing late ancient theologians with their apostolic forebears. Todd Still and David Wilhite, together with their contributors, take steps in the direction of such an approach, and for this we may be sincerely grateful.

---

contrasting of Paulinism and Jewish Christianity, in which Paulinism is made equivalent to Gentile Christianity. . . . This judgment is confirmed by a glance at the fate of Pauline Theology in the 120 years that followed. Marcion was the only Gentile Christian who understood Paul, and even he misunderstood him: the rest never got beyond the appropriation of particular Pauline sayings, and exhibited no comprehension especially of the theology of the Apostle, so far as in it the universalism of Christianity as a religion is proved, even without recourse to Moralism and without putting a new construction on the Old Testament religion" (Harnack, *History of Dogma*, 1:89–90).

12

# ANTI-JUDAISM AND PHILO-JUDAISM IN
# PAULINE STUDIES, THEN AND NOW

According to Epiphanius, the Ebionites thought the theology of Paul so anti-Jewish that they reasoned he could not have been a Jew, but was a gentile proselyte who, when he learned too late that he could not marry a woman from a priestly family, channelled all his resentment into writing his apostolic letters (*Pan.* 30.16.8–9). This story is melodramatic fantasy, but the debate over anti-Judaism in Paul goes back before Epiphanius and the Ebionites[1] to our earliest post-Pauline sources. It is a major theme already in Acts (turn of the second century, plus or minus). When Paul comes to Jerusalem, the Jerusalem apostles warn him, "[The Jewish Christ-believers in Judea] have been instructed about you that you teach all the Jews who are among the gentiles apostasy from Moses, saying that they should not circumcise their children or walk according to the customs" (Acts 21:21). And when Paul's opponents apprehend him a few verses later, they level that very accusation: "This is the person who teaches everyone everywhere against the people and the law and this place [viz. the temple]" (Acts 21:28). The author of Acts, however, insists that these reports about Paul are false. He narrates a scene of Paul bringing a votive offering at the temple (Acts 21:23–26), proving, to the author's

---

1. On whom see A. F. J. Klijn and G. J. Reinink, *Patristic Evidence for Jewish-Christian Sects* (Leiden: Brill, 1973), 19–43; Sakari Häkkinen, "Ebionites," in *A Companion to Second-Century Christian "Heretics,"* ed. Antti Marjanen and Petri Luomanen (Leiden: Brill, 2008), 247–78.

satisfaction, at least, that "there is nothing to what they have been instructed about you, but that you yourself walk by guarding the law" (Acts 21:24).[2] In short, by the turn of the second century, if not before, some Christ-believers hold up Paul as a champion of Judaism, others as an enemy of Judaism.

## PAUL, JUDAISM, AND PROTESTANTISM

The more things change, the more they stay the same. One could organize a textbook on the modern critical study of Paul following the template of this ancient debate recounted in Acts 21.[3] Hence my title: Anti-Judaism and Philo-Judaism in Pauline Studies, Then and Now. Although reams of material could be discussed under this heading,[4] this chapter necessarily selects just a few of the most important figures to illustrate some main points. But first, a brief word on terminology. In my title, I have used the pair "anti-Judaism and philo-Judaism" in a bid for symmetry and accuracy, but the latter term is admittedly awkward and not widely current (although the cognate adjective "philo-Judaic" does have some traction, at least). If one searches for "philo-Judaism" in the standard journal databases and library catalogues, one finds studies of the Judaism of Philo of Alexandria. We, as a linguistic community, have the well-established paired terms "antisemitism" and "philosemitism," and we have the additional term "anti-Judaism" (often used to cover cases where "antisemitism" is considered anachronistic or otherwise not quite right), but we lack a standard contrast term for "anti-Judaism." "Philo-Judaism" would be an obvious choice, clumsy though it may be.[5] It solves the same kinds of conceptual problems that "anti-Judaism" does vis-à-vis "antisemitism." I will therefore use it in this essay as a kind of linguistic experiment.

My central claim is as follows: There is a crucial ambiguity baked into our topic, the importance of which is hard to overestimate. Namely, an anti-

---

2. On this episode and Luke's view of Paul's law observance, see Matthew Thiessen, *Contesting Conversion: Genealogy, Circumcision, and Identity in Ancient Judaism and Christianity* (New York: Oxford University Press, 2011), 111–41.

3. Indeed, Magnus Zetterholm has effectively done so in his *Approaches to Paul: A Student's Guide to Recent Scholarship* (Minneapolis: Fortress, 2009).

4. See further Daniel R. Langton, *The Apostle Paul in the Jewish Imagination* (Cambridge: Cambridge University Press, 2010); Anders Gerdmar, *Roots of Theological Anti-Semitism*, SJHC 20 (Leiden: Brill, 2009); Patrick Gray, *Paul as a Problem in History and Culture* (Grand Rapids: Baker, 2016).

5. There is express warrant for using it in the *Oxford English Dictionary*, s.v. "philo-."

Jewish (or, *mutatis mutandis*, a philo-Judaic) reading of Paul might mean one in which the interpreter exposes *the apostle's* position as anti-Jewish, or it might mean one in which *the interpreter's own* anti-Judaism colors or even determines his or her exegesis of Paul. Indeed, the story of anti-Judaism and philo-Judaism in Pauline studies is, in large part, the story of this ambiguity. Hyam Maccoby, for instance, offers an anti-Jewish reading of Paul in the former sense,[6] while F. C. Baur, to cite an eminent example, offers an anti-Jewish reading of Paul in the latter sense.[7] The plot thickens, however, because Baur thought that he was doing the former, but we, with the benefit of hindsight, know that he was doing the latter (or I, at least, think we know that). Baur's Paul ends up championing Baur's own anti-Jewish hobby-horses.[8] This collapsing of the distinction between Paul's view and the interpreter's view is *the* hermeneutical issue in the matter before us. But here is the thing: in the history of Protestant interpretation, in particular, the collapsing of the distinction between Paul's view and the interpreter's view is, as we say nowadays, not a bug but a feature. Exhibit A: these classic lines from the preface to Karl Barth's monumental commentary on Paul's Letter to the Romans:

> I have nothing whatever to say against historical criticism. I recognize it, and once more state quite definitely that it is both necessary and justified. My complaint is that recent commentators confine themselves to an interpretation of the text which seems to me to be no commentary at all, but merely the first step towards a commentary. . . . Place the work of Jülicher side by side with that of Calvin: how energetically Calvin, having first established what stands in the text, sets himself to re-think the whole material and to wrestle with it, till the walls which separate the sixteenth century from the first become transparent! Paul speaks, and the man of the sixteenth century hears. The conversation between the original record and the reader moves round the subject-matter, until a distinction between yesterday and to-day becomes impossible.[9]

6. Hyam Maccoby, *The Mythmaker: Paul and the Invention of Christianity* (San Francisco: Harper & Row, 1986); and see the review by J. Louis Martyn, "A Gentile in Spite of Himself," *New York Times* (July 20, 1986).

7. F. C. Baur, *Paul the Apostle of Jesus Christ*, trans. Eduard Zeller, 2 vols. (London: Williams & Norgate, 1876 [German original 1845]).

8. See further Gerdmar, *Roots of Theological Anti-Semitism*, 97–120.

9. Karl Barth, "Preface to the Second Edition" (1921), in Barth, *The Epistle to the Romans*, trans. Edwyn C. Hoskyns (Oxford: Oxford University Press, 1933), 6–7.

In this venerable tradition, to collapse the distinction between Paul and the modern interpreter is the whole point of exegesis. In the matter before us, then, we could try to (and in this essay, I sometimes do) introduce terminology to eliminate this ambiguity, but to do so is also to miss the point of most modern Pauline studies, whose whole raison d'être has been to trade on this ambiguity. We will come back to this.

The history of Protestant interpretation of the Bible is littered with instances of anti-Judaism and, less so, of philo-Judaism. This is the case because Protestants (like other Christians, but in our own way) have always used Jews and Judaism as tools for thinking our Christian and Protestant identities. (I say "our" because I am a Protestant myself, though because I come from a family of mixed Jewish, Catholic, and Protestant backgrounds, I am more sharply aware of the contingencies of Protestant history than I might otherwise have been.) There are obvious ethical problems with this phenomenon, but some form of it or other was virtually inevitable once the ancient church rejected Marcionism for a two-testament Christian Bible.[10] (And had the church opted in favour of Marcionism, they would have been stuck with yet another form of the same problem.) At the risk of oversimplifying, we may say that, historically, Protestants have needed the idea of Jews and Judaism in order to know what we, Protestants and Protestantism, are.[11]

Protestant interpretation of all parts of the Bible illustrates this point, but the letters of Paul are a special case. Never are Protestants more Protestant, we might say, than when they are reading Paul.[12] At least part of the reason for this is congenital. Martin Luther, forefather of the Protestant churches, famously prized Paul's letters above the rest of the biblical canon, and Galatians above all else. "The Epistle to the Galatians is my epistle, to which I am betrothed. It is my Katie von Bora"—the name, of course, of Luther's human wife. (Not coincidentally, Galatians is the only book of the New Testament in

10. This problem was perceptively theorized by Brevard Childs, among other places, in his *Biblical Theology of the Old and New Testaments: Theological Reflection on the Christian Bible* (Minneapolis: Fortress, 1992), 55–69.

11. As did many ancient Christians, a phenomenon Paula Fredriksen has perceptively characterized with the phrase "Jews in the head."

12. A point well made by Robert Morgan, "Introduction: The Nature of New Testament Theology," in Morgan, ed., *The Nature of New Testament Theology*, SBT (London: SCM, 1973), 53: "The field of Pauline interpretation . . . is where Protestant theologians since Luther have generally heard the gospel 'clearest of all.' This is, therefore, the point at which their interpretation of the tradition and their own theology are most likely to coincide. In saying what Christianity *was* for Paul, they are often saying what it *is* for themselves" (emphasis original).

which the Greek word Ἰουδαϊσμός, commonly translated *Judentum* or Judaism, occurs: twice in Gal 1:13–14.)[13] I single out Luther here because he is the originator, but it is not only Luther. Many key contributions to the history of Protestant theology have taken the form of interpretations of Paul: Luther's *Lectures on Galatians* (1519 and 1535, not two editions of the same commentary, but two different commentaries), John Calvin's interpretation of Rom 9–11 in his *Institutes of the Christian Religion*, John Wesley's *Explanatory Notes upon the New Testament*, Albrecht Ritschl's *Christian Doctrine of Justification and Reconciliation*, Karl Barth's commentary on Romans (all six editions), Rudolf Bultmann's *Theology of the New Testament* (in which Paul's only equal is John), Thomas Torrance's *Doctrine of Grace in the Apostolic Fathers* (in which Clement, Polycarp, and Ignatius are measured against Paul and found wanting), and many more beside.[14]

Because Protestants have done a great deal of their theology by reading Paul, the modern critical study of Paul has tended to happen especially (though by no means exclusively) in Protestant institutional spaces: Tübingen, Marburg, Cambridge, Durham, Princeton, New Haven, etc. Not so much Rome, Leuven, South Bend, or Jerusalem—until relatively recently, that is, much to the benefit of the discipline.[15] What is more, although the modern critical study of Paul is, in theory, independent of the history of dogma and free to pursue whatever lines of inquiry it may choose, in practice, it has most often run in the grooves carved out by Luther and his successors. Some recent commentators consider this fact a happy one, others think it tragic,[16] but there is little or no dispute that it is the case. In particular, the modern critical study of Paul has

13. On which see Matthew V. Novenson, "Paul's Former Occupation in *Ioudaismos*," in *Galatians and Christian Theology*, ed. Mark W. Elliott et al. (Grand Rapids: Baker Academic, 2014), 24–39.

14. Luther's two sets of *Lectures on Galatians*, of 1519 and 1535, are translated in *Luther's Works*, vols. 26 and 27, respectively. And see John Calvin, *Institutes of the Christian Religion*, trans. Elsie Anne McKee (Grand Rapids: Eerdmans, 2009); John Wesley, *Explanatory Notes upon the New Testament* (London, 1813 [1755]); Albrecht Ritschl, *The Christian Doctrine of Justification and Reconciliation*, trans. H. R. Mackintosh and A. B. Macaulay (Edinburgh: T&T Clark, 1902); Barth, *Romans*; Rudolf Bultmann, *Theology of the New Testament*, trans. Kendrick Grobel, 2 vols. (New York: Scribner's, 1951–1955); Thomas F. Torrance, *The Doctrine of Grace in the Apostolic Fathers* (Edinburgh: Oliver & Boyd, 1948).

15. See, e.g., the excellent Catholic/Jewish/Protestant collaboration *Paul's Jewish Matrix*, ed. Thomas G. Casey and Justin Taylor (Rome: Gregorian and Biblical Press, 2011).

16. See, e.g., Stephen Westerholm, *Justification Reconsidered: Rethinking a Pauline Theme* (Grand Rapids: Eerdmans, 2013) for the former perspective; and J. Albert Harrill, *Paul the Apostle: His Life and Legacy in Their Roman Context* (New York: Cambridge University Press, 2012) for the latter.

often taken for granted what Luther took for granted: that the interpretation of Paul consists in explaining where, how, and why Paul departs from Judaism. Historically, to do Protestant theology is to interpret Paul, and to interpret Paul is to explain Paul's relation to Judaism.

But this state of affairs is contingent, not inevitable. Catholic exegesis of Paul naturally shares with its Protestant counterpart a number of inherited theological problematics, but it is, on the whole, considerably less anxious than Protestant exegesis of Paul is. Compare the Romans commentaries by Joseph Fitzmyer and Brendan Byrne on the one hand with their Protestant counterparts by James Dunn and Robert Jewett on the other.[17] Reading Catholic exegesis of Paul, one gets the sense that there is less at stake, because, well, there is less at stake. Catholic theology has recourse not only to the rest of the canon but also to tradition and magisterium, whereas Protestant theology stands or falls on its interpretation of Paul. (I generalize and exaggerate, but not by much.) Of course, this is also why some Protestant exegesis of Paul (e.g., Barth's commentary on Romans, or part 2 of Bultmann's *Theology of the New Testament*, or J. Louis Martyn's commentary on Galatians) can be so exciting to read, because one can tell that, for the author, life and death hang in the balance.[18] This is bracing stuff, but it has not always yielded the most sober, disciplined historical judgments.

## ANTI-JUDAISM IN PAULINE STUDIES

While there certainly have been egregious examples of racist antisemitism in Protestant New Testament scholarship (one thinks immediately of Walter Grundmann's quixotic quest for an Aryan Jesus),[19] in Pauline studies, it seems

17. Joseph A. Fitzmyer, *Romans: A New Translation with Introduction and Commentary*, AYB (New Haven: Yale University Press, 2008 [1993]); Brendan Byrne, *Romans*, SP (Collegeville, MN: Liturgical Press, 1996); James D. G. Dunn, *Romans*, 2 vols., WBC (Dallas: Word Books, 1988); Robert Jewett, *Romans: A Commentary*, Hermeneia (Minneapolis: Fortress, 2007).

18. Barth, *Romans*; Bultmann, *Theology of the New Testament*; J. Louis Martyn, *Galatians: A New Translation with Introduction and Commentary*, AYB (New Haven: Yale University Press, 2010 [1997]). Another, more recent example is Douglas A. Campbell, *The Deliverance of God: An Apocalyptic Rereading of Justification in Paul* (Grand Rapids: Eerdmans, 2009).

19. Walter Grundmann, *Jesus der Galiläer und das Judentum* (Leipzig: Georg Wigand, 1940), on which see Gerdmar, *Roots of Theological Anti-Semitism*, 531–76; and Susannah Heschel, *The Aryan Jesus: Christian Theologians and the Bible in Nazi Germany* (Princeton: Princeton University Press, 2008).

to me, the glaring problem is theological anti-Judaism. Most Protestant theologies of Paul require a foe for the apostle to vanquish, and most have made
Judaism play the part of that foe, however it may need to be constructed in
order so to serve (e.g., as legalism, ritualism, or ethnocentrism). "The apostle's
message of justification is a fighting doctrine, directed against Judaism," as
Ernst Käsemann put it,[20] and an overwhelming number of modern interpreters have agreed.

This is true already of Luther's *Lectures on Galatians*, mentioned above.
Luther casts Paul's anonymous opponents in the letter, whom Paul himself
only calls "agitators" (Gal 1:7; 5:10), as representatives of Judaism. "Right after
he [Paul] had gone away false teachers among the Galatians had destroyed
what he had built up so painstakingly. These false apostles, adherents of Judaism and Pharisaism at that, were men of great prestige and authority."[21] For
Luther, Paul's fight is with Judaism, which is assumed to teach a false gospel
of justification from works of the law. But Luther also makes this supposed
Jewish false gospel stand in for all the sixteenth-century theologies with which
he, Luther, has a quarrel. He writes, "If the doctrine of justification is lost, the
whole of Christian doctrine is lost. And those in the world who do not teach
it are either Jews or Turks or papists or sectarians. For between these two
kinds of righteousness, the active righteousness of the Law and the passive
righteousness of Christ, there is no middle ground."[22] For Luther, the imagined
Jews of Galatians represent Jews in his own present, but they also represent
Turks (i.e., Muslims), papists (i.e., Roman Catholics), and sectarians (i.e., other
non-Lutheran churches). This is a rhetorically powerful kind of theological
anti-Judaism, different in interesting ways, however, from the crass antisemitism of old man Luther's *On the Jews and Their Lies* of 1543.[23]

If Luther marks the beginning of Protestant interpretation of Paul, then
Baur marks the beginning of modern, critical interpretation of Paul, which,
not coincidentally, has also been largely Protestant.[24] "Anti-Judaism" (*Antiju-
daismus*) is actually Baur's own term for the apostle's theology. Arguing, for

---

20. Ernst Käsemann, "Justification and Salvation History in the Letter to the Romans,"
in *Perspectives on Paul*, trans. Margaret Kohl (London: SCM, 1971), 70.

21. Luther, *Lectures on Galatians* (1535), 14.

22. Luther, *Lectures on Galatians* (1535), 9.

23. On which see Thomas Kaufmann, *Luther's Jews: A Journey into Anti-Semitism*, trans.
Lesley Sharpe and Jeremy Noakes (Oxford: Oxford University Press, 2017).

24. On Baur's tremendous significance, see the essays collected in *Ferdinand Christian
Baur and the History of Early Christianity*, ed. Martin Bauspiess et al., trans. Robert F. Brown
and Peter C. Hodgson (Oxford: Oxford University Press, 2017).

instance, that Marcion's fourteen-chapter recension of Romans was in fact the original text, Baur writes, "The criticism of the last chapters [i.e., Rom 15–16] leads to but one result: they must be held to be the work of a Paulinist, writing in the spirit of the Acts of the Apostles, seeking to soothe the Judaists, and to promote the cause of unity, and therefore tempering the keen anti-Judaism of Paul with a milder and more conciliatory conclusion to his Epistle."[25] Baur's overarching historical question is how Christianity managed to break free of its origins in Judaism.[26] As he puts it, "How Christianity, instead of remaining a mere form of Judaism, and ultimately being absorbed in it, asserted itself as a separate, independent principle, broke loose from it and took its stand as a new form of religious thought and life, essentially differing from Judaism, and freed from all its national exclusiveness, is the point of next greatest importance in the primitive history of one Christianity."[27] On Baur's telling, the hero of this story is Paul, whose genius lies in his anti-Judaism, his realization that Judaism itself is the problem.[28] "The element of the Jewish religion, which must have excited the most lively repugnance in the fully formed Christian consciousness, as it appeared for the first time in Paul, was undoubtedly its empty confidence in outward works. From this it was necessary to appeal to the inner disposition—to faith."[29] With Baur we need not lay the charge of anti-Judaism; he confesses to it openly. It is his own name for Paul's guiding theological principle.[30]

Most (though not all) subsequent interpreters have been far more subtle. In the twentieth century, Protestant interpreters tended to favor the idea that, for Paul, Jews and Judaism represent *homo religiosus*, humanity at its pious best.[31] There are myriad examples, but one standout is Ernst Käsemann, a student of Bultmann and one of the foremost Paulinists writing after the Second World War. Käsemann writes, "The apostle's real adversary is the devout Jew, not only as the mirror-image of his own past—though that, too—but as the reality of the religious man. . . . Religion always provides man with his

---

25. Baur, *Paul the Apostle*, 1:365.

26. See Anders Gerdmar, "Baur and the Creation of the Judaism-Hellenism Dichotomy," in Bauspiess, *Baur and the History of Early Christianity*, 96–115.

27. Baur, *Paul the Apostle*, 1:3.

28. See Christof Landmesser, "Ferdinand Christian Baur as Interpreter of Paul: History, the Absolute, and Freedom," in Bauspiess, *Baur and the History of Early Christianity*, 147–76.

29. Baur, *Paul the Apostle*, 2:307.

30. See further Gerdmar, *Roots of Theological Anti-Semitism*, 97–120.

31. On which theme, see the critical but sympathetic discussion by Francis Watson, *Paul, Judaism, and the Gentiles*, rev. ed. (Grand Rapids: Eerdmans, 2007), 27–56.

most thoroughgoing possibility of confusing an illusion with God. Paul sees this possibility realized in the devout Jew."[32] There are echoes here of Luther's idea that the Jews represent not only themselves but also Muslims, Catholics, and heretics—that is, religious people who nevertheless do not grasp the (Lutheran, or Käsemannian) gospel of Christian righteousness. Käsemann argues further in the same essay, "Israel has exemplary significance for [Paul]; in and with Israel he strikes at the hidden Jew in all of us, at the man who validates rights and demands over against God on the basis of God's past dealings with him and to this extent is serving not God but an illusion."[33] Here the Jew is not just a historical but a psychological phenomenon, "the hidden Jew in all of us," that aspect of the human self that makes demands of God.[34] Käsemann is much less contemptuous of actual Jews than Luther or Baur had been, but his use of Jewishness as a cipher in this way is another kind of theological anti-Judaism.[35]

The New Perspective on Paul, a movement so named by James Dunn in 1982, fits rather awkwardly in this story.[36] Dunn credited E. P. Sanders's 1977 *Paul and Palestinian Judaism* with catalyzing the movement, but Sanders himself has never owned the label and arguably does not do what Dunn's New Perspective does.[37] Sanders showed with devastating effectiveness that the traditional (read: Protestant) interpretation of Paul depended on a colossal straw man, a theory of a supposedly ubiquitous Jewish doctrine of salvation by works (as, e.g., in Ferdinand Weber's *Jüdische Theologie*).[38] Sanders showed that there was no such doctrine, which left New Testament scholars wonder-

---

32. Ernst Käsemann, "Paul and Israel," in *New Testament Questions of Today*, trans. W. J. Montague (Philadelphia: Fortress, 1969), 184.

33. Käsemann, "Paul and Israel," 186.

34. On this theme in Käsemann, see the devastating criticism of Daniel Boyarin, *A Radical Jew: Paul and the Politics of Identity* (Berkeley: University of California Press, 1994), 209–14.

35. See further R. Barry Matlock, *Unveiling the Apocalyptic Paul*, JSNTSup 127 (Sheffield: Sheffield Academic, 1996), 186–246.

36. The movement was spoken into being by James D. G. Dunn, "The New Perspective on Paul," *BJRL* 65 (1983): 95–122, which is reprinted together with Dunn's other major Pauline essays in Dunn, *The New Perspective on Paul*, rev. ed. (Grand Rapids: Eerdmans, 2008).

37. The landmark book was E. P. Sanders, *Paul and Palestinian Judaism: A Comparison of Patterns of Religion* (Philadelphia: Fortress, 1977). Sanders's own reading of Paul is more fully laid out in his *Paul, the Law, and the Jewish People* (Philadelphia: Fortress, 1983); and his most recent statement is Sanders, *Paul: The Apostle's Life, Letters, and Thought* (Minneapolis: Fortress, 2015).

38. Ferdinand Weber, *Jüdische Theologie*, 2nd ed. (Leipzig: Dörffling & Franke, 1897).

ing what, then, Paul was so exercised about. Sanders himself appealed to the simple thatness of Christ: "The law is good, even doing the law is good, but salvation is only by Christ; therefore the entire system represented by the law is worthless for salvation."[39] Or, more tersely and famously: "In short, this is what Paul finds wrong in Judaism: It is not Christianity."[40]

For Dunn's New Perspective, however, this is too arbitrary an answer. Dunn complains, "The Lutheran Paul has been replaced by [Sanders's] idiosyncratic Paul who in arbitrary and irrational manner turns his face against the glory and greatness of Judaism's covenant theology."[41] Unlike Sanders, Dunn needs to diagnose a problem in the Judaism of Paul's day to which the apostle can respond and over which he can triumph. Dunn finds it not, as previous generations of Protestant interpreters had done, in legalism but rather in nationalism: "Judaism had itself invested so much significance in these particular works, so that the test of loyalty to covenant and law was precisely the observance of circumcision, food laws and Sabbath. . . . They had become the expression of a too narrowly nationalistic and racial conception of the covenant, because they had become a badge not of Abraham's faith but of Israel's boast."[42] Similar but more measured is the New Perspective à la N. T. Wright, who writes, "Paul's critique of Israel was aimed not at proto-Pelagianism or 'moralism' but at ethnocentric covenantalism."[43] Sanders had the closest thing I know of in Pauline studies to a genuinely new insight: that the entire scholarly quest for "Paul's critique of Judaism" was and had always been a mistake. With Dunn's New Perspective, however, the quest was re-entrenched,[44] but now it was Pauline universalism over against Jewish ethnocentrism, in contrast to the older freedom-versus-legalism rubric.

## PHILO-JUDAISM IN PAULINE STUDIES

Not at all coincidentally, it is in the aftermath of the Holocaust that we begin to see significant strands of philo-Judaism in academic Pauline studies. This development was part of the reckoning, happening in many corners of Christian

---

39. Sanders, *Paul and Palestinian Judaism*, 550.
40. Sanders, *Paul and Palestinian Judaism*, 552.
41. Dunn, "New Perspective on Paul," 103.
42. Dunn, "New Perspective on Paul," 118–19.
43. Wright, "Romans and the Theology of Paul," 66.
44. A point well made by Matthew Thiessen, *Paul and the Gentile Problem* (New York: Oxford University Press, 2016), 4–7.

theology, with the long history of Christian anti-Judaism and antisemitism.[45] There had been earlier dissenters from the mainstream of anti-Jewish interpretation of Paul. One thinks especially of Albert Schweitzer's *Paul and His Interpreters* (1912) and *Mysticism of Paul the Apostle* (1931) and W. D. Davies's *Paul and Rabbinic Judaism* (1948),[46] both of whom interpreted Paul's theology in inner-Jewish terms: apocalyptic Jewish for Schweitzer, rabbinic Jewish for Davies, but both firmly against the majority view that Paul marshalled the resources of Hellenism to transcend Judaism.[47] But these earlier scholars dissented on historicist grounds, not ecumenical ones. They were correcting an error in historical-critical interpretation, not doing anti-supersessionist theology for the churches.

In the 1950s and following, though, a number of interpreters undertook to do the latter in addition to the former. The foremost figure in this movement was Krister Stendahl, longtime professor of New Testament at Harvard and latterly also Lutheran bishop of Stockholm in his native Sweden. Stendahl's argument—now justly famous—is that Paul's gospel is not about salving the guilty conscience but about bringing unwashed gentiles into covenant with the God of Abraham.[48] For Stendahl's Paul, it is gentiles, not Jews, who are the problem. He writes, for instance:

> Paul does not say that when the time of God's kingdom, the consummation, comes Israel will accept Jesus as the Messiah. He says only that the time will come when "all Israel will be saved" ([Rom] 11:26). It is stunning to note that Paul writes this whole section of Romans (10:17–11:36) without using the name of Jesus Christ. . . . Paul's reference to God's mysterious plan is an affirmation of a God-willed coexistence between Judaism and Christianity in which the missionary urge to convert Israel is held in check.[49]

---

45. On this period, see William Baird, *From C. H. Dodd to Hans Dieter Betz*, vol. 3 of Baird, *History of New Testament Research* (Minneapolis: Fortress, 2013).

46. Albert Schweitzer, *Paul and His Interpreters: A Critical History*, trans. W. Montgomery (London: Black, 1912); Schweitzer, *The Mysticism of Paul the Apostle*, trans. W. Montgomery (London: Black, 1931); W. D. Davies, *Paul and Rabbinic Judaism: Some Rabbinic Elements in Pauline Theology* (London: SPCK, 1948).

47. On this older majority view and its discontents, see Troels Engberg-Pedersen, ed., *Paul beyond the Judaism/Hellenism Divide* (Louisville: Westminster John Knox, 2001).

48. Esp. in his *Paul among Jews and Gentiles, and Other Essays* (Philadelphia: Fortress, 1976); but see also his later *Final Account: Paul's Letter to the Romans* (Minneapolis: Fortress, 1995).

49. Stendahl, "Paul among Jews and Gentiles," in *Paul among Jews and Gentiles*, 4.

That last sentence hints at Stendahl's post-Holocaust ecumenical stance, which becomes quite explicit later in the same essay:

> The United States of today [1963] is the first place in the modern world since Philo's Alexandria where Jews and Christians as people, as religious communities, and as learned communities, live together in a manner and in sufficient numbers to allow for open dialogue. It is the first time in recent history where there could be an open relation between Christians and Jews and where the conversation which Paul started in Romans 9–11, but which was broken off mainly by Christian expansion and superiority feelings, can start again. The pain of history and the shame of the holocaust interfere with real dialogue, but the possibility really exists and, it is to be hoped, will increase.[50]

Above I suggested that Baur illustrates the collapsing of the distinction between Paul's view and the Protestant interpreter's view: both Baur and Baur's Paul are contemptuous of a Judaism supposedly preoccupied with legal externalism. But Stendahl, too, illustrates this Protestant collapsing of horizons, albeit in a much more ethically praiseworthy direction. In this connection, there is a poignant story about Stendahl related by the German Jewish philosopher Jacob Taubes, a friend and almost exact contemporary of Stendahl who, however, pre-deceased Stendahl by more than twenty years. In his brilliant *Political Theology of Paul*, Taubes writes:

> [Krister Stendahl] visited me once in New York, and we were standing in front of a very large fireplace. And Krister—he's a real warrior type, you know, Goebbels would have envied him his figure—he says to me that his deepest worry is whether he belongs (we were speaking English) to the "commonwealth of Israel." So I said to myself, Krister, you super-Aryan from Sweden, at the end of the world, as viewed from the Mediterranean, other worries you don't have? No, he has no other worries! There I saw what Paul had done: that someone in the jungles of Sweden—as seen from where I'm standing—is worrying about whether he belongs to the "commonwealth of Israel," that's something that's impossible without Paul. (I was able to reassure him: as far as I'm concerned he's in.)[51]

---

50. Stendahl, "Paul among Jews and Gentiles," 37.
51. Jacob Taubes, *The Political Theology of Paul*, trans. Dana Hollander (Stanford: Stanford University Press, 2004), 41.

This is a lovely story of a Jewish/Christian friendship forged in the aftermath of twentieth-century atrocity, but it also illustrates our point about Protestant exegesis of Paul. Stendahl the exegete argues that Paul's apostolate is about bringing gentiles into the people of God, and Stendahl the gentile Christian worries whether he himself will be counted among that people. The wall between the first century and the twentieth becomes transparent, Barth might have said.

If Stendahl saw in Paul's letters "a God-willed coexistence between Judaism and Christianity," some of his successors went further still, arguing that Paul has a fully formed two-covenant theology: gentiles are to be saved through Christ-faith, Jews through the Sinai covenant.[52] One standout figure here is the North American Presbyterian Lloyd Gaston, whose 1987 book *Paul and the Torah* is a landmark in this tradition of liberal Protestant exegesis.[53] Gaston starts from the theological problematic famously posed by Rosemary Radford Ruether in her 1974 *Faith and Fratricide*: "Possibly anti-Judaism is too deeply embedded in the foundations of Christianity to be rooted out entirely without destroying the whole structure."[54] Whereas Ruether the Catholic thinks this problem theologically, Gaston the Protestant answers it with—lo and behold—an exegesis of Paul. To Ruether's sobering claim that "anti-Judaism is the left hand of Christology," Gaston answers, "It may be that Paul, and Paul alone among the New Testament writers, has no left hand. . . . I believe that it is possible to interpret Paul in this manner. That it is necessary to do so is the implication of the agonized concern of many in the post-Auschwitz situation."[55] Note Gaston's Protestant reasoning: In the agonized post-Auschwitz situation, Christian theology is on the ropes, but a fresh reading of the letters of Paul will save us. Or, as he says elsewhere, "A Christian church with an anti-Semitic New Testament is abominable, but a Christian church without a New

---

52. For a retrospect on and thoughtful criticism of this hypothesis, see Terence L. Donaldson, "Jewish Christianity, Israel's Stumbling, and the *Sonderweg* Reading of Paul," *JSNT* 29 (2006): 27–54.

53. Lloyd Gaston, *Paul and the Torah* (Vancouver: University of British Columbia Press, 1987). Also important here is Gaston's contemporary John G. Gager, who reads Paul similarly but without Gaston's theological commitments. See John G. Gager, *The Origins of Anti-Semitism: Attitudes toward Judaism in Pagan and Christian Antiquity* (New York: Oxford University Press, 1983), 193–264; Gager, *Reinventing Paul* (New York: Oxford University Press, 2000).

54. Rosemary Radford Ruether, *Faith and Fratricide: The Theological Roots of Anti-Semitism* (New York: Seabury, 1974), 228.

55. Gaston, *Paul and the Torah*, 34.

Testament is inconceivable."[56] Philo-Judaic exegesis of the New Testament becomes a moral imperative, and Paul is the canon within the canon who will admit of such an exegesis.

## CONCLUSION

The state of anti-Judaism and philo-Judaism in Pauline studies now is both like and unlike what it was then—that is, in generations past. It is *unlike*, in many respects, for the better. One is not likely to find the racist antisemitism of the later Luther or the interreligious contempt of a Baur in any work of critical Pauline studies nowadays. That it took an evil on the scale of the Holocaust to effect this change in scholarship is shameful, but we may be grateful, at least, that change did come. But the state of affairs now is also *like* what it was then in some respects. Pauline studies is still a disproportionately Protestant project. And although the extreme sentiments of a Luther or a Baur have become déclassé, other, cooler-headed anti-Jewish interpretations of Paul survive and even thrive.[57] Claims such as Käsemann's—"Paul's real opponent is the devout Jew," "Paul strikes at the hidden Jew in all of us"—are still quite close to the mainstream, which—and this, I think, is the key—continues to look for Paulinism at just those points where Paul supposedly departs from his ancestral religion. If Paulinism is, as per a Protestant axiom, *true* and, as per the aforementioned model, *not Judaism*, then some form of theological anti-Judaism, however soft, is virtually inevitable. Hence while almost all interpreters nowadays line up to affirm that Paul is a Jew, most also hasten to qualify that affirmation: he is an anomalous Jew, a radical Jew, a transformed Jew, a redefined Jew[58] (where it is assumed that, say, the Teacher of Righteousness, or Philo, or Bar Kokhba was not anomalous or radical each in his own way).

56. Gaston, *Paul and the Torah*, 15.

57. A number of such interpretations are footnoted in Paula Fredriksen, *Paul: The Pagans' Apostle* (New Haven: Yale University Press, 2017). See also Matthew Thiessen, "Conjuring Paul and Judaism Forty Years after *Paul and Palestinian Judaism*," *JJMJS* 5 (2018): 6–20.

58. E.g., John M. G. Barclay, *Jews in the Mediterranean Diaspora* (Edinburgh: T&T Clark, 1996), 381–96: "Paul: an anomalous diaspora Jew"; Love Sechrest, *A Former Jew: Paul and the Dialectics of Race*, LNTS 410 (London: T&T Clark, 2009); N. T. Wright, *Paul and the Faithfulness of God*, 2 vols. (London: SPCK, 2013), 2:774–1042: "the people of God [Israel, Jews], freshly reworked"; Michael F. Bird, *An Anomalous Jew: Paul among Jews, Greeks, and Romans* (Grand Rapids: Eerdmans, 2016), 1–30: "Paul the Jew . . . of sorts."

Significantly, however, the popular anomalous-Jewish or radical-Jewish
Pauls of recent interpretation are not at all anomalous or radical relative to
the theological views of their proponents. Quite the contrary. Indeed, what all
of the various anti-Jewish and philo-Judaic Pauls we have discussed have in
common is their extremely close affinity with the theologies of their respective
modern interpreters. Whether Paul is presented as blisteringly anti-Jewish or
humanely philo-Judaic, he almost never fails to agree with the person doing
the presenting.[59] This is why it is so jarring to read the rare interpretation
of Paul (e.g., Albert Schweitzer's or Paula Fredriksen's) in which the apostle
comes out looking genuinely strange, holding views that no modern person,
of whatever theological persuasion, holds.[60]

With Schweitzer, I would argue that it makes for both better history *and*
better theology to let Paul be Paul and then to take responsibility for whatever
theological and ethical steps we need to take beyond or away from him.[61]
(Easier said than done, I realize; most of the interpreters discussed above have
said that they were letting Paul be Paul. But it is possible to do better.) This
rule applies to a great many topics, but Judaism is certainly one of the most
important. E. P. Sanders, representing a road unfortunately not taken in the
subsequent New Perspective debates of the 1980s and 1990s, made this point
in one of his early discussions. He writes:

> It perhaps should go without saying . . . that Paul's view does not provide
> an adequate basis for a Jewish-Christian dialogue. Generations have come
> and gone, and Paul's expectations have not been fulfilled. His references to
> the fullness of the Gentiles and to all Israel depend on his expectation that
> the Redeemer would come soon, and they have in view only the generation

---

59. Recall Robert Morgan's observation: "In saying what Christianity *was* for Paul,
they are often saying what it *is* for themselves" ("Nature of New Testament Theology," 53;
emphasis original).

60. Schweitzer, *Mysticism of Paul*; Fredriksen, *Pagans' Apostle*. One also thinks here of
Rudolf Bultmann's famous demythologizing project, which, whatever weaknesses it may
have had, paid Paul the compliment of allowing him to hold strange ancient views.

61. See Schweitzer, *Mysticism of Paul*, x: "My methods have remained old-fashioned, in
that I aim at setting forth the ideas of Paul in their historically conditioned form. I believe
that the mingling of ours ways of regarding religion with those of former historical periods,
which is now so much practised, often with dazzling cleverness, is of no use as an aid to
historical comprehension, and of not much use in the end for our religious life." For an
impressive recent effort to think theology along similar lines, see Dale B. Martin, *Biblical
Truths: The Meaning of Scripture in the Twenty-First Century* (New Haven: Yale University
Press, 2017).

during which Paul worked. Thus they cannot be used in any simple way to determine what Paul would have thought of the fate of future generations of either Gentiles or Jews. We may put the matter this way: what Paul would have thought, had he foreseen that God would not do what he based his entire life on expecting him to do, is simply imponderable. That will not, however, keep us from pondering it.[62]

It should go without saying, Sanders writes, but it really does not. It needs careful, repeated saying. As I have argued here, it is in the disciplinary DNA of academic Pauline studies (especially but not only of the Protestant variety) to assume that Paul's view on anything, but on Judaism above all, *does* provide an adequate basis for a modern view on that thing. Barth's ideal of the hermeneutical dissolution of the wall between the first and twenty-first centuries remains an ideal for many, perhaps most. That ideal, however, will strongly press the interpreter to read Paul as saying what she herself believes to be theologically true—for example, that Judaism is a religion of empty ritual (thus Baur), or that Christ came to save gentiles only (thus Gaston), or any of a thousand other passionately held views. There may be no other ancient author whom we have such a hard time just letting him be himself, letting him hold the views that he holds. On average, non-Christian interpreters can perform this hermeneutical feat more easily than Christian ones can, and Catholics more easily than Protestants,[63] but almost no one does it effortlessly (see, e.g., Daniel Boyarin's *A Radical Jew*, or Alain Badiou's *The Foundation of Universalism*).[64] The story of anti-Judaism and philo-Judaism in Pauline studies is a classic story of what happens when we moderns use an ancient person's words to do our thinking for us.

62. Sanders, *Paul, the Law, and the Jewish People*, 197.

63. See, e.g., Claudia Setzer, "Does Paul Need to Be Saved?" *BibInt* 13 (2005): 289–97; Gregory Tatum, "Did Paul Find Anything Wrong with Judaism?" *JJMJS* 5 (2018): 38–44.

64. Boyarin, *Radical Jew*; Alain Badiou, *Saint Paul: The Foundation of Universalism*, trans. Ray Brassier (Stanford: Stanford University Press, 2003).

# BIBLIOGRAPHY

Adam, A. K. M. *Making Sense of New Testament Theology: "Modern" Problems and Prospects.* Macon, GA: Mercer University Press, 1995.

Agamben, Giorgio. *The Time That Remains: A Commentary on the Letter to the Romans.* Translated by Patricia Dailey. Stanford: Stanford University Press, 2005.

Ahuvia, Mika. *On My Right Michael, On My Left Gabriel: Angels in Ancient Jewish Culture.* Berkeley: University of California Press, 2021.

Albini, Umberto, ed. *Lisia: I discorsi.* Florence: Sansoni, 1955.

Aleith, Eva. *Paulusverständnis in der alten Kirche.* BZNW 18. Berlin: Töpelmann, 1937.

Arneson, Hans K. "Revisiting the Sense and Syntax of Romans 2:28–29." Forthcoming.

Arnold, Matthew. *St. Paul and Protestantism.* Pop. ed. London: Smith & Elder, 1887.

Aslan, Reza. *Zealot: The Life and Times of Jesus of Nazareth.* New York: Random House, 2013.

Badiou, Alain. *Saint Paul: The Foundation of Universalism.* Translated by Ray Brassier. Stanford: Stanford University Press, 2003.

Bain, Andrew M. "Tertullian: Paul as Teacher of the Gentile Churches." Pp. 207–25 in *Paul and the Second Century.* Edited by Michael F. Bird and Joseph R. Dodson. LNTS 412. London: T&T Clark, 2011.

Baird, William. *History of New Testament Research*, Volume 3: *From C. H. Dodd to Hans Dieter Betz.* Minneapolis: Fortress, 2013.

Bakker, Arjen, Rene Bloch, Yael Fisch, Paula Fredriksen, and Hindy Najman, eds. *Antisemitism and Philosemitism in Protestant Bible Scholarship*. JSJSup. Leiden: Brill, forthcoming.

Barclay, John M. G. "Deviance and Apostasy: Some Applications of Deviance Theory to First-Century Judaism and Christianity." Pp. 123–39 in *Pauline Churches and Diaspora Jews*. Grand Rapids: Eerdmans, 2016.

_____. "An Identity Received from God: The Theological Configuration of Paul's Kinship Discourse." *EC* 8 (2017): 354–72.

_____. "*Ioudaios*: Ethnicity and Translation." Pp. 46–58 in *Ethnicity, Race, Religion*. Edited by Katherine M. Hockey and David G. Horrell. London: T&T Clark, 2018.

_____. *Jews in the Mediterranean Diaspora*. Edinburgh: T&T Clark, 1996.

_____. *Obeying the Truth: Paul's Ethics in Galatians*. Vancouver: Regent College Publishing, 1988.

_____. "Paul among Diaspora Jews: Anomaly or Apostate?" *JSNT* 60 (1995): 89–120.

_____. "Paul and Philo on Circumcision: Romans 2.25–9 in Social and Cultural Context." *NTS* 44 (1998): 536–56.

_____. *Paul and the Gift*. Grand Rapids: Eerdmans, 2015.

_____. *Pauline Churches and Diaspora Jews*. Grand Rapids: Eerdmans, 2016.

_____. "Tertullian, Paul, and the Nation of Israel: A Response to Geoffrey D. Dunn." Pp. 98–103 in *Tertullian and Paul*. Edited by Todd D. Still and David E. Wilhite. London: T&T Clark, 2013.

_____. "What Makes Paul Challenging Today?" Pp. 299–318 in *The New Cambridge Companion to St. Paul*. Edited by Bruce W. Longenecker. Cambridge: Cambridge University Press, 2020.

_____. "Who Was Considered an Apostate in the Jewish Diaspora?" Pp. 141–56 in *Pauline Churches and Diaspora Jews*. Grand Rapids: Eerdmans, 2016.

Barrett, C. K. *A Commentary on the Epistle to the Romans*. HNTC. New York: Harper & Row, 1957.

_____. *The Epistle to the Romans*. 2nd ed. BNTC. London: Black, 1991.

Barth, Fritz. "Tertullians Auffassung des Apostels Paulus und seines Verhältnisses zu den Uraposteln." *JPT* 8 (1882): 706–56.

Barth, Karl. *The Epistle to the Romans*. Translated by Edwyn D. Hoskyns. London: Oxford University Press, 1933.

Barth, Markus. *The People of God*. JSNTSup 5. Sheffield: Sheffield Academic, 1983.

Bauckham, Richard. "Gamaliel and Paul." Pp. 87–106 in *Earliest Christianity within the Boundaries of Judaism: Essays in Honor of Bruce Chilton*. Edited by Alan J. Avery-Peck, Craig Evans, and Jacob Neusner. BRLJ 49. Leiden: Brill, 2016.

_____. "Paul's Christology of Divine Identity." Pp. 182–232 in *Jesus and the God of Israel*. Grand Rapids: Eerdmans, 2009.

Bauer, Walter, F. W. Danker, William F. Arndt, and F. Wilbur Gingrich. *A Greek-English Lexicon of the New Testament and Other Early Christian Literature.* 3rd ed. Chicago: University of Chicago Press, 2000.

Baur, F. C. *Paul the Apostle of Jesus Christ.* Translated by Eduard Zeller. Revised by A. Menzies. 2 vols. London: Williams & Norgate, 1876.

Bauspiess, Martin, Christof Landmesser, and David Lincicum, eds. *Ferdinand Christian Baur and the History of Early Christianity.* Translated by Robert F. Brown and Peter C. Hodgson. Oxford: Oxford University Press, 2017.

Beckheuer, Burkhard. *Paulus und Jerusalem.* Frankfurt: Peter Lang, 1997.

Berger, Klaus. "Jesus als Pharisäer und frühe Christen als Pharisäer." *NovT* 30 (1988): 231–62.

*Biblia Hebraica Stuttgartensia.* Edited by K. Elliger and W. Rudolph. 5th ed. Stuttgart: Deutsche Bibelgesellschaft, 1997.

Bickermann, Elias J. "The Warning Inscriptions of Herod's Temple." *JQR* 37 (1946–1947): 387–405.

Bindley, T. H., trans. *Tertullian: On the Testimony of the Soul and On the Prescription of Heretics.* London: SPCK, 1914.

Bird, Michael F. *An Anomalous Jew: Paul among Jews, Greeks, and Romans.* Grand Rapids: Eerdmans, 2016.

_____. "Paul, Tertullian, and the God of the Christians: A Response to Andrew B. McGowan." Pp. 16–21 in *Tertullian and Paul*. Edited by Todd D. Still and David E. Wilhite. London: T&T Clark, 2013.

Blanton, Ward. *A Materialism for the Masses: Saint Paul and the Philosophy of Undying Life.* New York: Columbia University Press, 2014.

Blount, Brian K. *Cultural Interpretation: Reorienting New Testament Criticism.* Minneapolis: Fortress, 1995.

Boakye, Andrew K. *Death and Life: Resurrection, Restoration, and Rectification in Paul's Letter to the Galatians.* Eugene, OR: Pickwick, 2017.

Boccaccini, Gabriele, and Carlos A. Segovia, eds. *Paul the Jew: Rereading the Apostle as a Figure of Second Temple Judaism.* Minneapolis: Fortress, 2016.

Bockmuehl, Markus. "'The Form of God' (Phil 2:6): Variations on a Theme of Jewish Mysticism." *JTS* 48 (1997): 1–23.

Bockmuehl, Markus, and Alan J. Torrance, eds. *Scripture's Doctrine and Theology's Bible.* Grand Rapids: Baker Academic, 2008.

Bonar, Chance. "Epistles of Paul and Seneca." *e-Clavis: Christian Apocrypha.* http://www.nasscal.com/e-clavis-christian-apocrypha/epistles-of-paul-and-seneca/.

Bond, Helen K. *The First Biography of Jesus: Genre and Meaning in Mark's Gospel.* Grand Rapids: Eerdmans, 2020.

Bowens, Lisa M. *African American Readings of Paul: Reception, Resistance, and Transformation.* Grand Rapids: Eerdmans, 2020.

Bowersock, G. W. "Who Was Saint Paul?" *New York Review of Books* (November 5, 2015).

Boyarin, Daniel. *The Jewish Gospels: The Story of the Jewish Christ.* New York: Free Press, 2012.

_____. *Judaism: The Genealogy of a Modern Notion.* New Brunswick, NJ: Rutgers University Press, 2018.

_____. *A Radical Jew: Paul and the Politics of Identity.* Berkeley: University of California Press, 1994.

Brandom, Robert B. "Hermeneutic Practice and Theories of Meaning." *SATS Northern European Journal of Philosophy* 5 (2004): 1–22.

_____. *Tales of the Mighty Dead: Historical Essays in the Metaphysics of Intentionality.* Cambridge, MA: Harvard University Press, 2002.

Breed, Brennan W. *Nomadic Text: A Theory of Biblical Reception History.* Bloomington: Indiana University Press, 2014.

Brooten, Bernadette. "'Junia . . . Outstanding among the Apostles' (Romans 16:7)." Pp. 141–44 in *Women Priests: A Catholic Commentary on the Vatican Declaration.* Edited by Leonard Swidler and Arlene Swidler. New York: Paulist, 1977.

Brown, Alexandra R. *The Cross and Human Transformation: Paul's Apocalyptic Word in 1 Corinthians.* Minneapolis: Fortress, 1995.

Buell, Denise Kimber. *Why This New Race: Ethnic Reasoning in Early Christianity.* New York: Columbia University Press, 2005.

Buell, Denise Kimber, and Caroline Johnson Hodge. "The Politics of Interpretation: The Rhetoric of Race and Ethnicity in Paul." *JBL* 123 (2004): 235–51.

Bultmann, Rudolf. *Der Stil der paulinischen Predigt und die kynisch-stoische Diatribe.* FRLANT 13. Göttingen: Vandenhoeck & Ruprecht, 1910.

_____. *New Testament and Mythology, and Other Basic Writings.* Translated by Schubert M. Ogden. Philadelphia: Fortress, 1984.

_____. *Theology of the New Testament.* Translated by Kendrick Grobel. 2 vols. New York: Scribner's, 1951–1955.

Butcher, S. H., ed. *Demosthenis orationes.* 3 vols. Oxford: Clarendon, 1903.

Byrne, Brendan. *Romans.* SP. Collegeville, MN: Liturgical Press, 1996.

Calvin, John. *Institutes of the Christian Religion.* Translated by Elsie Anne McKee. Grand Rapids: Eerdmans, 2009.

Campbell, Douglas A. *The Deliverance of God: An Apocalyptic Rereading of Justification in Paul.* Grand Rapids: Eerdmans, 2009.

_____. *Pauline Dogmatics: The Triumph of God's Love.* Grand Rapids: Eerdmans, 2020.

Campbell, William S. "I Rate All Things as Loss: Paul's Puzzling Accounting System." Pp. 39–61 in *Celebrating Paul.* Edited by Peter Spitaler. CBQMS 48. Washington, DC: Catholic Biblical Association, 2011.

_____. *Paul and the Creation of Christian Identity.* LNTS 322. London: T&T Clark, 2006.

Campenhausen, Hans von. *The Formation of the Christian Bible.* Translated by J. A. Baker. Philadelphia: Fortress, 1972.

Carleton Paget, James. "Schweitzer and Paul." *JSNT* 33 (2011): 223–56.

Carraway, George. *Christ Is God Over All: Romans 9:5 in the Context of Romans 9–11.* LNTS 489. London: T&T Clark, 2013.

Casey, Thomas G., and Justin Taylor, eds. *Paul's Jewish Matrix.* Rome: Gregorian and Biblical Press, 2011.

Chaniotis, Angelos. "Megatheism: The Search for the Almighty God and the Competition of Cults." Pp. 112–40 in *One God: Pagan Monotheism in the Roman Empire.* Edited by Stephen Mitchell and Peter van Nuffelen. Cambridge: Cambridge University Press, 2010.

Charles, R. H., trans. *The Book of Jubilees, or The Little Genesis.* London: SPCK, 1917.

Charles, Ronald. *Paul and the Politics of Diaspora.* Minneapolis: Fortress, 2014.

Chester, Andrew. "The Sibyl and the Temple." Pp. 37–69 in *Templum Amicitiae: Essays on the Second Temple Presented to Ernst Bammel.* Edited by William Horbury. JSNTSup 48. Sheffield: Sheffield Academic, 1991.

Chester, Stephen J. *Reading Paul with the Reformers: Reconciling Old and New Perspectives.* Grand Rapids: Eerdmans, 2017.

Childs, Brevard S. *Biblical Theology of the Old and New Testaments: Theological Reflection on the Christian Bible.* Minneapolis: Fortress, 1992.

Chin, C. M. "Marvelous Things Heard: On Finding Historical Radiance." *Massachusetts Review* 58 (2017): 478–91.

Clark, Elizabeth A. "*Status Feminae*: Tertullian and the Uses of Paul." Pp. 127–55 in *Tertullian and Paul.* Edited by Todd D. Still and David E. Wilhite. London: T&T Clark, 2013.

Cohen, Shaye J. D. *The Beginnings of Jewishness: Boundaries, Varieties, Uncertainties.* Hellenistic Culture and Society 31. Berkeley: University of California Press, 1999.

_____. "The Significance of Yavneh: Pharisees, Rabbis, and the End of Jewish Sectarianism." *HUCA* 55 (1984): 27–53.

_____. Review of *Contesting Conversion*, by Matthew Thiessen. *CBQ* 75 (2013): 379–81.

Collins, John J., trans. "Sibylline Oracles." Pp. 317–472 in vol. 1 of *The Old Testament Pseudepigrapha*. Edited by James H. Charlesworth. 2 vols. New York: Doubleday, 1983.

_____. "The Zeal of Phinehas: The Bible and the Legitimation of Violence." *JBL* 122 (2003): 3–21.

Collman, Ryan D. "Apostle to the Foreskin: Circumcision in the Letters of Paul." PhD diss., University of Edinburgh, 2021.

_____. "Beware the Dogs! The Phallic Epithet in Philippians 3:2." *NTS* 67 (2021): 105–20.

Concannon, Cavan W. "Paul Is Dead. Long Live Paulinism! Imagining a Future for Pauline Studies." *Ancient Jew Review* (November 1, 2016). www.ancientjewreview.com/read/2016/11/1/paul-is-dead-long-live-paulinism-imagining-a-future-for-pauline-studies.

_____. *Profaning Paul*. Chicago: University of Chicago Press, 2021.

_____. *When You Were Gentiles: Specters of Ethnicity in Roman Corinth and Paul's Corinthian Correspondence*. Synkrisis. New Haven: Yale University Press, 2014.

Cooper, Stephen. "*Communis Magister Paulus*: Altercation over the Gospel in Tertullian's *Against Marcion*." Pp. 224–246 in *Tertullian and Paul*. Edited by Todd D. Still and David E. Wilhite. London: T&T Clark, 2013.

Cover, Michael B. "Now and Above, Then and Now (Gal 4:21–31): Platonizing and Apocalyptic Polarities in Paul's Eschatology." Pp. 220–29 in *Galatians and Christian Theology*. Edited by Mark W. Elliott, Scott J. Hafemann, N. T. Wright, and John Frederick. Grand Rapids: Baker Academic, 2014.

_____. "Paulus als Yischmaelit? The Personification of Scripture as Interpretive Authority in Paul and the School of Rabbi Ishmael." *JBL* 135 (2016): 617–37.

Cranfield, C. E. B. *The Epistle to the Romans*. 2 vols. ICC. London: T&T Clark, 2010.

Dahl, Nils A. "The Future of Israel." Pp. 137–58 in Dahl, *Studies in Paul: Theology for the Early Christian Mission*. Minneapolis: Augsburg, 1977.

_____. "The Neglected Factor in New Testament Theology." Pp. 153–63 in Dahl, *Jesus the Christ: The Historical Origins of Christological Doctrine*. Edited by Donald H. Juel. Minneapolis: Fortress, 1991.

_____. "The Particularity of the Pauline Letters as a Problem in the Ancient Church." Pp. 165–78 in Dahl, *Studies in Ephesians*. WUNT 131. Tübingen: Mohr Siebeck, 2000.

Davies, J. P. *Paul among the Apocalypses? An Evaluation of the "Apocalyptic Paul" in the Context of Jewish and Christian Apocalyptic Literature.* LNTS 562. London: T&T Clark, 2016.

Davies, W. D. *Paul and Rabbinic Judaism: Some Rabbinic Elements in Pauline Theology.* London: SPCK, 1948.

De Boer, Martinus C. *The Defeat of Death: Apocalyptic Eschatology in 1 Corinthians 15 and Romans 5.* JSNTSup 22. Sheffield: JSOT Press, 1988.

de Jonge, Marinus, ed. *Testamenta xii patriarcharum.* 2nd ed. Leiden: Brill, 1970.

Deissmann, Adolf. *St. Paul: A Study in Social and Religious History.* Translated by Lionel R. M. Strachan. London: Hodder & Stoughton, 1912.

Derrida, Jacque. "Différance." Pp. 1–28 in *Margins of Philosophy.* Translated by Alan Bass. Chicago: University of Chicago Press, 1982.

Dimant, Devorah. "Jerusalem and the Temple in the Animal Apocalypse (1 Enoch 85–90) in Light of the Qumran Community Worldview." Pp. 119–137 in *From Enoch to Tobit.* FAT 114. Tübingen: Mohr Siebeck, 2017. Hebrew original 1983.

Dindorf, Ludwig August, and Theodorus Büttner-Wobst, eds. *Polybii Historiae.* Leipzig: Teubner, 1867–1885.

Dingeldein, Laura B. "Gaining Virtue, Gaining Christ: Moral Development in the Letters of Paul." PhD diss., Brown University, 2014.

Dinkler, Michal Beth. *Literary Theory and the New Testament.* AYBRL. New Haven: Yale University Press, 2019.

Dio Cassius. *Roman History.* Translated by Earnest Carey. LCL. Cambridge, MA: Harvard University Press, 1914.

Dochhorn, Jan. "Der Vorwurf des Tempelraubs in Röm 2,22b und seine politischen Hintergründe." *ZNW* 109 (2018): 101–17.

Dodd, C. H. *The Epistle to the Romans.* MNTC. London: Hodder & Stoughton, 1932.

Donaldson, Terence L. "Jewish Christianity, Israel's Stumbling, and the *Sonderweg* Reading of Paul." *JSNT* 29 (2006): 27–54.

———. *Judaism and the Gentiles: Jewish Patterns of Universalism (to 135 CE).* Waco, TX: Baylor University Press, 2007.

———. *Paul and the Gentiles: Remapping the Apostle's Convictional World.* Minneapolis: Fortress, 1997.

———. "Zealot and Convert: The Origin of Paul's Christ-Torah Antithesis." *CBQ* 51 (1989): 655–82.

Donfried, Karl P., ed. *The Romans Debate.* Rev. ed. Edinburgh: T&T Clark, 1991.

Donfried, Karl P., and Johannes Beutler, eds. *The Thessalonians Debate.* Grand Rapids: Eerdmans, 2000.

Downs, David J. *The Offering of the Gentiles: Paul's Collection for Jerusalem in Its Chronological, Cultural, and Cultic Contexts.* Grand Rapids: Eerdmans, 2016.

du Toit, Andrie. Review of *Paul's Interlocutor in Romans 2*, by Runar M. Thorsteinsson. *Neot* 38 (2004): 152–54.

Dunn, Geoffrey D. *Tertullian*. London: Routledge, 2004.

_____. "Tertullian's Scriptural Exegesis in *De praescriptione haereticorum*." *JECS* 14 (2006): 141–55.

Dunn, James D. G. "The New Perspective on Paul." *BJRL* 65 (1983): 95–122

_____. *The New Perspective on Paul*. Rev. ed. Grand Rapids: Eerdmans, 2005.

_____. *Romans*. 2 vols. WBC. Nashville: Nelson, 1988.

Eastman, David L. *Paul the Martyr: The Cult of the Apostle in the Latin West*. Atlanta: SBL Press, 2011.

Ehrensperger, Kathy. *Paul at the Crossroads of Cultures: Theologizing in the Space Between*. LNTS 456. London: T&T Clark, 2013.

Ehrman, Bart D. *Forgery and Counterforgery: The Use of Literary Deceit in Early Christian Polemics*. New York: Oxford University Press, 2013.

_____. *How Jesus Became God: The Exaltation of a Jewish Preacher from Galilee*. San Francisco: HarperOne, 2014.

Eisenbaum, Pamela. "Paul, Polemics, and the Problem of Essentialism." *BibInt* 13 (2005): 224–38.

Elliott, J. K. *The Apocryphal New Testament*. Oxford: Clarendon, 1993.

Elliott, John H. "Jesus the Israelite Was Neither a 'Jew' nor a 'Christian': On Correcting Misleading Nomenclature." *JSHJ* 5 (2007): 119–54.

Engberg-Pedersen, Troels. *Cosmology and Self in the Apostle Paul: The Material Spirit*. Oxford: Oxford University Press, 2010.

_____. *Paul and the Stoics*. Edinburgh: T&T Clark, 2000.

_____, ed. *Paul beyond the Judaism/Hellenism Divide*. Louisville: Westminster John Knox, 2001.

Epictetus. *Discourses*. Translated by W. A. Oldfather. LCL. Cambridge, MA: Harvard University Press, 1925.

Epp, Eldon Jay. *Junia: The First Woman Apostle*. Minneapolis: Fortress, 2005.

Euripides. Translated by David Kovacs. LCL. Cambridge, MA: Harvard University Press, 1995.

Evans, Ernest, ed. *Tertullian: Adversus Marcionem*. 2 vols. Oxford: Clarendon, 1972.

_____, trans. *Tertullian's Homily on Baptism*. London: SPCK, 1964.

Eyl, Jennifer. "'I Myself Am an Israelite': Paul, Authenticity, and Authority." *JSNT* 40 (2017): 148–68.

_____. *Signs, Wonders, and Gifts: Divination in the Letters of Paul*. New York: Oxford University Press, 2019.

Fairchild, Mark R. "Paul's Pre-Christian Zealot Associations: A Re-examination of Gal 1:14 and Acts 22:3." *NTS* 45 (1999): 514–32.

Fee, Gordon D. *Paul's Letter to the Philippians*. NICNT. Grand Rapids: Eerdmans, 1995.

Fitzmyer, Joseph A. *Romans: A New Translation with Introduction and Commentary*. AYB. New Haven: Yale University Press, 2008.

Frankfurter, David. "Jews or Not? Reconstructing the 'Other' in Rev 2:9 and 3:9." *HTR* 94 (2001): 403–25.

Fredriksen, Paula. *Augustine and the Jews: A Christian Defense of Jews and Judaism*. New Haven: Yale University Press, 2010.

_____, ed. *Augustine on Romans*. Chico, CA: Scholars Press, 1982.

_____. "Augustine's Early Interpretation of Paul." PhD diss., Princeton University, 1979.

_____. *From Jesus to Christ: The Origins of the New Testament Images of Jesus*. New Haven: Yale University Press, 1988.

_____. "How High Can Early High Christology Be?" Pp. 293–319 in *Monotheism and Christology in Greco-Roman Antiquity*. Edited by Matthew V. Novenson. NovTSup 180. Leiden: Brill, 2020.

_____. "How Later Contexts Affect Pauline Content, or: Retrospect Is the Mother of Anachronism." Pp. 17–51 in *Jews and Christians in the First and Second Centuries: How to Write Their History*. Edited by Peter J. Tomson and Joshua Schwartz. CRINT 13. Leiden: Brill, 2014.

_____. *Jesus of Nazareth, King of the Jews: A Jewish Life and the Emergence of Christianity*. New York: Knopf, 1999.

_____. "Judaism, the Circumcision of Gentiles, and Apocalyptic Hope: Another Look at Galatians 1 and 2." *JTS* 42 (1991): 532–64.

_____. "Judaizing the Nations: The Ritual Demands of Paul's Gospel." *NTS* 56 (2010): 232–52.

_____. "Mandatory Retirement: Ideas in the Study of Christian Origins Whose Time Has Come to Go." *SR* 35 (2006): 231–46.

_____. "Paul the 'Convert'?" In *Oxford Handbook of Pauline Studies*. Edited by Matthew V. Novenson and R. Barry Matlock. Oxford: Oxford University Press, forthcoming.

_____. *Paul: The Pagans' Apostle*. New Haven: Yale University Press, 2017.

_____. "Paul's Letter to the Romans, the Ten Commandments, and Pagan Justification by Faith." *JBL* 133 (2014): 801–8.

_____. "The Philosopher's Paul and the Problem of Anachronism." Pp. 61–73 in *St. Paul among the Philosophers*. Edited by John D. Caputo and Linda Martin Alcoff. Bloomington: Indiana University Press, 2009.

_____. *Sin: The Early History of an Idea*. Princeton: Princeton University Press, 2012.

_____. "What 'Parting of the Ways'? Jews, Gentiles, and the Ancient Mediterranean City." Pp. 35–63 in *The Ways That Never Parted: Jews and Christians in Late Antiquity and the Early Middle Ages*. Edited by Adam H. Becker and Annette Yoshiko Reed. Minneapolis: Fortress, 2007.

Frei, Hans W. *The Eclipse of Biblical Narrative: A Study in Eighteenth and Nineteenth Century Hermeneutics*. New Haven: Yale University Press, 1974.

Frey, Jörg. "Contextualizing Paul's 'Works of the Law': MMT in New Testament Scholarship." Pp. 743–62 in Frey, *Qumran, Early Judaism, and New Testament Interpretation: Kleine Schriften III*. Edited by Jacob N. Cerone. WUNT 424. Tübingen: Mohr Siebeck, 2019.

Furnish, Victor Paul. *1 Thessalonians, 2 Thessalonians*. ANTC. Nashville: Abingdon, 2007.

Gadamer, Hans-Georg. *Truth and Method*. 2nd rev. ed. Translated by Joel Weinsheimer and Donald G. Marshall. London: Bloomsbury, 2013.

Gager, John G. *The Origins of Anti-Semitism: Attitudes toward Judaism in Pagan and Christian Antiquity*. New York: Oxford University Press, 1983.

_____. *Reinventing Paul*. New York: Oxford University Press, 2000.

_____. *Who Made Early Christianity? The Jewish Lives of the Apostle Paul*. New York: Columbia University Press, 2015.

Gager, John G., and E. Leigh Gibson. "Violent Acts and Violent Language in the Apostle Paul." Pp. 11–21 in *Violence in the New Testament*. Edited by Shelly Matthews and E. Leigh Gibson. London: T&T Clark, 2005.

Gamble, Harry. *The Textual History of the Letter to the Romans*. SD 42. Grand Rapids: Eerdmans, 1979.

Garroway, Joshua D. "The Circumcision of Christ: Romans 15:7–13." *JSNT* 34 (2012): 303–22.

_____. "Paul: Within Judaism, Without Law." Pp. 49–66 in *Law and Lawlessness in Early Judaism and Early Christianity*. Edited by David Lincicum, Ruth Sheridan, and Charles M. Stang. WUNT 420. Tübingen: Mohr Siebeck, 2019.

_____. "Paul's Gentile Interlocutor in Romans 3:1–20." Pp. 85–100 in *The So-Called Jew in Paul's Letter to the Romans*. Edited by Rafael Rodriguez and Matthew Thiessen. Minneapolis: Fortress, 2016.

_____. *Paul's Gentile-Jews: Neither Jew nor Gentile, but Both*. New York: Palgrave Macmillan, 2012.

_____. "The Pharisee Heresy: Circumcision for Gentiles in the Acts of the Apostles." *NTS* 60 (2014): 20–36.

Gaston, Lloyd. *Paul and the Torah*. Vancouver: University of British Columbia Press, 1987.

Gaventa, Beverly Roberts, ed. *Apocalyptic Paul: Cosmos and Anthropos in Romans 5–8*. Waco, TX: Baylor University Press, 2013.

_____. "The Cosmic Power of Sin in Paul's Letter to the Romans." *Int* 58 (2004): 229–40.

_____. *Our Mother Saint Paul*. Louisville: Westminster John Knox, 2007.

_____. *Romans*. NTL. Louisville: Westminster John Knox, forthcoming.

_____. "The Singularity of the Gospel." Pp. 101–12 in *Our Mother Saint Paul*. Louisville: Westminster John Knox, 2007.

Georgi, Dieter. *Remembering the Poor: The History of Paul's Collection for Jerusalem*. Nashville: Abingdon, 1992. German original 1965.

Gerdmar, Anders. "Baur and the Creation of the Judaism–Hellenism Dichotomy." Pp. 96–115 in *Ferdinand Christian Baur and the History of Early Christianity*. Edited by Martin Bauspiess, Christof Landmesser, and David Lincicum. Translated by Robert F. Brown and Peter C. Hodgson. Oxford: Oxford University Press, 2017.

_____. *Roots of Theological Anti-Semitism*. SJHC 20. Leiden: Brill, 2009.

Goodman, Martin. *A History of Judaism*. Princeton: Princeton University Press, 2018.

_____. *Mission and Conversion: Proselytizing in the Religious History of the Roman Empire*. Oxford: Clarendon, 1994.

_____. "The Persecution of Paul by Diaspora Jews." Pp. 145–52 in *Judaism in the Roman World: Collected Essays*. AJEC 67. Leiden: Brill, 2007.

Goodman, Martin, George H. van Kooten, and Jacques T. A. G. M. van Ruiten, eds. *Abraham, the Nations, and the Hagarites: Jewish, Christian, and Islamic Perspectives on Kinship with Abraham*. Leiden: Brill, 2010.

Gray, Patrick. *Paul as a Problem in History and Culture*. Grand Rapids: Baker Academic, 2016.

Gregory, Eric. *Politics and the Order of Love: An Augustinian Ethic of Democratic Citizenship*. Chicago: University of Chicago Press, 2010.

Grundmann, Walter. *Jesus der Galiläer und das Judentum*. Leipzig: Georg Wigand, 1940.

Gupta, Nijay K., and John K. Goodrich, eds. *Sin and Its Remedy in Paul*. Eugene, OR: Cascade, 2020.

Hahn, Ferdinand. *Mission in the New Testament*. SBT 47. London: SCM, 1965.

Häkkinen, Sakari. "Ebionites." Pp. 247–78 in *A Companion to Second-Century Christian "Heretics."* Edited by Antti Marjanen and Petri Luomanen. Leiden: Brill, 2008.

Hall, Jonathan M. *Ethnic Identity in Greek Antiquity*. Cambridge: Cambridge University Press, 1997.

Hamerton-Kelly, Robert G. *Sacred Violence: Paul's Hermeneutic of the Cross*. Minneapolis: Fortress, 1992.

Hanson, R. P. C. "Notes on Tertullian's Interpretation of Scripture." *JTS* 12 (1961): 273–79.

Harnack, Adolf von. *History of Dogma*. Translated by Neil Buchanan. 7 vols. London: Williams & Norgate, 1894–1899.

_____. "Tertullians Bibliothek christlicher Schriften." *Sitzungsberichte der königlich preussischen Akademie der Wissenschaften* 10 (1914): 303–34.

_____. *What Is Christianity?* Translated by Thomas Bailey Saunders. New York: Harper, 1957.

Harrill, J. Albert. *Paul the Apostle: His Life and Legacy in Their Roman Context*. New York: Cambridge University Press, 2012.

Harvey, Graham. *The True Israel: Uses of the Names Jew, Hebrew, and Israel in Ancient Jewish and Early Christian Texts*. AGJU 35. Leiden: Brill, 1996.

Hayes, Christine. *What's Divine about Divine Law? Early Perspectives*. Princeton: Princeton University Press, 2015.

Hays, Richard B. "Christ Prays the Psalms: Israel's Psalter as Matrix of Early Christology." Pp. 101–18 in *The Conversion of the Imagination: Paul as Interpreter of Israel's Scripture*. Grand Rapids: Eerdmans, 2005.

_____. *Echoes of Scripture in the Letters of Paul*. New Haven: Yale University Press, 1989.

_____. "Have We Found Abraham to Be Our Forefather according to the Flesh? A Reconsideration of Rom 4:1." *NovT* 27 (1985): 76–98.

Heath, Malcom. *Menander: A Rhetor in Context*. Oxford: Oxford University Press, 2004.

Heine, Ronald E. "In Search of Origen's Commentary on Philemon." *HTR* 93 (2000): 117–33.

Hengel, Martin. *The Pre-Christian Paul*. Translated by John Bowden. London: SCM, 1991.

_____. *The Zealots*. Translated by John Bowden. Edinburgh: T&T Clark, 1989. Translation of *Die Zeloten*. Leiden: Brill, 1961.

Hengel, Martin, and Roland Deines. "Common Judaism, Jesus, and the Pharisees." *JTS* 46 (1995): 1–70.

Heschel, Susannah. *The Aryan Jesus: Christian Theologians and the Bible in Nazi Germany*. Princeton: Princeton University Press, 2008.

Hewitt, J. Thomas. "Ancient Messiah Discourse and Paul's Expression *achris hou elthe to sperma* in Galatians 3:19." *NTS* 65 (2019): 398–411.

_____. *Messiah and Scripture: Paul's "in Christ" Idiom in Its Ancient Jewish Context*. WUNT 2.522. Tübingen: Mohr Siebeck, 2020.

Hicks-Keeton, Jill. "Already/Not Yet: Eschatological Tension in the Book of Tobit." *JBL* 132 (2013): 97–117.

_____. "Putting Paul in His Place: Diverse Diasporas and Sideways Spaces in Hellenistic Judaism." *JJMJS* 6 (2019): 1–21.

Hill, Wesley. *Paul and the Trinity: Persons, Relations, and the Pauline Letters.* Grand Rapids: Eerdmans, 2015.

Holder, R. Ward, ed. *A Companion to Paul in the Reformation.* Leiden: Brill, 2009.

Holl, Karl. "Tertullian als Schriftsteller." Pp. 1–12 in vol. 3 of *Gesammelte Aufsätze zur Kirchengeschichte.* Tübingen: Mohr, 1928.

Horbury, William. "Jewish and Christian Monotheism in the Herodian Age." Pp. 2–33 in *Herodian Judaism and New Testament Study.* WUNT 193. Tübingen: Mohr Siebeck, 2006.

Horn, Friedrich Wilhelm. Review of *Paul's Interlocutor in Romans 2*, by Runar M. Thorsteinsson. *TLZ* 130 (2005): 786–89.

Horsley, Richard A. "The Zealots: The Origin, Relationships, and Importance in the Jewish Revolt." *NovT* 28 (1986): 159–92.

Hultin, Jeremy. "Who Rebuked Cephas? A New Interpretation of Gal 2:14–17." Paper presented at the Annual Meeting of the Society of Biblical Literature, Baltimore, MD, November 2013.

Humphreys, S. H. "Social Relations on Stage: Witnesses in Classical Athens." *History and Anthropology* 1 (1985): 313–69.

Hurtado, Larry W. *Lord Jesus Christ: Devotion to Jesus in Earliest Christianity.* Grand Rapids: Eerdmans, 2003.

Irmscher, J., F. Paschke, and B. Rehm, eds. *Die Pseudoklementinen I. Homilien.* 2nd ed. GCS. Berlin: Akademie Verlag, 1969.

Jenson, Robert W. "On the Authorities of Scripture." Pp. 146–54 in *The Triune Story: Collected Essays on Scripture.* Edited by Brad East. Oxford: Oxford University Press, 2019.

Jeremias, Joachim. "Paulus als Hillelit." Pp. 88–94 in *Neotestamentica et Semitica: Studies in Honour of Matthew Black.* Edited by E. Earle Ellis and Max Wilcox. Edinburgh: T&T Clark, 1969.

Jewett, Robert. *Romans: A Commentary.* Hermeneia. Minneapolis: Fortress, 2007.

Jipp, Joshua W. *Christ Is King: Paul's Royal Ideology.* Minneapolis: Fortress, 2015.

_____. *The Messianic Theology of the New Testament.* Grand Rapids: Eerdmans, 2020.

Johnson Hodge, Caroline. *If Sons Then Heirs: A Study of Kinship and Ethnicity in the Letters of Paul.* New York: Oxford University Press, 2007.

Jones, Christopher P. *Between Pagan and Christian.* Cambridge, MA: Harvard University Press, 2014.

Josephus. *Jewish Antiquities, Volume IV: Books 9-11.* Translated by Ralph Marcus. Loeb Classical Library 326. Cambridge, MA: Harvard University Press, 1937.

———. *The Jewish War, Volume II: Books 3-4.* Translated by H. St. J. Thackeray. Loeb Classical Library 487. Cambridge, MA: Harvard University Press, 1927.

Kalmin, Richard. "Pharisees in Rabbinic Literature of Late Antiquity." *Sidra* 24–25 (2010): 7–28.

Käsemann, Ernst. *Commentary on Romans.* Translated by Geoffrey W. Bromiley. Grand Rapids: Eerdmans, 1980.

———. *New Testament Questions of Today.* Translated by W. J. Montague. Philadelphia: Fortress, 1969.

———. *Perspectives on Paul.* Translated by Margaret Kohl. London: SCM, 1971.

Kattan Gribetz, Sarit. "The Shema in the Second Temple Period: A Reconsideration." *JAJ* 6 (2015): 58–84.

Kaufmann, Thomas. *Luther's Jews: A Journey into Anti-Semitism.* Translated by Lesley Sharpe and Jeremy Noakes. Oxford: Oxford University Press, 2017.

Keck, Leander E. "The Function of Rom 3:10–18: Observations and Suggestions." Pp. 141–57 in *God's Christ and His People: Studies in Honour of Nils Alstrup Dahl.* Edited by Jacob Jervell and Wayne A. Meeks. Oslo: Universitetsforlaget, 1977.

———. "The Poor among the Saints in the New Testament." *ZNW* 56 (1965): 100–129.

———. *Romans.* ANTC. Nashville: Abingdon, 2005.

Kennedy, George A. *Classical Rhetoric and Its Christian and Secular Tradition from Ancient to Modern Times.* 2nd ed. Chapel Hill: University of North Carolina Press, 1999.

Kim, Seyoon. "Paul and Violence." *Ex Auditu* 34 (2018): 67–89.

Kimelman, Reuven. "Rabbinic Prayer in Late Antiquity." Pp. 573–611 in vol. 4 of *The Cambridge History of Judaism.* Edited by Steven T. Katz. Cambridge: Cambridge University Press, 2006).

King, Donald B. "The Appeal to Religion in Greek Rhetoric." *CJ* 50 (1955): 363–76.

Klausner, Joseph. *History of the Second Temple.* 5 vols. Jerusalem: Ahiasaf, 1949. Hebrew.

Klawans, Jonathan. *Josephus and the Theologies of Ancient Judaism.* New York: Oxford University Press, 2012.

Klijn, A. F. J., and G. J. Reinink. *Patristic Evidence for Jewish-Christian Sects.* Leiden: Brill, 1973.

Koch, Dietrich-Alex. *Die Schrift als Zeuge des Evangeliums.* BHT 69. Tübingen: Mohr Siebeck, 1986.

Kohler, Kaufmann. "Saul of Tarsus." Pp. 79–87 in vol. 11 of *Jewish Encyclopedia.* New York: Funk & Wagnalls, 1906.

Kugel, James L. *The Bible As It Was.* Cambridge, MA: Harvard University Press, 1997.

_____. *How to Read the Bible: A Guide to Scripture, Then and Now.* New York: Free Press, 2007.

Kuhn, K. G. "Ἰουδαῖος." *TDNT* 3:356–69.

Lake, Kirsopp. "Appendix A: The Zealots." Pp. 421–25 in vol. 1 of *The Beginnings of Christianity, Part 1: The Acts of the Apostles.* Edited by F. J. Foakes Jackson and Kirsopp Lake. 5 vols. New York: Macmillan, 1920–1933.

Lambrecht, Jan. *Second Corinthians.* SP. Collegeville, MN: Liturgical Press, 1999.

Lampe, Peter. *From Paul to Valentinus: Christians at Rome in the First Two Centuries.* London: T&T Clark, 2003.

_____. "The Roman Christians of Romans 16." Pp. 216–30 in *The Romans Debate.* Edited by Karl P. Donfried. Rev. ed. Edinburgh: T&T Clark, 1991.

Landmesser, Christof. "Ferdinand Christian Baur as Interpreter of Paul: History, the Absolute, and Freedom." Pp. 147–76 in *Ferdinand Christian Baur and the History of Early Christianity.* Edited by Martin Bauspiess, Christof Landmesser, and David Lincicum. Translated by Robert F. Brown and Peter C. Hodgson. Oxford: Oxford University Press, 2017.

Lang, T. J. *Mystery and the Making of a Christian Historical Consciousness: From Paul to the Second Century.* BZNW 219. Berlin: de Gruyter, 2015.

Langton, Daniel R. *The Apostle Paul in the Jewish Imagination.* Cambridge: Cambridge University Press, 2010.

Lappenga, Benjamin L. *Paul's Language of Zelos: Monosemy and the Rhetoric of Identity and Practice.* BIS 137. Leiden: Brill, 2016.

Lee, Bryan D. Review of *Paul's Interlocutor in Romans 2,* by Runar M. Thorsteinsson. *RBL* (2005).

Legaspi, Michael C. *The Death of Scripture and the Rise of Biblical Studies.* New York: Oxford University Press, 2010.

Lentz, John C. *Luke's Portrait of Paul.* SNTSMS 77. Cambridge: Cambridge University Press, 1993.

Liddell, H. G., R. Scott, and H. S. Jones. *Greek-English Lexicon.* Oxford: Clarendon, 1996.

Lieu, Judith M. "'As Much My Apostle as Christ Is Mine': The Dispute over Paul between Tertullian and Marcion." *EC* 1 (2010): 41–59.

Lim, Timothy H. *Holy Scripture in the Qumran Commentaries and Pauline Letters.* Oxford: Clarendon, 1997.

Limor, Ora, and Guy G. Stroumsa, eds. *Contra Iudaeos: Ancient and Medieval Polemics between Christians and Jews.* TSMEMJ 10. Tübingen: Mohr Siebeck, 1996.

Lincicum, David. "Martin Luther in Modern New Testament Scholarship." In *Oxford Encyclopedia of Martin Luther.* Edited by Derek R. Nelson and Paul R. Hinlicky. 3 vols. Oxford: Oxford University Press, 2017.

Lindbeck, George A. *The Nature of Doctrine: Religion and Theology in a Postliberal Age.* Louisville: Westminster John Knox, 1984.

Lindemann, Andreas. *Paulus Apostel und Lehrer der Kirche: Studien zu Paulus und zum frühen Paulusverständnis.* Tübingen: Mohr Siebeck, 1999.

_____. *Paulus im ältesten Christentum.* BHT 58. Tübingen: Mohr Siebeck, 1979.

Linebaugh, Jonathan A. *God, Grace, and Righteousness in Wisdom of Solomon and Paul's Letter to the Romans.* NovTSup 152. Leiden: Brill, 2013.

Litwa, M. David. *Iesus Deus: The Early Christian Depiction of Jesus as a Mediterranean God.* Minneapolis: Fortress, 2014.

Longenecker, Bruce W. "Did Tertullian Succeed? Reflections on Tertullian's Appropriation of Paul in His Response to Marcion." Pp. 247–58 in *Tertullian and Paul.* Edited by Todd D. Still and David E. Wilhite. London: T&T Clark, 2013.

_____. "What Did Paul Think Is Wrong in God's World?" Pp. 171–86 in *The New Cambridge Companion to St. Paul.* Edited by Bruce W. Longenecker. Cambridge: Cambridge University Press, 2020.

Longenecker, Richard N. *The Epistle to the Romans.* NIGTC. Grand Rapids: Eerdmans, 2016.

Lortz, Joseph. *Tertullian als Apologet.* 2 vols. Münster: Aschendorff, 1927–1928.

*Lucian.* Edited by A. M. Harmon. LCL. Cambridge, MA: Harvard University Press, 1913.

Luther, Martin. *Lectures on Galatians (1519)* and *Lectures on Galatians (1535).* Volumes 26–27 of *Luther's Works.* Edited by Jaroslav Pelikan and Helmut T. Lehmann. St. Louis: Concordia, 1955–1976.

Maccoby, Hyam. *The Mythmaker: Paul and the Invention of Christianity.* San Francisco: Harper & Row, 1986.

Malherbe, Abraham J. "'Gentle as a Nurse': The Cynic Background to 1 Thessalonians 2." *NovT* 12 (1970): 203–17.

_____. *The Letters to the Thessalonians.* AB. New York: Doubleday, 2000.

Manson, T. W. "St. Paul's Letter to the Romans—and Others." Pp. 3–15 in *The Romans Debate.* Edited by Karl P. Donfried. Rev. ed. Edinburgh: T&T Clark, 1991.

Marshall, John W. *Parables of War: Reading John's Jewish Apocalypse.* ESCJ 10. Waterloo: Wilfred Laurier University Press, 2001.

_____. Review of *Contesting Conversion,* by Matthew Thiessen. *JTS* 64 (2013): 617–20.

Marshall, Mary. *The Portrayals of the Pharisees in the Gospels and Acts.* FRLANT 254. Göttingen: Vandenhoeck & Ruprecht, 2015.

Martin, Dale B. *Biblical Truths: The Meaning of Scripture in the Twenty-First Century.* New Haven: Yale University Press, 2017.

_____. *The Corinthian Body*. New Haven: Yale University Press, 1995.

_____. "Heterosexism and the Interpretation of Romans 1:18–32." *BibInt* 3 (1995): 332–55.

_____. *Sex and the Single Savior: Gender and Sexuality in Biblical Interpretation*. Louisville: Westminster John Knox, 2006.

Martin, V., and G. de Budé, eds. *Eschine. Discours*, vol. 2. Paris: Belles Lettres, 1928.

Martyn, J. Louis. *Galatians: A New Translation with Introduction and Commentary*. AYB. New Haven: Yale University Press, 2004.

_____. "A Gentile in Spite of Himself." *New York Times* (July 20, 1986).

_____. "A Tale of Two Churches." Pp. 25–36 in *Theological Issues in the Letters of Paul*. Edinburgh: T&T Clark, 1997.

Mason, Steve. *Flavius Josephus on the Pharisees: A Composition-Critical Study*. Leiden: Brill, 2001.

_____. *A History of the Jewish War, AD 66–74*. New York: Cambridge University Press, 2016.

_____. "Jews, Judaeans, Judaizing, Judaism: Problems of Categorization in Ancient History." *JSJ* 38 (2007): 457–512.

_____. *Josephus and the New Testament*. 2nd ed. Peabody, MA: Hendrickson, 2003.

_____. "N. T. Wright on Paul the Pharisee and Ancient Jews in Exile." *SJT* 69 (2016): 432–52.

Matera, Frank J. *II Corinthians: A Commentary*. NTL. Louisville: Westminster John Knox, 2003.

Matlock, R. Barry. *Unveiling the Apocalyptic Paul*. JSNTSup 127. Sheffield: Sheffield Academic, 1996.

Matthews, Shelly. *Perfect Martyr: The Stoning of Stephen and the Construction of Christian Identity*. New York: Oxford University Press, 2010.

McCaulley, Esau. *Sharing in the Son's Inheritance: Davidic Messianism and Paul's Worldwide Interpretation of the Abrahamic Land Promise in Galatians*. LNTS 608. London: T&T Clark, 2019.

McGowan, Andrew B. "God in Christ: Tertullian, Paul, and Christology." Pp. 1–15 in *Tertullian and Paul*. Edited by Todd D. Still and David E. Wilhite. London: T&T Clark, 2013.

McKechnie, Paul. "Paul among the Jews." Pp. 103–23 in *All Things to All Cultures: Paul among Jews, Greeks, and Romans*. Edited by Mark Harding and Alanna Nobbs. Grand Rapids: Eerdmans, 2013.

Meeks, Wayne A. *The First Urban Christians: The Social World of the Apostle Paul*. 2nd ed. New Haven: Yale University Press, 2003.

Metzger, Bruce M. *The Canon of the New Testament: Its Origin, Development, and Significance*. Oxford: Clarendon, 1987.

_____. "Literary Forgeries and Canonical Pseudepigrapha." *JBL* 91 (1972): 3–24.

_____. "The Punctuation of Romans 9:5." Pp. 95–112 in *Christ and the Spirit in the New Testament*. Edited by Barnabas Lindars and Stephen S. Smalley. Cambridge: Cambridge University Press, 1973.

Meyer, Paul W. "The Worm at the Core of the Apple: Exegetical Reflections on Romans 7." Pp. 57–77 in Meyer, *The Word in This World: Essays in New Testament Exegesis and Theology*. Edited by John T. Carroll. NTL. Louisville: Westminster John Knox, 2004.

Minear, Paul S. *The Obedience of Faith: The Purposes of Paul in the Epistle to the Romans*. London: SCM, 1971.

Mirhady, David C. "Athens' Democratic Witnesses." *Phoenix* 56 (2002): 255–74.

Mitchell, Margaret M. "Paul and Judaism now, Quo vadimus?" *JJMJS* 5 (2018): 55–78.

_____. *Paul and the Rhetoric of Reconciliation: An Exegetical Investigation of the Language and Composition of 1 Corinthians*. Tübingen: Mohr Siebeck, 1991.

_____. "Pauline Accommodation and 'Condescension' (ΣΥΓΚΑΤΑΒΑΣΙΣ): 1 Cor 9:19–23 and the History of Influence." Pp. 197–214 in *Paul beyond the Judaism/Hellenism Divide*. Edited by Troels Engberg-Pedersen. Louisville: Westminster John Knox, 2001.

Moberly, R. W. L. "What Is Theological Interpretation of Scripture?" *JTI* 3 (2009): 161–78.

Momigliano, Arnaldo. Review of *Tertullian: A Historical and Literary Study*, by Timothy D. Barnes. *JRS* 66 (1976): 273–76.

Moo, Douglas J. *The Epistle to the Romans*. NICNT. Grand Rapids: Eerdmans, 1996.

Moore, G. F. "Fate and Free Will in the Jewish Philosophies according to Josephus." *HTR* 22 (1929): 371–89.

Moore, Stephen D., and Yvonne Sherwood. *The Invention of the Biblical Scholar: A Critical Manifesto*. Minneapolis: Fortress, 2011.

Morgan, Robert. "Introduction: The Nature of New Testament Theology." Pp. 1–67 in Morgan, ed., *The Nature of New Testament Theology*. London: SCM, 1973.

_____, ed. *The Nature of New Testament Theology*. SBT 2.25. London: SCM, 1973.

_____. "*Sachkritik* in Reception History." *JSNT* 33 (2010): 175–90.

Morgan, Teresa. *Roman Faith and Christian Faith: Pistis and Fides in the Early Roman Empire and Early Churches*. Oxford: Oxford University Press, 2015.

Moxnes, Halvor. *Theology in Conflict: Studies in Paul's Understanding of God in Romans*. NovTSup 53. Leiden: Brill, 1980.

Mroczek, Eva. *The Literary Imagination in Jewish Antiquity*. New York: Oxford University Press, 2016.

Müller, C. F. W., ed. *M. Tullii Ciceronis Scripta quae manserunt omnia*. Leipzig: Teubner, 1879.

Munck, Johannes. *Paul and the Salvation of Mankind.* Translated by Frank Clarke. Atlanta: John Knox, 1959.

Murphy-O'Connor, Jerome. *Paul: A Critical Life.* Oxford: Oxford University Press, 1996.

Nanos, Mark D., and Magnus Zetterholm, eds. *Paul within Judaism: Restoring the First-Century Context to the Apostle.* Minneapolis: Fortress, 2015.

Nasrallah, Laura Salah. *Archaeology and the Letters of Paul.* Oxford: Oxford University Press, 2019.

Neusner, Jacob. "Mr. Sanders' Pharisees and Mine." *SJT* 44 (1991): 73–95.

_____. "Preface." Pp. ix–xiv in *Judaisms and Their Messiahs at the Turn of the Christian Era.* Edited by Jacob Neusner, William S. Green, and Ernest Frerichs. Cambridge: Cambridge University Press, 1987.

_____. *The Rabbinic Traditions about the Pharisees before 70.* 3 vols. Leiden: Brill, 1971.

Neusner, Jacob, and Bruce D. Chilton, eds. *In Quest of the Historical Pharisees.* Waco, TX: Baylor University Press, 2007.

Neutel, Karin B. *A Cosmopolitan Ideal: Paul's Declaration "Neither Jew Nor Greek, Neither Slave Nor Free, Nor Male and Female" in the Context of First-Century Thought.* LNTS 513. London: T&T Clark, 2015.

Nickelsburg, George W. E., and James C. VanderKam. *1 Enoch: A New Translation.* Minneapolis: Fortress, 2004.

Nickle, Keith F. *The Collection: A Study in Paul's Strategy.* SBT 48. Naperville, IL: Allenson, 1966.

Niebuhr, Karl-Wilhelm. *Heidenapostel aus Israel: Die jüdische Identität des Paulus nach ihrer Darstellung in seinen Briefen.* WUNT 62. Tübingen: Mohr Siebeck, 1992.

Niese, B., ed. *Flavii Iosephi opera.* Berlin: Weidmann, 1895.

Nongbri, Brent. *Before Religion: A History of a Modern Concept.* New Haven: Yale University Press, 2013.

Novak, David. "Jewish Eschatology." Pp. 113–31 in *The Oxford Handbook of Eschatology.* Edited by Jerry L. Walls. Oxford: Oxford University Press, 2007.

Novenson, Matthew V. "Beyond Compare, or: Some Recent Strategies for Not Comparing Early Christianity with Other Things." Pp. 79–94 in *The New Testament in Comparison: Validity, Method, and Purpose in Comparing Traditions.* Edited by John M. G. Barclay and Benjamin G. White. LNTS 600. London: T&T Clark, 2020.

_____. *Christ among the Messiahs: Christ Language in Paul and Messiah Language in Ancient Judaism.* New York: Oxford University Press, 2012.

_____. *The End of the Law and the Last Man: Paul between Judaism and Christianity.* New York: Cambridge University Press, forthcoming.

_____. "Gentile Sinners: A Brief History of an Ancient Stereotype." In *Negotiating Identities.* Edited by Anders Runesson, Cecilia Wassen, Karin Zetterholm, and Magnus Zetterholm. Minneapolis: Fortress, forthcoming.

_____. "The Jewish Messiahs, the Pauline Christ, and the Gentile Question." *JBL* 128 (2009): 357–73.

_____. "On *The Grammar of Messianism*, in Dialogue with N. T. Wright." *ExpTim* 129 (2018): 303–6.

_____. "Paul's Former Occupation in *Ioudaismos*." Pp. 24–39 in *Galatians and Christian Theology.* Edited by Mark W. Elliott, Scott J. Hafemann, N. T. Wright, and John Frederick. Grand Rapids: Baker Academic, 2014.

_____. Review of *Who Made Early Christianity?* by John G. Gager. *Theology Today* 73 (2017): 396–97.

_____. "The Universal Polytheism and the Case of the Jews." Pp. 32–60 in *Monotheism and Christology in Greco-Roman Antiquity.* Edited by Matthew V. Novenson. NovTSup 180. Leiden: Brill, 2020.

_____. "What the Apostles Did Not See." Pp. 55–72 in *Reactions to Empire: Sacred Texts in Their Socio-Political Contexts.* Edited by John Anthony Dunne and Dan Batovici. WUNT 2.372. Tübingen: Mohr Siebeck, 2014.

*Novum Testamentum Graece.* Edited by Kurt Aland et al. 28th ed. Stuttgart: Deutsche Bibelgesellschaft, 2012.

O'Brien, Peter T. *Introductory Thanksgivings in the Letters of Paul.* NovTSup 49. Leiden: Brill, 1977.

Oehler, Franz, ed. *Q. S. F. Tertulliani opera omnia.* 3 vols. Leipzig, 1851–1854.

Ollenburger, Ben C. "What Krister Stendahl 'Meant': A Normative Critique of 'Descriptive Biblical Theology.'" *HBT* 8 (1986): 61–98.

O'Malley, T. P. *Tertullian and the Bible: Language, Imagery, Exegesis.* LCP 21. Nijmegen: Dekker & Van De Vegt, 1967.

Origen. *Commentary on the Epistle to the Romans, Books 1–5.* Translated by Thomas P. Scheck. FC 103. Washington, DC: Catholic University of America Press, 2001.

Osborn, Eric. *Tertullian: First Theologian of the West.* Cambridge: Cambridge University Press, 1997.

Overbeck, Franz. *Christentum und Kultur: Gedanken und Anmerkungen zur modernen Theologie.* Basel: Benno Schwabe, 1919.

Overman, J. Andrew. "*Kata Nomon Pharisaios*: A Short History of Paul's Pharisaism." Pp. 180–93 in *Pauline Conversations in Context: Essays in Honor of Calvin J. Roetzel.* Edited by Janice Capel Anderson, Philip Sellew, and Claudia Setzer. JSNTSup 221. Sheffield: Sheffield Academic, 2002.

Pardes, Ilana. *The Song of Songs: A Biography*. Princeton: Princeton University Press, 2019.

Peppard, Michael. *The Son of God in the Roman World: Divine Sonship in Its Social and Political Context*. New York: Oxford University Press, 2011.

Perelman, Chaim, and Lucie Olbrechts-Tyteca. *The New Rhetoric: A Treatise on Argumentation*. Notre Dame: University of Notre Dame Press, 1969.

Pervo, Richard I. *The Acts of Paul: A New Translation with Introduction and Commentary*. Eugene, OR: Cascade, 2014.

———. *The Making of Paul: Constructions of the Apostle in Early Christianity*. Minneapolis: Fortress, 2010.

*Philo*. 10 vols. Translated by F. H. Colson and G. H. Whitaker. LCL. Cambridge, MA: Harvard University Press, 1929–1962.

Quispel, Gilles. "African Christianity before Minucius Felix and Tertullian." Pp. 257–335 in *Actus: Studies in Honour of H. L. W. Nelson*. Edited by J. den Boeft and A. H. M. Kessels. Utrecht: Institute of Classical Languages, 1982.

Rahlfs, A., ed. *Septuaginta*. 2 vols. Stuttgart: Deutsche Bibelgesellschaft, 1935.

Räisänen, Heikki. *Paul and the Law*. Philadelphia: Fortress, 1986.

———. "Paul, God, and Israel: Romans 9–11 in Recent Research." Pp. 178–206 in *The Social World of Formative Christianity and Judaism: Essays in Tribute to Howard Clark Kee*. Edited by Jacob Neusner, Peder Borgen, Ernest S. Frerichs, and Richard Horsley. Philadelphia: Fortress, 1988.

———. "Zion Torah and Biblical Theology: Thoughts on a Tübingen Theory." Pp. 225–51 in *Jesus, Paul, and Torah: Collected Essays*. Translated by David E. Orton. JSNTSup 43. Sheffield: Sheffield Academic, 1992.

Rambaux, Claude. "La composition et l'exégèse dans les deux lettres *Ad uxorem*, le *De exhortations castitatis*, et le *De monogamia*, ou la construction de la pensée dans les traités de Tertullien sur la remarriage." *REA* 22 (1976): 3–28, 201–17, and 23 (1977): 18–55.

———. *Tertullien face aux morales des trois premiers siècles*. Paris: Belles Lettres, 1979.

Reasoner, Mark. *Romans in Full Circle: A History of Interpretation*. Louisville: Westminster John Knox, 2005.

Reed, Annette Yoshiko. "When Did Rabbis Become Pharisees? Reflections on Christian Evidence for Post-70 Judaism." Pp. 859–96 in vol. 2 of *Envisioning Judaism: Studies in Honor of Peter Schäfer on the Occasion of His Seventieth Birthday*. Edited by Ra'anan S. Boustan, Klaus Herrmann, Reimund Leicht, Annette Yoshiko Reed, and Giuseppe Veltri. Tübingen: Mohr Siebeck, 2013.

Refoulé, Francois. "Unité de l'Épitre aux Romains et histoire du salut." *RSPT* 71 (1987): 219–42.

Reinhartz, Adele, Steve Mason, Daniel Schwartz, Annette Yoshiko Reed, Joan Taylor, Malcolm Lowe, Jonathan Klawans, Ruth Sheridan, and James Crossley.

"Jew and Judean: A Forum on Politics and Historiography in the Trans-
    lation of Ancient Texts." *Marginalia* (August 26, 2014). https://marginalia
    .lareviewofbooks.org/jew-judean-forum/.

Rensberger, David K. "As the Apostle Teaches: The Development of the Use of Paul's
    Letters in Second-Century Christianity." PhD diss., Yale University, 1981.

Reumann, John. *Philippians: A New Translation with Introduction and Commen-
    tary*. AYB. New Haven: Yale University Press, 2008.

Richard, Earl J. *First and Second Thessalonians*. SP. Collegeville, MN: Liturgical
    Press, 1995.

Riches, John. *Galatians through the Centuries*. Oxford: Wiley-Blackwell, 2007.

Ritschl, Albrecht. *The Christian Doctrine of Justification and Reconciliation*. Trans-
    lated by H. R. Mackintosh and A. B. Macaulay. Edinburgh: T&T Clark, 1902.

Rivkin, Ellis. "Defining the Pharisees: The Tannaitic Sources." *HUCA* 40 (1969):
    205–49.

Roberts, J. J. M. *The Bible and the Ancient Near East: Collected Essays*. Winona
    Lake, IN: Eisenbrauns, 2002.

———. "The End of War in the Zion Tradition." *HBT* 26 (2004): 2–22.

Rochefort, G., ed. *L'empereur Julien. Oeuvres complètes*. Paris: Belles Lettres, 1963.

Rodriguez, Rafael. *If You Call Yourself a Jew: Reappraising Paul's Letter to the Ro-
    mans*. Eugene, OR: Cascade, 2014.

Rodriguez, Rafael, and Matthew Thiessen, eds. *The So-Called Jew in Paul's Letter
    to the Romans*. Minneapolis: Fortress, 2016.

Roensch, Hermann. *Das neue Testament Tertullians*. Leipzig, 1871.

Roetzel, Calvin J. "Paul in the Second Century." Pp. 227–41 in *The Cambridge
    Companion to St Paul*. Edited by James D. G. Dunn. Cambridge: Cambridge
    University Press, 2003.

Rollens, Sarah E. "'The God Came to Me in a Dream': Epiphanies in Voluntary
    Associations as a Context for Paul's Vision of Christ." *HTR* 111 (2018): 41–65.

Rorty, Richard. "The Historiography of Philosophy: Four Genres." Pp. 49–76 in
    *Philosophy in History: Essays on the Historiography of Philosophy*. Edited by
    Richard Rorty, J. B. Schneewind, and Quentin Skinner. Cambridge: Cam-
    bridge University Press, 1984.

Ross, W. D., ed. *Aristotelis ars rhetorica*. Oxford: Clarendon, 1959.

Rudolph, David J. *A Jew to the Jews: Jewish Contours of Pauline Flexibility in 1 Cor-
    inthians 9:19–23*. 2nd ed. Eugene, OR: Pickwick, 2016.

Ruether, Rosemary Radford. *Faith and Fratricide: The Theological Roots of Anti-
    Semitism*. New York: Seabury, 1974.

Ruiten, Jacques T. A. G. M. van. *Abraham in the Book of Jubilees: The Rewriting of Gen-
    esis 11:26–25:10 in the Book of Jubilees 11:14–23:8*. JSJSup 161. Leiden: Brill, 2012.

Sanders, E. P. *Jewish Law from Jesus to the Mishnah*. London: SCM, 1990.

_____. *Judaism: Practice and Belief, 63 BCE-66 CE*. London: SCM, 1992.

_____. *Paul and Palestinian Judaism: A Comparison of Patterns of Religion*. Philadelphia: Fortress, 1977.

_____. *Paul: The Apostle's Life, Letters, and Thought*. Minneapolis: Fortress, 2015.

_____. *Paul, the Law, and the Jewish People*. Philadelphia: Fortress, 1983.

Sanders, Paul. "So May God Do To Me!" *Bib* 85 (2004): 91–98.

Satlow, Michael L. "Defining Judaism: Accounting for 'Religions' in the Study of Religion." *JAAR* 74 (2006): 837–60.

_____. *How the Bible Became Holy*. New Haven: Yale University Press, 2014.

_____. "Jew or Judean?" Pp. 165–75 in *The One Who Sows Bountifully: Essays in Honor of Stanley K. Stowers*. Edited by Caroline Johnson Hodge, Saul M. Olyan, Daniel Ullucci, and Emma Wasserman. BJS 356. Atlanta: SBL Press, 2013.

_____. "Paul, a Jew from Jerusalem." *The Bible and Interpretation* (September 2014). https://bibleinterp.arizona.edu/articles/2014/09/sat388024.

_____. "Paul's Scriptures." Pp. 257–74 in *Strength to Strength: Essays in Honor of Shaye J. D. Cohen*. Edited by Michael Satlow. BJS 363. Providence: Brown University Press, 2018.

Schäfer, Peter. *Two Gods in Heaven: Jewish Concepts of God in Antiquity*. Translated by Allison Brown. Princeton: Princeton University Press, 2020.

Schellenberg, Ryan S., and Heidi Wendt, eds. *Handbook to the Historical Paul*. London: T&T Clark, forthcoming.

Schnelle, Udo. "Über Judentum und Hellenismus hinaus: Die paulinische Theologie als neue Wissensystem." *ZNW* 111 (2020): 124–55.

Schoeps, Hans-Joachim. *Paul: The Theology of the Apostle in the Light of Jewish Religious History*. Translated by H. Knight. Philadelphia: Westminster, 1961.

Scholem, Gershom. *Major Trends in Jewish Mysticism*. New York: Schocken, 1995.

_____. *The Messianic Idea in Judaism and Other Essays on Jewish Spirituality*. New York: Schocken, 1995.

_____. *Sabbatai Zevi: Mystical Messiah, 1626–1676*. Translated by R. J. Zwi Werblowsky. Princeton: Princeton University Press, 1973.

Schubert, Paul. *The Form and Function of the Pauline Thanksgivings*. Berlin: Töpelmann, 1939.

Schüssler Fiorenza, Elisabeth. "The Ethics of Biblical Interpretation: Decentering Biblical Scholarship." *JBL* 107 (1988): 3–17.

Schwartz, Daniel R. "'Judaean' or 'Jew'? How Should We Translate *Ioudaios* in Josephus?" Pp. 3–28 in *Jewish Identity in the Greco-Roman World*. Edited by Jörg Frey, Daniel R. Schwartz, and Stephanie Gripentrog. AJEC 71. Leiden: Brill, 2007.

Schwartz, Seth. "How Many Judaisms Were There?" *JAJ* 2 (2011): 208–38.

Schweitzer, Albert. *The Mysticism of Paul the Apostle.* Translated by W. Montgomery. London: Black, 1931.

_____. *Paul and His Interpreters: A Critical History.* Translated by W. Montgomery. London: Black, 1912.

_____. *The Quest of the Historical Jesus.* Translated by W. Montgomery. London: Black, 1910.

Sechrest, Love. *A Former Jew: Paul and the Dialectics of Race.* LNTS 410. London: T&T Clark, 2009.

Segal, Alan F. *Paul the Convert: The Apostolate and Apostasy of Saul the Pharisee.* New Haven: Yale University Press, 1990.

_____. "Paul's Jewish Presuppositions." Pp. 159–72 in *The Cambridge Companion to St. Paul.* Edited by James D. G. Dunn. Cambridge: Cambridge University Press, 2003.

Setzer, Claudia. "Does Paul Need to Be Saved?" *BibInt* 13 (2005): 289–97.

Sider, Robert D. "Literary Artifice and the Figure of Paul in the Writings of Tertullian." Pp. 99–120 in *Paul and the Legacies of Paul.* Edited by William S. Babcock. Dallas: Southern Methodist University Press, 1986.

Smith, Jonathan Z. *Drudgery Divine: On the Comparison of Early Christianities and the Religions of Late Antiquity.* Chicago: University of Chicago Press, 1990.

Smith, Mark S. *The Origins of Biblical Monotheism: Israel's Polytheistic Background and the Ugaritic Texts.* Oxford: Oxford University Press, 2001.

Smith, Morton. "Zealots and Sicarii, Their Origins and Relation." *HTR* 64 (1971): 1–19.

Smith, Rowland. *Julian's Gods: Religion and Philosophy in the Thought and Action of Julian the Apostate.* London: Routledge, 1995.

Snyder, Glenn E. "Paul beyond the Jew/Gentile Dichotomy: A Perspective from Benjamin." *Expositions* 9 (2015): 125–37.

Sommerstein, Alan H., and Isabelle C. Torrance. *Oaths and Swearing in Ancient Greece.* Berlin: de Gruyter, 2014.

Stählin, Gustav. "Zum Gebrauch von Beteuerungsformeln im Neuen Testament." *NovT* 5 (1962): 115–43.

Stanley, Christopher D. *Paul and the Language of Scripture.* SNTSMS 74. Cambridge: Cambridge University Press, 1992.

Staples, Jason A. *The Idea of Israel in Second Temple Judaism: A New Theory of People, Exile, and Israelite Identity.* New York: Cambridge University Press, 2021.

_____. "What Do the Gentiles Have to Do with 'All Israel'? A Fresh Look at Romans 11:25–27." *JBL* 130 (2011): 371–90.

Stendahl, Krister. "The Apostle Paul and the Introspective Conscience of the West." *HTR* 56 (1963): 199–215.

_____. "Biblical Theology, Contemporary." Pp. 418–32 in vol. 1 of *The Interpreter's Dictionary of the Bible*. 4 vols. Nashville: Abingdon, 1981.

_____. *Final Account: Paul's Letter to the Romans*. Minneapolis: Fortress, 1995.

_____. *Paul among Jews and Gentiles, and Other Essays*. Philadelphia: Fortress, 1976.

Stern, Menahem. "Aspects of Jewish Society: The Priesthood and Other Classes." Pp. 561–630 in vol. 2 of *The Jewish People in the First Century*. Edited by Shmuel Safrai and Menahem Stern. CRINT. Assen: Van Gorcum, 1976.

_____. *Greek and Latin Authors on Jews and Judaism*. 3 vols. Jerusalem: Israel Academy of Sciences and Humanities, 1974–1984.

Still, Todd D. "Afterword: Tertullian and Pauline Studies." Pp. 282–84 in *Tertullian and Paul*. Edited by Todd D. Still and David E. Wilhite. London: T&T Clark, 2013.

_____, ed. *God and Israel: Providence and Purpose in Romans 9–11*. Waco, TX: Baylor University Press, 2017.

_____. "Martyrdom as Sacrament: Tertullian's (Mis)Use of 'the Apostle' (Paul)." Pp. 119–26 in *Tertullian and Paul*. Edited by Todd D. Still and David E. Wilhite. London: T&T Clark, 2013.

Still, Todd D, and David E. Wilhite, eds. *Tertullian and Paul*. London: T&T Clark, 2013.

Stout, Jeffrey. *Democracy and Tradition*. Princeton: Princeton University Press, 2004.

_____. *Ethics after Babel: The Languages of Morals and Their Discontents*. 2nd ed. Princeton: Princeton University Press, 2001.

_____. "The Relativity of Interpretation." *Monist* 69 (1986): 103–18.

_____. "What Is the Meaning of a Text?" *New Literary History* 14 (1982): 1–12.

Stowers, Stanley K. *The Diatribe and Paul's Letter to the Romans*. SBLDS 57. Chico, CA: Scholars Press, 1981.

_____. "Kinds of Myths, Meals, and Power: Paul and the Corinthians." Pp. 105–50 in *Redescribing Paul and the Corinthians*. Edited by Ron Cameron and Merrill P. Miller. Atlanta: SBL Press, 2011.

_____. *A Rereading of Romans: Justice, Jews, and Gentiles*. New Haven: Yale University Press, 1994.

_____. Review of *Paul's Interlocutor in Romans 2*, by Runar M. Thorsteinsson. *JTS* 56 (2005): 561–65.

Strawbridge, Jennifer R. *The Pauline Effect: The Use of the Pauline Epistles by Early Christian Writers*. SBR 5. Berlin: de Gruyter, 2015.

Strecker, Georg. "Befreiung und Rechtfertigung." Pp. 479–508 in *Rechtfertigung: Festschrift für Ernst Käsemann zum 70. Geburtstag*. Edited by Johannes Friedrich, Wolfgang Pöhlmann, and Peter Stuhlmacher. Tübingen: Mohr Siebeck, 1976.

Stroumsa, Gedaliahu G. "Form(s) of God: Some Notes on Metatron and Christ." *HTR* 76 (1983): 269–88.

Stroup, Christopher. *The Christians Who Became Jews: Acts of the Apostles and Ethnicity in the Roman City*. New Haven: Yale University Press, 2020.

Stuckenbruck, Loren T. "'Angels' and 'God': Exploring the Limits of Early Jewish Monotheism." Pp. 45–70 in *Early Christian and Jewish Monotheism*. Edited by Loren T. Stuckenbruck and Wendy E. S. North. JSNTSup 263. London: T&T Clark, 2004.

Stuhlmacher, Peter. *Paul's Letter to the Romans*. Translated by Scott J. Hafemann. Louisville: Westminster John Knox, 1994. German original 1989.

Sweeney, James. Review of *Paul's Interlocutor in Romans 2*, by Runar M. Thorsteinsson. *RBL* (2004).

Tanner, Kathryn. *Theories of Culture: A New Agenda for Theology*. Minneapolis: Fortress, 1997.

Tatum, Gregory. "Did Paul Find Anything Wrong with Judaism?" *JJMJS* 5 (2018): 38–44.

Taubes, Jacob. *The Political Theology of Paul*. Translated by Dana Hollander. Stanford: Stanford University Press, 2004.

Tertullian. *La pudicité*. Edited by Charles Munier. 2 vols. SC 394–95. Paris: Cerf, 1993.

———. *Traité de la prescription contre les hérétiques*. Edited by R. F. Refoulé. SC 46. Paris: Cerf, 1957.

Thiel, Nathan. "'Israel' and 'Jew' as Markers of Jewish Identity in Antiquity: The Problems of Insider/Outsider Classification." *JSJ* 45 (2014): 80–99.

Thielman, Frank. *From Plight to Solution: A Jewish Framework for Understanding Paul's View of the Law in Galatians and Romans*. NovTSup 61. Leiden: Brill, 1989.

Thiessen, Matthew. "Conjuring Paul and Judaism Forty Years after *Paul and Palestinian Judaism*." *JJMJS* 5 (2018): 6–20.

———. *Contesting Conversion: Genealogy, Circumcision, and Identity in Ancient Judaism and Christianity*. New York: Oxford University Press, 2011.

———. *Paul and the Gentile Problem*. New York: Oxford University Press, 2016.

———. "Paul's Argument against Gentile Circumcision in Rom 2:17–29." *NovT* 56 (2014): 373–91.

———. "Paul's So-Called Jew and Lawless Lawkeeping." Pp. 59–84 in *The So-Called Jew in Paul's Letter to the Romans*. Edited by Rafael Rodriguez and Matthew Thiessen. Minneapolis: Fortress, 2016.

_____. "The Text of Genesis 17:14." *JBL* 128 (2009): 625–42.

Thiselton, Anthony C. *The Two Horizons: New Testament Hermeneutics and Philosophical Description.* Grand Rapids: Eerdmans, 1980.

Thorsteinsson, Runar M. *Paul's Interlocutor in Romans 2: Function and Identity in the Context of Ancient Epistolography.* ConBNT 40. Stockholm: Almqvist & Wiksell, 2003.

Tomson, Peter J. "The Names Israel and Jew in Ancient Judaism and in the New Testament." *Bijdragen* 47 (1986): 120–40, 266–89.

_____. *Paul and the Jewish Law: Halakha in the Letters of the Apostle to the Gentiles.* CRINT. Assen: Van Gorcum, 1990.

Torrance, Thomas F. *The Doctrine of Grace in the Apostolic Fathers.* Edinburgh: Oliver & Boyd, 1948.

Trevett, J. C. "Aristotle's Knowledge of Athenian Oratory." *CQ* 46 (1996): 371–79.

Trocmé, Etienne. "The Jews as Seen by Paul and Luke." Pp. 145–61 in *To See Ourselves as Others See Us: Christians, Jews, "Others" in Late Antiquity.* Edited by Jacob Neusner and Ernest S. Frerichs. Chico, CA: Scholars Press, 1985.

Turner, E. G. "Tiberius Julius Alexander." *JRS* 44 (1954): 54–64.

Unnik, W. C. van. *Tarsus or Jerusalem? The City of Paul's Youth.* Translated by George Ogg. London: Epworth, 1962.

VanderKam, James C. "The Pharisees and the Dead Sea Scrolls." Pp. 225–36 in *In Quest of the Historical Pharisees.* Edited by Jacob Neusner and Bruce D. Chilton. Waco, TX: Baylor University Press, 2007.

Waddell, James A. *The Messiah: A Comparative Study of the Enochic Son of Man and the Pauline Kyrios.* JCTCRS 10. London: T&T Clark, 2011.

Wagner, J. Ross. "The Christ, Servant of Jew and Gentile: A Fresh Approach to Rom 15:8–9." *JBL* 116 (1997): 473–85.

_____. *Heralds of the Good News: Isaiah and Paul in Concert in the Letter to the Romans.* NovTSup 101. Leiden: Brill, 2002.

_____. *Opening the Sealed Book: Old Greek Isaiah and the Problem of Septuagint Hermeneutics.* FAT 88. Tübingen: Mohr Siebeck, 2013.

Wasserman, Emma. *Apocalypse as Holy War: Divine Politics and Polemics in the Letters of Paul.* AYBRL. New Haven: Yale University Press, 2018.

_____. *The Death of the Soul in Romans 7: Sin, Death, and the Law in Light of Hellenistic Moral Psychology.* WUNT 256. Tübingen: Mohr Siebeck, 2008.

Watson, Francis. *Paul and the Hermeneutics of Faith.* 2nd ed. London: T&T Clark, 2016.

_____. *Paul, Judaism, and the Gentiles.* Rev. ed. Grand Rapids: Eerdmans, 2007.

Weber, Ferdinand. *Jüdische Theologie.* 2nd ed. Leipzig: Dörffling & Franke, 1897.

Wendland, P., ed. *Philonis Alexandrini opera quae supersunt.* Berlin: Reimer, 1897. Repr., Berlin: de Gruyter, 1962.

Wendt, Heidi. *At the Temple Gates: The Religion of Freelance Experts in the Roman Empire*. New York: Oxford University Press, 2016.

Wesley, John. *Explanatory Notes upon the New Testament*. London, 1813.

Westerholm, Stephen. *Justification Reconsidered: Rethinking a Pauline Theme*. Grand Rapids: Eerdmans, 2013.

_____. "The 'New Perspective' at Twenty-Five." Pp. 1–38 in vol. 2 of *Justification and Variegated Nomism*. Edited by D. A. Carson, Peter T. O'Brien, and Mark A. Seifrid. WUNT 2.181. Tübingen: Mohr Siebeck, 2004.

_____. *Perspectives Old and New on Paul: The "Lutheran" Paul and His Critics*. Grand Rapids: Eerdmans, 2004.

_____. *Understanding Paul: The Early Christian Worldview of the Letter to the Romans*. Grand Rapids: Baker Academic, 2004.

White, Benjamin L. "*Imago Pauli*: Memory, Tradition, and Discourses on the 'Real' Paul in the Second Century." PhD diss., University of North Carolina, 2011.

_____. *Remembering Paul: Ancient and Modern Contests over the Image of the Apostle*. New York: Oxford University Press, 2014.

Wiles, Maurice F. *The Divine Apostle: The Interpretation of St. Paul's Epistles in the Early Church*. Cambridge: Cambridge University Press, 1967.

Wilhite, David E. "Introduction: Reading Tertullian Reading Paul." Pp. xvii–xxiv in *Tertullian and Paul*. Edited by Todd D. Still and David E. Wilhite. London: T&T Clark, 2013.

Wilk, Florian. *Die Bedeutung des Jesajabuches für Paulus*. FRLANT 179. Göttingen: Vandenhoeck & Ruprecht, 1998.

Wilk, Florian, and J. Ross Wagner, eds. *Between Gospel and Election: Explorations in the Interpretation of Romans 9–11*. WUNT 257. Tübingen: Mohr Siebeck, 2010.

Willitts, Joel. "Davidic Messiahship in Galatians: Clearing the Deck for a Study of the Theme in Galatians." *JSPL* 2 (2012): 143–61.

_____. *Matthew's Messianic Shepherd-King: In Search of "the Lost Sheep of the House of Israel."* BZNW 147. Berlin: de Gruyter, 2007.

Windsor, Lionel J. "The Named Jew and the Name of God." *NovT* 63 (2021): 229–48.

Winston, David. *The Wisdom of Solomon*. AB. New York: Doubleday, 1979.

Winterbottom, Michael, ed. *M. Fabi Quintiliani Institutionis oratoriae libri duodecim*. 2 vols. Oxford: Clarendon, 1970.

Wolff, H. W. "Swords into Plowshares: Misuse of a Word of Prophecy?" *CurTM* 12 (1985): 133–47.

Wright, N. T. *The Climax of the Covenant: Christ and the Law in Pauline Theology*. Edinburgh: T&T Clark, 1991.

_____. "Messiahship in Galatians?" Pp. 3–23 in *Galatians and Christian Theology*.

Edited by Mark W. Elliott, Scott J. Hafemann, N. T. Wright, and John Frederick. Grand Rapids: Baker Academic, 2014.

_____. "Messianic Grammar? A Response to Matthew V. Novenson, *The Grammar of Messianism: An Ancient Jewish Political Idiom and Its Users.*" *ExpTim* 129 (2018): 295–302.

_____. *Paul and His Recent Interpreters: Some Contemporary Debates.* Minneapolis: Fortress, 2015.

_____. *Paul and the Faithfulness of God.* 2 vols. London: SPCK, 2013.

Yarbro Collins, Adela. "Insiders and Outsiders in the Book of Revelation." Pp. 187–218 in *To See Ourselves as Others See Us: Christians, Jews, "Others" in Late Antiquity.* Edited by Jacob Neusner and Ernest S. Frerichs. Chico, CA: Scholars Press, 1985.

_____. "Jesus as Messiah and Son of God in the Letters of Paul." Pp. 101–22 in John J. Collins and Adela Yarbro Collins, *King and Messiah as Son of God: Divine, Human, and Angelic Messianic Figures in Biblical and Related Literature.* Grand Rapids: Eerdmans, 2008.

_____. "Vilification and Self-Definition in the Book of Revelation." *HTR* 79 (1986): 308–20.

Young, Stephen L. "Paul the Mythmaker." PhD diss., Brown University, 2016.

_____. "Paul's Eschatological Myth of Judean Sin." *NTS* (forthcoming).

Zahn, Theodor. *Einleitung in das Neuen Testament.* 2 vols. Leipzig, 1897–1900.

Zeitlin, Solomon. "Spurious Interpretations of Rabbinic Sources in the Studies of the Pharisees and Pharisaism." *JQR* 65 (1974): 122–35.

Zeller, Dieter. "Zur Transformation des Χριστός bei Paulus." Pp. 155–67 in *Der Messias.* Edited by Ingo Baldermann, Ernst Dassmann, and Ottmar Fuchs. JBT 8. Neukirchen-Vluyn: Neukirchener Verlag, 1993.

Zetterholm, Magnus. *Approaches to Paul: A Student's Guide to Recent Scholarship.* Minneapolis: Fortress, 2009.

_____. *The Formation of Christianity in Antioch: A Sociological Approach to the Separation between Judaism and Christianity.* London: Routledge, 2003.

Zoccali, Christopher. *Reading Philippians after Supersessionism.* Eugene, OR: Cascade, 2017.

# INDEX OF MODERN AUTHORS

# INDEX OF SUBJECTS

*pneuma*, 29–30, 38, 45, 55, 61, 69,
71–73, 76, 78–79, 84–85, 95–96, 106,
179
polemic, 9, 15, 68–69, 83, 86–87,
101n40, 106, 108n57, 169
polytheism, 62
prayer, 34–35, 56n40, 103n44, 127,
131–32, 141, 145, 148, 173
present age, the, 55, 66, 71, 79, 83, 122,
124
priest, 28, 32n31, 39–40, 61, 119–20,
146n2, 180
profane, 2n3, 10–11, 104, 145
prophecy, prophets, 46, 53, 77, 123,
128–30, 141, 146–49, 160, 170, 173, 179
proselyte, 20, 27, 36n48, 38n55, 68,
70–72, 77, 92–93, 102–3, 147, 155, 180
Protestantism, 17, 67–68, 75, 83–85,
110n67, 175, 180–95
pseudepigraphy, pseudonymity, 2, 59,
81, 171
psychology, 43–44, 79, 188

rabbis, 28n19, 32, 38n54, 40n61, 47, 56,
104, 163, 190
rational reconstruction, 176–78
reception history. *See* effective history
Reformation. *See* Protestantism
relativity, 4–5, 11–12, 54–55, 68, 105,
107, 194
religion, 6n14, 16–17, 22–23, 38, 47–50,
55, 63, 65–66, 86, 90, 114, 179n50, 187,
193–95
resurrection, 38, 49–50, 60, 62, 78,
82n38, 85, 122, 154n30, 166, 169,
173–74, 179
rhetoric, 15–16, 21, 29–31, 39, 76, 91–92,
97, 108n58, 116, 119–20, 125–44, 146,
159, 177n44, 186
righteous, righteousness, 7, 20, 37, 44,

54–55, 65–66, 68, 70–71, 73, 76–79,
82, 84–85, 87, 89–90, 97n23, 105,
107–17, 133, 141–42, 148, 154n30, 160,
174, 186, 188, 193
ritual, 31n31, 35, 56n40, 59, 70, 78n29,
83, 99, 159, 186, 195
Roman Catholicism, 17, 68, 175,
183–86, 188, 192, 195
Roman Empire, 43, 65n70, 80, 139n45
Rome, 40, 42, 68–69, 73–74, 76, 80–81,
101, 103n45, 131, 139n45, 151n15, 172,
184

Sabbath, 101, 107, 145, 189
*Sache, Sachkritik*, 9–10, 161
sacrilege, 96, 102–4, 116
Sadducees, 32–34, 38
salvation, 15, 17, 51, 83, 91n2, 113n74,
115–16, 148n6, 154–55, 174, 188–90,
192, 195
Sarah, 72, 84
Satan, 19, 63–64
science, 6n14, 8, 17n15
scripture, 4–6, 13–15, 23, 38n54, 53, 62,
67–68, 72, 77, 108–9, 111, 113, 118–20,
124, 140, 147n5, 151, 153, 159, 171–74
Seneca, 1–2
sex, 20, 92, 170, 173, 175
Shammai, 40
Shema, 56–57
sicarii, 41
sin, 7, 14–15, 17, 30, 39, 55, 63, 76–80,
83, 86, 88–89, 92, 97–98, 103, 108–9,
111, 115, 122, 136, 142, 158, 174, 178
Sinai, 56, 65, 192
sinners, 29–30, 92, 103, 109n62, 111
slavery, 7, 30n27, 43–44, 51–52, 61,
72–73, 76, 84–85, 174
Socrates, 46, 65, 138
son of God, 55–56, 59–61, 64, 70, 166

# INDEX OF ANCIENT SOURCES